Proof, Evidence and Hate Crime

Proof is the property of a disputed fact being established inferentially from an extant fact. This book explicates the structural components of this phenomenon in the context of hate crimes across various jurisdictions around the world. It departs from the orthodox conception of evidence and proof as being a general, value-neutral (or non-normative) and epistemic subject, and offers a relativistic conception of this area of law. The core argument is that proof is both semantically and methodologically determined by three conditions of materiality, process and probativity. This argument is then justified by the context-specific application of this relativistic theory of proof to hate crimes. This theoretical application of proof is sustained throughout the book using multiple examples and illustrations of hate crimes around the world. The discussion, both at the level of proof and hate crimes, while focusing on the grounds of race, religion and ethnicity specifically, is framed in jurisprudential, cross-jurisdictional and interdisciplinary terms. The book will be of interest to academics and researchers working in the areas of criminal law, legal philosophy and procedural law.

Tshepo Bogosi Mosaka is Senior Lecturer, Advocate of the High Court and Young Fellow of the University of Cape Town's (UCT) College of Fellows, South Africa, as well as a Visiting Fellow at the Max Planck Institute of Crime, Security and Law, Freiburg, Germany.

Proof, Evidence and Hate Crime

A Study in Criminal Jurisprudence

Tshepo Bogosi Mosaka

Routledge
Taylor & Francis Group
LONDON AND NEW YORK

First published 2026
by Routledge
4 Park Square, Milton Park, Abingdon, Oxon OX14 4RN

and by Routledge
605 Third Avenue, New York, NY 10158

Routledge is an imprint of the Taylor & Francis Group, an informa business

British Library Cataloguing-in-Publication Data
A catalogue record for this book is available from the British Library

ISBN: 978-1-032-76453-5 (hbk)
ISBN: 978-1-032-79620-8 (pbk)
ISBN: 978-1-003-49300-6 (ebk)

DOI: 10.4324/9781003493006

Typeset in Galliard
by Apex CoVantage, LLC

Contents

Abstract

Proof is the property of a disputed fact being established inferentially from an extant fact (evidence). *Proof, Evidence and Hate Crime: A Study in Criminal Jurisprudence* explicates the structural components of this phenomenon in the context of hate crimes across various jurisdictions around the world. The book departs from orthodox conceptions of evidence and proof that are general, value-neutral (absent normative aspects) and epistemic, and offers a relativistic framing that is bound up with doctrinal considerations. The core argument is that proof is both semantically and methodologically determined by three conditions of *process*, *materiality* and *probativity*. The first two conditions determine, firstly, the nature of the inferential conclusions of probative judgements (materiality) and secondly, the type of premisses (evidentiary facts) that are acceptable grounds from which to infer these conclusions. The third condition defines the nature of the inferential chains that are drawn to connect the pertinent evidential premisses (process) to their corresponding conclusions (materiality). This core argument is then justified by the context-specific application of this relativistic (three-part) theory of proof to hate crimes. This theoretical application of proof is sustained throughout the book using multiple examples and illustrations of hate crimes around the world. The discussion, both at the level of proof and hate crimes (while focusing on the grounds of race, religion and ethnicity specifically), is framed in jurisprudential, cross-jurisdictional (theoretical), and interdisciplinary terms.

Acknowledgements

The completion of this book would not have been possible without the funding and research support of the University of Cape Town, the Max Planck Institute for the Study of Crime, Security and Law (Freiburg) and the Department of Higher Education's Future Professors Programme. I am also indebted to the comments and feedback of my colleagues in the University of Cape Town's Department of Public Law and at the Zurich *Standards of Proof* workshop, particularly John Jackson and Sarah Summers. The book is dedicated to my son Tshepo Bogosi Mosaka Jr, who was born in the year in which the book was completed, and my supportive wife Pontso Mosaka.

Illustrations

Figures

Tables

Table of Cases

Agarwal v Johnson (1979) 25 Cal.3d 932.
Diane Soares da Costa (2013) No. 0098040–18.2010.8.26.0050 (Sao Paulo Ct. of Just., 23 May).
Eatock v Bolt [2011] [FCA 1103].
EEOC v AA Foundries Inc. (2012) No. 11–792 (W.D. Tex.).
EEOC v Tyson Foods, Inc. (2006) No. cv-05-BE-1704-E (N.D. Ala.).
Ferguson v R [1979] 1 WLR 94, PC.
Glimmerveen and Hagenbeek v Netherlands (1979) Nos. 8348/78 and 8406/78 (ECtHR, 11 Oct.).
Jersild v Denmark [1994] EHRR 1.
Keira McCormack (2010) [80 Adjudication issued 04/01/10] (unreported).
Mbatha v Van Staden (1982) (2) SA 260 (N).
Ortenberg v Plamondon (1915) [24 B.R. 69, 385 (Quebec).
Phelps-Roper v City of Manchester 697 F.3d 678 (8th Cir. 2012).
Phelps-Roper v Strickland 539 F.3d 356, 359 (6th Cir. 2008).
R v Alikor [2004] EWCA Crim 1646.
R *v* Bracewell (1979) 68 Cr App R 44, CA.
R v Derek William Bentley [2001] 1 Cr App R 326 (CA).
R v Hepworth (George Alfred) [1955] 2 Q.B. 600.
R v Majid [2009] EWCA Crim 2563.
R v Miah (2018) EWCA Crim 563.
R v Summers [1952] 1 All ER 1059, CCA.
R v Yap Chuan Ching (1976) 63 Cr App Rep 7.
S v Basson 2005 (1) SA 171 (CC).
Snyder v Phelps 131 S.Ct. 1207, 1213, 179 L.Ed.2d 172 (2011).
Turley v ISG Lackawanna Inc. (2013) No. 1:2006-cv-00794, Doc. 251 (W.D.N.Y.).
Walters v R [1969] 2 AC 26, PC.
Wiggs v Courshon (1973) 355 F. Supp. 206 (S.D. Fla.).

Table of Statutes

18 United States Code.
Additional Protocol to the Convention on Cybercrime, Concerning the African Charter on Human and People's Rights of 1986.
California Penal Code of 1978.
Canada Criminal Code, 1985.
Cape Evidence Ordinance of 1830.
Code Pénal (1992) (France).
Código Penal decreto ley 10426 de 23 Agosto de 1972 (Bolivia).
Connecticut General Statutes (1978).
Constituição da República de Moçambique, 2004.
Constitution de la Niger République, 2010.
Constitution de la République de Guinée, 2010.
Constitution de la République du Sénégal, 2001.
Constitution of the Arabic Republic of Egypt, 2014.
Constitution of the Republic of Namibia, 1990.
Crime and Disorder Act, 1998 (England and Wales).
Criminal Code Compilation Act, 1913 (Western Australia).
Criminalisation of Acts of a Racist and Xenophobic Nature Committed through Computer Systems of 2003.
Decreto-Lei No 2.848, De 7 de Dezembro de 1940, Código Penal (Brazil).
English Draft Criminal Code (1989).
European Union Charter of Fundamental Rights of 2000.
Hate Crime and Public Order (Scotland) Act of 2021.
Hate Crime Statistics Act, 1990.
International Convention on the Elimination of all forms of Racial Discrimination of 1965.
International Covenant on Civil and Political Rights of 1966.
La Constitution de la Guinée équatoriale, 1991.
Law Determining Offences and Penalties in General no. 68 of 2018.
Legge Mancino, decreto-legge Nr. 205/1993 (Italy).
Ley contra el racism y toda forma de discriminacion no. 045 (2010) (Bolivia).
Ley Orgánica 10/1995, de 23 de noviembre, del Código Penal (Spain).

Loi du 30 juillet 1981 tendant à réprimer certains actes inspirés par le racisme ou la xénophobie (Belgium).
Loi n 72–545 du 1 juillet 1972 contre le racism (France).
New York State Penal Law (1965).
Prevention and Combatting of Hate Crimes and Hate Speech Act 13 of 2023.
Public Order Act, 1986 (England and Wales).
Revised Code of Washington (1981).
Strafgesetzbuch (1998) (Germany).
United Nations Charter (1945).
Universal Declaration of Human Rights (1948).
West Virginia Code (1995).
Wetboek van Strafrecht (1881) (Netherlands).

1 Introduction

1.1 The Basic Problem of the Swimming Pool Incident

The primary focus of this book is on the structure and application of evidential proof. The contested phenomenon of hate crimes is used to explicate the structure and meaning of evidential proof in the forensic context. While there are many books about 'evidence and proof',[1] hate crimes[2] and procedural law,[3] it is rare to encounter all three of these areas within a single project. The closest scholarly home for a project of this nature is in the burgeoning field

1 See Kevin M. Clermont *A general theory of evidence and proof: Forming beliefs in truth* (Cham: Springer, 2024); Christian Dahlman et al, eds. *Philosophical foundations of evidence law* (Oxford: Oxford University Press, 2021); Frederick Schauer *Uses of evidence in law, politics and everything else* (Cambridge: Harvard University Press, 2022); Donald Nicolson *Evidence and proof in Scotland: Context and critique* (Edinburgh: Edinburgh University Press, 2019); Chris Carey et al, eds. *Evidence and proof in ancient Greece* (Newcastle: Cambridge Scholars Publishing, 2024); Verena Klappstein and Maciej Dybowski, eds. *Theory of legal evidence – Evidence in legal theory* (Cham: Springer, 2021).

2 See Leah Burch and David Wilkin, eds. *Disability hate crime: Perspectives for change* (London: Routledge, 2025); Stevie-Jade Hardy and Neil Chakraborti *Blood, threats and fears: The hidden worlds of hate crime victims* (Cham: Palgrave Macmillan, 2020); Paul Iganski and Abe Sweiry "Hate crime," in *The Cambridge handbook of social problems*, ed. Javier A. Treviño vol 2 (Cambridge: Cambridge University Press, 2018) Ch 23. See also the recent books in the Palgrave Macmillan series edited by Neil Chakraborti and Barbara Perry: Kim Barker and Olga Jurasz *Violence against women, hate and law: Perspectives from contemporary Scotland* (Cham: Palgrave Macmillan, 2022); Mark A. Walters *Criminalising hate: Law and social justice liberalism* (Cham: Palgrave Macmillan, 2022); Lucille Micheletto *Assessing hate crime laws: A multidisciplinary perspective* (Cham: Palgrave Macmillan, 2023); Jen Neller *Stirring up hatred: Myth, identity and order in the regulation of hate speech* (Cham: Palgrave Macmillan, 2023); Rachel Keighley *Researching hate as an activist: Exploring LGBTQ+ online hate, its impacts, and our responsibility toward equality* (Cham: Palgrave Macmillan, 2024).

3 Joanna Gomula and Stephan Wittich, eds. *Research handbook on international procedural law* (Cheltenham: Elgar, 2024); Torsten Stirner *The procedural law governing facts and evidence in international human rights proceedings* (Leiden: Brill Nijhoff, 2021); Christina Peristeridou and André Klip *Comparative perspectives of criminal procedure* (Cambridge: Intersentia, 2024); Thomas Weigend "Criminal law and criminal procedure," in *Elgar encyclopedia of comparative law*, eds. Jan M. Smits et al (Cheltenham: Elgar, 2023).

DOI: 10.4324/9781003493006-1

of 'evidence theory,'[4] which is a subset of the broader area of jurisprudence or legal philosophy.[5] Hate crime incidents are varied in their motivations, the kinds of actions they entail and the degree of harm they inflict upon their targets. While all kinds of hate crime incidents present difficulties of proof,[6] each scenario generates its own unique legal problem. Hate crimes that culminate in violence often do not produce novel problems of proof that are different from the kind that ordinarily occur in violent crimes such as murder and assault. Therefore, the primary focus of this book will be on non-contact hate crimes that are committed under racial, religious and ethnic (citizenship) motivations. The following scenario illustrates the kind of problem that this book focuses on: X_1 and her swimming coach X_2 decide to undertake a swimming lesson at a communal pool in X_1's residential complex. Upon their arrival, they find Y_1, Y_2, Y_3 and Y_4 swimming in the pool. The swimming lesson commences with a few stretches and warm-up exercises after which X_1 dives into the pool. Y_1, Y_2, Y_3 and Y_4 immediately desist from swimming and they start vacating the pool upon recognising X_1's entry into the pool. The four swimmers then approach Z, who is the caretaker of the complex, to complain about X_1's entry into the pool. Z decides to start draining the water from the pool while X_1 is still swimming, thereby prompting her to stop her lesson and to leave the pool. Once all of the water is drained, and X_1 has left the pool, Z refills the pool and installs a "~X_n" ("No X_n allowed") sign next to the pool. X_1 sees the sign and that Y_1, Y_2, Y_3 and Y_4 are returning to the pool to continue swimming in her absence. X_1 and X_2 are outraged by these events and they wonder whether any of the actions by Y_1, Y_2, Y_3, Y_4 and Z are legally actionable.[7]

4 Paul Roberts "Theorising evidence law" (2023) 43(3) *Oxford Journal of Legal Studies* 629 at 630.

5 Paul Roberts "Rethinking the law of evidence: A twenty-first century agenda for teaching and research" (2002) 55(1) *Current Legal Problems* 297 at 310. Twining himself sees 'jurisprudence' simply as 'the theoretical part of law as a discipline,' see William Twining *General jurisprudence: Understanding law from a global perspective* (Cambridge: Cambridge University Press, 2008) xiii and 8–9. See also William Twining "Some jobs for jurisprudence" (1974) 1(2) *British Journal of Law and Society* 149; William Twining "Evidence and legal theory" (1984) 47(3) *Modern Law Review* 261.

6 Nicola Lacey "Legislation against sex discrimination: Questions from a female perspective" (1987) 14(4) *Journal of Law & Society* 411 at 412; Loretta de Plevitz "The Briginshaw 'standard of proof' in anti-discrimination law: 'Pointing with a wavering finger'" (2003) 27(2) *Melbourne University Law Review* 308 at 325 ('The elements are notoriously difficult to prove'); Richard Moon "Discrimination and its justification: Coping with equality rights under the Charter" (1988) 26(4) *Osgoode Hall Law Journal* 673 at 687 ('Intention to discriminate is difficult to discover and difficult to prove'); Howard Varney "Forging new tools: A note on *Fose v Minister of Safety and Security* CCT 14/96" (1998) 14(2) *South African Journal of Human Rights* 336 at 346.

7 This illustrative scenario is drawn from the real personal account of Cornel West in Sacramento, California, United States; see Cornel West *Brother West: Living and loving out loud, a memoir* (New York: Smiley Books, 2009) 37–38. See Marta Araújo "A very 'prudent integration': White flight, school segregation and depoliticization of (anti)-racism" (2016) 19(2) *Race, Ethnicity and Education* 300 at 309, n15: 'The term *white flight* was popularised in the 1970s debates on desegregation in US public schools, due to the significant number of white families moving to the suburbs to avoid integrated schooling.'

If X_1 and X_2 was to institute legal proceedings against Y_1, Y_2, Y_3, Y_4 and Z, there generally would be three notional outcomes: the defendants are found guilty (KaPR), they are found not guilty (Ka~PR) or there is insufficient evidence to decide the matter one way or the other (i.e. a stalemate) (~KaPR).[8] If X instituted a civil action, her burden to prove that KaPR > Ka~PR ∨ ~KaPR is normatively symmetrical to that of the defendants,[9] whereas in a criminal case the State bears a heavier burden to establish that KaPR > Ka~PR ∧ ~KaPR.[10] In the event that the defendants are charged with hate crimes and they deny having been involved at all in the swimming pool incident, the core question that confronts X is *how can she prove the claim that the defendants committed hate crimes?* ($Y_n \pm Z_n < P_m + P_{proc} + P_p$): This question in turn depends on the meaning given to the terms 'hate crime' and 'proof.'

1.2 The Orthodoxy of Evidential Proof

Proof in the context of legal trials commonly is understood in epistemological terms; that is, as an 'epistemic engine'[11] or 'fundamentally an epistemological

8 See Samuel Bray "Not proven: Introducing a third verdict" (2005) 72 *University of Chicago Law Review* 1299 at 1299–1300; Larry Laudan "Need verdicts come in pairs?" (2010) 14 *International Journal of Evidence & Proof* 1; Federico Picinali "Do theories of punishment necessarily deliver a binary system of verdicts? An exploratory essay" (2018) 12 *Criminal Law and Philosophy* 555; Federico Picinali *Justice in-between: A study of intermediate criminal verdicts* (Oxford: Oxford University Press, 2022). However, exceptional jurisdictions such as Scotland, Italy and Israel deploy systems of three verdicts, see Yaniv Vaki and Yoram Rabin "Two kinds of acquittals – Different kinds of doubts" (2021) 32 *Criminal Law Forum* 97; Peter Duff "Scottish criminal jury: A very peculiar institution" (1999) 62 *Law and Contemporary Problems* 173.

9 Dale Nance *The burdens of proof: Discriminatory power, weight of evidence and tenacity of belief* (Cambridge: Cambridge University Press, 2016) 244; Edward K. Cheng "Reconceptualising the burden of proof" (2013) 122 *Yale Law Journal* 1254 at 1275. For philosophical accounts, see Douglas Walton *Burden of proof, presumption and argumentation* (New York: Cambridge University Press, 2014) Chs 2 and 3; Petar Bodlović "On presumptions, burdens of proof and explanations" (2020) 2(40) *Informal Logic* 255; Avital Fried "Statistical evidence and the criminal verdict asymmetry" (2022) 200 *Synthese* 472.

10 Paul Roberts "Presumptuous or pluralistic presumptions of innocence? Methodological diagnosis towards conceptual reinvigoration" (2021) 198 *Synthese* 8901 at 8927; Larry Laudan *Truth, error and criminal law: An essay in legal epistemology* (New York: Cambridge University Press, 2006) 109–110; John D. Jackson "Managing uncertainty and finality: The function of the criminal trial in legal inquiry," in *Trial on trial: Truth and due process*, eds. Antony Duff et al vol 1 (Portland: Oregon, 2004) 121 at 127. Cf. Thomas Weigend "Assuming that the defendant is not guilty: The presumption of innocence in the German system of criminal justice" (2014) 8 *Criminal Law and Philosophy* 285 at 290 ('The German system of criminal procedure knows no "parties" with active roles at the trial, and it knows nothing about a burden of proof being placed on either party; in the German tradition, the criminal process is conceived of as the court's unilateral endeavour to find the truth, with the prosecution and the defence standing at the side-lines').

11 Laudan *Truth, error and criminal law: An essay in legal epistemology*, 2.

event.'[12] According to Haack, 'the law is up to its neck in epistemology.'[13] This conception isolates proof into a discrete and 'non-legal' part of the adjudication. This separation implies three things: a conceptual and institutional segregation between fact-finding, a value-neutral epistemic exercise, and value preferences that arise in the context of normative judgements. The general faith in the 'human epistemic competence' of fact-finders, according to Stein, warrants them being accorded a 'Freedom of Proof' to decide factual disputes without the intrusion of legal doctrine and normative reasoning.[14] Secondly, proof is separated from procedural law rules that regulate, among other things, the investigation of facts; the authentication and admissibility of evidence; the presentation of evidence; and the processing of interlocutory challenges. According to Wigmore, the general process of vindicating or enforcing 'public and private jural rights and duties falls naturally into five stages': (1) the securing of the attendance of the parties to the trial; (2) the determination of the facts in dispute from the pleadings or the *dossier*; (3) the demonstration of proof of the facts in dispute; (4) the rendering of a verdict by the fact-finder; and (5) the enforcement of the verdict.[15] Wigmore regards proof as falling 'somewhere in the third stage,'[16] whereas the first and fifth stages 'involve and rest upon certain larger aspects of procedure that are independent of the evidential material.'[17] Moreover, Wigmore also makes a similar distinction between the 'presentation of . . . elemental facts' and 'the piecing of them together,' through 'the invocation, by counsel, of ordinary rules of logic and rhetoric.'[18] The latter process, which Wigmore designates as '[a]rgumentation,' he regards as a subject falling outside the discipline of law.[19] The third implication of the epistemic conception of trials involves the separation of proof from substantive law, which is regarded as the determiner of legal rights and duties as well as the facts in dispute.[20] On this conception, the nature and meaning of criminal prohibitions and civil actions are contained in the

12 Michael S. Pardo "The field of evidence and the field of knowledge" (2005) 24(5) *Law and Philosophy* 321 at 321; Jeremy Bentham "An introductory view of the rationale of evidence," in *The works of Jeremy Bentham*, ed. John Bowring vol 6 (London: Simpkin, Marshall & Co., 1843) 5: 'The field of evidence is no other than the field of knowledge.'

13 Susan Haack "Epistemology legalized: Or, truth, justice and the American way" (2004) 49 *American Journal of Jurisprudence* 43 at 44.

14 Alex Stein "The refoundation of evidence law" (1996) 9 *Canadian Journal of Law & Jurisprudence* 279 at 296–297.

15 John H. Wigmore *Evidence in trials at common law* vol 1 (revised by Peter Tillers) (Boston: Little Brown, 1983) 2.

16 Wigmore "Evidence in trials at common law," 2.

17 Wigmore "Evidence in trials at common law," 689.

18 Wigmore "Evidence in trials at common law," 6–7.

19 Wigmore "Evidence in trials at common law," 7.

20 Wigmore "Evidence in trials at common law," 8.

pleadings and regulated by substantive law, whereas the logical and rhetorical canons of proof form part of a separate subject entirely.

This segregated conception of adjudication also has firm institutional roots. In particular, legal scholarship and teaching likewise reflects the kind of segregation described earlier as consisting of the facts in dispute being determined by *substantive law*; the investigation, presentation and authentication of the relevant evidence being regulated by *procedural rules*; and the extra-legal canons of *logic* and *rhetoric* being deployed to evaluate the probative weight of evidence. For example, teaching materials and courses mostly focus on substantive law at university-level legal education, and procedural courses tend to be taught in vocational and professional contexts.[21] Common law students are taught about substantive law rules and duties as they are clarified and applied in binding (mostly appellate-level) cases, whereas the civilian student is given their staple diet of substantive law doctrine and the *travaux préparatoires* of the provisions of the relevant legislative codes.[22] It is rare to find this segregation being bridged by substantive and procedural law being taught in the same course. Furthermore, there are journals such as the *Journal of Criminal Law*,[23] *Criminal Law Forum*,[24] *Criminal Law and Philosophy*,[25] *Journal of International Criminal Justice*,[26] *New Criminal Law Review*[27] and the *Criminal Law Review*,[28] which self-evidently have a substantive law focus. Similarly, the *International Journal of Procedural Law*,[29] *Civil Justice* Quarterly[30] and the *Journal für Strafrecht*[31] are three examples of periodicals that focus exclusively on procedural law. Moreover, procedural law is also institutionalised by scholarly associations such as the *International Association of Procedural Law*[32] and the *Max Planck Institute Luxembourg for International, European*

21 Paul Roberts "Five foundational fallacies of common law evidence" (translated by Ping Yang and Baosheng Zhang) (2018) 26 *Evidence Science* 93–108; Carlson Anyangwe *Cameroonian judicial system* (Yaoundé: CEPER, 1987) 144, also 125–135 and 197–210; Philip M. Genty "Celebrating the difference: A U.S. educator's perspective on legal education under the civil and common law," in *Re-thinking legal education under the civil and common law*, ed. Richard Grimes (London: Routledge, 2018) 2 at 4.

22 Genty "Celebrating the difference," 3. See also Kris Gledhill and Ben Livings, eds. *The teaching of criminal law: The pedagogical imperatives* (London: Routledge, 2017); Warren Swain and David Campbell, eds. *Reimaging contract law pedagogy: A new agenda for teaching* (London: Routledge, 2019).

23 Available at: www.journals.sagepub.com (accessed: 24 July 2024).

24 Available at: www.jhs.gonzagu.edu (accessed: 24 July 2024).

25 Available at: www.link.springer.com (accessed: 24 July 2024).

26 Available at: www.academic.oup.com (accessed: 24 July 2024).

27 Available at: www.online.ucpress.edu (accessed: 24 July 2024).

28 Available at: www.sweetandmaxwell.co.uk (accessed: 24 July 2024).

29 Available at: www.jurisquare.be (accessed: 24 July 2024).

30 Available at: www.sweetandmaxwell.co.uk (accessed: 24 July 2024).

31 Available at: www.verlagoesterreich.at (accessed: 24 July 2024).

32 See www.iaplaw.org (accessed: 24 July 2024).

and Regulatory Procedural Law.[33] This scholarly[34] and pedagogic divide tracks the orthodox segregated and bifurcated conception of adjudication described earlier. This orthodoxy of adjudication leaves no room for proof within the discipline of law. As a result, the study and scholarship of proof has almost no institutional reach.

Whereas legal scholarship and teaching are dominated by substantive law, and to a lesser extent procedural law, materials, proof hardly has a comparable institutional footprint. As Twining's 'taking facts seriously' thesis has shown,[35] proof is hardly taught as a separate self-standing specialisation in legal education. It is customary for law students to be given an assumed set of facts in their assessments and to be requested to discuss the applicable doctrinal rules. Proof scholarship is currently the preoccupation of a multidisciplinary group of scholars, some of whom are not lawyers, under the New Evidence Scholarship banner.[36]

This book aims to break from this orthodoxy by offering a much more integrated conception of proof. By definition, proof (PR) is *the property of a*

33 See www.mpi.lu (accessed: 24 July 2024).

34 Notable institutional exceptions to the substantive law–procedural law divide, such as the *International Journal of Evidence & Proof* (available at: www.journals.sagepub.com (accessed: 24 July 2024)); *Quaestio facti: International Journal on Evidential Legal Reasoning* (available at: www.quaestiofacti.com (accessed: 24 July 2024)); and the *Michele Taruffo Girona Evidence Week* (www.gironaevidenceweek.com [accessed: 24 July 2024)), that focus on evidence and proof are rare.

35 William Twining "Taking facts seriously – Again," in *Rethinking evidence: Exploratory essays*, ed. William Twining 2nd ed (Cambridge: Cambridge University Press, 2009) 417 at 417. Twining took up this 'daunting task', with largely pedagogical motivations, of 'taking facts seriously' in earnest in 1982 (William Twining "Taking facts seriously," in *Essays on legal education*, ed. Neil Gold (Toronto: Butterworths, 1982), but regretfully later acknowledged that his clarion call had 'failed to persuade.' The insistence on trial courts and 'factual questions', as opposed to appellate 'legal questions', has strong roots in the sceptical American Realist movement, see Karl Llewellyn "A realistic jurisprudence – the next step" (1930) 3(4) *Columbia Law Review* 431; Karl N. Llewellyn "Some realism about realism – Responding to Dean Pound" (1931) 44 *Harvard Law Review* 1222; Jerome Frank *Law and the modern mind* (New York: Brentano's, 1930); Jerome Frank "Why not a clinical lawyer-school?" (1933) 81(8) *University of Pennsylvania Law Review and American Law Register* 907; William Twining *Karl Llewellyn and the realist movement* 2nd ed (Cambridge: Cambridge University Press, 2012).

36 Richard Lempert "The new evidence scholarship: Analysing the process of proof" (1986) 66(3) *Boston University Law Review* 439 at 439–440. Lempert is credited widely for coining the term 'New Evidence Scholarship,' see William Twining "The new evidence scholarship" (1999) 40 *South Texas Law Review* 351 at 352, n4; William Twining "Evidence as a multi-disciplinary subject," 91 at 91; Susan Haack *Evidence matters: Science, proof, and truth in the law* (New York: Cambridge University Press, 2014) 20, n91; William Twining "The new evidence scholarship" (1991) 13 *Cardozo Law Review* 295 at 297; Ian Dennis *The law of evidence* 6th ed (London: Sweet & Maxwell, 2017) [129]. For an overview of the explosion of scholarship under the "New Evidence Scholarship" banner, see Roger Park et al "Bayes wars redivivus – An exchange" (2010) 8(1) *International Commentary on Evidence* 1; Michael S. Pardo "The nature and purpose of evidence theory" (2013) 2(3) *Vanderbilt Law Review* 547 at 553.

disputed fact (P_m) *being established inferentially* (P_p) *from an extant fact (evidence)* (P_{proc}).[37] On the narrow orthodox conception described earlier, proof is the equivalent of the drawing of inferences using the extra-legal canons of logic and rhetoric to establish disputed facts, namely $PR = P_p$. As indicated earlier, this institutionalised orthodoxy is far too narrow and thus, prone to conceptual and contextual errors.[38] By contrast, proof is defined in this book to include the disputed and extant facts that are the object (P_m) and foundation (P_{proc}), respectively, of inferential reasoning. The implications of this move will be made clearer, particularly in Chapters 5 and 6, but the difference between this integrated conception of proof from the orthodoxy is one of scope. On the integrated conception, proof consists of three *material* (P_m), *processual* (P_{proc}) and *probative* (P_p) conditions in conjunctive combination; that is, $PR = P_m \wedge P_{proc} \wedge P_p$.

The material condition refers to the objects of proof in the forensic context. These objects are facts about which the parties are in dispute.[39] The nature and eligibility of these facts usually correspond to the rights and duties, that have been violated or threatened, of the parties as determined by substantive law.[40] The term 'materiality' is deployed, in the law of evidence in common law jurisdictions, to define the quality of a fact being disputed and corresponding (usually) to a substantive law provision.[41] Material facts are also known, following Wigmore,[42] as *ultimate probanda* on account of their potential to spiral into several sub-layers of disputed facts. There is material variation not only with different crimes and causes of actions, but also with varying disputed facts that affects the structure and application of proof. This contingent quality of proof makes it inherently relativistic. To satisfy the materiality condition, our complainant (X) from the swimming pool incident described earlier will have to know legal meaning and elements of the hate crimes with which the defendants are charged. The history, meaning, types and elements of hate crimes across the world are discussed in Chapter 2. However, in its broadest sense the term 'hate crime' refers, according to Levin, to 'discriminatory criminal acts committed because of someone's actual or perceived membership in a particular socially identifiable status group.'[43] The overlap between the terms 'hate crime' and 'discrimination' will also be discussed in Chapter 2.

37 See Pamela-Jane Schwikkard and Tshepo B. Mosaka *Principles of evidence* 5th ed (Claremont: Juta, 2023) 607.
38 See Roberts "Theorising evidence law," 632–633.
39 Wigmore "Evidence in trials at common law," 20, n4.
40 Terence Anderson et al *Analysis of evidence* 2nd ed (Cambridge: Cambridge University Press, 2005) 46.
41 James L. Montrose "Basic concepts of the law of evidence" (1954) 70 *Law Quarterly Review* 527 at 529; Wigmore "Evidence in trials at common law," 18–19.
42 Wigmore "Evidence in trials at common law," 13–20.
43 Brian Levin "The long arc of justice: Race, violence and the emergence of hate crime law," in *Hate crimes*, eds. Barbara Perry and Brian Levin vol 1 (Westport: Praeger, 2009) 1 at 2. See

The processual condition regulates the extant facts that serve as the foundation from which inferences are drawn to prove the material facts discussed earlier. In order to preserve their authenticity,[44] most jurisdictions attach a multitude of rules and procedures to the *presentation* of these extant facts.[45] These presentational procedures are also affected by the type of adjudicator (e.g. lay, professional or *sui generis*) before whom the extant facts will be adduced. In order to distinguish the material and processual conditions of proof, the common law orthodoxy is to distinguish between *facta probanda* or 'principal facts' (material) and *facta probans* or 'evidentiary facts.'[46] Similar to material facts, extant facts under the processual condition are also varied in their nature and areas of application. They range from 'brute facts' (e.g. bloodstained knives, cell phone location data or bullet cartridges) to multi-layered propositions of facts (e.g. motives, opportunities or means).[47] In general, extant facts are either 'events' (occurrences) or 'states of affairs,' which either exist or not.[48] The procedures pertaining to the presentation of the extant facts of hate crimes are discussed in Chapter 4.

Having discussed the material and processual conditions of proof, we now turn to the third condition that will take up the bulk of this book. The probative condition is the subject of Chapters 3, 5 and 6. It is by the probative condition of proof that the nature of the inference to be drawn from the processual (extant) facts to establish the material (disputed) facts is determined and evaluated. As indicated earlier, proof on the orthodox conception is limited to the probative condition, about which the law has little to say. According to Thayer, '[t]he law has no *mandamus* to the logical faculty,'[49] whereas

---

also Erik Bleich "From race to hate: A historical perspective," in *Hate, politics, law: Critical perspectives on combating hate*, eds. Thomas Brudholm and Birgitte S. Johansen (New York: Oxford University Press, 2018) 15 at 33: '[I]t is now common to refer to 1960s – and 1970s – era laws penalising racist expressions as hate speech laws.'

44 Larry May *Ancient legal thought: Equity, justice and humaneness from Hammurabi and the Pharaohs to Justinian and the Talmud* (New York: Cambridge University Press, 2019) 43–44.

45 Wigmore "Evidence in trials at common law," 6–7.

46 Bentham "An introductory view of the rationale of evidence; for the use of non-lawyers as well as lawyers" 15; Jeremy Bentham *Rationale of judicial evidence* vol 1 (edited by J.S Mill) (London: Hunt & Clark, 1827) 19–20; James J.F. Stephen *A digest on the law of evidence* (London: Macmillan, 1887) art 1 ('any two facts . . . so related to each other that according to the common course of events one either taken by itself or in connection with other facts proves or renders probable the past, present, or future existence or non-existence of the other'); James B. Thayer *A preliminary treatise on evidence at common law* (Boston: Little Brown and Co., 1898) 263 ('a matter of fact which is to be used as a basis of inference to another matter of fact'); Wigmore "Evidence in trials at common law," 13–20 ('*factum probandum*' and '*facta probans*').

47 Montrose "Basic concepts of the law of evidence," 534.

48 Bentham "Rationale of judicial evidence," 21.

49 Thayer "A preliminary treatise on evidence at common law," 314; James B. Thayer "Law and logic" (1900) 14 *Harvard Law Review* 139 at 140–141; William Twining *Rethinking evidence: Exploratory essays* (Evanston, IL: Northwestern University Press, 1994) 196; Hock-Lai Ho *A philosophy of evidence law* (Oxford: Oxford University Press, 2008) 38.

Damaška has identified an enduring culture of rule-scepticism in civilian jurisdictions with respect to the evaluation of evidence.[50] However, as this book will show, an approach to the probative condition that simply ignores the material and processual conditions in the overall assessment of proof is prone to error. The aim of this book is to show how these three conditions of proof can be met in the context of non-contact hate crimes around the world.

1.3 An Introduction to 'The Problem of Hate'

The belated emergence of hate crime statutes in the second half of the twentieth century[51] gives the false impression that inter-social hate or hate-inspired violence is new. However, the prevalence of inter-social hatred has endured since the beginning of human history.[52] Hatred is a biological (neurological) phenomenon that ranges from 'relatively mild and unaggressive dislikes' (e.g. when somebody says they 'hate the smell of eggs') to 'vicious animosities' 'with or without a passionately violent component.'[53] According to Steenberg and Steenberg, hatred comprises three components: the *negation of intimacy* between the hater and the target, a *passion* that expresses itself as a combination of anger and fear on the part of the hater, and the *commitment* to devalue or diminish the targeted individual or group.[54]

The opposite of the negation of intimacy between the hater and the target is either an inclination for connection or indifference. For most people, their relations with other people are characterised by an indifference or inclination for connection, but for the hater, the feeling is one of repulsion or disgust,[55] which become motivations for fostering the negation of social intimacy between her and the target. The hater's negative appraisal of the

50 Mirjan R. Damaška "Evidentiary barriers to conviction and two models of criminal procedure: A comparative study" (1973) 121(3) *University of Pennsylvania Law Review* 507 at 515, n10; Damaška *Evaluation of evidence: Premodern and modern approaches*, 128; Joëlle Vuille "Forensic science evidence in non-adversary criminal justice systems," in *Forensic science evidence and expert witness testimony: Reliability through reform*, eds. Paul Roberts and Michael Stockdale (Cheltenham: Elgar, 2018) 354 at 365.

51 Valerie Jenness and Ryken Grattet *Making a hate crime: From social movement to law enforcement* (New York: Russell Sage Foundation, 2001) 17–18; Erik Bleich "From race to hate: A historical perspective," 15 at 16 and 20; Erik Bleich "The rise of hate speech and hate crime laws in liberal democracies" (2011) 37(6) *Journal of Ethnic and Migration Studies* 917 at 920.

52 Thomas F. Gossett *Race: The history of an idea in America* (Dallas: Southern Methodist University Press, 1965) 3; Ryken Grattet and Valerie Jenness "Examining the boundaries of hate crime law: Disabilities and the 'dilemma of difference'" (2001) 91(3) *Journal of Criminal Law and Criminology* 653 at 658: '[W]hat is now commonly understood as "bias" or "hate" crime is an age-old problem approached with a new conceptual lens and sense of urgency.'

53 Nick Haslam and Sean C. Murphy "Hate, dehumanization and 'hate'," in *Perspectives on hate: How it originates, develops, manifests and spreads*, ed. Robert J. Sternberg (Washington: American Psychological Association, 2020) 27 at 33.

54 Sternberg and Sternberg "The nature of hate," 18.

55 Sternberg "A duplex theory of hate," 305.

target, as being 'immoral,' 'malicious' or 'dangerous,' generates a social barrier between the two that may or may not lead to violence.[56] The second component of hate focuses on the hater's *passion* in order to distinguish the kind of disposition involved from a gratuitous or mild antipathy towards the target. According to Sternberg, a hateful *passion* consists in underlying feelings of anger and/or fear on the part of the hater.[57] The target is appraised as being a threat or transgressor coupled with the hater feeling a sense of powerlessness to do anything about it.[58] It is within this particular context that hatred has been associated by neuroscience researchers with the insula and amygdala parts of the human brain.[59] The amygdala functions as a crude 'early warning system' that detects threats, whereas the pyramid-shaped insula processes and recalls incidents of perceptive pain.[60] According to Williams, fMRI (functional magnetic resonance imaging) scans of these two parts of the brains of test subjects show increased levels of oxygenation and activation in reaction to pictures of what or whom they fear (and hate).[61] The hateful impulses generated by the amygdala and the insula are usually controlled, and where necessary, corrected, by our prefrontal cortex that is responsible for our executive decisions.[62] However, for the hateful transgressor of hate crimes, it may be that the amygdala and insula have a stronger influence than the prefrontal cortex.[63]

The third component of hate consists of the hater's *commitment* towards the devaluation and diminution of the target.[64] This component typically manifests towards groups because, according to Allport, it is far easier for most haters to devalue abstract groups than specific individuals with whom they may or may not have some social relationship.[65] Furthermore, it is also easier to devalue vulnerable minority groups than ubiquitous and conspicuous members of the population. This devaluation typically is grounded upon the extropunitive effect of hatred, namely that the target is saddled with a degree of blameworthiness for the hater's anxiety or fear.[66] According to Brudholm, the defining proposition of hatred is that 'the target is evil and worthy

56 Agneta Fischer et al "Why we hate," in *The moral psychology of hate*, ed. Noelle Birondo (Lanham: Rowman & Littlefield, 2022) 137 at 154.
57 Sternberg "A duplex theory of hate," 307.
58 Fischer et al "Why we hate," 154.
59 Michael Williams *The science of hate: How prejudice becomes hate and what we can do to stop it* (London: Faber & Faber, 2021) Ch 3.
60 Williams "The science of hate," Ch 3.
61 Williams "The science of hate," Ch 3.
62 Williams "The science of hate," Ch 3.
63 Williams "The science of hate," Ch 3:
64 Sternberg "A duplex theory of hate," 308.
65 Gordon W. Allport *The nature of prejudice* (Cambridge, MA: Addison-Wesley Publishing Company, 1954) 363–364.
66 Allport "The nature of prejudice," 363.

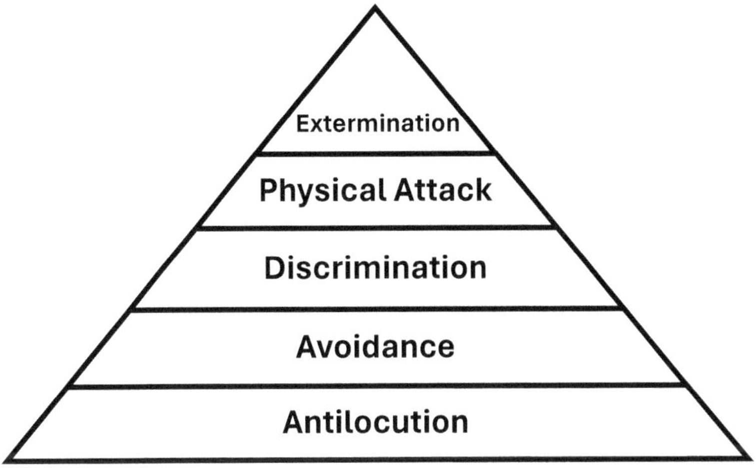

Figure 1.1 Pyramid of Hatred

of damage, suffering and destruction.'[67] Exhortations to violence or destruction in this way flow much more readily when grounded upon the sustained devaluation of the humanity, character or actions of the target.

Although it is potent and catalysing, hatred does not always lead to the perpetration of violence or the contravention of hate crime laws.[68] It is for this reason, among others, that hatred, as we will see later in Chapter 2, is not a requirement for the successful prosecution of a hate crime.[69] However, where hatred does end up contributing to violence, this transition can be formulated into five stages: the *antilocution, avoidance, discrimination, physical attack* and *extermination*.[70]

Antilocution consists of hateful opinions, jokes and outright slurs commonly being directed towards the target individual or group. Although regulated mainly through civil or constitutional sanctions in some jurisdictions, the first stage of the Pyramid of Hatred in Figure 1.1 rarely attracts criminal sanction. Haters at this stage often contend that their speech is protected

67 Thomas Brudholm "What is hate," in *Perspectives on hate: How it originates, develops, manifests and spreads*, ed. Robert J. Sternberg (Washington: American Psychological Association, 2020) 65 at 80, citing Robert C. Roberts *Emotions: An essay in aid of moral psychology* (Cambridge: Cambridge University Press, 2003) 251.

68 Sternberg and Sternberg "The nature of hate," 7.

69 Frederick M. Lawrence *Punishing hate: Bias crimes under American law* (Cambridge: Harvard University Press, 1999) 9; James B. Jacobs and Kimberly Potter *Hate crimes: Criminal law & identity politics* (New York: Oxford University Press, 1998) 11; Joanna Botha and Avinash Govindjee "Regulating cases of 'extreme hate speech' in South Africa: A suggested framework for a legislated criminal sanction" (2014) 27(2) *South African Journal of Criminal Justice* 117 at 119: 'Actual hatred or hostility is not necessary to found the offence.'

70 See Williams "The science of hate," Ch 1.

by the right to freedom of expression.[71] The second stage entails the social separation of the haters, as the in-group, and the target, as the out-group, particularly in public institutions as such schools, public transport and housing.[72] One of the most infamous examples of the avoidance stage of hateful violence is the historic South African policy of apartheid that divided citizens according to their race.[73] Subsequent to the Avoidance stage, the third stage of discrimination follows where the target group is denied access to opportunities and goods and services in order to stifle their ability to advance in society.[74] The last two stages of the Pyramid of Hate turn from non-contact to contact actions. The fourth stage consists of the hater manifesting their hatred through a physical attack against the target. This type of action, considered in isolation, would qualify for a common assault criminal charge. In the fifth stage of the Pyramid of Hate, the hater commits further acts of violence with the aim of exterminating the target and destroying their ethnicity within a particular society.[75]

It is the potential that hate-motivated violence has to contribute towards incidents of terrorism, genocide, massacres and ethnic cleansing[76] that has prompted legislatures around the world to enact legislative prohibitions and to designate them as 'hate crimes.' For example, an estimated 190,000 incidents of hate crime are reported every year in England and Wales.[77] The Federal Bureau of Investigation reported 11,634 incidents of hate crimes were recorded across 14 631 state-level law enforcement agencies in the United States in 2022.[78] Over 7200 incidents of hate crime were reported across 37 countries in Europe in 2020,[79] whereas in 2022 Sweden and Canada

71 See generally, Adrienne Stone and Frederick Schauer, eds. *The Oxford handbook of freedom of speech* (Oxford: Oxford University Press, 2021).

72 Williams "The science of hate," Ch 1.

73 See Nancy L. Clark and William H. Worger *South Africa: The rise and fall of apartheid* 3rd ed. (London: Routledge, 2016); Terry Bell and Dumisa B. Ntsebeza *Unfinished business: South Africa, apartheid and truth* (London: Verso, 2003); Saul Dubow *Apartheid, 1948–1994* (Oxford: Oxford University Press, 2014); Nancy L. Clark "South Africa: Apartheid and post-apartheid," in *The Palgrave handbook of African colonial and postcolonial history*, eds. Martin S. Shanguhyia and Toyin Falola (New York: Palgrave Macmillan, 2018) Ch 40.

74 Williams "The science of hate," Ch 1.

75 Williams "The science of hate," Ch 1.

76 Robert J. Sternberg and Karin Sternberg *The nature of hate* (New York: Cambridge University Press, 2008) 7; Robert J. Sternberg "A duplex theory of hate: Development and application to terrorism, massacres and genocide" (2003) 7(3) *Review of General Psychology* 219 at 304–305.

77 United Kingdom House of Commons *Hate crime statistics* (15 January 2024), available at: www.researchbriefings.files.parliament.uk (accessed: 28 July 2024).

78 United States Federal Bureau of Investigation *FBI Releases 2022 hate crime statistics* (16 October 2023), available at: www.justice.gov (accessed: 28 July 2024). The United States Department of Justice reported that race-based and religion-based hate crimes constituted the largest chunk of the total reported hate crimes in the United States.

79 Organisation for Security and Co-Operation in Europe *2020 Hate Crime Data Key Findings* (15 November 2021) 2, available at: www.hatecrime.osce.org (accessed: 28 July 2024). The

reported 4788[80] incidents and 3576 incidents[81] of hate crime, respectively. In addition to these rising statistics of hate crimes, legislators have also been influenced by historic examples of genocidal incidents of hate-related violence such as the infamous Holocaust of more than 6 million Jews through 'mass bludgeoning . . . shootings, starvation and . . . asphyxiation' in Nazi Germany.[82] The massacre of almost 2 million Buddhist, Vietnamese, Muslim Cham, Chinese and other religious minorities in Cambodia between 1975 and 1979 is another well-known example.[83] Other examples are the killing of over 8000 Bosnian-Muslim men and the raping and torture of no fewer than 20,000 Bosnian-Muslim women in Yugoslavia in the early 1990s;[84] the Rwandan genocide of approximately 75% of the Tutsi population (between 500,000 and 600,000 civilians) within less than 100 days in 1994;[85] and the Islamic State's mass attack of 350,000 Yazidis, including adolescent children, in the Sinjar region of Iraq on 3 August 2014.[86] Most recently, an estimated

---

OSCE's membership consists of 57 states from North America, Europe and Asia, including France, Germany, Belgium, United States, United Kingdom, Italy, Russia, Spain, Switzerland, Portugal and the Netherlands.

80 Swedish National Council for Crime Prevention *Hate crimes reported to the police in 2022: A compilation of the cases that were classified as hate crimes by the police* (Report No. 17) (2023) 9, available at: www.bra.se (accessed 28 July 2024).

81 Statistique Canada *Police-reported hate crime, 2022* (13 March 2024), available at: www150.statcan.gc.ca (accessed: 28 July 2024).

82 Karin Orth "Camps," in *The Oxford handbook of Holocaust studies*, eds. Peter Hayes and John K. Roth (Oxford: Oxford University Press, 2010) 364 at 375–376; Mary Fulbrook "Systematic and ad hoc persecution and mass murder in the Holocaust: Killings in eastern Europe outside the camps," in *The Cambridge world history of genocide: Genocide in the contemporary era*, eds. Ben Kiernan et al (Cambridge: Cambridge University Press, 2023) 235 at 235.

83 Jay Winter "War and genocide in the twentieth century," in *The Cambridge world history of genocide: Genocide in the contemporary era*, eds. Ben Kiernan et al (Cambridge: Cambridge University Press, 2023) 44 at 59; Alexander L. Hinton *Why did they kill? Cambodia in the shadow of genocide* (Berkeley: University of California Press, 2005); Ben Kiernan "The genocides in Cambodia," in *The Cambridge world history of genocide: Genocide in the contemporary era*, eds. Ben Kiernan et al (Cambridge: Cambridge University Press, 2023) 518.

84 Winter "War and genocide in the twentieth century," 62; Edina Bećirević "Genocide in Bosnia and Herzegovina," in *The Cambridge world history of genocide: Genocide in the contemporary era*, eds. Ben Kiernan et al (Cambridge: Cambridge University Press, 2023) 627; Sternberg and Sternberg "The nature of hate," 4–5.

85 Scott Straus "The Rwandan genocide in context," in *The Cambridge world history of genocide: Genocide in the contemporary era*, eds. Ben Kiernan et al (Cambridge: Cambridge University Press, 2023) 647 at 668–669; Winter "War and genocide in the twentieth century," 63; William A. Schabas "Hate speech in Rwanda: The road to genocide," in *Genocide and human rights*, ed. Mark Lattimer (London: Routledge, 2017) Ch 8.

86 Sareta Ashraph "The Yazidi genocide," in *The Cambridge world history of genocide: Genocide in the contemporary era*, eds. Ben Kiernan et al (Cambridge: Cambridge University Press, 2023) 722 at 722.

1.4 million Rohingyas were expelled, including being killed and having their houses burned, from their homes in Myanmar.[87]

1.4 Three Jurisprudential Aims of Evidence Theory

The project of this book, which is to explicate the evidential proof of hate crimes, is a theoretical one within the discipline of law.[88] The application of the kinds of theoretical models of proof developed in Chapters 5 and 6 of the book is a form of middle-order theorising that is not commonly associated with first-order jurisprudence.[89] The project of this book is also distinguishable by its three methodological aims of undertaking a form of theorising that is *trans-disciplinary, cross-jurisdictional* and *post-colonial.*

The first aim of the book is to combine the analytic techniques of argumentation theory with the contextual foundation of evidential, procedural and substantive law doctrine. The argumentation models developed in Chapters 5 and 6 of the book are used to explicate the structure and meaning of proof of the elements of hate crime that are developed in Chapter 2 within the institutional context of the procedural rules described in Chapters 3 and 4. It is in that sense that this book is first and foremost, *trans-disciplinary.*

Secondly, the book aims to be *cross-jurisdictional* in that the kind of theorising that is undertaken throughout is framed in general terms that widen its scope of application across several jurisdictions around the world. In any case, phenomena such as hate crimes and proof are germane and familiar to most jurisdictions across the world. Proof is encountered by any jurisdiction that

87 Azeem Ibrahim "Genocide in Myanmar: The assault on the Rohingya, 2010–2019," in *The Cambridge world history of genocide: Genocide in the contemporary era*, eds. Ben Kiernan et al (Cambridge: Cambridge University Press, 2023) 746 at 749 and 760.

88 Twining defined jurisprudence simply as 'theoretical part of law as a discipline,' see William Twining *General jurisprudence: Understanding law from a global perspective* (Cambridge: Cambridge University Press, 2009) xiii. For further definitions, see Richard Posner *The problems of jurisprudence* (Cambridge: Harvard University Press, 1990) xi; Jerome Hall *Foundations of jurisprudence* (Indiana: Bobbs-Merrill Company, 1973) 13–15; Roger Cotterrell "The jurist's conscience: Reflections around Radbruch," in *The anxiety of the jurist: Legality, exchange and judgement*, eds. Maksymilian Del Mar and Cláudio Michelon (Farnham: Ashgate, 2013) 13 at 13–15; Maksymilian Del Mar and Cláudio Michelon "Introduction," in *The anxiety of the jurist: Legality, exchange and judgement*, eds. Maksymilian Del Mar and Cláudio Michelon (Farnham: Ashgate, 2013) 1 at 1–2; Michael Freeman *Lloyd's introduction to jurisprudence* 9th ed (London: Sweet & Maxwell, 2014) 3 and 10.

89 For the five kinds of jurisprudential theorising (i.e. the 'jobs for jurisprudence'), see William Twining "Evidence and legal theory," in *Law in context: Enlarging a discipline*, ed. Williams Twining (Oxford: Oxford University Press, 1997) 110 at 112–113; Twining "Some jobs for jurisprudence," 149 at 160 (on 'the development of working theories and of theories of the middle order' being a 'job for jurisprudence'); William Twining "General jurisprudence," 9.

has to adjudicate legal disputes using rational means,[90] while hate crimes have increasingly become a global phenomenon.[91]

The third aim of the book is to produce theorising that is *post-colonial*. The book associates the tradition of evidence law that is dominated by doctrinal rules of procedure[92] with coloniality; that is, the adjudication rules and procedures that were exported mainly from Europe throughout the world, especially in the Global South where vestiges of these colonial transplants continue to endure.[93] For example, Stephen's tripartite model of 'relevancy,' 'proof of facts' (meaning, the decision rules associated with burdens and standards of proof) and 'production . . . of relevant facts'[94] was exported from the Indian Evidence Act of 1872 throughout the British commonwealth and its colonial allies and subjects.[95] The colonial transplantation of the civilian Napoleonic and Prussian codes, coupled with a historical scepticism towards the imposition of judicial rules of proof,[96] is an analogous example of a similar form of coloniality.[97] While

90 Michael Freeman *Lloyd's introduction to jurisprudence* 9th ed (London: Sweet & Maxwell, 2014) 1551; Lon Fuller "The forms and limits of adjudication" (1978) 92(2) *Harvard Law Review* 353; Michael S. Pardo "Judicial proof, evidence and pragmatic meaning: Towards evidentiary holism" (2000) 95(1) *Northwestern University Law Review* 399.

91 Jennifer Schweppe and Mark A. Walters, eds. *The globalisation of hate: Internationalising hate crime?* (New York: Oxford University Press, 2016); Paul Iganski and Jack Levin *Hate crime: A global perspective* (New York: Routledge, 2015).

92 John H. Wigmore "The problem of proof" (1913) 8(2) *Illinois Law Review* 77 at 77–78: 'The study of the principles of Evidence, for a lawyer, falls into two distinct parts. One is Proof in the general sense . . . The other part is Admissibility, the procedural rules devised by law . . . Hitherto, the latter has loomed largest in our formal studies, – has, in fact, monopolized them; while the former, virtually ignored . . . Here we have been wrong.'

93 Máximo Langer "The long shadow of the adversarial and inquisitorial categories," in *The Oxford handbook of criminal law*, eds. Markus D. Dubber and Tatjana Hörnle (Oxford: Oxford University Press, 2014) 887.

94 James F. Stephen *The Indian Evidence Act (I of 1872): With an introduction on the principles of judicial evidence* (London: Macmillan, 1872) 9; James F. Stephen *A digest on the law of evidence* 12th ed (London: Macmillan, 1876–1948) articles 1–57 ('Relevancy'); 58–92 ('On proof'); 93–143 ('Production and effect of evidence').

95 Howard B. Miller "Beyond the law of evidence" (1966) 40(1) *Southern California Law Review* 1 at 3; Ronald J. Allen et al "Reforming the law of evidence of Tanzania (Part one): The social and legal challenges" (2013) 31(1) *Boston University International Law Journal* 217; Henry F. Morris *Evidence in East Africa* (1968) 1–23; Zacchaeus Adangor "What is innovative in the Evidence Act, 2011?" (2015) 43 *Journal of Law, Policy and Globalisation* 34. Cf. William Twining *Rethinking evidence: Exploratory essays* (Cambridge: Cambridge University Press, 2006) 210: 'Thayer's picture of the Law of Evidence has dominated Anglo-American discussions of the subject during the twentieth century.'

96 Damaška "Evidentiary barriers to conviction and two models of criminal procedure: A comparative study," 507 at 515, n10; Mirjan R. Damaška *Evaluation of evidence: Premodern and modern approaches* (Cambridge: Cambridge University Press, 2019) 125.

97 Bart Wauters and Marco de Benito *The history of law in Europe: An introduction* (Cheltenham: Elgar, 2017) 123 and 128; Arthur T. Von Mehren and James R. Gordley *The civil law system: An introduction to the comparative study of law* 2nd ed (Boston: Little Brown & Company,

established procedural and evidential doctrine are outlined in Chapters 3 and 4, respectively, as a contextual foundation to the theoretical work undertaken in subsequent chapters of the book, the third aim of the book is to break with this established tradition by theorising, as it does in Chapters 5 and 6, about the structure and content of proof with respect to the phenomenon of hate crimes.

1.5 Conclusion

The first chapter of this book introduces the subject matter unlike a lawyer usually would; for example, by describing the history and 'main thesis' to be defended, but rather like a mathematician by beginning with the problem. The chapter, in sum, says what the problem is and then proceeds to tell the reader how it is proposed to be answered in the remaining chapters of the book. The problem pertains to *how hate crimes can be proven in forensic adjudication*. It is broken down and its features are illustrated through a swimming pool incident involving an inter-racial conflict. The next two sections develop the problem even further with a preliminary discussion of the meaning of 'proof' and 'hate crime.' Orthodox discussions of proof often narrowly focus on burdens and standards of proof in isolation of the substantive and procedural law contexts to which they apply. The project of this book is introduced as one focusing on evidential proof, but it is actually about *applied proof*, where the field of application is hate crimes. The main argument being defended is that theorising about proof as applied in the relevant context is far less prone to contextual error than orthodox narrow forms of theorising.

The phenomenon of hate crimes is the particular context to which the probative theorising is applied. Hate crimes not only present several complex theoretical problems, but they are also globally appealing to many jurisdictions around the world. The book aims to be *trans-disciplinary, cross-jurisdictional* and *post-colonial*, thereby aligning itself to the globalised readership of scholars of hate crimes, evidence and proof and jurisprudence more generally. The theoretical models developed in the remaining chapters of the book specifically focus on the non-contact variant of hate crimes that are committed on the grounds of race, religion and ethnicity (citizenship) in the main.

1.6 Bibliography

Books and Book Chapters

Adrienne Stone and Frederick Schauer, eds. *The Oxford handbook of freedom of speech* (Oxford: Oxford University Press, 2021).

1977) 51 ('By 1811, four additional codes had come into force: the *Code de Procédure Civile* (1807), the *Code de Commerce* (1808), the *Code d'Instruction Criminelle* (1811), and the Code Pénal (1811)'); Serge Dauchy "French law and its expansion in the early modern period," in *The Oxford handbook of European legal history*, eds. Heikki Pihlajamäki et al (Oxford: Oxford University Press, 2018) 760 at 780.

Agneta Fischer et al "Why we hate," in *The moral psychology of hate*, ed. Noelle Birondo (Lanham: Rowman & Littlefield, 2022) 137.
Alexander L. Hinton *Why did they kill? Cambodia in the shadow of genocide* (Berkeley: University of California Press, 2005).
Arthur T. Von Mehren and James R. Gordley *The civil law system: An introduction to the comparative study of law* 2nd ed (Boston: Little Brown & Company, 1977).
Azeem Ibrahim "Genocide in Myanmar: The assault on the Rohingya, 2010–2019," in *The Cambridge world history of genocide: Genocide in the contemporary era*, eds. Ben Kiernan et al (Cambridge: Cambridge University Press, 2023) 746.
Bart Wauters and Marco de Benito *The history of law in Europe: An introduction* (Cheltenham: Elgar, 2017).
Ben Kiernan "The genocides in Cambodia," in *The Cambridge world history of genocide: Genocide in the contemporary era*, eds. Ben Kiernan et al (Cambridge: Cambridge University Press, 2023) 518.
Brian Levin "The long arc of justice: Race, violence and the emergence of hate crime law," in *Hate crimes*, eds. Barbara Perry and Brian Levin vol 1 (Westport: Praeger, 2009) 1.
Carlson Anyangwe *Cameroonian judicial system* (Yaoundé: CEPER, 1987).
Chris Carey et al, eds. *Evidence and proof in ancient Greece* (Newcastle: Cambridge Scholars Publishing, 2024).
Christian Dahlman et al, eds. *Philosophical foundations of evidence law* (Oxford: Oxford University Press, 2021).
Christina Peristeridou and André Klip *Comparative perspectives of criminal procedure* (Cambridge: Intersentia, 2024).
Cornel West *Brother West: Living and loving out loud, a memoir* (New York: Smiley Books, 2009).
Dale Nance *The burdens of proof: Discriminatory power, weight of evidence and tenacity of belief* (Cambridge: Cambridge University Press, 2016).
Donald Nicolson *Evidence and proof in Scotland: Context and critique* (Edinburgh: Edinburgh University Press, 2019).
Douglas N. Walton *Burden of proof, presumption and argumentation* (New York: Cambridge University Press, 2014).
Edina Bećirević "Genocide in Bosnia and Herzegovina," in *The Cambridge world history of genocide: Genocide in the contemporary era*, eds. Ben Kiernan et al (Cambridge: Cambridge University Press, 2023) 627.
Erik Bleich "From race to hate: A historical perspective," in *Hate, politics, law: Critical perspectives on combating hate*, eds. Thomas Brudholm and Birgitte S. Johansen (New York: Oxford University Press, 2018) 15.
Federico Picinali *Justice in-between: A study of intermediate criminal verdicts* (Oxford: Oxford University Press, 2022).
Frederick M. Lawrence *Punishing hate: Bias crimes under American law* (Cambridge: Harvard University Press, 1999).
Frederick Schauer *Uses of evidence in law, politics and everything else* (Cambridge: Harvard University Press, 2022).
Gordon W. Allport *The nature of prejudice* (Cambridge, MA: Addison-Wesley Publishing Company, 1954).
Hock-Lai Ho *A philosophy of evidence law* (Oxford: Oxford University Press, 2008).
Ian Dennis *The law of evidence* 6th ed (London: Sweet & Maxwell, 2017).
James B. Jacobs and Kimberly Potter *Hate crimes: Criminal law & identity politics* (New York: Oxford University Press, 1998).
James B. Thayer *A preliminary treatise on evidence at common law* (Boston: Little Brown and Co., 1898).
James F. Stephen *A digest on the law of evidence* (London: Macmillan, 1887).
James F. Stephen *The Indian Evidence Act (I of 1872): With an introduction on the principles of judicial evidence* (London: Macmillan, 1872).

Jay Winter "War and genocide in the twentieth century," in *The Cambridge world history of genocide: Genocide in the contemporary era*, eds. Ben Kiernan et al (Cambridge: Cambridge University Press, 2023) 44.
Jen Neller *Stirring up hatred: Myth, identity and order in the regulation of hate speech* (Cham: Palgrave Macmillan, 2023).
Jennifer Schweppe and Mark A. Walters, eds. *The globalisation of hate: Internationalising hate crime?* (New York: Oxford University Press, 2016).
Jeremy Bentham "An introductory view of the rationale of evidence; for the use of non-lawyers as well as lawyers," in *The works of Jeremy Bentham*, ed. Jeremy Bowring vol 6 (Edinburgh: Tait, 1843) 15.
Jeremy Bentham "An introductory view of the rationale of evidence," in *The works of Jeremy Bentham*, ed. John Bowring vol 6 (London: Simpkin, Marshall & Co., 1843) 5.
Jeremy Bentham *Rationale of judicial evidence*, ed. J.S. Mill vol 1 (London: Hunt & Clark, 1827).
Jerome Frank *Law and the modern mind* (New York: Brenato's, 1930).
Jerome Hall *Foundations of jurisprudence* (Indiana: Bobbs-Merrill Company, 1973).
Joanna Gomula and Stephan Wittich, eds. *Research handbook on international procedural law* (Cheltenham: Elgar, 2024).
Joëlle Vuille "Forensic science evidence in non-adversary criminal justice systems," in *Forensic science evidence and expert witness testimony: Reliability through reform*, eds. Paul Roberts and Michael Stockdale (Cheltenham: Elgar, 2018) 354.
John D. Jackson "Managing uncertainty and finality: The function of the criminal trial in legal inquiry," in *Trial on trial: Truth and due process*, eds. Antony Duff et al vol 1 (Portland: Oregon, 2004) 121.
John H. Wigmore *Evidence in trials at common law* (revised by Peter Tillers) vol 1 (Boston: Little Brown, 1983).
Karin Orth "Camps," in *The Oxford handbook of Holocaust studies*, eds. Peter Hayes and John K. Roth (Oxford: Oxford University Press, 2010) 364.
Kevin M. Clermont *A general theory of evidence and proof: Forming beliefs in truth* (Cham: Springer, 2024).
Kim Barker and Olga Jurasz *Violence against women, hate and law: Perspectives from contemporary Scotland* (Cham: Palgrave Macmillan, 2022).
Kris Gledhill and Ben Livings, eds. *The teaching of criminal law: The pedagogical imperatives* (London: Routledge, 2017).
Larry Laudan *Truth, error and criminal law: An essay in legal epistemology* (New York: Cambridge University Press, 2006).
Larry May *Ancient legal thought: Equity, justice and humaneness from Hammurabi and the pharaohs to Justinian and the Talmud* (New York: Cambridge University Press, 2019).
Leah Burch and David Wilkin, eds. *Disability hate crime: Perspectives for change* (London: Routledge, 2025).
Lucille Micheletto *Assessing hate crime laws: A multidisciplinary perspective* (Cham: Palgrave Macmillan, 2023).
Maksymilian Del Mar and Cláudio Michelon "Introduction," in *The anxiety of the jurist: Legality, exchange and judgement*, eds. Maksymilian Del Mar and Cláudio Michelon (Farnham: Ashgate, 2013) 1.
Mark A. Walters *Criminalising hate: Law and social justice liberalism* (Cham: Palgrave Macmillan, 2022).
Mary Fulbrook "Systematic and ad hoc persecution and mass murder in the Holocaust: Killings in eastern Europe outside the camps," in *The Cambridge world history of genocide: Genocide in the contemporary era*, eds. Ben Kiernan et al (Cambridge: Cambridge University Press, 2023) 235.

Máximo Langer "The long shadow of the adversarial and inquisitorial categories," in *The Oxford handbook of criminal law*, eds. Markus D. Dubber and Tatjana Hörnle (Oxford: Oxford University Press, 2014) 887.
Michael Freeman *Lloyd's introduction to jurisprudence* 9th ed (London: Sweet & Maxwell, 2014).
Michael Williams *The science of hate: How prejudice becomes hate and what we can do to stop it* (London: Faber & Faber, 2021).
Mirjan R. Damaška *Evaluation of evidence: Premodern and modern approaches* (Cambridge: Cambridge University Press, 2019).
Nancy L. Clark "South Africa: Apartheid and post-apartheid," in *The Palgrave handbook of African colonial and postcolonial history*, eds. Martin S. Shanguhyia and Toyin Falola (New York: Palgrave Macmillan, 2018) Ch 40.
Nancy L. Clark and William H. Worger *South Africa: The rise and fall of apartheid* 3rd ed (London: Routledge, 2016).
Nick Haslam and Sean C. Murphy "Hate, dehumanization and 'hate'," in *Perspectives on hate: How it originates, develops, manifests and spreads*, ed. Robert J. Sternberg (Washington: American Psychological Association, 2020) 27.
Pamela-Jane Schwikkard and Tshepo B. Mosaka *Principles of evidence* 5th ed (Claremont: Juta, 2023).
Paul Iganski and Abe Sweiry "Hate crime," in *The Cambridge handbook of social problems*, ed. Javier A. Treviño vol 2 (Cambridge: Cambridge University Press, 2018) Ch 23.
Paul Iganski and Jack Levin *Hate crime: A global perspective* (New York: Routledge, 2015).
Philip M. Genty "Celebrating the difference: A U.S. educator's perspective on legal education under the civil and common law," in *Re-thinking legal education under the civil and common law*, ed. Richard Grimes (London: Routledge, 2018) 2.
Rachel Keighley *Researching hate as an activist: Exploring LGBTQ+ online hate, its impacts, and our responsibility toward equality* (Cham: Palgrave Macmillan, 2024).
Richard Posner *The problems of jurisprudence* (Cambridge: Harvard University Press, 1990).
Robert C. Roberts *Emotions: An essay in aid of moral psychology* (Cambridge: Cambridge University Press, 2003).
Robert J. Sternberg and Karin Sternberg *The nature of hate* (New York: Cambridge University Press, 2008).
Roger Cotterrell "The jurist's conscience: Reflections around Radbruch," in *The anxiety of the jurist: Legality, exchange and judgement*, eds. Maksymilian Del Mar and Cláudio Michelon (Farnham: Ashgate, 2013) 13.
Sareta Ashraph "The Yazidi genocide," in *The Cambridge world history of genocide: Genocide in the contemporary era*, eds. Ben Kiernan et al (Cambridge: Cambridge University Press, 2023) 722.
Saul Dubow *Apartheid, 1948–1994* (Oxford: Oxford University Press, 2014).
Scott Straus "The Rwandan genocide in context," in *The Cambridge world history of genocide: Genocide in the contemporary era*, eds. Ben Kiernan et al (Cambridge: Cambridge University Press, 2023) 647.
Serge Dauchy "French law and its expansion in the early modern period," in *The Oxford handbook of European legal history*, eds. Heikki Pihlajamäki et al (Oxford: Oxford University Press, 2018) 760.
Stevie-Jade Hardy and Neil Chakraborti *Blood, threats and fears: The hidden worlds of hate crime victims* (Cham: Palgrave Macmillan, 2020).
Susan Haack *Evidence matters: Science, proof, and truth in the law* (New York: Cambridge University Press, 2014).
Terence Anderson, William Twining and David Schum *Analysis of evidence* 2nd ed (Cambridge: Cambridge University Press, 2005).

Terry Bell and Dumisa B. Ntsebeza *Unfinished business: South Africa, apartheid and truth* (London: Verso, 2003).
Thomas Brudholm "What is hate," in *Perspectives on hate: How it originates, develops, manifests and spreads*, ed. Robert J. Sternberg (Washington: American Psychological Association, 2020) 65.
Thomas F. Gossett *Race: The history of an idea in America* (Dallas: Southern Methodist University Press, 1965).
Thomas Weigend "Criminal law and criminal procedure," in *Elgar encyclopedia of comparative law*, eds. Jan M. Smits et al (Cheltenham: Elgar, 2023) 483.
Torsten Stirner *The procedural law governing facts and evidence in international human rights proceedings* (Leiden: Brill Nijhoff, 2021).
Valerie Jenness and Ryken Grattet *Making a hate crime: From social movement to law enforcement* (New York: Russell Sage Foundation, 2001).
Verena Klappstein and Maciej Dybowski, eds. *Theory of legal evidence – Evidence in legal theory* (Cham: Springer, 2021).
Warren Swain and David Campbell, eds. *Reimaging contract law pedagogy: A new agenda for teaching* (London: Routledge, 2019).
William A. Schabas "Hate speech in Rwanda: The road to genocide," in *Genocide and human rights*, ed. Mark Lattimer (London: Routledge, 2017) Ch 8.
William Twining "Evidence and legal theory," in *Law in context: Enlarging a discipline*, ed. Williams Twining (Oxford: Oxford University Press, 1997) 110.
William Twining *General jurisprudence: Understanding law from a global perspective* (Cambridge: Cambridge University Press, 2008).
William Twining *Karl Llewellyn and the realist movement* 2nd ed (Cambridge: Cambridge University Press, 2012).
William Twining *Rethinking evidence: Exploratory essays* (Evanston, IL: Northwestern University Press, 1994).
William Twining *Rethinking evidence: Exploratory essays* 2nd ed (Cambridge: Cambridge University Press, 2006).
William Twining "Taking facts seriously – Again," in *Rethinking evidence: Exploratory essays*, ed. William Twining 2nd ed (Cambridge: Cambridge University Press, 2009) 417.
William Twining "Taking facts seriously," in *Essays on legal education*, ed. Neil Gold (Toronto: Butterworths, 1982) 51.

Periodicals

Alex Stein "The refoundation of evidence law" (1996) 9 *Canadian Journal of Law & Jurisprudence* 279.
Avital Fried "Statistical evidence and the criminal verdict asymmetry" (2022) 200 *Synthese* 472.
Edward K. Cheng "Reconceptualising the burden of proof" (2013) 122 *Yale Law Journal* 1254.
Federico Picinali "Do theories of punishment necessarily deliver a binary system of verdicts? An exploratory essay" (2018) 12 *Criminal Law and Philosophy* 555.
Howard Varney "Forging new tools: A note on *Fose v Minister of Safety and Security* CCT 14/96" (1998) 14(2) *South African Journal of Human Rights* 336.
Larry Laudan "Need verdicts come in pairs?" (2010) 14 *International Journal of Evidence & Proof* 1.
Loretta de Plevitz "The Briginshaw 'standard of proof' in anti-discrimination law: 'Pointing with a wavering finger'" (2003) 27(2) *Melbourne University Law Review* 308.

Marta Araújo "A very 'prudent integration': White flight, school segregation and depoliticization of (anti)-racism" (2016) 19(2) *Race, Ethnicity and Education* 300.
Michael S. Pardo "The field of evidence and the field of knowledge" (2005) 24(5) *Law and Philosophy* 321.
Nicola Lacey "Legislation against sex discrimination: Questions from a female perspective" (1987) 14(4) *Journal of Law & Society* 411.
Paul Roberts "Five foundational fallacies of common law evidence" (translated by Ping Yang and Baosheng Zhang) (2018) 26 *Evidence Science* 93–108.
Paul Roberts "Presumptuous or pluralistic presumptions of innocence? Methodological diagnosis towards conceptual reinvigoration" (2021) 198 *Synthese* 8901.
Paul Roberts "Rethinking the law of evidence: A twenty-first century agenda for teaching and research" (2002) 55(1) *Current Legal Problems* 297.
Paul Roberts "Theorising evidence law" (2023) 43(3) *Oxford Journal of Legal Studies* 629.
Petar Bodlović "On presumptions, burdens of proof and explanations" (2020) 2(40) *Informal Logic* 255.
Peter Duff "Scottish criminal jury: A very peculiar institution" (1999) 62 *Law and Contemporary Problems* 173.
Richard Moon "Discrimination and its justification: Coping with equality rights under the charter" (1988) 26(4) *Osgoode Hall Law Journal* 673.
Samuel Bray "Not proven: Introducing a third verdict" (2005) 72 *University of Chicago Law Review* 1299.
Susan Haack "Epistemology legalized: Or, truth, justice and the American way" (2004) 49 *American Journal of Jurisprudence* 43.
Thomas Weigend "Assuming that the defendant is not guilty: The presumption of innocence in the German system of criminal justice" (2014) 8 *Criminal Law and Philosophy* 285.
William Twining "Evidence and legal theory" (1984) 47(3) *Modern Law Review* 261.
William Twining "Some jobs for jurisprudence" (1974) 1(2) *British Journal of Law and Society* 149.
Yaniv Vaki and Yoram Rabin "Two kinds of acquittals – Different kinds of doubts" (2021) 32 *Criminal Law Forum* 97.

Online Resources

Civil Justice Quarterly, available at: www.sweetandmaxwell.co.uk (accessed: 24 July 2024).
Criminal Law and Philosophy, available at: www.link.springer.com (accessed: 24 July 2024).
Criminal Law Forum, available at: www.journals.sagepub.com (accessed: 24 July 2024).
Criminal Law Review, available at: www.sweetandmaxwell.co.uk (accessed: 24 July 2024).
International Association of Procedural Law, available at: www.iaplaw.org (accessed: 24 July 2024).
International Journal of Evidence & Proof, available at: www.journals.sagepub.com (accessed: 24 July 2024).
International Journal of Procedural Law, available at: www.jurisquare.be (accessed: 24 July 2024).
Journal für Strafrecht, available at: www.verlagoesterreich.at (accessed: 24 July 2024).
Journal of Criminal Law, available at: www.journals.sagepub.com (accessed: 24 July 2024).

Journal of International Criminal Justice, available at: www.academic.oup.com (accessed: 24 July 2024).

Max Planck Institute Luxembourg for International, European and Regulatory Procedural Law, available at: www.mpi.lu (accessed: 24 July 2024).

Michele Taruffo Girona Evidence Week, see www.gironaevidenceweek.com (accessed: 24 July 2024).

New Criminal Law Review, available at: www.online.ucpress.edu (accessed: 24 July 2024).

Organisation for Security and Co-Operation in Europe *2020 Hate Crime Data Key Findings* (15 November 2021), available at: www.hatecrime.osce.org (accessed: 28 July 2024).

Quaestio facti: International Journal on Evidential Legal Reasoning, available at: www.quaestiofacti.com (accessed: 24 July 2024).

Statistique Canada *Police-Reported Hate Crime, 2022* (13 March 2024), available at: www150.statcan.gc.ca (accessed: 28 July 2024).

Swedish National Council for Crime Prevention *Hate crimes reported to the police in 2022: A compilation of the cases that were classified as hate crimes by the police* (Report No. 17) (2023), available at: www.bra.se (accessed 28 July 2024).

United Kingdom House of Commons *Hate crime statistics* (15 January 2024), available at: www.researchbriefings.files.parliament.uk (accessed: 28 July 2024).

United States Federal Bureau of Investigation *FBI releases 2022 hate crime statistics* (16 October 2023), available at: www.justice.gov (accessed: 28 July 2024).

2 The Material Condition

2.1 An Introduction to the Criminal Law of Hate

A hate crime is a manifested hostility towards an individual or group of persons on the ground of their actual or perceived membership of a defined social demographic.[1] This manifested hostility usually takes the form of a criminal act[2] (e.g. a murder, assault or malicious damage to property) or a non-criminal violation of a constitutional or human rights norm.[3] Hate crimes have the effect of 'nullifying or impairing the recognition, enjoyment or exercise, on an equal footing, of human rights and fundamental freedoms in the political, economic, social, cultural or any other field of public life.'[4] There are two theoretical features that characterise all forms of hate crimes: differentiation and subordination.[5] By this hostile action, the perpetrator of a hate crime

1 See Levin "The long arc of justice: Race, violence and the emergence of hate crime law," 1 at 2; David Kostan "Hate and the state in ancient Greece," in *Hate, politics, law: Critical perspectives on combating hate*, eds. Thomas Brudholm and Birgitte S. Johansen (New York: Oxford University Press, 2018) 34 at 36; Randy Blazak "Isn't every crime a hate crime?: The case for hate crime laws" (2011) 5(4) *Sociology Compass* 244 at 245; Jennifer Schweppe "What is a hate crime?" (2021) 7 *Cogent Social Sciences* 1 at 11: '[A] crime recognised by the law which is committed with an additional 'hate' element, which element is directed at one or more (presumed) characteristics of the victim.'

2 Thomas Brudholm "Conceptualising hatred globally: Is hate crime a human rights violation?," in *The globalization of hate: Internationalising hate crime*, eds. Jennifer Schweppe and Mark A. Walters (Oxford: Oxford University Press, 2016) 31 at 34.

3 Barbara Perry *In the name of hate: Understanding hate crimes* (New York: Routledge, 2001) 8.

4 See International Convention on the Elimination of All Forms of Racial Discrimination 1965, Article 1; Office for Democratic Institutions and Human Rights *Hate crime laws: A practical guide* (2009) 16: 'Hate crimes are criminal acts committed with a bias motive.' Available at: www.osce.org (accessed: 2 January 2023); English Law Commission Hate crime laws: Final report no. 402 (2021) 1: '"Hate crime" . . . is generally used to refer to the aggravation of the seriousness of existing criminal offences – such as assault, harassment or criminal damage – because there is an additional "hostility" element.' Available at: www.gov.uk (accessed: 2 January 2022).

5 See Steve Biko *I write what I like: A selection of his writings* (Johannesburg: Heinemann, 1987) 25; Mabogo P. More "Biko: Africana existentialist philosopher" (2004) 11(1) *Alternation* 79 at 87–88; Kwame A. Appiah "Racisms," in *Anatomy of racism*, ed. Theo D. Goldberg (Minneapolis: University of Minnesota Press, 1990) 3; Paul Gilroy "One nation under a

DOI: 10.4324/9781003493006-2

firstly targets and isolates a particular individual or group on the basis of their actual or perceived affiliation to a particular social group.[6] This differentiation usually is a manifestation of a prejudice or bias on the part of the perpetrator, who isolates the target on the basis solely of their biological, psychosomatic or social traits. Secondly, a differentiation is innocuous unless it is coupled with the isolated target being additionally subordinated or subjugated.[7] The subordination of the target may take many forms, including the denial of access to a particular facility, the creation of higher barriers to enter certain professions, public humiliation or restrictions to public movement.

Hate crimes are a global phenomenon.[8] They appear on the statute books of several countries around the world. For example, the 182 countries that have ratified the International Convention on the Elimination of All Forms of Racial Discrimination are bound to criminally punish

> all dissemination of ideas based on racial superiority or hatred, incitement to racial discrimination, as well as all acts of violence or incitement to such acts against any race or group of persons of another colour or ethnic origin, and also the provision of any assistance to racist activities, including the financing thereof.[9]

Similarly, hate crimes, including specified acts of discrimination, incitement and intimidation, are punishable criminally across several African[10] and South

---

groove: The cultural politics of 'race' and racism in Britain," in *Anatomy of racism*, ed. David T. Goldberg (Minneapolis: University of Minnesota Press, 1990) 263.

6 Robert Miles and Malcolm Brown *Racism* 2nd ed (London: Routledge, 2003) 103; Kimberlé Crenshaw et al "Introduction," in *Critical race theory: The key writings that formed the movement*, eds. Kimberlé Crenshaw et al (New York: The New Press, 1995) xiii at xiv; Howard Winant "Race and race theory" (2000) *Annual Review of Sociology* 169 at 172; Tanya Golash-Boza "A critical and comprehensive sociological theory of race and racism" (2016) 2(2) *Sociology of Race and Racism* 129 at 130. See generally, Martin Bulmer and John Solomons, eds. *Racism* (Oxford: Oxford University Press, 1999) Chs 42–47; Tania Das Gupta et al, eds. *Race and racialization: Essential readings* (Toronto: Canadian Scholars' Press, 2007); David T. Goldberg *Racist culture: Philosophy and the politics of meaning* (Oxford: Blackwell, 1993) Ch 3; Michael Banton *Racial theories* (New York: Cambridge University Press, 1987)).

7 Miles and Brown "Racism," 104.

8 Schweppe and Walters, eds. *The globalisation of hate: Internationalising hate crime?*; Iganski and Levin *Hate crime: A global perspective*.

9 International Convention on the Elimination of all forms of Racial Discrimination of 1965, article 4; International Covenant on Civil and Political Rights of 1966, article 20(1): 'Any advocacy of national, racial or religious hatred that constitutes incitement to discrimination, hostility or violence shall be prohibited by law.' (ratified by 173 countries). See also African Charter on Human and People's Rights of 1986, articles 2 and 18(3) (ratified by 54 countries); European Union Charter of Fundamental Rights of 2000, article 21; Additional Protocol to the Convention on Cybercrime, Concerning the Criminalisation of Acts of a Racist and Xenophobic Nature Committed through Computer Systems of 2003.

10 Constitution of the Arabic Republic of Egypt, article 53; Law Determining Offences and Penalties in General no. 68 of 2018, article 163; *Constitution de la Niger République*,

American[11] jurisdictions. Criminal prohibitions against manifestations of 'discrimination, hatred or violence, against a person on account of his so-called race, colour, descent, origin or nationality' also appear in several European penal statutes.[12] Although there is no general hate crime statute (and certainly not of the kind that would prohibit the kind of incident described earlier) in England and Wales, certain specified hate-related actions, such as incitement (stirring up hatred)[13] and the commission of specified existing offences with racial or religious motives,[14] are subject to criminal prohibition.[15] It is in the United States, however, that hate crime statutes feature most prominently (e.g. only three states, Arkansas, South Carolina and Wyoming, currently have not enacted any hate crime laws),[16] both at federal[17] and state[18] levels. For example, 18 United States Code § 245(2)(F) sanctions anybody who 'wilfully injures, intimidates or interferes with, or attempts to injure, intimidate or interfere with . . . any person [that is] . . . enjoying the goods, services, facilities, privileges, advantages, or accommodations of' any public place of entertainment, such as 'any motion picture house, theatre, concert hall, sports arena, stadium, or any other place of exhibition or entertainment which serves the public.'[19] This federal sanction applies if the latter

---

2010, article 4; *Constitution de la République du Sénégal*, 2001, article 5; *Constituição da República de Moçambique*, 2004, article 39; *Constitution de la République de Guinée*, 2010, article 4; *La Constitution de la Guinée équatoriale*, 1991, article 15(1). Cf. Constitution of the of Namibia, 1990, article 23(1). See also the Prevention and Combatting of Hate Crimes and Hate Speech Act 13 of 2023 (South Africa); *Mbatha v Van Staden* (1982) (2) SA 260 (N) (on the commission of the crime of criminal *iniuria* by a person expressing racial epithets to another).

11 *Decreto-Lei No 2.848, De 7 de Dezembro de 1940, Código Penal*, article 140(3) (Brazil); *Ley contra el racism y toda forma de discriminacion* no. 045 (2010) article 23, read with article 281 of *Código Penal decreto ley 10426 de 23 Agosto de 1972* (Bolivia).

12 *Loi du 30 juillet 1981 tendant à réprimer certains actes inspirés par le racisme ou la xénophobie*, article 1(3) (Belgium); *Ley Orgánica 10/1995, de 23 de noviembre, del Código Penal*, article 510(2)(a) (Spain); *Legge Mancino, decreto-legge* Nr. 205/1993, article 1 (Italy); *Code Pénal* (1992), article 225–222 (France); *Wetboek van Strafrecht* (1881) article 137 (Netherlands). Cf. *Strafgesetzbuch* (1998) § 185 (on the general crime of insult).

13 Public Order Act, 1986, section 18.

14 Crime and Disorder Act, 1998, section 28–32.

15 Cf. Canada Criminal Code, 1985, sections 318–319; Criminal Code Compilation Act, 1913, sections 77–80G (Western Australia); Hate Crime and Public Order (Scotland) Act of 2021.

16 Donald Altschiller *Hate crimes: A reference handbook* 3rd ed (Santa Barbara: ABC-CLIO, 2015) 30; Nathan Hall et al, eds. *The Routledge international handbook on hate crime* (New York: Routledge, 2015) 153 at 156.

17 See 18 United States Code § 245(b)(2)(F). However, prosecutions under this federal statute are prohibited unless certified by the Attorney General (see § 245(a)(1)).

18 See, e.g., Connecticut General Statutes (1978) § 53–37; West Virginia Code (1995) § 61–16–21; New York State Penal Law § 485.05; Revised Code of Washington (1981) § 9A.36.080. For a full list of state statutes, see Lawrence *Punishing hate: Bias crimes under American law*, Appendix A (pp. 178–189).

19 18 United States Code § 245(b)(2)(F).

targeted person is interfered with in this way 'because of [their] race, colour, religion or national origin.'[20]

Most of these hate crime prohibitions take the form of one or more of three models focusing on penalty enhancement, sentence aggravation or a separate substantive offence.[21] The most common among these at the moment is the penalty enhancement model, particularly in Europe and the United States.[22] A hate crime statute on the penalty enhancement model specifies an additional maximum, or sometimes a minimum, penalty on some or all pre-existing offences if their perpetration is motivated or aggravated by prejudice or bias against a person from a protected demographic.[23] For example, the hate crime statute of England and Wales increases the penalty for assault from five to seven years' imprisonment if it is motivated by racial or religious bias.[24] Penalty enhancement hate crime statutes aim do not create new offences, but they serve only to 'top up' the penalties of existing offences that are motivated by bias or prejudice.[25] Secondly, hate crime prohibitions on the sentence aggravation model provide that a bias motivation for the perpetration of an existing offence against a protected demographic must be regarded as an aggravating factor by sentencing adjudicators.[26] For example, the Canadian hate crime prohibition obliges adjudicators to regard a motivation by 'by bias, prejudice or hate based on race, national or ethnic origin, language, colour, religion, sex, age, mental or physical disability, sexual orientation, or any other similar factor' as an aggravating factor when sentencing an offender.[27] The third category of hate crime offences consists of statutes that establish separate substantive offences for hostile actions that are motivated by bias against a person or group from a protected demographic.[28] Most of these 'parallel offences' are comparable to ordinary offences, such as assault, murder and malicious damage to property, except that they are motivated by prejudice towards a protected demographic.[29] Their effect typically is stymied by their resemblance to their comparable existing counterparts, thereby leading law enforcement officials to charge offenders with the latter more familiar category of offences.[30] It is a separate substantive offence, under Californian criminal law, 'to injure,

20 18 United States Code § 245(b)(2)(F).
21 Gail Mason "Legislating against hate," in *The Routledge international handbook on hate crime*, eds. Nathan Hall et al (New York: Routledge, 2015) 59 at 60; Jacobs and Potter *Hate crimes: Criminal law & identity politics*, 29.
22 Jacobs and Kimberly *Hate crimes: Criminal law & identity politics*, 29.
23 Mason "Legislating against hate," 60.
24 See Crime and Disorder Act, 1998, section 29(2)(b).
25 Mason "Legislating against hate," 61.
26 Mason "Legislating against hate," 61.
27 Canada Criminal Code, 1985, section 718.2(a)(i).
28 Mason "Legislating against hate," 61; Jacobs and Kimberly *Hate crimes: Criminal law & identity politics*, 33–36.
29 Mason "Legislating against hate," 61.
30 Mason "Legislating against hate," 61.

intimidate, interfere with, oppress or threaten another person, by force or threat of force, in the free exercise or enjoyment of Constitutional rights or privileges' on account of their actual or perceived membership of a protected demographic.[31] Although this model is not common in Europe, there are many jurisdictions, such as Canada, England and Wales, and some parts of Australia, that have hate crime statutes on the substantive offence model.[32]

The theorising in this book will pay heed to normative and institutional prescriptions, including the form and content of hate crime laws, but the scope is much wider than a single or particular jurisdiction, hate crime statute or model of hate crime laws. This book's theoretical aims are to develop a sufficient, and accurate, substantive and institutional base that is framed in broad, cross-jurisdictional and general terms to which the theoretical models of evidential proof that are developed later are applied. Therefore, the discussion of specific requirements of elements of hate crimes that follows later in this chapter is an extrapolation of the general features that are applicable mostly to the substantive model of statutes, but nevertheless consistent with the penalty enhancement and sentence aggravation models as well.

2.2 The History of Hate Crimes

The hostile targeting or isolation of individuals on the basis of their actual or perceived membership of a specific demographic group or class has been prevalent for several millennia in human history, but legal prohibitions against this kind of conduct are only a few decades old.[33] For example, the term 'hate crime' first appeared in a bill tabled in the US House of Representatives in 1985,[34] whereas discriminatory social practices have a much longer history stretching back to antiquity. As Jenness and Grattet say, 'the history of human societies is a history of intergroup conflict.'[35] For example, the Indu people

31 California Penal Code of 1978, § 422.6(2)(a).

32 Mason "Legislating against hate," 61.

33 Thomas F. Gossett *Race: The history of an idea in America* (Dallas: Southern Methodist University Press, 1965) 3; Blazak "Isn't every crime a hate crime?: The case for hate crime laws," 245: 'Acts that look and feel like hate crimes have occurred throughout history, but the legal concept is relatively new'; Ryken Grattet and Valerie Jenness "Examining the boundaries of hate crime law: Disabilities and the 'dilemma of difference'" (2001) 91(3) *Journal of Criminal Law and Criminology* 653 at 658: 'what is now commonly understood as "bias" or "hate" crime is an age-old problem approached with a new conceptual lens and sense of urgency'; Bleich "The rise of hate speech and hate crime laws in liberal democracies," 917 at 919: 'There were few meaningful legal restrictions on racist expressions in pre–World War Two Europe.'

34 The bill was ultimately promulgated in 1990 as the Hate Crime Statistics Act, see Jacobs and Potter *Hate crimes: Criminal law & identity politics*, 4; Erik Bleich "From race to hate: A historical perspective," in *Hate, politics, law: Critical perspectives on combating hate*, eds. Thomas Brudholm and Birgitte S. Johansen (New York: Oxford University Press, 2018) 15 at 22; Altschiller *Hate crimes: A reference handbook*, 5.

35 Valerie Jenness and Ryken Grattet *Making a hate crime: From social movement to law enforcement*, 18.

were commonly described as 'noseless people' (*Anasahs*), whose skin had been darkened and noses 'flattened' by Indra (the god of the Aryas) in ancient India (ca. 3000 BCE).[36] Persons who were yellow-haired and green-eyed in the ancient Chinese Han dynasty (ca. 200 BCE) were caricatured as resembling monkeys.[37] Various ancient Egyptian minorities, of varying races, were associated with evil and depravity because of their peculiar skin colour (ca. 1350 BCE).[38] There is also the infamous biblical example of the dark skin of the son of Ham, Canaan, being attributed to a curse bestowed by his grandfather Noah in the book of Genesis.[39]

Despite these references to antiquity, the term 'hate crimes' did not exist until the mid-1980s.[40] Soon after the Hate Crime Statistics Bill was introduced by Representatives John Conyers, of Michigan; Barbara Kennelly, of Connecticut; and Mario Biaggi, of New York, in the US House of Representatives in 1985,[41] the term later appeared in an American magazine on 9 October 1989.[42] The term then began to spread into public discourse through debates about university campus speech codes in the late 1980s and early 1990s.[43] Notwithstanding this belated emergence of the term in the late twentieth century, statutes that purported to sanction various species of hateful actions stretch back to the nineteenth century. Following the abolition of slavery in the United States in 1865, the Civil Rights Act of 1866, the Enforcement Act of 1870, the Ku Klux Klan Act of 1871 and the Civil Rights Act of 1875 were all passed at a federal level to sanction bias-related offences against African Americans.[44] However, many of the lofty objects of this legislation were not achieved, largely because they were not enforced at the state level in the United States.[45]

36 Thomas F. Gossett *Race: The history of an idea in America* (Dallas: Southern Methodist University Press, 1965) 3–4.
37 Gossett "Race: The history of an idea in America," 4.
38 Gossett "Race: The history of an idea in America."
39 Gossett "Race: The history of an idea in America," 5. The era portrayed in the book of genesis is ca. 2500 BCE.
40 Jacobs and Kimberly "Hate crimes: Criminal law & identity politics," 3. Cf. Blazak "Isn't every crime a hate crime?: The case for hate crime laws," 245: 'It was not until after the passage of the landmark civil rights legislation of the 1960s that 'hate crime' entered the criminal codes.'
41 Jacobs and Kimberly *Hate crimes: Criminal law & identity politics*, 4.
42 See John Leo 'The politics of hate' *U.S. News & Report* (9 October 1989), cited in Jacobs and Kimberly *Hate crimes: Criminal law & identity politics*, 4.
43 Bleich "From race to hate: A historical perspective," 22.
44 Altschiller *Hate crimes: A reference handbook*, 5–6; Ely Aaronson *From slave abuse to hate crime: The criminalisation of racial violence in American history* (New York: Cambridge University Press, 2014) Ch 2 (on the early slavery era, 1619–1860), Ch 3 (covering the Reconstruction and Post-Reconstruction periods, 1865–1909), Ch 4 (on the early twentieth century) and Ch 5 (for the post-1970s era). A comprehensive and insightful historical exposition is given in Brian Levin 'From slavery to hate crime laws: The emergence of race and status-based protection in American criminal law' (2002) 58(2) *Journal of Social Issues* 227.
45 Bleich "From race to hate: A historical perspective," 20–21.

Contemporary hate crime legislation dates back to the middle of the twentieth century across the world. The insertion of article 130 into the German Penal Code on 20 May 1960 was pioneering in many ways in the history of contemporary hate crime legislation.[46] This provision prohibits the incitement of hatred, the hateful insult of the dignity of another person, the dissemination of hateful ideas and Holocaust denialism.[47] The English Race Relations Act of 1965 was enacted by the Labour government of Harold Wilson to prohibit the intentional use of threatening, abusive or insulting language that was likely to stir up hatred against sections of public on the grounds of colour, race or ethnic or national origins in England and Wales.[48] For reasons that will be discussed in the next section of this chapter, England's stirring up prohibition was later re-enacted initially into the Public Order Act of 1986 and subsequently into the current Crime and Disorder Act of 1998.[49] Following France's ratification of the International Convention on the Elimination of All Forms of Racial Discrimination in 1971, the 'Pleven Law,' named after the then Minister of Justice, René Pleven, was promulgated in 1972 to prohibit defamatory and provocative acts of hatred and violence on the grounds of race, ethnicity, nationality and religion.[50] The first state-level hate crime prohibition in the United States was enacted by the State of Connecticut in 1978.[51] Section 53–37 of the Connecticut General Statutes of 1970 prohibits the ridiculing or 'holding up to contempt' of any individual or group on account of their 'creed, religion, colour, denomination, nationality or race.'[52] Building on this post-war history of hateful criminalisation, hate crime statutes have continued to spread to jurisdictions across the world. Most recently, the Hate Crime and Public Order Act of 2021 and the Prevention and Combatting of Hate Crimes and Hate Speech Act 13 of 2023 were enacted in Scotland and South Africa, respectively. Furthermore, Rwanda's Law Determining Offences and Penalties in General no. 68 of 2018[53] and Bolivia's *Ley contra el racism y toda forma de discriminacion* no. 045 (2010)[54] also add to this global suite of hate crime prohibitions.

46 Eric Stein "History against free speech: The new German law against the 'Auschwitz' – and other – lies" (1986) 85 *Michigan Law Review* 277 at 282–283; Erik Bleich "The rise of hate speech and hate crime laws in liberal democracies" (2011) 37(6) *Journal of Ethnic and Migration Studies* 917, 920 (on the inclusion of articles 86 and 130 into the German Criminal Code).
47 *Strafgesetzbuch* (1998) § 130.
48 Bleich "From race to hate: A historical perspective," 19.
49 Bleich "The rise of hate speech and hate crime laws in liberal democracies," 920.
50 *Loi n 72–545 du 1 juillet 1972 contre le racism.*
51 Blazak "Isn't every crime a hate crime?: The case for hate crime laws," 245.
52 53 Connecticut General Statutes § 53–37 (1978).
53 Law Determining Offences and Penalties in General no. 68 of 2018, articles 163–164 (prohibiting various acts of discrimination and instigating divisions).
54 *Ley contra el racism y toda forma de discriminacion* no. 045 (2010) article 23, read with article 281 of *Código Penal decreto ley* 10426 de 23 Agosto de 1972 (Bolivia).

2.3 Post-War Identity Politics

Hateful actions and inter-social conflict along demographic lines are not new, as shown earlier in the chapter, but contemporary hate crime laws only appeared from the middle of the twentieth century. This begs the question as to what about this period provided fertile ground for the origination and spread of hate crime legislation.[55] At its founding meeting in San Francisco on 26 June 1945, the members of the United Nations signed a charter as a display of their commitment, among other things, to 'save succeeding generations from the scourge of war,' to 'reaffirm faith in fundamental human rights' and to 'promote and encourage respect for human rights and for fundamental freedoms for all without distinction as to race, sex, language or religion.'[56] This seminal event introduced a post-war era of human rights, globalisation and identity politics. Three years after its formation, the United Nations adopted the Universal Declaration of Human Rights, which prohibited slavery and provided that 'everyone is entitled to all the rights and freedoms set forth in [the] Declaration, without distinction of any kind, such as race, colour, sex, language, religion, political or other opinion, national or social origin, property, birth or other status.'[57] According to Bleich, this renewed focus on human rights exposed the plight of marginalised minority groups and taught the world that racial or demographic hatred can eventually lead to violence and war.[58]

This post-war era of human rights also led to the consolidation of various movements of ethnic and social groups into a larger anti-hate crime movement. There were two fundamental problems that the anti-hate crime movement was grappling with.[59] Firstly, it was that bigoted violence had multiple consequences that transcended the bodily pain or injury of an individual. Some of these included the enslavement of the minds of victims, an increase in the daily anxiety levels of individual victims and the denigration of the self-worth and self-belief of victims. Secondly, the anti-hate crime movement also contended that bias-motivated violence, unlike orthodox individualised crimes, negatively affected social groups. The anti-hate crime movement contended

55 Jenness and Grattet "Making a hate crime: From social movement to law enforcement," 17: 'So why is it only in the latter part of the twentieth century that hate crime has come to the fore as a major social problem worthy of public attention, legislative action, judicial review, and punitive response? Why and how has "hate crime" become a part of our social and legal lexicon? How did such an issue come into being?'

56 United Nations Charter (1945), Preamble and Article 1(3).

57 Universal Declaration of Human Rights (1948), Articles 2 and 4.

58 Bleich "From race to hate: A historical perspective," 16; Bleich "The rise of hate speech and hate crime laws in liberal democracies," 920: 'All told, therefore, racial incitement provisions in the major European democracies originated primarily in the 1960s and 1970s, and not earlier, as might be supposed.'

59 See Jenness and Grattet "Making a hate crime: From social movement to law enforcement," 17–18.

that these two problems could not be addressed effectively by existing legislation and policies.

The anti-hate crime movement was a consolidation of several movements with a much longer history.[60] The first of these was the African Decolonisation movement that fought primarily against racial domination of Africa by Europe. Between the arrival of the Portuguese in the 1400s[61] and the twentieth-century period of independence, only 2 out of 54 African countries – Liberia and Ethiopia – had escaped European colonisation.[62] Secondly, the work of the Anti-Semitism movement, mobilised by lobby organisations such as the Anti-Defamation League,[63] the American Jewish Committee[64] and the Religious Action Center of Reform Judaism,[65] in advocating for the protection of ethnic and religious groups made a significant contribution towards the promulgation of hate crime legislation, particularly in the United States. Thirdly, the American Civil Rights movement undertook various protests against the enslavement of the 6.5 million people at the peak of the Atlantic slave trade.[66] Fourthly, feminist organisations such as the National Organization for Women[67] agitated for equal employment opportunities and the protection of sexual and reproductive rights for women.[68] Fifthly, organisations such as the Gay Liberation Front and the Gay Activists Alliance (both 1969) in the United States, the Campaign for Homosexual Equality (1964) in Britain,[69] the *Front de libération homosexuelle* (1969) and the Community Homophile Association of Toronto (1972) in Canada, the Dorian Society (1964) in New Zealand, the Campaign Against Moral Persecution (1971) in Australia, the Homosexualle Aktion Westberlin (1971) in Germany and the Front *homosexuel d'action révolutionnaire* (1971) in France all championed gay and lesbian

60 Jacobs and Kimberly *Hate crimes: Criminal law & identity politics*, 66: 'The hate crime laws were passed because of the lobbying efforts of organisations that advocate on behalf of blacks, Jews, gays and lesbians, a few other ethnic and nationality groups, and in some cases, women.'

61 Rosina Beckman *Colonial and postcolonial Africa* (New York: Britannica, 2017) 44.

62 At the height of colonialism, about 70% of the world's land surface was controlled by Europe: Mary E. Townsend *European colonial expansion since 1871* (Philadelphia: J.B. Lippincott Company, 1941) 15.

63 The Anti-Defamation League was founded in 1913; see www.adl.org (accessed: 3 September 2024).

64 The American Jewish Committee is a Jewish advocacy group that was founded on 11 November 1906; see www.ajc.org (accessed: 3 September 2024).

65 The Religious Action Center of Reform Judaism was founded in 1961 in Washington DC; see www.rac.org (accessed: 3 September 2024).

66 Roland Oliver and Anthony Atmore *Medieval Africa, 1250–1800* (Cambridge: Cambridge University Press, 2001) 228.

67 The National Organisation for Women was founded in 1966; see www.now.org (accessed: 3 September 2024).

68 For an exposition of the second wave of feminist history, see Sue Thornham "Second wave feminism," in *The Routledge companion to feminism and postfeminism*, ed. Sarah Gamble (London: Routledge, 2001) Ch 3.

69 See www.c-h-e.org.uk (accessed: 4 September 2024).

rights.[70] According to Jacobs and Potter, the convergence of these organisations under the broader banner of the anti-hate crime movement spawned a new 'identity politics' that led to individuals defining themselves according to their race, religion, gender, sexual orientation or ethnicity.[71]

The 'identity politics' slogan is traceable back to the Combahee River Collective's state of 1977[72] in which it was contended that: '[T]he most profound and potentially most radical politics come directly out of our own identity, as opposed to working to end somebody else's oppression.'[73] On the one hand, identity politics describes the intersection of the political influence garnered from the relative success of the activist work of the constituent organisations of the anti-hate crime movements. On the other hand, the intersectional and manifold impact that oppressive systems and practices have on particular demographic groups (e.g. members of a particular gender and race) also defines identity politics. The potential pitfall of identity politics is a form of essentialism that privileges one or some identities to the exclusion of others.[74] A comprehensive discussion of this pitfall is beyond the scope of this chapter, but it suffices to note that this potential pitfall extends to the criminal law doctrine and theory of hate crimes.

2.4 A Typology of Hateful Actions

Hateful actions generally, and at a minimum, are characterised by the *differentiation* or isolation of an actual or perceived member of a demographic group as well as their *subordination* or subjugation by denying or impairing their access or enjoyment of one or more of the freedoms of being human.[75] The manifestation of these actions can take various forms ranging from the communication of threatening and prejudicial telephone messages against a member of a particular demographic group to bias-motivated physical violence and

70 See generally, Barry D. Adam *The rise of a gay and lesbian movement* (revised edition) (New York: Twayne, 1995) Ch 5; Jeffrey Weeks "Gay liberation and its legacies," in *The Ashgate research companion to lesbian and gay activism*, eds. Manon Tremblay and David Paternotte (Farnham: Ashgate, 2015) Ch 3.

71 Jacobs and Kimberly *Hate crimes: Criminal law & identity politics*, 65.

72 Named after the military action led by Harriet Tubman along the Combahee River in South Carolina in 1863, the Combahee River Collective was a black feminist and lesbian organisation based in Boston, Massachusetts.

73 Combahee River Collective "A black feminist statement," in *Feminist manifestos: A global documentary reader*, ed. Penny A. Weiss (New York: New York University Press, 2018) Ch 59; Tivadar Vervoort "Towards a critical identity politics: Butler, Adorno and the force of non-identity," in *Feminism and the Early Frankfurt School*, eds. Christine A. Payne and Jeremiah Morelock (Leiden: Brill, 2024) 113; Jaime S. Miller "Identity politics," in *Encyclopaedia of queer studies in education*, eds. Kamden K. Strunk and Stephanie A. Shelton (Leiden: Brill, 2022) 294.

74 Jaime S. Miller "Identity Politics," 295.

75 See the literature cited at footnotes 4 and 5 earlier in this chapter.

mass murder.[76] There is an even greater variety in the multitude of types of actions that can be grouped under the broader category of discrimination.[77] Some scholars prefer to categorise these actions on the grounds of the motivations that distinguish them,[78] while others develop identity-based typologies.[79] The typology that is preferred in this chapter is action orientated.[80] It distinguishes between various racial hate crimes based on the qualitative properties of the various actions aside from their surrounding motivations or the identity of the victims that they target. As depicted in Figure 2.1, a primary distinction can be drawn between a paradigmatic type of hateful action that lies in the nucleus of racialised hate crime prohibitions in general and at least six different manifestations (or variations) of this core. The core will be referred to as 'hateful expression,' while its six manifestations are designated: criminal defamation, negative stereotyping, denialism, discriminatory harassment, incitement and intimidation.

Hateful expression (HE) has been designated a nucleus status because it involves the most direct (face-to-face), unequivocal and aggressive expression of contempt.[81] HE consists of verbal or symbolic insults or slurs that directly express contempt or hostility towards another person or group on the ground of their perceived membership within a particular social group or class. Examples abound within this category: hurling racial epithets such as 'tranny'[82] (towards transgender or queer individuals), 'towel head'[83]

76 Altschiller *Hate crimes: A reference handbook*, 5.

77 For the avoidance of ambiguity, the terms 'discrimination,' 'hateful action' and 'hate crime' are used interchangeably for the purposes of describing the myriad of actions associated with these terms.

78 For a typology consisting of 'mission hate crimes,' 'retaliatory hate crimes,' 'defensive hate crimes' and 'thrill hate crimes,' see Paul Iganski and Jack Levin *Hate crime: A global perspective* (New York: Routledge, 2015), 43–51. This typology draws heavily on the work of Jack Levin and Jack McDevitt *Hate crimes: The rising tide of bigotry and bloodshed* (New York: Plenum Press, 1993), Chs 4–7 and Jack Levin and Jack McDevitt *Hate crimes revisited: America's war on those who are different* (Boulder, CO: Westview Press, 2002), Chs 3–7. See also Kamban Naidoo 'Hate crimes: Some theoretical considerations and their possible application to the South African context' (2016) 29(2) *Acta Criminologica* 37, 39–41.

79 Here scholars categorise crimes according to race, sexual orientation, religion, disability and analogous grounds. See Neil Chakraborti and Jon Garland *Hate crime: Impact, causes and responses* 2nd ed (London: Sage, 2015) 12–13; Jenniffer Schweppe et al *Lifecycle of a hate crime: Comparative report* (2018) 8, report commissioned by the Irish Council for Civil Liberties and is available at: www.iccl.ie (accessed 5 January 2023) (where a hate crime is described as a 'identity-based hostility').

80 A comparable typology is deployed in Alexander Brown *Hate speech law: A philosophical examination* (New York: Routledge, 2015) 7–8.

81 Cf. Brown "Hate speech law: A philosophical examination," 30 and 33 (who prefers to categorise this as 'defamation').

82 Keira McCormack (2010) [80 Adjudication issued 04/01/10] (unreported), but discussed in Brown "Hate speech law: A philosophical examination," 23–24.

83 Altschiller *Hate crimes: A reference handbook*, 55.

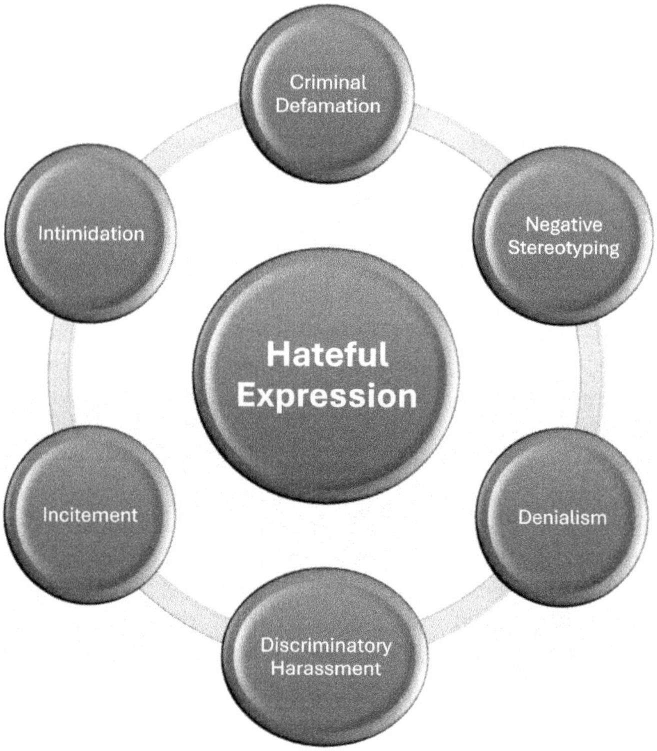

Figure 2.1 A cycle chart of hateful actions

(referring to the dress of Muslims), 'nigger',[84] 'kaffir',[85] 'monkey' or 'boy.'[86] The six manifestations of HE, in varying degrees, are a lot more subtle and indirect. Criminal defamation (CD) is similar to HE, except that it is limited to statements that are false and damaging to the dignity or reputation of a person from a specified group.[87] For example, the propagation of false or unverified conspiracy theories against certain groups[88] (e.g. purple-haired people are evil witches), and the generalised classification of certain groups

84 See *Wiggs v Courshon* (1973) 355 F. Supp. 206 (S.D. Fla.); *Agarwal v Johnson* (1979) 25 Cal.3d 932; *Turley v ISG Lackawanna Inc.* (2013) No. 1:2006-cv-00794, Doc. 251 (W.D.N.Y.).

85 See *Mbatha v Van Staden* (1982) (2) SA 260 (N).

86 See *Diane Soares da Costa* (2013) No. 0098040–18.2010.8.26.0050 (Sao Paulo Ct. of Just., 23 May); *Turley v ISG Lackawanna Inc.* (2013) No. 1:2006-cv-00794, Doc. 251 (W.D.N.Y.).

87 Cf. Brown "Hate speech law: A philosophical examination," 20.

88 Brown "Hate speech law: A philosophical examination," 31 (on antisemitism propagated against Jewish people by a newspaper).

as 'criminals,'[89] 'liars'[90] or 'lazy,' would fall within the CD category of hate crime.

The kind of hateful action involved in discriminatory harassment (DH), incitement (INC) and intimidation (INT) is comparatively more direct and deliberate than the actions of negative stereotyping (NS) and denialism (DEN). DEN is committed when a perpetrator denies, trivialises, approves of, condones, justifies or glorifies acts of mass cruelty or violence against a particular group of people,[91] whereas NS consists of public statements towards a particular social group (usually in the media) that, although not necessarily false (unlike CD actions described earlier), are unbalanced, oversimplified or misleading.[92] Very few countries (criminally) punish DEN,[93] whereas examples of NS include displaying savage or barbaric caricatures as symbolising the culture or ethnicity of indigenous communities;[94] selecting the worst members of a social group to misleadingly portray the entirety of this group to outsiders;[95] and the suggestive promises of politicians to 'remove all immigrants' if the public votes for them, thereby portraying immigrants as generally being problematic and deserving of removal.[96]

Furthermore, DH entails barring, inhibiting or interfering with the enjoyment of the rights of a person or group.[97] The display of 'whites only' signs (or the equivalent) in public areas;[98] the application of black grease to the offices or furniture occupied by black employees;[99] and the locking of bathrooms, while giving only white patrons or employees the keys,[100] are all examples of DH. DH has some overlap with INT, as is the case with several other categories of this action-orientated typology. For example, the display of a noose in a work area occupied by black employees may fall within either DH or INT categories.[101] More generally, INT consists of actions that instil fear into a

89 See *Jersild v Denmark* [1994] EHRR 1; *Ortenberg v Plamondon* (1915) [24 B.R. 69, 385] (Quebec).
90 See *Eatock v Bolt* [2011] [FCA 1103].
91 Brown "Hate speech law: A philosophical examination," 29.
92 Brown "Hate speech law: A philosophical examination," 23.
93 One such country is Germany, where Holocaust denialism is prohibited, see Howard J. Ehrlich "Campus ethnoviolence," in *Race and Ethnic conflict: Contending views on prejudice, discrimination and ethnoviolence*, eds. Fred J. Pincus and Howard J. Ehrlich, 2nd ed (New York: Westview Press, 1999) 271, 280.
94 Cf. Brown "Hate speech law: A philosophical examination," 34–35.
95 Altschiller "*Hate crimes: A reference handbook*," 77.
96 See *Glimmerveen and Hagenbeek v Netherlands* (1979) Nos. 8348/78 and 8406/78 (ECtHR, 11 Oct.).
97 Cf. Brown "Hate speech law: A philosophical examination," 33.
98 See the example of the Sweet Briar College incident in Virginia discussed in Altschiller *Hate crimes: A reference handbook*, 126.
99 *Turley v ISG Lackawanna Inc.* (2013) No. 1:2006-cv-00794, Doc. 251 (W.D.N.Y.).
100 *EEOC v Tyson Foods, Inc.* (2006) No. cv-05-BE-1704-E (N.D. Ala.).
101 See *EEOC v AA Foundries Inc.* (2012) No. 11–792 (W.D. Tex.).

targeted individual or social group usually through verbal or symbolic threats or provocation.[102] Other examples of INT include cross burnings at social spaces that are occupied by targeted individuals or groups[103] and the symbolic vandalism of monuments or institutions that are held sacred by targeted individuals or groups.[104] The last type of action (INC) is also punished, aside from hate crime statutory law, at common law. The main difference here would be the motivation. INC entails the 'stirring up' or propagation for one or more individuals (or the public in general) to express hatred (or violence) towards certain groups.[105] The spreading of hateful protest messages (e.g. banners written 'God hates gays') at funerals of members of targeted groups[106] and threatening the (white) neighbours of black or immigrant residents with violence if they did not make these residents leave their homes and the community,[107] are both examples of INC.

2.5 Four General Elements of Hate Crimes

Hate crime statutes around the world generally fit into one or more of the three penalty-enhancement, sentence-aggravation and substantive models discussed earlier in this chapter. However, the content and definitional elements of each statute differ from one jurisdiction to the next. The purpose of this section of the chapter is to discuss the basic elements[108] that apply generally to offences on the substantive model. This theoretical generalisation is undertaken with the usual caveat that permits exceptions. While substantive hate crime offences from some jurisdictions may specify more requirements, and using different language, the argument in this chapter is that there is a generalised minimum that is germane to most jurisdictions within this category. There are four minimum requirements of substantive hate crime offences: (1) the manifest isolation or discriminatory targeting of an individual or group, (2) the target or victim being a member of the protected social group, (3) a bias or

102 See Brown "Hate speech law: A philosophical examination," 34–35.
103 Altschiller *Hate crimes: A reference handbook*, 49.
104 On the torching and defacing of churches and mosques, see Altschiller *Hate crimes: A reference handbook*, 48–49 and 77. On acts of shredding copies of the Holy Koran at the Islamic Foundation of Central Ohio in Columbus, see Altschiller *Hate crimes: A reference handbook*, 78.
105 Brown "Hate speech law: A philosophical examination," 26.
106 See *Phelps-Roper v City of Manchester* 697 F.3d 678 (8th Cir. 2012) at 683. See also *Phelps-Roper v Strickland* 539 F.3d 356, 359 (6th Cir. 2008); *Snyder v Phelps* 131 S.Ct. 1207, 1213, 179 L.Ed.2d 172 (2011).
107 The related incident of Robert Keller in Hurricane, Utah, is discussed in Altschiller *Hate crimes: A reference handbook*, 50–51.
108 The terms 'elements' and 'requirements' are used synonymously in this section of the chapter.

Table 2.1 General elements of substantive hate crimes

GENERAL ELEMENTS OF HATE CRIMES		
1. Base Offence		*2. Responsibility*
(a) Manifest Discriminatory Targeting	**(b) Protected Demographic**	**(d) Prejudice** **(e) Intention**

prejudicial motivation and (4) intention.[109] As Table 2.1 shows, the first two requirements, which are also known as the 'base offence' element, are taken as generally expressing the *wrongdoing* of hate crimes, whereas the third and fourth are a measurement of the *responsibility* that is to be attributed to an individual perpetrator in the circumstances. Therefore, for the sake of this discussion, I take wrongdoing and responsibility to be the minimum grounds of general criminal liability.[110]

109 There is no consistency in number of requirements that are listed in the literature. For example, see Brudholm "Conceptualising hatred globally: Is hate crime a human rights violation?" 31 at 33–34 (listing four requirements); Blazak "Isn't every crime a hate crime?: The case for hate crime laws," 245: '[F]our basic elements: (1) criminal offense, (2) intent, (3) perception, and (4) protected statuses.'; Jenness and Grattet "Making a hate crime: From social movement to law enforcement," 78: 'First, the law must propose a state policy action. That is, it must create a new criminal category, alter an existing law, or enhance penalties for select crimes. Second, it must contain an "intent standard." . . . Finally, for a state law to qualify as a hate crime law it must specify a list of protected social statuses, such as religious affiliation, race, ethnicity, or sexual orientation.'

110 See generally, George P. Fletcher *Rethinking criminal law* (Boston: Little, Brown, 1978) 455; Victor Tadros *Wrongs and crimes* (Oxford: Oxford University Press, 2016) 12–13 (distinguishing between 'wrongdoing' and 'public blame'); Michael S. Moore *Placing blame: A theory of the criminal law* (Oxford: Oxford University Press, 1997) 193 (on 'wrongdoing' and 'culpability'). Standard common law approaches draw an *actus reus-mens rea* (and defences) distinction: English Draft Criminal Code (1989) vol 2, para 7.2; Paul Robinson *Structure and function in criminal law* (Oxford: Oxford University Press, 1997) 5; David Ormerod and Karl Laird *Smith and Hogan's criminal law* 15th ed (Oxford: Oxford University Press, 2021) 26–27; Joshua Dressler *Understanding criminal law* 9th ed (Durham: Carolina Academic Press, 2022) § 9.01. Cf. The Francophone *'l'élément matériel'* (*actus reus*) and *'l'élément moral'* (*mens rea*): Catherine Elliot *French criminal law* (New York: Routledge, 2001) 59; John Bell "Criminal law," in *Principles of French law*, eds. John Bell et al 2nd ed (Oxford: Oxford University Press, 2008) 201 at 204–205. Further compare this to the German three-part classification: Michael Bohlander *The German criminal code: A modern English translation* (Portland: Hart, 2008) 6; R. Antony Duff *Answering for crime: Responsibility and liability in the criminal law* (2007) 205–206. For further general and comparative discussion, see Mohamed E. Badar & Iryna Marchuk 'A comparative study of the principles governing criminal responsibility in the major legal systems of the world (England, United States, Germany, France, Denmark, Russia, China, and Islamic legal tradition' (2013) 24 *Criminal Law Forum* 1; George P. Fletcher *The grammar of criminal law: American, comparative and international* vol 1 (Oxford: Oxford University Press, 2007) 43–58.

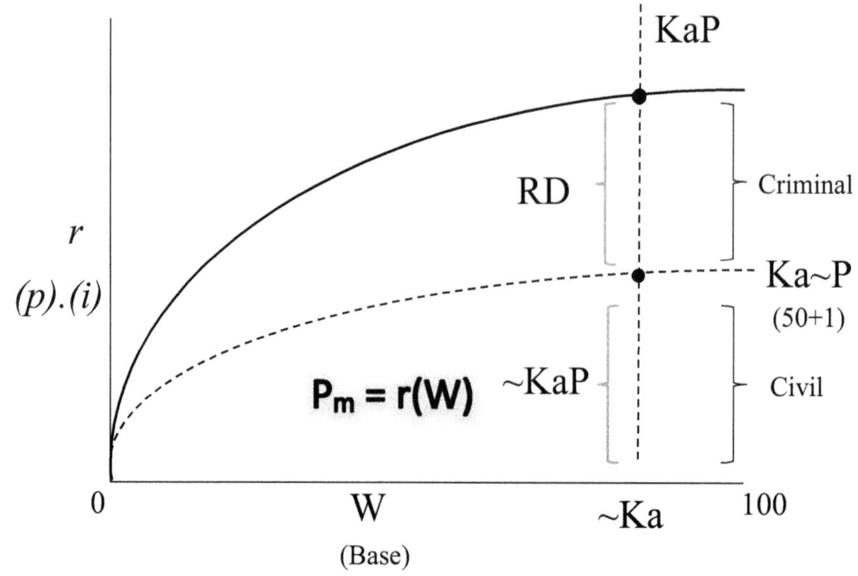

Figure 2.2 A graph of criminal wrongdoing and responsibility

Wrongdoing (W) and responsibility (*r*) have a linear one-to-one relationship ($P_m = r(W)$),[111] where an increase in the reprehensibility (or dangerousness) of a particular incident of wrongdoing results (defences and excuses aside)[112] in a corresponding increase in the level of responsibility that is attributed to its perpetrator. Likewise, increased levels of wrongdoing (ranging from zero to 100) and responsibility (zero to one) are also likely to result in a higher degree of punishment.[113] The relationship between wrongdoing and responsibility is reflected graphically in Figure 2.2.

Therefore, the materiality (P_m) of hate crime consists of the wrongdoing of the base discriminatory targeting of a member of a protected social group for a prejudicial motive (responsibility). Each of these requirements will now be discussed in turn.

According to Brudholm and other commentators, 'if there is no crime, there can be no hate crime.'[114] By this they mean that unless the manifest isolation or

111 This formulation is an adaptation to that originally developed by Robert Nozick, see Robert Nozick *Philosophical explanations* (Cambridge: Harvard University Press, 1981) 363.

112 Defences and excuses can decrease or entirely exclude the levels of reprehensibility (or dangerousness) of wrongdoing and responsibility respectively.

113 Cf. Fletcher "Rethinking criminal law," 43–58.

114 Brudholm "Conceptualising hatred globally: Is hate crime a human rights violation?," 34; Blazak "Isn't every crime a hate crime?: The case for hate crime laws," 245–246; 'Hate crime laws only characterize already criminal acts, like murder or arson. These statutes do not

discriminatory targeting of an individual or group results in an assault, murder, arson or some other extant offence, the first 'base offence' requirement would not be met.[115] In my view, this interpretation is far too narrow to achieve the broader purposes of hate crime legislation. On this interpretation of the first requirement, a large pool of hateful actions, such as the dissemination of hateful (sexist, racist or xenophobic) posters, flyers or placards;[116] cross burnings;[117] the display of 'no red-heads allowed' (or the equivalent) signs on public bathrooms or buildings;[118] and sending provocative objects such as nooses, parts of dead animals or swastikas to certain targeted groups,[119] most likely would be excluded from the prohibition. In any event, the international formulation[120] of the prohibition is wide enough to encompass hateful expressions that are linked to extant offences and those that are not. Therefore, the first 'base' requirement for purposes of this book is interpreted in the same wide sense to include both (narrow and broad) categories of hateful expressions. However, the discriminatory targeting of individuals or groups through these various actions is one thing, but characterising these as being wrongful in the legal (criminal) sense (i.e. without legal justification) is quite another. This latter aspect will be discussed in further detail later in Chapter 6 (discussing the probative condition of proof), but it suffices at this stage to note that the first base requirement at the very least consists of the isolation or discriminatory targeting (selection) of a particular group (or one of its members) as being deserving of hostility or hateful expression.

Secondly, the perpetrator's actions must target or be against individuals from statutorily specified groups.[121] Jurisdictions typically select demographic

---

create any new categories of criminalized behaviour.'; Perry "In the name of hate: Understanding hate crimes," 8: 'The hate crime designation may be applied only where a "predicate offense," or underlying crime, is committed.'

115 For a similar view, see Office for Democratic Institutions and Human Rights *Hate crime laws: A practical guide* 2nd ed (2022) 15: 'Hate crimes are criminal acts committed with a bias motive.' Available at: www.osce.org (accessed: 2 January 2023); English Law Commission *Hate crime laws: Final report* no. 402 (2021) 13, para 2.3. Available at: www.gov.uk (accessed: 2 January 2022). Botha and Govindjee "Regulating cases of 'extreme hate speech' in South Africa: A suggested framework for a legislated criminal sanction," 117, 119; Joanna Botha 'The selection of victim groups in hate-crime legislation' (2019) 136 *South African Law Journal* 781, 784.

116 Ehrlich "Campus ethnoviolence," 271. For example, the display of a poster showing the image of a black person with a red diagonal line across it on the door of a black resident, see Mari J. Matsuda "Public response to racist speech: Considering the victim's story," in *Words that wound: Critical race theory, assaultive speech and the first amendment*, eds. Mari J. Matsuda et al (New York: Westview Press, 1999) 17 at 17.

117 Ehrlich "Campus ethnoviolence," 280.

118 Cf. Altschiller *Hate crimes: A reference handbook*, 127.

119 Matsuda "Public response to racist speech: Considering the victim's story," 20–11.

120 See the sources cited at notes 4 and 9 earlier.

121 Brudholm "Conceptualising hatred globally: Is hate crime a human rights violation?," 34–35.

groupings for legislative protection given their peculiar history with incidents of mass violence and social unrest. However, given the global post-war history of hate crimes that was outlined earlier, religion, sexual orientation, race and ethnicity (or social origin) appear to be common to most jurisdictions.[122] Therefore, once our swimming pool prosecutor (from our earlier scenario in Chapter 1) can show that the base actions (vacating and draining the pool and erecting a 'whites only' sign) of the perpetrators had isolated or targeted X and that X is a member of a specified racial demographic, this *prima facie* would constitute wrongdoing. This is a preliminary observation because, as intimated earlier, wrongdoing, as the term is used in this book, is a loaded concept requiring both the prohibited conduct and the absence of a legal justification. The latter component will be discussed later in Chapter 6 of the book.

The third requirement is that the wrongdoing (in the respects defined above) must have been perpetrated with a prejudicial motivation.[123] This requirement fulfils two functions. Firstly, it demands an explanation as to *why* the base discriminatory targeting was committed.[124] Secondly, it limits the extent of criminal liability by distinguishing discriminatory actions that are perpetrated for the wrong (or illegitimate) reasons from those that are committed for acceptable reasons. However, this explanatory requirement of a motivation has little to do with the state of mind of a perpetrator.[125] Therefore, it would be no defence for our swimming pool perpetrators to contend that they 'did not intend cause any harm to X.'[126] Similarly, there is a hidden irony in the 'hate' crime designation because, as Jacobs and Potter say, '"Hate" crime is not really about hate, but about bias or prejudice.'[127] This is the case for three reasons: firstly, the work of Levin and McDevitt shows that hate crimes can be committed by opponents for various intentional and unintentional reasons, including 'to rid the world of evil' (mission hate crimes);[128] 'to blame others

122 Blazak "Isn't every crime a hate crime?: The case for hate crime laws," 247; English Law Commission *Hate crime laws: Final report* no. 402 (2021) 61, para 3.1: 'There are currently five characteristics recognised in hate crime laws in England and Wales: race, religion, sexual orientation, disability and transgender identity.' Available at: www.gov.uk (accessed: 2 January 2022).

123 This requirement is also sometimes referred to as a 'bias,' see Office for Democratic Institutions and Human Rights *Hate crime laws: A practical guide* 2nd ed (2022) 15; English Law Commission (n119), 15, para 2.11; Botha and Govindjee "Regulating cases of 'extreme hate speech' in South Africa: A suggested framework for a legislated criminal sanction," 119, n4; Botha "The selection of victim groups in hate-crime legislation," 784: 'The bias motive against the victim's group status distinguishes the hate crime from an ordinary crime.'

124 Brudholm "Conceptualising hatred globally: Is hate crime a human rights violation?," 34.

125 Lawrence "Punishing hate: Bias crimes under American law," 9.

126 It could well sincerely be, to borrow a trope from Kierkegaard, that 'it is agony to breathe in the same world where the hated one breathes,' see Søren Kierkegaard *Works of Love* edited and translated by H.V Hong & E.H. Hong (Princeton: Princeton University Press, 1995) 308.

127 Jacobs and Kimberly *Hate crimes: Criminal law & identity politics*, 11.

128 Levin and McDevitt "Hate crimes: The rising tide of bigotry and bloodshed," Ch 7; Levin and McDevitt "Hate crimes revisited: America's war on those who are different," Ch 7.

for their loss' (resentful or retaliatory hate crimes);[129] 'to protect themselves against [perceived] outsiders' (defensive hate crimes);[130] and 'for the thrill of it' (thrill-seeking hate crimes).[131] Secondly, the impact and structure of base discriminatory wrongdoing typically transcends the idiosyncratic context of an individual victim. As Brudholm argues, hate crimes typically have an 'us and them' (as opposed to 'me and you') dimension.[132] The perpetrator's actions communicate a much wider message about the particular demographic that the victim represents. Thirdly, most hate crime statutory provisions do not use the language of *mens rea* or 'hate' at all, but they rather focus on the disposition or character (as a source of their prejudice) of the perpetrator.[133]

The bottom line, according to Jacobs and Potter, is that 'we all have prejudices for and against individuals, groups, foods, countries and weather.'[134] 'Sometime,' Jacobs and Potter argue further, 'these prejudices are rooted in experience, sometimes in fantasy and in irrationality, and sometimes they are passed down to us by family, friends, school, religion, and culture.'[135] However, some of these prejudices are good or innocuous (e.g. preferring tall basketball players and educated presidents), while others are reprehensible (e.g. racism, anti-Semitism, misogyny). Acting out any of these latter prejudices generally will attract criminal responsibility, but it will only be for actions that amount to wrongdoing (i.e. the discriminatory targeting of a specified group) that the actor's liability will arise. According to Levin and McDevitt, these prejudices could be conceived as lying on a spectrum from one innocuous end to the other hateful and bigoted end.[136] The line of where innocuous preference ends and hateful bigotry begins will have to be decided by legislatures in each jurisdiction.

Not many theorists discuss a fourth intention requirement of substantive hate crimes. This largely is because one does not need to hate their victim to be guilty of a hate crime, as contended earlier. However, the imposition of a

129 Levin and McDevitt "Hate crimes: The rising tide of bigotry and bloodshed," Ch 4; Levin and McDevitt "Hate crimes revisited: America's war on those who are different," Ch 4.
130 Levin and McDevitt "Hate crimes: The rising tide of bigotry and bloodshed," Ch 6; Levin and McDevitt "Hate crimes revisited: America's war on those who are different," Ch 6.
131 Levin and McDevitt "Hate crimes: The rising tide of bigotry and bloodshed," Ch 5; Levin and McDevitt "Hate crimes revisited: America's war on those who are different," Ch 5.
132 Brudholm "Conceptualising hatred globally: Is hate crime a human rights violation?," 34, n6.
133 Heidi M. Hurd 'Why liberals should hate "Hate crime legislation' (2001) 20(2) *Law & Philosophy* 215, 219; Lawrence "Punishing hate: Bias crimes under American law," 29–39 and appendices B and C (on the 'animus' and 'discriminatory selection' models). Cf. Paul H. Robinson 'Hate crimes: Crimes of motive, character or group terror' (1992) *Annual Survey of American Law* 605 (on the plausibility of the recklessness model to capture the motivational requirement of hate crimes). See generally, Michael D. Bayles "Character, purpose and criminal responsibility" (1982) 1 *Law & Philosophy* 5; R. Antony Duff "Choice, character and criminal liability" (1993) 12 *Law & Philosophy* 345.
134 Jacobs and Kimberly *Hate crimes: Criminal law & identity politics*, 11.
135 Jacobs and Kimberly *Hate crimes: Criminal law & identity politics*, 11–12.
136 Levin & McDevitt "Hate crimes revisited: America's war on those who are different," 97.

culpability requirement is what the general principles of criminal law demand for most offences, unless expressly excluded by the legislature.[137] Lawrence contends that '[t]here is no justification for an application of strict liability principles in the criminal context.'[138] This sentiment is shared across many jurisdictions around the world, as indicated by the ***principio de culpabilidad*** ('principle of culpability') in the Spanish-speaking parts of South America,[139] the Chinese[140] and Russian[141] 'psychological' or 'subjective' components of crime in the Far East,[142] the common law presumption of ***mens rea***[143] and the civilian culpability principle[144] (e.g. the French ***culpabilité***[145] and the German ***Schuldprinzip***).[146]

137 Lawrence "Punishing hate: Bias crimes under American law," 64; Blazak "Isn't every crime a hate crime?: The case for hate crime laws," 245; Jenness and Grattet "Making a hate crime: From social movement to law enforcement," 77.

138 Lawrence "Punishing hate: Bias crimes under American law," 65.

139 See Marcelo Ferrante "Argentina," in ***The handbook of comparative criminal law***, eds. Kevin J. Heller and Markus D. Dubber (Stanford: Stanford University Press, 2011) 12 at 24. See *Antiñir*-2006 (Fallos: 329:2367) (Argentinian Supreme Court decision on ***principio de culpabilidad***).

140 Criminal Code of the People's Republic of China, 1997, articles 14–15; Wei Luo "China," in ***The handbook of comparative criminal law***, eds. Kevin J. Heller and Markus D. Dubber (Stanford: Stanford University Press, 2011) (Stanford: Stanford University Press, 2011) 137 at 148.

141 Stephen Thaman "Russia," in ***The handbook of comparative criminal law***, eds. Kevin J. Heller and Markus D. Dubber (Stanford: Stanford University Press, 2011) 414 at 420 ('Today the focus of "guilt" is psychological, rather than the ideological laden ethical or sociopolitical content that prevailed in socialist times and facilitated the repression of innocent persons').

142 See also John O. Haley "Japan," in ***The handbook of comparative criminal law***, eds. Kevin J. Heller and Markus D. Dubber (Stanford: Stanford University Press, 2011) 393 at 400; 刑法 Keihō (Japan Penal Code), 1907, article 38.

143 *Sherras v De Rutzen* [1895] 1 Q.B. 918 at 921; *R. v Beaver* [1957] S.C.R. 531 at 21–22; *Sweet v Parsley* [1970] A.C. 132 at 148; *R v M and B* [2010] 2 Cr. App. R. 33 at 388; *B v Director of Public Prosecutions* [2000] 2 A.C. 428 at 460; C.S. Kenny *Outlines of criminal law* 2nd ed (Cambridge: Cambridge University Press, 1904) 39; United States Model Penal Code, 1962, § 2.02(3) and (4); Kent Roach "Canada," in ***The handbook of comparative criminal law***, eds. Kevin J. Heller and Markus D. Dubber (Stanford: Stanford University Press, 2011) 97 at 103; Dressler *Understanding criminal law* § 10.01; Andrew Ashworth "United Kingdom," in ***The handbook of comparative criminal law***, eds. Kevin J. Heller and Markus D. Dubber (Stanford: Stanford University Press, 2011) 531 at 536; Simon Bronitt "Australia," in ***The handbook of comparative criminal law***, eds. Kevin J. Heller and Markus D. Dubber (Stanford: Stanford University Press, 2011) 49 at 58: 'Australia strongly subscribes to an orthodox subjective approach to fault.'

144 John R. Spencer and Antje Pedain "Approaches to strict and constructive liability in Continental criminal law," in ***Appraising strict liability***, ed. Andrew Simester (Oxford: Oxford University Press, 2005) 237 at 252, citing Reinhard Frank "Über den Aufbau des Schuldbegriffs," in ***Festschrift für die juristische Fakultät Giessen Zum Universitäts-Jubiläum***, ed. Reinhard Frank (Giessen: A. Töpelmann, 1907) 3.

145 *Code Pénal* (1992), article 121–123; Spencer and Pedain "Approaches to strict and constructive liability in Continental criminal law," 267; Catherine Elliot "France," in ***The handbook of comparative criminal law***, eds. Kevin J. Heller and Markus D. Dubber (Stanford: Stanford University Press, 2011) 209 at 216. Cf. Carlos G. Diez and Luis E. Chiesa 'Spain' in ***The handbook of comparative criminal law***, eds. Kevin J. Heller and Markus D. Dubber (Stanford: Stanford University Press, 2011) 488 at 491.

146 *Strafgesetzbuch* (1998) § 15 (Germany); Spencer and Pedain "Approaches to strict and constructive liability in continental criminal law," 250; Weigend (n 19) 261. See also

African approaches, largely because of their European colonial heritage, to criminal fault reflect a similar 'subjectivity.'[147] From a theoretical point of view, Lawrence demonstrates the relevance of an intention requirement by distinguishing three kinds of cases: the clever bias criminal (CIC), the unconscious bigot (UB) and the ignorant offensive actor (IOA).[148] Of the three, only the IOA would be exculpated from criminal liability for a lack of intention. Unlike the CIC and the UB, the IOA is unaware of the negative or discriminatory effect of their discriminatory actions and that their victim is a member of a protected demographic.[149] The IOA instead thinks their actions will breach some other non-criminal societal norm, by shocking the general public, but not that a particular demographic group will be specifically offended.[150] The UB, on the other hand, is aware of the discriminatory effect of their actions, but nevertheless thinks either that he is justified or that his own motivation (e.g. ridding the world of evil) deserves greater protection.[151] Therefore, the UB genuinely believes in the righteousness, which in some cases may well be legally or morally justified, of his own cause. The CIC is the aware of the three actors. She is aware of both the potentially negative or discriminatory impact of her actions and the membership of her target within a protected demographic. In addition to this, it is the CIC's gratuitous desire to bring harm to her target. The CIC is also well informed about the history, main arguments and agendas of the broader anti-hate crime movement yet offers a duplicitous non-bias motivation in order to justify her wrongdoing.[152] A robust and properly theorised intention requirement performs the task of distinguishing the range of liability and/or punishment between the CIC, the UB and the IOA.

2.6 Conclusion

The study of hate crimes has spread across the globe and to a variety of disciplines. However, the scholarship is not dominated by lawyers or criminal law theorists. It is rather political theorists, sociologists, anthropologists, gender theorists, educationists and many other social scientists. The seminal

BverfGE 80, 244 (255), available at: www.bundesverfassungsgericht.de (accessed: 12 February 2023).

147 See Sadiq Reza "Egypt," in *The handbook of comparative criminal law*, eds. Kevin J. Heller and Markus D. Dubber (Stanford: Stanford University Press, 2011) 179 at 187; Lawrence Atsegbua et al *Criminal law in Nigeria: A modern approach* (Lagos: Malthouse Press, 2022) 18; Callie R. Snyman "The tension between legal theory and policy considerations in the general principles of criminal law" (2003) *Acta Juridica* 1 at 2; Shannon V. Hoctor "The concept of *dolus eventualis* in South African law – An historical perspective" (2008) 14(2) *Fundamina* 14 at 19.

148 Lawrence "Punishing hate: Bias crimes under American law," 65.

149 Lawrence "Punishing hate: Bias crimes under American law," 66.

150 Lawrence "Punishing hate: Bias crimes under American law," 66.

151 Lawrence "Punishing hate: Bias crimes under American law," 65–66. For examples of the raising of a jest defence, see Matsuda "Public response to racist speech: Considering the victim's story," 20–21.

152 Lawrence "Punishing hate: Bias crimes under American law," 65.

monographs by Frederick Lawrence (*Punishing Hate: Bias Crimes Under American Law*) and James Jacobs and Kimberly Potter (*Hate Crimes: Criminal Law & Identity Politics*) are rare pieces of scholarship that contain criminal law theory and doctrine. This chapter has attempted to fill this void by discussing the meaning, history, types and models of hate crimes around the world. These together constitute the material condition of evidential proof, as defined in this book. The chapter has attempted to apply criminal law theorising and doctrine to the contested terrain of hate crimes around the world. As a result, the substantive criminal law account of hate crimes in this chapter is not meant to reflect the existing doctrine of a single particular country or region. It is cross-jurisdictional, theoretical and framed in sufficiently wide terms as to be germane to various parts of the model.

There are three models of hate crime statutes: penalty enhancement provisions, sentence aggravating laws and substantive criminal prohibitions. Most countries around the world that have enacted hate crime legislation would fall within one or more of these three categories. Much of the doctrinal theorising of this chapter focuses on substantive criminal prohibitions. This includes the four general elements discussed towards the end of the chapter. However, much of the general definitions, arguments and conceptual clarifications that are discussed in the chapter also may find application to the sentencing and penalty enhancing contexts as well.

The chapter has explicated the first of the three (*material*, *processual* and *probative*) conditions of evidential proof described in Chapter 1. Having now described the objects of the evidential proof of hate crimes, the next chapter will proceed to discuss the second *processual* condition before concluding with the *probative* condition in the remaining three chapters of the book.

2.7 Bibliography

Books and Book Chapters

Alexander Brown *Hate speech law: A philosophical examination* (New York: Routledge, 2015).

Andrew Ashworth "United Kingdom," in *The handbook of comparative criminal law*, eds. Kevin J. Heller and Markus D. Dubber (Stanford: Stanford University Press, 2011) 531.

Barbara Perry *In the name of hate: Understanding hate crimes* (New York: Routledge, 2001).

Barry D. Adam *The rise of a gay and lesbian movement* revised ed (New York: Twayne, 1995).

Brian Levin "The long arc of justice: Race, violence and the emergence of hate crime law," in *Hate crimes*, eds. Barbara Perry and Brian Levin vol 1 (Westport: Praeger, 2009) 1.

Carlos G. Diez and Luis E. Chiesa "Spain," in *The handbook of comparative criminal law*, eds. Kevin J. Heller and Markus D. Dubber (Stanford: Stanford University Press, 2011) 488.

Catherine Elliot "France," in *The handbook of comparative criminal law*, eds. Kevin J. Heller and Markus D. Dubber (Stanford: Stanford University Press, 2011) 209.

Catherine Elliot *French criminal law* (New York: Routledge, 2001).
Combahee River Collective "A black feminist statement," in *Feminist manifestos: A global documentary reader*, ed. Penny A. Weiss (New York: New York University Press, 2018) Ch 59.
Courtney S. Kenny *Outlines of criminal law* 2nd ed (Cambridge: Cambridge University Press, 1904).
David Kostan "Hate and the state in ancient Greece," in *Hate, politics, law: Critical perspectives on combating hate*, eds. Thomas Brudholm and Birgitte S. Johansen (New York: Oxford University Press, 2018) 34.
David Ormerod and Karl Laird *Smith and Hogan's criminal law* 15th ed (Oxford: Oxford University Press, 2021).
David T. Goldberg *Racist culture: Philosophy and the politics of meaning* (Oxford: Blackwell, 1993).
Donald Altschiller *Hate crimes: A reference handbook* 3rd ed (Santa Barbara: ABC-CLIO, 2015).
Ely Aaronson *From slave abuse to hate crime: The criminalisation of racial violence in American history* (New York: Cambridge University Press, 2014).
Erik Bleich "From race to hate: A historical perspective," in *Hate, politics, law: Critical perspectives on combating hate*, eds. Thomas Brudholm and Birgitte S. Johansen (New York: Oxford University Press, 2018) 15.
Frederick M. Lawrence *Punishing hate: Bias crimes under American law* (Cambridge: Harvard University Press, 1999).
Gail Mason "Legislating against hate," in *The Routledge international handbook on hate crime*, eds. Nathan Hall et al (New York: Routledge, 2015) 59.
George P. Fletcher *The grammar of criminal law: American, comparative and international* vol 1 (Oxford: Oxford University Press, 2007).
George P. Fletcher *Rethinking criminal law* (Boston: Little, Brown, 1978).
Howard J. Ehrlich "Campus ethnoviolence," in *Race and ethnic conflict: Contending views on prejudice, discrimination and ethnoviolence*, eds. Fred J. Pincus and Howard J. Ehrlich 2nd ed (New York: Westview Press, 1999) 271.
Jack Levin and Jack McDevitt *Hate crimes revisited: America's war on those who are different* (Boulder, CO: Westview Press, 2002).
Jack Levin and Jack McDevitt *Hate crimes: The rising tide of bigotry and bloodshed* (New York: Plenum Press, 1993).
Jaime S. Miller "Identity politics," in *Encyclopaedia of queer studies in education*, eds. Kamden K. Strunk and Stephanie A. Shelton (Leiden: Brill, 2022) 294.
James B. Jacobs and Kimberly Potter *Hate crimes: Criminal law & identity politics* (New York: Oxford University Press, 1998).
Jeffrey Weeks "Gay liberation and its legacies," in *The Ashgate research companion to lesbian and gay activism*, eds. Manon Tremblay and David Paternotte (Farnham: Ashgate, 2015).
Jennifer Schweppe and Mark A. Walters, eds. *The globalisation of hate: Internationalising hate crime?* (New York: Oxford University Press, 2016).
Jennifer Schweppe et al *Lifecycle of a hate crime: Comparative report* (2018) 8, report commissioned by the Irish Council for Civil Liberties and is available at: www.iccl.ie (accessed 5 January 2023).
John Bell "Criminal law," in *Principles of French law*, eds. John Bell et al 2nd ed (Oxford: Oxford University Press, 2008) 201.
John O. Haley "Japan," in *The handbook of comparative criminal law*, eds. Kevin J. Heller and Markus D. Dubber (Stanford: Stanford University Press, 2011) 393.
John R. Spencer and Antje Pedain "Approaches to strict and constructive liability in continental criminal law," in *Appraising strict liability*, ed. Andrew Simester (Oxford: Oxford University Press, 2005) 237.

Joshua Dressler *Understanding criminal law* 9th ed (Durham: Carolina Academic Press, 2022).

Kent Roach "Canada," in *The handbook of comparative criminal law*, eds. Kevin J. Heller and Markus D. Dubber (Stanford: Stanford University Press, 2011) 97.

Kimberlé Crenshaw et al "Introduction," in *Critical race theory: The key writings that formed the movement*, eds. Kimberlé Crenshaw et al (New York: The New Press, 1995).

Kwame A. Appiah "Racisms," in *Anatomy of racism*, ed. Theo D. Goldberg (Minneapolis: University of Minnesota Press, 1990) 3.

Lawrence Atsegbua et al *Criminal law in Nigeria: A modern approach* (Lagos: Malthouse Press, 2022).

Marcelo Ferrante "Argentina," in *The handbook of comparative criminal law*, eds. Kevin J. Heller and Markus D. Dubber (Stanford: Stanford University Press, 2011) 12.

Mari J. Matsuda "Public response to racist speech: Considering the victim's story," in *Words that wound: Critical race theory, assaultive speech and the first amendment*, eds. Mari J. Matsuda, Charles R. Lawrence, Richard Delgado and Kimberlé W. Crenshaw (New York: Westview Press, 1999) 17.

Martin Bulmer and John Solomons, eds. *Racism* (Oxford: Oxford University Press, 1999).

Mary E. Townsend *European colonial expansion since 1871* (Philadelphia: J.B. Lippincott Company, 1941).

Michael Banton *Racial theories* (New York: Cambridge University Press, 1987).

Michael Bohlander *The German criminal code: A modern English translation* (Portland: Hart, 2008).

Michael S. Moore *Placing blame: A theory of the criminal law* (Oxford: Oxford University Press, 1997).

Nathan Hall et al, eds. *The Routledge international handbook on hate crime* (New York: Routledge, 2015).

Neil Chakraborti and Jon Garland *Hate crime: Impact, causes and responses* 2nd ed (London: Sage, 2015).

Paul Gilroy "One nation under a groove: The cultural politics of 'race' and racism in Britain," in *Anatomy of racism*, ed. David T. Goldberg (Minneapolis: University of Minnesota Press, 1990) 263.

Paul Iganski and Jack Levin *Hate crime: A global perspective* (New York: Routledge, 2015).

Paul Robinson *Structure and function in criminal law* (Oxford: Oxford University Press, 1997).

R. Antony Duff *Answering for crime: Responsibility and liability in the criminal law* (2007).

Reinhard Frank "Über den Aufbau des Schuldbegriffs," in *Festschrift für die juristische Fakultät Giessen Zum Universitäts-Jubiläum*, ed. Reinhard Frank (Giessen: A. Töpelmann, 1907) 3.

Robert Miles and Malcolm Brown *Racism* 2nd ed (London: Routledge, 2003).

Robert Nozick *Philosophical explanations* (Cambridge: Harvard University Press, 1981).

Roland Oliver and Anthony Atmore *Medieval Africa, 1250–1800* (Cambridge: Cambridge University Press, 2001).

Rosina Beckman *Colonial and postcolonial Africa* (New York: Britannica, 2017).

Sadiq Reza "Egypt," in *The handbook of comparative criminal law*, eds. Kevin J. Heller and Markus D. Dubber (Stanford: Stanford University Press, 2011) 179.

Simon Bronitt "Australia," in *The handbook of comparative criminal law*, eds. Kevin J. Heller and Markus D. Dubber (Stanford: Stanford University Press, 2011) 49.

Søren Kierkegaard *Works of love* (edited and translated by H.V. Hong and E.H. Hong) (Princeton: Princeton University Press, 1995).

Stephen Thaman "Russia," in *The handbook of comparative criminal law*, eds. Kevin J. Heller and Markus D. Dubber (Stanford: Stanford University Press, 2011) 414.
Steve Biko *I write what I like: A selection of his writings* (Johannesburg: Heinemann, 1987).
Sue Thornham "Second wave feminism," in *The Routledge companion to feminism and postfeminism*, ed. Sarah Gamble (London: Routledge, 2001).
Tania Das Gupta et al, eds. *Race and racialization: Essential readings* (Toronto: Canadian Scholars' Press, 2007).
Thomas Brudholm "Conceptualising hatred globally: Is hate crime a human rights violation?," in *The globalization of hate: Internationalising hate crime*, eds. Jennifer Schweppe and Mark A. Walters (Oxford: Oxford University Press, 2016) 31.
Thomas F. Gossett *Race: The history of an idea in America* (Dallas: Southern Methodist University Press, 1965).
Tivadar Vervoort "Towards a critical identity politics: Butler, Adorno and the force of non-identity," in *Feminism and the early Frankfurt School*, eds. Christine A. Payne and Jeremiah Morelock (Leiden: Brill, 2024) 113.
Valerie Jenness and Ryken Grattet *Making a hate crime: From social movement to law enforcement* (New York: Russell Sage Foundation, 2001).
Victor Tadros *Wrongs and crimes* (Oxford: Oxford University Press, 2016).
Wei Luo "China," in *The handbook of comparative criminal law*, eds. Kevin J. Heller and Markus D. Dubber (Stanford: Stanford University Press, 2011) 137.

Periodicals

Brian Levin "From slavery to hate crime laws: The emergence of race and status-based protection in American criminal law" (2002) 58(2) *Journal of Social Issues* 227.
Callie R. Snyman "The tension between legal theory and policy considerations in the general principles of criminal law" (2003) *Acta Juridica* 1.
Eric Stein "History against free speech: The new German law against the 'Auschwitz' – and other – lies" (1986) 85 *Michigan Law Review* 277.
Erik Bleich "The rise of hate speech and hate crime laws in liberal democracies" (2011) 37(6) *Journal of Ethnic and Migration Studies* 917.
Heidi M. Hurd "Why liberals should hate 'hate crime legislation'" (2001) 20(2) *Law & Philosophy* 215.
Howard Winant "Race and race theory" (2000) *Annual Review of Sociology* 169.
Jennifer Schweppe "What is a hate crime?" (2021) 7 *Cogent Social Sciences* 1.
Joanna Botha "The selection of victim groups in hate-crime legislation" (2019) 136 *South African Law Journal* 781.
Joanna Botha and Avinash Govindjee "Regulating cases of 'extreme hate speech' in South Africa: A suggested framework for a legislated criminal sanction" (2014) 27(2) *South African Journal of Criminal Justice* 117.
Kamban Naidoo "Hate crimes: Some theoretical considerations and their possible application to the South African context" (2016) 29(2) *Acta Criminologica* 37.
Mabogo P. More "Biko: Africana existentialist philosopher" (2004) 11(1) *Alternation* 79.
Michael D. Bayles "Character, purpose and criminal responsibility" (1982) 1 *Law & Philosophy* 5.
Paul H. Robinson "Hate crimes: Crimes of motive, character or group terror" (1992) *Annual Survey of American Law* 605.
R. Antony Duff "Choice, character and criminal liability" (1993) 12 *Law & Philosophy* 345.
Randy Blazak "Isn't every crime a hate crime?: The case for hate crime laws" (2011) 5(4) *Sociology Compass* 244.

Ryken Grattet and Valerie Jenness "Examining the boundaries of hate crime law: Disabilities and the 'dilemma of difference'" (2001) 91(3) *Journal of Criminal Law and Criminology* 653.

Shannon V. Hoctor "The concept of *dolus eventualis* in South African law – An historical perspective" (2008) 14(2) *Fundamina* 14.

Tanya Golash-Boza "A critical and comprehensive sociological theory of race and racism" (2016) 2(2) *Sociology of Race and Racism* 129.

Online Resources

American Jewish Committee, available at: www.ajc.org (accessed: 3 September 2024).

Anti-Defamation League, available at: www.adl.org (accessed: 3 September 2024).

Campaign for Homosexual Equality, available at: www.c-h-e.org.uk (accessed: 4 September 2024).

English Law Commission *Hate Crime Laws: Final Report no. 402* (2021) 1, available at: www.gov.uk (accessed: 2 January 2022).

National Organisation for Women, available at: www.now.org (accessed: 3 September 2024).

Office for Democratic Institutions and Human Rights *Hate Crime Laws: A Practical Guide* (2009) 16,' available at: www.osce.org (accessed: 2 January 2023).

Religious Action Center of Reform Judaism, available at: www.rac.org (accessed: 3 September 2024).

3 The Processual Condition

3.1 Introducing Processual Coloniality

Evidential proof, by definition, is the property of a *disputed fact* (materiality) being established *inferentially* (probativity) from an *extant fact* (processual).[1] The material and probative conditions are discussed in Chapter 2 as well as Chapters 5 and 6, respectively, whereas the processual condition is the subject of the present chapter. The processual condition refers to the full range of 'mechanisms',[2] 'methods and principles'[3] or 'institutions, procedures and practices'[4] that regulate, among others, the investigation, presentation, authentication and evaluation of the (processual) extant facts upon which evidential proof depends. Processual practices are the mechanisms through which the state responds officially to the perpetration of crime.[5] Using its monopoly over criminal law enforcement,[6] the state must mediate between society's interest in effective criminal law enforcement and the rights and freedoms of all individuals that are suspected of, arrested for, charged with, convicted of, or sentenced for crime.[7] As a result, processual practices have been defined as consisting of 'a series of compromises.'[8]

1 See Pamela-Jane Schwikkard and Tshepo B. Mosaka *Principles of evidence* 5th ed (Claremont: Juta, 2023) 607.
2 Liz Campbell et al *The Criminal Process* 5th ed (Oxford: Oxford University Press, 2019) 1.
3 Victor G. Hiemstra *Introduction to the law of criminal procedure* (Durban: Butterworths, 1977) 1.
4 Paul Roberts et al "Introduction," in *The integrity of criminal process: From theory into practice*, eds. Jill Hunter et al (Oxford: Hart, 2016) 3 at 8.
5 Liz Campbell et al "The Criminal Process," 1–2.
6 Ronald J. Allen et al *Comprehensive criminal procedure* 5th ed (New York: Wolters Kluwer, 2020) 55.
7 Allen et al "Comprehensive criminal procedure," 8. See also Herbert Packer "Two models of the criminal process" (1964) 113(1) *University of Pennsylvania Law Review* 1 (on the 'criminal control' and 'due process' models); Herbert Packer "The courts, the police and the rest of us" (1966) 57(3) *Journal of Criminal Law, Criminology and Police Science* 238.
8 Stephen E. Van der Merwe "A basic introduction to criminal procedure," in *Criminal procedure handbook*, ed. J. Johannes Joubert (Claremont: Juta, 2020) 3 at 7–8.

DOI: 10.4324/9781003493006-3

From its commencement with the identification of a suspect until its completion when the accused person is sentenced and subsequently decides to exercise their post-sentencing remedies (e.g. appeals or reviews),[9] criminal process consists of a series of decisions[10] taken by various institutional actors, including police officers, prosecutors, defence lawyers, adjudicators, probation officers and prison warders.[11] Some of these decisions, such as the charging of a suspect, the decision to prosecute, the granting of bail and the decision to remand an accused person[12] and decisions on whether and how to investigate various suspects, are 'processual' decisions. Processual decisions facilitate the progression of the accused through the various stages of the criminal process.[13] On the other hand, 'dispositive' decisions consist of all the opportunities that are available to the accused to exit the criminal process.[14] These include the decision to divert the accused to alternative (non-criminal) dispute resolution processes, the accused's decision to plead guilty, adjudicative decisions on the merits or sentencing, preliminary decisions on whether or not to commit the accused to trial and prosecutorial decisions to withdraw the charges.[15] The granting of an order to dismiss the indictment or criminal charges due to insufficient evidence is another example of a dispositive decision.

Processual practices around the world generally are dominated by two traditions from Europe. One is the civil law or 'inquisitorial' tradition and the other is the common law or 'accusatorial' tradition.[16] The civilian

9 See generally, Van der Merwe "A basic introduction to criminal procedure," 7; Allen et al "Comprehensive criminal procedure," 5 (stipulating 11 characteristics of criminal prosecutions of serious crimes from the 'initial enforcement responsibility . . . [of] police agencies . . . to involve individuals in the criminal justice process' to the vindication of the right of '[a] convicted defendant . . . to some form of appellate review').

10 Liz Campbell et al "The Criminal Process," 1–2.

11 Liz Campbell et al "The Criminal Process," 2.

12 Cf. Liz Campbell et al "The Criminal Process," 11, where bail and remand decisions are regarded as being neither processual nor dispositive.

13 Liz Campbell et al "The Criminal Process," 10.

14 Liz Campbell et al "The Criminal Process," 10–11.

15 Liz Campbell et al "The Criminal Process," 11.

16 Craig M. Bradley "Overview," in *Criminal procedure: A worldwide study*, ed. Craig M. Bradley (Durham: Carolina Academic Press, 1999) xv at xv; Jospeter M. Mbuba "Introduction," in *Comparative criminal justice*, ed. Jospeter M. Mbuba (Lanham: Rowman & Littlefield, 2023) 1 at 2 ('Court trials take on different forms, the main ones being adversarial and inquisitorial'); Cliff Roberson and Dilip K. Das *An introduction to comparative legal models of criminal justice* 2nd ed (Boca Raton: CRC Press, 2016) 13 ('The two major legal models in the modern Western world are the civil law and the common law models'); Ed Johnston and Tom Smith *Criminal procedure and punishment* 3rd ed (Saltford: Hall and Stitt, 2023) 1 ('It is widely accepted that the criminal justice process of a jurisdiction, and

tradition, which is rooted historically in continental Europe, is the 'older' and 'more widely distributed' of the two.[17] The common law was developed and exported primarily from England. It is reported that approximately 72% of the world's jurisdictions (140 out of 195 countries surveyed) are 'either completely or partially based on the civil-law tradition,' whereas only 39% (76 out of 195 countries) affiliate to the common law.[18] The remaining countries often are designated into categories such as 'socialist law' and 'sacred law.'[19] A sample of countries and their affiliation to these dominant traditions is reflected in Table 3.1. As a result, processual practices are commonly characterised as 'the gift of the west to the rest.'[20] According to Langer, the European roots of these practices 'has conferred a premier role to England and the United States [common law] and to France, Germany, and Italy [civil law]' as the primary founders, developers and exporters of these two dominant traditions.[21] Processual reform initiatives, under the 'westernisation', 'modernisation', 'development' and 'globalisation' banners,[22] end up replicating one or a combination of the civil law or common law tradition.[23] This processual dominance, as Baxi argues, 'reduces the diversity of the world's legal systems to a common Euro-American measure.'[24]

---

the rules governing it, will fall under one of two broad legal traditions, adversarialism or inquisitorialism').

17 John H. Merryman and Rogelio Pérez-Perdomo *The civil law tradition: An introduction to the legal systems of Europe and Latin America* 4th ed (Stanford: Stanford University Press, 2019) 1.

18 Sanja K. Ivković and Valerie P. Hans "A worldwide perspective on lay participation," in *Juries, lay judges and mixed courts: A global perspective*, eds. Sanja Ivković et al (New York: Cambridge University Press, 2021) 323 at 334.

19 See Harry R. Dammer and Jay S. Albanese *Comparative criminal justice systems* 5th ed (Wadsworth Cengage Learning, 2014) 11.

20 Upendra Baxi "The colonialist heritage," in *Comparative legal studies: Transitions and transitions*, eds. Pierre Legrand and Roderick Munday (Cambridge: Cambridge University Press, 2003) 46 at 49. Similarly, Twining describes orthodox comparative law as follows: 'It focuses almost exclusively on Western capitalist societies in Europe and the United States, with little or no detailed consideration of 'the East' (former and surviving socialist countries, including China), the 'South' (poorer countries) and richer countries of the Pacific Basin (Japan, Asian tigers)', at William Twining *Globalisation and legal theory* (New York: Cambridge University Press, 2000) 185.

21 Langer "The long shadow of the adversarial and inquisitorial categories" 887 at 906.

22 Baxi "The colonialist heritage," 49.

23 Langer "The long shadow of the adversarial and inquisitorial categories," 901–902.

24 Baxi "The colonialist heritage," 49.

Table 3.1 Common law and civil law countries

	SAMPLE OF JURISDICTIONS[25]
Traditional Roots	*Representative Countries*
Civil law tradition	Algeria, Argentina, Austria, Belgium, Benin, Bolivia, Brazil, Burkina Faso, Burundi, Central African Republic, Chad, Chile, Colombia, Congo, Costa Rica, Côte d'Ivoire, Denmark, Dominican Republic, Ecuador, Egypt, El Salvador, Finland, France, Gabon, Germany, Greece, Guatemala, Guinea-Bissau, Haiti, Honduras, Indonesia, Iran, Iraq, Italy, Japan, Jordan, Luxembourg, Madagascar, Mali, Mauritania, Mexico, Morocco, Netherlands, Nicaragua, Niger, Norway, Panama, Paraguay, Peru, Philippines, Portugal, Rwanda, Senegal, South Korea, Spain, Suriname, Sweden, Switzerland, Syria, Togo, Tunisia, Turkey, Uruguay, Venezuela
Common law	Australia, Bangladesh, Barbados, Botswana, Canada, Cyprus, Gambia, Ghana, Hong Kong, India, Ireland, Israel, Jamaica, Kenya, Lesotho, Liberia, Malawi, Malaysia, Malta, Mauritius, Nepal, New Zealand, Nigeria, Pakistan, Papua New Guinea, Sierra Leone, Singapore, South Africa, Sri Lanka, Swaziland, Tanzania, Thailand, Trinidad and Tobago, Uganda, United Kingdom, United States, Zambia, Zimbabwe
Socialist legal tradition	China, Cuba, North Korea, Vietnam

The colonial imposition, and the post-colonial continuation, of processual practices throughout the world, especially in the Global South, is a feature of coloniality. Coloniality describes the legal, political and economic endurance of colonial institutions beyond the historical period of formal colonialism.[26] According to Quijano, who originally coined the term,[27] coloniality is characterised by the reidentification and 'making' of Africa, Asia and Oceania in the image of America and Europe.[28] This form of 'neo-colonialism'[29] or 'indirect rule'[30] does not depend on the kind of militaristic and political force that characterised colonialism historically. It persists through legal,

25 Dammer and Albanese "Comparative criminal justice systems," 42; Paul G. Mahoney "The Common law and economic growth: Hayek might be right" (2001) 30(2) *Journal of Legal Studies* 503 at 524 (Appendix A).

26 Nelson Maldonado-Torres "On the coloniality of being," 240 at 243.

27 Sabelo J. Ndlovu-Gatsheni *Epistemic freedom in Africa: Deprovincialisation and decolonisation* (London: Routledge, 2018) 43 ('Anibal Quijano coined the concept of "coloniality"').

28 Anibal Quijano "Coloniality of power and Eurocentricism in Latin America" (2000) 1(3) *Nepantla: Views from South* 533 at 540. An abridged version was published in Anibal Quijano 'Coloniality of power and Eurocentricism in Latin America' (2000) 15(2) *International Sociology* 215. See also Walter D. Mignolo *The darker side of Renaissance: Literacy, territoriality and colonisation* 2nd ed (Ann Arbor: University of Michigan Press, 2003).

29 Kwame Nkrumah *Neo-colonialism: The last stage of imperialism* (1965, Panaf Books Ltd).

30 Ania Loomba *Colonialism/postcolonialism* 3rd ed (London: Routledge, 2015) 28–29.

economic and cultural institutions that were inherited from the Euro-American continuing to endure in the post-colonial context.[31] Ndlovu-Gatsheni associates post-modern phenomena such as genocides, historicides, epistemicides, and linguicides, especially in so far as they occur in the former colonies of Europe, with coloniality.[32] From a processual point of view, the overwhelming domination of two civilian and common law traditions of criminal process is a feature of an ongoing coloniality across the world. The processual systems of Euro-American regions, where less than 7% (approximately 530 million people) of the world's population lives, domineers over the rest of the world where about 7.5 billion people live.[33] For example, in Asia, where close to three-fifths of the world's population is based (approximately 4.8 billion people), most jurisdictions have civilian inquisitorial roots, but with contemporary common law influences. The processual practices of mainland China and Japan are two prominent examples in this mould. Both modelled their processual systems according to the German[34] and French[35] systems, respectively, but each later adopted several Anglo-American characteristics. These include the introduction of the beyond reasonable doubt standard[36] and a peremptory exclusionary rule in respect of illegally obtained evidence[37] in mainland China.[38] Japan

31 Ndlovu-Gatsheni "Epistemic freedom in Africa: Deprovincialisation and decolonisation," 3.
32 Ndlovu-Gatsheni "Epistemic freedom in Africa: Deprovincialisation and decolonisation," 3.
33 Evode Kayitana "The accusatorial and inquisitorial models of criminal procedure: A historical and comparative approach" (2019) 3(2) *African Journal of Law and Human Rights* 187 at 187; Callie R. Snyman "The accusatorial and inquisitorial approaches to criminal procedure: Some points of comparison between the South African and the continental systems" (1975) 8(1) *Comparative and International Law Journal of Southern Africa* 100; Joachim Herrmann "Various models of criminal proceedings" (1978) 2(1) *South African Journal of Criminal Law and Criminology* 3; Sandra F. Joireman "Inherited legal systems and effective rule of law: Africa and the colonial legacy" (2001) 39(4) *The Journal of Modern African Studies* 571; Louis T.C. Harms "Demystification of the inquisitorial system" (2011) 14(5) *Potchefstroom Electronic Law Journal* 1; Chukwunweike A. Ogbuabor "Inquisitorial and adversarial process in Nigeria's criminal justice system: The dilemma of a colonized state" (2015) 38(2) *University of Western Australia Law Review* 175.
34 Liling Yue "Chapter 2: The development of Chinese criminal procedure," in *Four criminal procedure case studies in comparative perspective: China–Italy–Russia–U.S.A.*, ed. Marco Fabri (Baden-Baden: Nomos, 2016) 23 at 23; May *Ancient legal thought: Equity, justice and humaneness from Hammurabi and the Pharaohs to Justinian and the Talmud* 249 ('I will argue that we can find in both Chinese and Greek legal systems precursors of the two most prominent forms of trial today, the Anglo-American jury and the Continental inquisitorial judge-based systems'). Cf. Dammer and Albanese "Comparative criminal justice systems," 53–57 (where China is classified as falling within an alternative 'Socialist' legal tradition).
35 Richard Terrill *World criminal justice systems: A comparative survey* 9th ed (New York: Routledge, 2016) 237.
36 Criminal Procedure Code of the People's Republic of China of 1996 (and revised in 2012 and 2018), article 55(3).
37 Criminal Procedure Code of the People's Republic of China of 1996 (and revised in 2012 and 2018), article 56.
38 Yue "Chapter 2: The development of Chinese criminal procedure," 37–38.

has also introduced open public trials;[39] a new criminal public defence system (*higisha kokusen bengo seido*) that includes defence rights to discovery (*shoko kaiji*), bail and the presence of counsel during an interrogation;[40] and a system of lay participation in criminal adjudication (*saiban-in seido*).[41] Furthermore, the criminal processes of Hong Kong,[42] Malaysia,[43] India[44] and Sri Lanka[45] are all modelled along British common law lines.

Processual domination is also prevalent in Africa, where approximately 19% (over 1.5 billion people) of the global population is situated, and South America, in which over 5% of the world's population can be found, as well. African processual practices are modelled in accordance either with civilian Napoleonic Codes, particularly the *Code d'instruction criminelle* of 1809,[46] or with Stephen's nineteenth-century model of evidence law.[47] According to

39 Terrill "World criminal justice systems: A comparative survey," 260.

40 David T. Johnson "Japan's lay judge system," in *Comparative criminal procedure*, eds. Jacqueline E. Ross and Stephen C. Thaman (Cheltenham: Elgar, 2016) 396 at 411.

41 Johnson "Japan's lay judge system," 396; Terrill "World criminal justice systems: A comparative survey," 248–249 ('The jury was introduced into the Japanese justice system in 1923 with the Jury Law . . . For a number of reasons, among them the fact that a court was not bound by a jury's decision, the jury gradually fell into disuse. The Jury Law . . . was suspended officially in 1943').

42 Yue "Chapter 2: The development of Chinese criminal procedure," 23.

43 Yik Koon "Introduction to the criminal justice system in Malaysia," in *Comparative criminal justice*, ed. Jospeter M. Mbuba (Lanham: Rowman & Littlefield, 2023) 107.

44 Roberson and Das "An introduction to comparative legal models of criminal justice," 232–233.

45 Roberson and Das "An introduction to comparative legal models of criminal justice," 239.

46 Anton Wekerle "Modern African criminal law and procedure codes" (1978) 35(4) *The Quarterly Journal of the Library of Congress* 282 at 282. There are five 'Napoleonic Codes' (*Les Cinq Codes*): the *Code Civile* (1804), the *Code de procédure civile* (1807), the *Code de commerce* (1803), the *Code d'instruction criminelle* (1809), and the *Code pénal* (1811), see Thomas Gergen "The reception of the Code Civil (Napoléonic Code) of 1804: An example of 'juridical migration'?" (2014) 1 *Journal of European History of Law* 26 at 27. The last two of these five codes were initially introduced into Senegal, through the decree of 6 March 1877, and later extended on a piecemeal basis by passing several further decrees (1892–1924) to other francophone jurisdictions in west and central Africa, see Jeswald W. Salacuse *An introduction to law in French-speaking Africa* vol I (1969) 22–23; Noah T. Fuashi "Statehood and the law-making process in Cameroon: From bifurcation to unification" (2012) 18(2) *Fundamina* 59 at 67; Anyopeuh S. Munzu 'Cameroon's search for a uniform legal system: The example of criminal justice' (1989) 1(1) *African Journal of International and Comparative Law* 46 at 50; Simon Tabetabe "A look at preliminary inquiry under the Cameroon criminal procedure code," in *Readings in the Cameroon criminal procedure code*, ed. Andrew E. Sone (2007) 49 at 50, n3.

47 Howard B. Miller "Beyond the law of evidence," 1 at 3; Andrew A.F. Massawe *The burden of proof: How to defend yourself in criminal cases* (2000) 116; Ronald J. Allen et al "Reforming the law of evidence of Tanzania (Part one): The social and legal challenges" (2013) 31(1) *Boston University International Law Journal* 217; Henry F. Morris *Evidence in East Africa* (Lagos: African Universities Press, 1968) 1–23; T. Akinola Aguda *The law of evidence in Nigeria* 3rd ed (London: Sweet & Maxwell, 1989) 3; Adangor "What is innovative in the evidence act, 2011?," 34; C. Eche Adah *The Nigerian law of evidence* (Lagos: Malthouse Press, 1997) 3. South Africa's evidence statutes are traced back to the common law-inspired Cape Evidence

Mahoney,[48] African jurisdictions are split roughly equally in their neo-colonial allegiance to the civil law[49] and common law[50] traditions. South American processual practices have generally followed the Spanish and Portuguese versions of the civilian tradition, since the promulgation of the *Las Siete Partidas* in 1265,[51] but this changed in the twentieth century when several adversarial elements from the common law tradition were introduced.[52] Some of these changes include open and oral public hearings, an institutional separation between the prosecutorial and judicial functions, the recognition of basic due process rights of accused persons, and the imposition of limitations against prosecutors' discretion to reduce the costs and time to institute legal proceedings.[53]

Processual coloniality generally produces two problematic consequences. Firstly, the processual systems of jurisdictions within the colonial paradigm are characterised by a systemic dualism that separates state law from a parallel regime of indigenous law.[54] This form of processual dualism is prevalent, for

Ordinance of 1830: Adrian Bellengère et al *The law of evidence in South Africa* (Cape Town: Oxford University Press, 2013) 5–6.

48 Mahoney "The common law and economic growth: Hayek might be right," 524 (Appendix A).

49 Algeria, Benin, Burkina Faso, Burundi, Central African Republic, Chad, Côte d'Ivoire, Egypt, Madagascar, Niger, Rwanda and Senegal are examples within this tradition.

50 Examples within this tradition include Ghana, Kenya, Malawi, Mauritius, Nigeria, South Africa, Tanzania, Uganda, Zambia and Zimbabwe.

51 Máximo Langer "Revolution in Latin American criminal procedure: Diffusion of legal ideas from the periphery" (2007) 55 *The American Journal of Comparative Law* 617 at 627; Alejandro Agüero "Latin American criminal law: A historical perspective," in *Göttingen handbook on Latin American public law and criminal justice*, eds. Kai Ambos and Jose Martinez (Baden-Baden: Nomos, 2023) 255 at 255.

52 Richard Vogler "Introduction," in *Criminal procedure in Europe*, eds. Richard Vogler and Barbara Huber (Berlin: Duncker & Humblot, 2008) 1 at 12: '[W]here 80% of all countries, including Nicaragua, Guatamala, and Chile have abandoned inquisitorial for more adversarial procedures in the last decade.' Langer "Revolution in Latin American Criminal Procedure: Diffusion of legal ideas from the periphery," 631: '[D]uring the last 15 years . . . 14 Latin American countries . . . and a number of Latin American province and state jurisdictions replaced their inquisitorial codes with accusatorial ones.'

53 Mauricio Duce J. and Claudio Fuentes M. "Trials and trial by jury in Latin America," in *Göttingen handbook on Latin American public law and criminal justice*, eds. Kai Ambos and Jose Martinez (Baden-Baden: Nomos, 2023) 517 at 518.

54 Eugene Cotran "The development and reform of the law in Kenya" (1983) 27(1) *Journal of African Law* 42 at 42–43; Mahmood Mamdani "Indirect rule, civil society and ethnicity: The African dilemma" (1996) 23(1) *Social Justice* 145; Stephen Humphreys "Laboratories of statehood: Legal intervention in colonial Africa and today" (2012) 75(4) *Modern Law Review* 475; Berihun A. Gebeye "Decoding legal pluralism in Africa" (2017) 49(2) *Journal of Legal Pluralism and Unofficial Law* 228; Anthony C. Diala "Legal pluralism and the future of personal family laws in Africa" (2021) 35(1) *International Journal of Law, Policy and the Family* 1; David Pimentel "Legal pluralism in post-colonial Africa: Linking statutory and customary adjudication in Mozambique" (2011) 14 *Yale Human Rights & Development Law Journal* 59; Francois du Bois and Danie Visser "The influence of foreign law in South Africa" (2003) 13 *Transnational Law & Contemporary Problems* 593.

example, in mainland China[55] and most African jurisdictions.[56] A concomitant feature of the coloniality of processual dualism is the inferiorisation of indigenous processual practices as being 'informal,' 'unofficial' and 'underdeveloped,' whereas the colonial-infused state-law regime is cloaked with the dominance of legal and political authority.[57] The second consequence of processual coloniality is the diffusion of processual practices from the Euro-American centre to the post-colonial periphery in the Global South.[58] For example, most of the common law jurisdictions that have modelled their systems of evidence law along the lines of Stephen's model[59] have inherited a largely antiquated doctrinal version[60] of the field that has now been eclipsed by developments within the New Evidence Scholarship movement.[61] Another example of an antiquated doctrinal inheritance is the Benthamist[62] substantive-adjectival law

55 Dammer and Albanese "Comparative criminal justice systems," 85.

56 Buluma Bwire "Integration of African customary legal concepts into modern law: Restorative justice – A Kenyan example" (2019) 9(1) *Societies* 17 at 19; James S. Read "Criminal law in the Africa of today and tomorrow" (1963) 7(1) *African Law Journal* 5 at 16; Jeanmarie Fenrich et al "Introduction," in *The future of African customary law*, ed. Jeanmarie Fenrich et al (New York: Cambridge University Press, 2011) 1 at 1.

57 Marius Pieterse "'It's a black thing': Upholding culture and customary law in a society founded on non-racialism" (2001) 17 *South African Journal of Human Rights* 364 at 372; Christa Rautenbach "Therapeutic jurisprudence in the customary courts of South Africa: Traditional authority courts as therapeutic agents" (2005) 21(2) *South African Journal of Human Rights* 323 at 328; Ivković and Hans "A worldwide perspective on lay participation," 332.

58 See Langer "Revolution in Latin American criminal procedure: Diffusion of legal ideas from the periphery," 620.

59 See Stephen *The Indian Evidence Act (I of 1872): With an introduction on the principles of judicial evidence*; Stephen *A digest on the law of evidence.*

60 Stephen understood the law of evidence as consisting of nothing else other than 'an enormous number of cases' and 'a comparatively small number of Acts of Parliament' (Stephen "A Digest on the Law of Evidence," x). According to Park, this is part of the 'golden age of doctrinal scholarship,' see Roger C. Park "Evidence scholarship, old and new" (1991) 75 *Minnesota Law Review* 849 at 854–855.

61 Tshepo Bogosi Mosaka "Here is a table: A prolegomenon to a future new evidence scholarship in Africa" (2022) 26(2) *International Journal of Evidence & Proof* 178 at 179. See also Wigmore "The problem of proof," 77 at 77–78; Christine Boyle "A principled approach to relevance: the Cheshire Cat in Canada," in *Innovations in evidence and proof: Integrating theory, research and teaching*, eds. Paul Roberts and Mike Redmayne (Oxford: Hart, 2007) 87 at 88: 'The most familiar part of the subject of Evidence is the extensive legal doctrine relating to rules of procedure.'; Peter W. Murphy "Some reflection on evidence and proof" (1999) 40 *Texas Law Review* 327 at 327; William Twining *Rethinking evidence: Exploratory essays* (Cambridge: Cambridge University Press, 2006) 227: '[T]he tendency to exaggerate the importance of the exclusionary rules remains valid.'; William Twining *Theories of evidence: Bentham and Wigmore* (London: Weidenfeld & Nicolson, 1985) 13: 'Since Thayer, the modern tendency has been to see the law of evidence largely as a collection of disparate constraints on freedom of proof and free evaluation of evidence.'

62 Jeremy Bentham *Rationale of judicial evidence* vol 1 (edited by J.S. Mill) (London: Hunt & Clark, 1827) 24–25; Thomas Starkie *A practical treatise of the law of evidence* 3rd ed (Philadelphia: T. & J.W. Johnson & Co., 1842) 1; Stephen "A Digest on the Law of Evidence," ix; Thayer *A preliminary treatise on evidence at common law,* 530; John H. Wigmore *Evidence in*

distinction that produces a trans-substantive and substance-blind procedural law. A trans-substantive procedural law is one that purports to apply generally to all substantive branches of law,[63] and it is substance-blind if it does not consider the variations on the meaning and implications of the varying substantive law crimes and causes of action.[64]

3.2 Global Systems of Criminal Adjudication

There are three catalytic historical events that have shaped the trajectory of the development systems of criminal adjudication around the globe. The first of these was the rise of the Catholic Church and its development of an inquisitorial system (*Inquisitionsprozess*) of fact-finding that was led by professional judges in the thirteenth century.[65] Following the collapse of the Roman empire in the fifth century,[66] the Church combined canon law doctrine (*Corpus iuris canonici*) with Roman law processual practices to establish a system of governance and fact-finding 'to regulate the rights and obligations of its members.'[67] The salient features of Roman-canonical process[68] were the development of a hierarchical judiciary, the use of university-educated lawyers, the elimination of ordeals, the introduction of

---

trials at common vol 1 (revised by Peter Tillers) (Boston: Little Brown and Co., 1983) ix and 41; Charles F. Chamberlayne *A treatise on the modern law of evidence* vol 3 (London: Sweet & Maxwell, 1911) 2230–2235.

63 Thomas O. Main "The procedural foundation of substantive law" (2003) 78 *Washington University Law Review* 801 at 822–823; Roberts "Five foundational fallacies of common law evidence", 93–108.

64 Cf. William Twining "Evidence as a multi-disciplinary subject," 91 at 99; William Twining "Evidence as a multi-disciplinary subject," 91 at 96 and 97; Anderson et al 78; Murphy "Some reflection on evidence and proof," 327; David Schum *Evidential Foundations of Probabilistic Reasoning* (Evanston, IL: Northwestern University Press, 1994); Richard D. Friedman '"E" is for eclectic: Multiple perspectives on evidence' (2001) 87 *Virginia Law Review* 2029.

65 Bart Wauters and Marco de Benito *The history of law in Europe: An introduction* (Cheltenham: Elgar, 2017) 73; Renée L. Lerner *The jury: A very short introduction* (New York: Oxford University Press, 2023) 16–17.

66 Arthur T. Von Mehren and James R. Gordley The Civil law system: An introduction to the comparative study of law 2nd ed (Boston: Little Brown & Company, 1977) 4 ('Much of what is today western Europe, including parts of England, had been romanized for some 400 years before the western Roman Empire was shattered by the German tribes and formally came to an end. In 476 Odovaker deposed Romulus Augustulus, the son of a leader among the Roman mercenaries and the last of the line of imperial rulers in the West. This act broke the western Empire's last tenuous bond of political unity').

67 Roberson & Das "An introduction to comparative legal models of criminal justice," 111; Lerner "The jury: A very short introduction," 16 ('The church had extensive needs for legal decision-making, both civil and criminal. It governed a vast personnel of priests, monks, and nuns who were exempt from criminal process in secular courts. It also held a large amount of land.').

68 A comprehensive discussion of this system will be discussed in Chapter 4, on the history of evidential proof, of this book.

written court records, the availability of appeals or reviews, and convention of written judgements.[69] Prior to the thirteenth century, fact-finding, in medieval Germania and elsewhere, was largely decentralised in the hands of lay 'local administrators, large landowners and even abbots and bishops,'[70] who dispensed justice in accordance with the *appeal of felony* procedure. A prosecution under the appeal of felony entailed criminal charges being initiated by private individuals and the parties being referred to a trial by battle or ordeal to resolve their dispute.[71] The Church's growth in wealth, size and influence enabled it to replace this system with the Roman-canon inquisitorial process. According to Langbein, Roman-canon procedure had spread throughout continental Europe[72] by the sixteenth century to become common to most jurisdictions in this region.[73] Through several centuries of evolution, contemporary systems of criminal process within the civil law tradition later modelled their processual practices on the Roman-canon system.

The second catalytic historical event is the promulgation of the Assize of Clarendon (the jury of accusation) by Henry II in 1166 to regulate English criminal process.[74] Henry II, who is credited with being 'the originator of the common law and juries,'[75] was only 21 years old when he assumed the English throne in a long line of Frankish rulers commencing with his great grandfather, William I of Normandy (1066–1087).[76] The *Assize*, meaning an

69 Wauters & de Benito "The history of law in Europe: An introduction," 73; John H. Langbein "Bifurcation and the bench: The influence of the jury on English conceptions of the judiciary," in *Judges and judging in the history of the common law and civil law: From antiquity to modern times*, eds. Paul Brand and Joshua Getzler (Cambridge: Cambridge University Press, 2012) 67 at 69.

70 Randall Lesaffer *European legal history: A cultural and political perspective* (translated by Jan Arriens) (Cambridge: Cambridge University Press, 2009) 134; Arthur T. Von Mehren and James R. Gordley *The civil law system: An introduction to the comparative study of law* 2nd ed (Boston: Little Brown & Company, 1977) 4 ('Western Europe became essentially a rural civilization').

71 John H. Langbein et al *History of the common law: The development of Anglo-American legal institutions* (New York: Aspen, 2009) 38; Harold J. Berman *Law and revolution: The formation of the western legal tradition* (Cambridge: Harvard University Press, 1983) 450 ('The primary motivation for bringing an appeal of felony was to avenge one's kindred or the feudal relation, or else to induce the other party to make a monetary settlement').

72 See, e.g., the *Constitutio Criminalis Carolina* of 1532 (Germany); the *ordonnance royale* of 1539 (France); and the *ordonnance criminelle* of 1570 (Spain).

73 John H. Langbein *Prosecuting crime in the Renaissance: England, Germany, France* (Cambridge: Harvard University Press, 1974) 129.

74 Langbein et al "History of the common law: The development of Anglo-American legal institutions," 37.

75 Lerner "The jury: A very short introduction," 11; Joshua C. Tate "Justice," in *A cultural history of law: In the middle ages*, ed. Emanuele Conte and Laurent Mayali vol 2 (London: Bloomsbury, 2019) 11 at 19 ('Henry II is known, for good reason, as the founder of the English common law').

76 Berman "Law and revolution: The formation of the western legal tradition," 438.

'ordinance, decree or statute,'[77] consisted of 14 provisions and was issued by Henry II at his hunting lodge in Clarendon in the South of England.[78] It was through this legislation that the 'jury of presentment' system was introduced to displace the privatised *appeal of felony* procedure.[79] Criminal prosecutions under the jury of presentment system were initiated by a group of no fewer than 12 lay jurors, who were entrusted with the responsibility of taking the preliminary decision of whether or not to refer the accused person to trial before the royal justices.[80] They did not hear any evidence, but decided the accused's committal to trial on the basis of their own personal knowledge as neighbours of the accused.[81] Juries of accusation, whose jurisdiction was limited to serious crimes (e.g. murder, theft and robbery),[82] then became the foundation for the establishment of the common law trial jury after the abolition of ordeals in 1215.[83] The presentment jury's pre-trial role of accusing the alleged offender later gave the common law system of criminal process its 'accusatorial' descriptor. Henry II's legal reforms, although not entirely unfamiliar to English communities before the twelfth century,[84] catalysed a break away from not only the ancient Germanic *appeal of felony* procedure, but also from the rest of continental Europe that adopted the Roman-canon inquisitorial procedure.

The third catalysing historical event is the multi-generational phenomenon of colonialism that facilitated the spread of the two domineering civil law and common law systems from Europe to the rest of the world. Formal colonialism spanned approximately four centuries, commencing with Spanish and Portuguese explorations in the Caribbean, the Americas, the Indies and

77 Langbein et al "History of the common law: The development of Anglo-American legal institutions," 37.
78 Langbein et al "History of the common law: The development of Anglo-American legal institutions," 37.
79 Langbein et al "History of the common law: The development of Anglo-American legal institutions," 4.
80 Berman "Law and revolution: The formation of the western legal tradition," 451.
81 Berman "Law and revolution: The formation of the western legal tradition," 449.
82 This list was later expanded in 1176 by the Assize of Northampton to include forgery, arson and 'almost all serious crimes,' see Langbein et al "History of the common law: The development of Anglo-American legal institutions," 40.
83 Berman "Law and revolution: The formation of the western legal tradition," 451; James Q. Whitman *The origins of reasonable doubt: Theological roots of the criminal trial* (New Haven: Yale University Press, 2008) 97.
84 For example, sworn lay groups were used during the ninth-century Carolingian empire to conduct inquests about fiscal matters, military preparedness and various other matters of the English crown, see Langbein et al "History of the common law: The development of Anglo American legal institutions," 43; Lerner "The jury: A very short introduction," 13 ('Henry and his advisors did not invent the idea of collecting groups of men and putting them on oath to give information. There were precedents, particularly in Germanic kingdoms, for using such groups. These were known as inquests . . . But was different, Henry's true innovation, was to make these inquests regular and uniform').

Africa.[85] By the beginning of the First World War, 'virtually the entire world,' with the exception of Japan, China, Siam, Liberia and Ethiopia, was under European colonial control.[86] Colonialism produced two kinds of systems of process and adjudication that are not exactly new and independent from the domineering civil law–common law paradigm: mixed and dualist systems. The constituent practices within these systems often are debased or slight modifications of one or both of the dominant civil law or common law systems. According to Palmer, mixed systems 'rule the lives of over 150 million people and occupy an area the size of a subcontinent'[87] in bi-jural countries such as South Africa, Canada, Puerto Rico, Cameroon, Scotland and the Philippines. Dualist systems, which were discussed earlier in this chapter, encompass two parallel, usually indigenous and state-level, systems within the same jurisdiction. The indigenous systems in most dualist jurisdictions pre-date the colonial era, whereas state-level processual mechanisms were introduced by historical colonial governments.

Therefore, we can distinguish between two distinct types of criminal process and adjudication around the globe: the adversarial procedure that is associated with the common law tradition and the inquisitorial process of the civil law tradition. Although they are not the only two types of systems across the world, they are two extremes along a very long continuum that encompasses a wide variety of systems.[88] The salient distinguishing features between adversarial and inquisitorial systems are presented in Table 3.2. Firstly, adversarial criminal process is a *contest* between two adversaries with each acting in their own interest, whereas the inquisitorial procedure is an *official* enquiry that

85 For example, the Portuguese colonialist Fernando Pó gave the west African country Cameroon its name, derived from the Portuguese word *camarões*, meaning shrimps, see Mathurin C. Tadonkeng "Land law and polygamy in the Bamiléké tribe in Cameroon," in *Property rights, land and territory in the European overseas empires*, ed. José V. Serrão (Lisbon: CEHC-IUL, 2014) 305 at 305.

86 Lesaffer "European legal history: A cultural and political perspective," 380.

87 Vernon V. Palmer "Introduction to the mixed jurisdictions," in *Mixed jurisdictions worldwide: The third legal family*, ed. Vernon V. Palmer 2nd ed (New York: Cambridge University Press, 2012) 3 at 3; Jacqueline S. Hodgson *The metamorphosis of criminal justice: A comparative account* (New York: Oxford University Press, 2020) 5 ('In discussing procedures here, I acknowledge that both the contemporary French system and that in England and Wales are more properly described as mixed systems, reflecting values and procedures that might be understood as belonging within both traditions. The roots and guiding ideas of these processes are, however, different and they are best understood as located within broadly adversarial or inquisitorial traditions').

88 Marco Fabri "Highlights of four case studies on criminal procedure," in *Four criminal procedure case studies in comparative perspective: China–Italy–Russia–U.S.A.*, ed. Marco Fabri (Baden-Baden: Nomos, 2016) 1 at 2; Hodgson "The metamorphosis of criminal justice: A comparative account," 5 ('The guiding ideas or principles of a procedural model can be identified, along with the related features (such as oral or written procedure) that they typically influence and shape, but modern legal systems are mixed').

Table 3.2 A comparison of adversarial and inquisitorial processes

ADVERSARIAL	*INQUISITORIAL*
Contest	Official inquiry
Party centred	State centred
Trial concentration	Pre-trial concentration
Evidence testing: cross-examination	Evidence testing: Judicial examination
Reactive state	Activist state

is undertaken by state officials on behalf of the disputing defendant and victim.[89] Secondly, the investigation and presentation of evidence before adversarial adjudicators is *party centred*, while inquisitorial process is dominated by *state officials*, particularly police officials and prosecutors.[90] Thirdly, adversarial procedure is focused primarily on the *trial stage* of the process where evidence is presented and tested before an impartial fact-finder.[91] The focal point of inquisitorial process is the pre-trial stage where most of the evidence is gathered, tested and recorded in preparation for a much shorter trial.[92] Fourthly, the principal mechanism of testing evidence in adversarial contexts is cross-examination by the parties, whereas the calling and questioning of witnesses in inquisitorial courts is primarily the responsibility of professional judges.[93] Fifthly, Damaška has used the 'reactive state' and 'activist state' political tropes to distinguish between adversarial and inquisitorial process more generally.[94] Adversarial criminal process usually is embedded within a reactive, 'laissez-faire administration' that has the liberal disposition to provide a basic framework of social interaction without intruding into the affairs of private

89 Mirjan R. Damaška *The faces of justice and state authority: A comparative approach to the legal process* (New Haven: Yale University Press, 1986) 3; Pamela-Jane Schwikkard 'Does cross-examination enhance accurate fact-finding?' (2019) 1 *South African Law Journal* 27; Richard Vogler *A world view of criminal justice* (New York: Routledge, 2005) Ch 7.

90 Schwikkard "Does cross-examination enhance accurate fact-finding?," 27; Hodgson "The metamorphosis of criminal justice: A comparative account," 7–8; Roberson & Das "An introduction to comparative legal models of criminal justice," 116.

91 Schwikkard "Does cross-examination enhance accurate fact-finding?," 27.

92 There is some variation in this regard among jurisdictions within the civilian tradition. For example, the German reforms of the nineteenth century moved that jurisdiction away from the medieval model of a secret pre-trial process towards the trial stage being the focal point in terms of the principle of immediacy, see John D. Jackson and Thomas Weigend "Witness evidence in pre-trial and trial procedure," in *Core concepts in criminal law and criminal justice*, eds. Kai Ambos et al (Cambridge: Cambridge University Press, 2022) 260 at 263–264 and 269–273.

93 Hodgson "The metamorphosis of criminal justice: A comparative account," 6–7; Schwikkard "Does cross-examination enhance accurate fact-finding?," 27.

94 Damaška "The faces of justice and state authority: A comparative approach to the legal process," 71.

individuals.[95] On the other hand, inquisitorial process exists typically within an activist and 'interventionist administration' that has the disposition to manage society.[96]

The remainder of the chapter will undertake a further comparative analysis of adversarial and inquisitorial criminal process with a focus on three specific questions that influence the structure and meaning of evidential proof: (1) Who is the fact-finder? (2) Which evidentiary or extant facts may be relied upon to draw inferential conclusions? (3) Against which standards or through which methods are these inferential conclusions to be evaluated?

3.3 Jurisdiction: Who Is the Fact-Finder?

The fulfilment of the processual condition of the evidential proof of hate crimes depends first and foremost on the competency and authority of the fact-finder within a particular jurisdiction. Criminal adjudication generally is controlled by a cadre of professional judges with or without the participation of lay fact-finders.[97] A survey of 195 countries has revealed that only about a third of countries in the world are without any form of lay participation in adjudicative fact-finding.[98] The majority of these jurisdictions are situated in South America where more than two-thirds of countries are without any lay participation, as well as in Asia where the number is close to 60% of countries being without lay participation.[99] The overwhelming majority of countries in the world – approximately 64% – have some form of lay participation in their fact-finding mechanisms.[100] The majority of jurisdictions with some form of lay participation are located in Australia and Oceania (93%), North America (78%), Europe (70%) and Africa (72%).[101] A statistical comparison of the levels lay participation across varying continents in the world is presented in Table 3.3.[102]

In the context of the two dominant traditions discussed earlier, lay participation is more prevalent in common law jurisdictions (73%) than it is in civilian jurisdictions (60%).[103]

From among the majority of countries (64%) that deploy lay fact-finders, there generally are four common types of lay participation: juries, lay

95 Damaška "The faces of justice and state authority: A comparative approach to the legal process," 71.
96 Damaška "The faces of justice and state authority: A comparative approach to the legal process," 71.
97 See Sanja Ivković et al "Introduction," in *Juries, lay judges and mixed courts: A global perspective*, eds. Sanja Ivković et al (New York: Cambridge University Press, 2021) 1 at 3.
98 Ivković and Hans "A worldwide perspective on lay participation," 334.
99 Ivković and Hans "A worldwide perspective on lay participation," 334.
100 Ivković and Hans "A worldwide perspective on lay participation," 334.
101 Ivković and Hans "A worldwide perspective on lay participation," 334.
102 Ivković and Hans "A worldwide perspective on lay participation," 334.
103 Ivković and Hans "A worldwide perspective on lay participation," 334.

Table 3.3 A comparison of lay participation by continent

LAY PARTICIPATION BY CONTINENT					
Continent	*No Lay Participation*		*Lay Participation*		*Total (Countries Surveyed)*
	Countries (N)	*%*	*Countries (N)*	*%*	
Africa	15	27.8	39	72.2	54
Asia	27	58.7	19	41.3	46
Australia & Oceania	1	7.1	13	92.9	14
Europe	14	30.4	32	69.6	46
North America	5	21.7	18	78.3	23
South America	8	66.7	4	33.3	12
Total	70	35.9	125	64.1	195

Table 3.4 Four types of lay participation

FORMS OF LAY PARTICIPATION (LP)					
	Countries With Any Form of Lay Participation	*Juries*	*Mixed Tribunals*	*Lay Magistrates (JP)*	*Lay (Popular) Courts*
Number of countries with LP	125	56	71	13	20
Percentage of all countries (i.e. 195)	64.1%	28.7%	36.4%	6.7%	10.3%
Percentage of countries (i.e. 125) with any form of LP	100%	44.8%	56.8%	10.4%	16%

magistrates, lay (indigenous) courts and mixed tribunals.[104] The most common form of lay participation are mixed tribunals (57%), followed by trial juries (45%), which combine professional judges with lay juries or assessors, as indicated in Table 3.4.[105]

More than half (37 out of 71) of the countries that deploy mixed benches are aligned to the civil law tradition.[106] Most of these countries are located in Europe (35%) and Africa (32%), as reflected in Table 3.5. For example, Germany's *Schöffen*, France's *juré d'assises*, Croatia's *suci porotnici*, and the Dutch

104 Valerie P. Hans et al "Global juries: A plan for research," in *The psychology of juries*, ed. Margaret B. Kovera (Washington: American Psychological Association, 2017) 131 at 132.

105 Ivković and Hans "A worldwide perspective on lay participation," 338–339.

106 Ivković and Hans "A worldwide perspective on lay participation," 340.

Table 3.5 A comparison of mixed tribunals by continent

CONTINENTAL FORMS OF LAY PARTICIPATION			
Continent	*Mixed Tribunals*		
	Number of Countries (N)	*% (Out of Total Countries on the Continent)*	*% (Countries With Mixed Tribunals)*
Africa	23	42.6	32.4
Asia	12	26.1	16.9
Australia & Oceania	7	50.0	9.9
Europe	25	54.3	35.2
North America	2	8.7	2.8
South America	2	16.7	2.8
Total	71	36.4	100

Table 3.6 A comparison of continental jury participation

CONTINENTAL FORMS OF LAY PARTICIPATION			
Continent	*Juries*		
	Number of countries (N)	*% (Out of Total Countries on the Continent)*	*% (Countries With Juries)*
Africa	16	29.6	28.6
Asia	6	13.0	10.7
Australia & Oceania	5	35.7	8.9
Europe	10	21.7	17.9
North America	16	69.6	28.6
South America	3	25.0	5.3
Total	56	28.7	100

gezworene all sit alongside professional judges in criminal courts.[107] Moreover, Finland, Sweden, Hungary, Poland, China and Czechoslovakia are further examples of civilian jurisdictions with mixed benches. Mixed benches in common law jurisdictions are rare: South Africa and Japan are two notable examples.[108]

A majority of countries (59%) that use juries for fact-finding are associated with the common law tradition. The United States, the United Kingdom, Australia, Canada, Ireland, New Zealand, Scotland, Ghana and Malawi are a few notable examples.[109] Most common law jurisdictions that deploy juries are located, as Table 3.6 shows, in North America (29%) and Africa (29%).[110]

107 Hans et al "Global juries: A plan for research," 135.

108 Hans et al "Global juries: A plan for research," 135.

109 Hans et al "Global juries: A plan for research," 133; John D. Jackson "Making juries accountable" (2002) 50 *The American Journal of Comparative Law* 477; Neil Vidmar *World Jury Systems* (Oxford: Oxford University Press, 2000) 425.

110 Ivković and Hans "A worldwide perspective on lay participation," 339.

However, juries can be found in several civilian jurisdictions as well, such as Austria, Belgium, Norway, Denmark, Greece, Spain, Russia, South Korea, Georgia and some Argentinian provinces.[111] There is also some variation in the type of juries that each of these countries deploy; for example, grand juries in the United States, trial juries both in the United Kingdom and the United States, and advisory juries in South Korea.

Given the seriousness of hate crimes, as discussed in Chapter 2, and the limited criminal jurisdiction of lay magistrates and popular (indigenous) lay courts to petty offences,[112] these courts will not be discussed in any great detail in this chapter. Lay magistrates, which are also known as 'justices of the peace,' are more prevalent in jurisdictions within the common law tradition (77%)[113] than they are among civilian jurisdictions (23%), whereas popular lay courts are inversely common to civilian jurisdictions (70%) and not to common law jurisdictions (25%).[114] Lay magistrates (32%) and popular indigenous courts (60%) are overwhelmingly prevalent in Africa than anywhere else in the world.[115] South American and Asian countries, by contrast, are regions where lay magistrates and popular courts are least prevalent. According to Ivković and Hans, popular courts and lay magistrates are not used at all (0%) in South America.[116] Lay magistrates are also not common to Asian jurisdictions, although there is some evidence of lay indigenous courts (e.g. the People's Mediation Committees of mainland China)[117] being deployed in some parts of the continent (15%).[118]

Proof judgements in the common law tradition are made within the context of a bifurcated court that upholds a functional distinction between the roles of the lay jury and the professional judge.[119] The finding of facts, which includes the evaluation of evidence and the making of probative judgements, is reserved for lay jurors, whereas the determination of questions of law and the imposition of punishment is the responsibility of judges in common law courts.[120] Civilian criminal courts, on the other hand, generally have a more

111 Hans et al "Global juries: A plan for research," 133.

112 Hans et al "Global juries: A plan for research," 133–134.

113 For example, the United Kingdom's 28,000 justices of the peace outnumber the amount of district judges in that jurisdiction. Moreover, justices of the peace process over 95% of criminal cases in the United Kingdom; see Hans et al "Global juries: A plan for research," 133.

114 Ivković and Hans "A worldwide perspective on lay participation," 340.

115 Ivković and Hans "A worldwide perspective on lay participation," 339. It is estimated that approximately 90% of the African population uses popular indigenous lay courts; see the sources cited at note 56 above.

116 Ivković and Hans "A worldwide perspective on lay participation," 339.

117 Hans et al "Global juries: A plan for research," 135.

118 Ivković and Hans "A worldwide perspective on lay participation," 339.

119 Mirjan R. Damaška *Evidence law adrift* (New Haven: Yale University Press, 1997) 26; Pieter J. Maartens and Pamela-Jane Schwikkard "A juryless jurisdiction and the epistemic rules of evidence" (2011) 128(3) *South African Law Journal* 513 at 520.

120 Hans et al "Global juries: A plan for research," 132; James B. Thayer '"Law" and "Fact" in jury trials' (1890) 4(4) *Harvard Law Review* 147 at 147 ('matters of law are for the court,

unitary structure that imposes no functional distinction between lay and professional judges.[121] Civilian lay and professional fact-finders each have a single vote to decide questions of both law and fact in the merits as well as sentencing phases of trials.[122] Unlike the common law judge, the civilian judge bears no responsibility to protect the lay assessors sitting with her against external influence and against the use of improper modes and patterns of proof.[123] It is the responsibility of all members of the civilian court, lay and professional, in equal measure to search for the truth.[124]

Secondly, the disposition of a civilian fact-finder is one of an activist investigator that is responsible for gathering, testing and evaluating evidence without being bound to the specific submissions made and evidence tendered by the parties.[125] On the other hand, common law judges, whose disposition and responsibility is described typically as one of an 'umpire,' 'referee' or 'arbiter,'[126] have no such liberty. Without suggesting that common law judges are or should be entirely 'passive,'[127] their decisions generally are dependent on and confined to the evidence and submissions tendered by the parties before

---

and matters of fact for the jury' – *ad quaestionem facti non respondent judices, ad quaestionem juris non respondent juratores*); Thayer "Preliminary treatise on Evidence," 183–262; Wigmore "Evidence in trials at common," 3, n2. Processual practices in some American states and South Korea are exceptions in this regard. In particular, only lay juries can sentence defendants to the death penalty in the American states that permit this form of punishment, while South Korean advisory juries decide both the merits and punishment, see Hans et al "Global juries: A plan for research," 131–132.

121 Damaška "Evidence law adrift," 50. Cf. John D. Jackson and Nikolay P. Kovalev 'Lay adjudication and human rights in Europe' (2006) 13 *Columbia Journal of European Law* 83.

122 Roberson and Das "An introduction to comparative legal models of criminal justice," 126.

123 Denis Salas "The role of the judge," in *European criminal procedures*, ed. Mireille Delmas-Marty and John R. Spencer (revised by Alejandro Alvarez) (Cambridge: Cambridge University Press, 2002) 488 at 501.

124 Kayitana "The accusatorial and inquisitorial models of criminal procedure: A historical and comparative approach," 189.

125 Salas "The role of the judge," 509; Michael Bohlander *Principles of German criminal procedure* (Oxford: Hart, 2021) 145–146 ('German law operates on an independent duty of the court to establish the truth (§ 244(2)) and not on the partisan presentation of the evidence by the parties; it is thus not really helpful to speak of the . . . "prosecution proving its case" or of the prosecution having a "burden of proof" in a German trial context. Once the case is admitted to trial and the hearings have begun, control is taken out of the hands of the prosecution and given to the court. In theory the court may initiate its own investigations as it deems fit, beyond what the prosecution and/or the defence may have presented in the dossier, any pre-trial motions or at trial').

126 Kayitana "The accusatorial and inquisitorial models of criminal procedure: A historical and comparative approach," 188–189. Cf. John D. Jackson and Sarah J. Summers *The internationalization of criminal evidence: Beyond the common law and civil law traditions* (New York: Cambridge University Press, 2012) 130.

127 Kayitana "The accusatorial and inquisitorial models of criminal procedure: A historical and comparative approach," 188; Damaška "The faces of justice and state authority: A comparative approach to the legal process," 3; Hodgson "The metamorphosis of criminal justice: A comparative account," 6–8.

them. According to Reichel, the civilian trial is 'more like a continuing investigation' and the court is 'another investigator with the added power of being able to decide the case.'[128] Civilian judges, in this capacity, are permitted, and indeed required, *mero motu* to call and examine their own witnesses (*Ermttlungsgrundsatz* or *Inquisitionsmaxime*) independent of any evidence tendered by the parties.[129] These differing judicial roles are also indicated by the effect of guilty pleas and plea bargains in the two respective traditions. Plea bargains are dispositive of a case in common law jurisdictions precisely because trials within this tradition are 'contests' between the parties and nobody else.[130] Therefore, the ending of the contest naturally terminates the proceedings. However, guilty pleas in civilian criminal process are not immediately dispositive of the case. They are no more than an additional piece of evidence to be considered by the fact-finders in the overall determination of the case.[131] This is a function of the degree of judicial control and activism that characterises the civilian judge's role, as compared to his common law counterpart.

Thirdly, common law fact-finders rely simply on their 'common sense' to adjudicate cases,[132] whereas civilians typically deploy doctrinal legal reasoning to interpret the relevant provision of the criminal code to fit the facts of the case.[133] For the civilian fact-finder, probative judgements, and generally all the answers to the questions that arise from the facts of the case, are guided by the legal solutions fashioned by the legislature in the applicable criminal code. According to Merryman and Pérez-Perdomo, civilian judges are 'operators of a machine designed and built by legislators.'[134] Therefore, although they write reasoned judgements in each case, their opinions do not create precedent in the same way that they would in the common law context.[135] It is

128 Philip L. Reichel, *Comparative criminal justice systems: A topical approach* 7th ed (New York: Pearson, 2018) 128.

129 Salas "The role of the judge," 509.

130 Kayitana "The accusatorial and inquisitorial models of criminal procedure: A historical and comparative approach," 188–189; Reichel "Comparative criminal justice systems: A topical approach," 125. See generally, Máximo Langer et al, eds. *Research handbook on plea bargaining and criminal justice* (Cheltenham: Elgar, 2024).

131 Reichel "Comparative criminal justice systems: A topical approach," 125: 'There is no civil law equivalent to the American model of plea bargaining.'

132 Paul Roberts *Roberts & Zuckerman's criminal evidence* 3rd ed (Oxford: Oxford University Press, 2022) 154–160; William Twining "Narrative and generationalisations in argumentation about questions of fact" (1999) 40 *Texas Law Review* 351; Ronald J. Allen "Common sense, rationality and the legal process," in *The dynamics of judicial proof: Computation, logic and common sense*, eds. Marilyn MacCrimmon and Peter Tillers (New York: Springer, 2002) 43; L. Jonathan Cohen "The role of evidential weight in criminal proof" (1986) 66(4) *Boston University Law Review* 635.

133 Merryman and Pérez-Perdomo "The civil law tradition: An introduction to the legal systems of Europe and Latin America," 36.

134 Merryman and Pérez-Perdomo "The civil law tradition: An introduction to the legal systems of Europe and Latin America," 36.

135 Salas "The role of the judge," 510.

thus no wonder that civilian judges do not garner as much popular acclaim and/or notoriety, as their common law counterparts do.[136] Common law lay fact-finders do not write reasoned judgements, although professional judges produce binding precedents on questions of law.[137]

3.4 Admissibility: Which Evidentiary Facts Are Admissible?

No system of adjudication permits untrammelled access to every item of evidence presented before it. Adjudicators typically aim to uphold multiple goals, including the search for the truth; avoiding unfairness or prejudice to any of the parties; avoiding excessive delays; upholding standards of integrity over the process as a whole; and avoiding the raising or pursuit of confusing, irrelevant or unnecessary points of dispute,[138] and one or more of these may require the exclusion of a particular item of evidence in a given case. Therefore, exclusionary processual practices, although they may differ in form and effect, occur in most jurisdictions across the world.[139] Nonetheless, there is a potential terminological pitfall that should be avoided here. Institutionalised concepts such as 'admissibility' and the demarcation between 'admissibility and weight' are as uncommon to most civilian jurisdictions as is a specialised field called 'the law of evidence.' The civilian criminal court is a unitary court that investigates, receives and evaluates evidence in a single continuous process,[140] and gives judgement on any excluded evidence, together with the reasons thereof, at the end of the case when the merits are decided. As a result, exclusionary doctrines of 'admissibility, relevancy and materiality,' as Nijboer clarifies,[141] 'are in a

136 Merryman and Pérez-Perdomo "The civil law tradition: An introduction to the legal systems of Europe and Latin America," 37: 'In the past, the great names of the civil law were not those of judges (who knows the name of a civil law judge?) but those of legislators . . . (Justinian, Napoleon, Andrés Bello) and scholars (Gaius, Irnerius, Bartolus, Mancini, Domat, Pothier, Savigny, and a host of other nineteenth- and twentieth-century European and Latin American scholars). Civil law judges are not culture heroes or parental figures, as they often are with us.'

137 John D. Jackson "The case for a hybrid jury in Europe," in *Juries, lay judges and mixed courts: A global perspective*, eds. Sanja Ivković et al (New York: Cambridge University Press, 2021) 304 at 308–309.

138 Richard Posner *The problems of jurisprudence* (Cambridge: Harvard University Press, 1990) 206; Jackson "Managing uncertainty and finality: The function of the criminal trial in legal inquiry" 121 at 124 and 128; Roberts "Roberts & Zuckerman's criminal evidence," 19–20; Terence Anderson et al *Analysis of evidence* 2nd ed (Cambridge: Cambridge University Press, 2005) 78–79.

139 Jenia I. Turner and Thomas Weigend "The purposes and functions of exclusionary rules," in *Do exclusionary rules ensure a fair trial?*, eds. Sabine Gless and Thomas Richter (Cham: Springer, 2019) 255 at 256; Damaška "Evidence law adrift," 12.

140 Cf. A distinction often is drawn between the preliminary, examination and trial phases, see Merryman and Pérez-Perdomo "The civil law tradition: An introduction to the legal systems of Europe and Latin America," 132–133. I am referring here especially to the trial phase.

141 Johannes F. Nijboer "Common law tradition in evidence scholarship observed from a continental perspective" (1993) 41(2) *The American Journal of Comparative law* 399 at 302.

certain way meaningless,' if they are understood as operating to bar the reception of a particular item of evidence during the proceedings. Instead, processual practices that regulate the exclusion of evidence in civilian jurisdictions generally are studied as part of procedural law.[142] Thayer famously remarked, by contrast, that 'the English law of evidence . . . is the child of the jury.'[143]

Evidence may be excluded in both civilian and common law jurisdictions for a number of reasons. In general, evidence may be excluded if it is rendered unreliable by the means through which it was obtained.[144] The torture or deceit of a witness is an archetypical example in this regard. Secondly, evidence may be excluded if admitting it would impugn the integrity of the court or the administration of justice.[145] An example of this would be evidence that is obtained by state actors breaching the law by, for example, failing to obtain a warrant. The rendering of a decision based on this type of evidence may taint the criminal process as a whole. Thirdly, the upholding of human rights may also be a basis for excluding evidence.[146] For example, a court may exclude evidence because the manner in which it was gathered contravenes the constitutional rights to privacy or freedom of expression of an individual or group. None of these rationales of exclusion is peculiar to one particular jurisdiction or legal tradition. Probative judgements that are not grounded upon admitted or extant evidence are 'matters of speculation' or 'conjecture.'[147]

Wigmore distinguishes between three types of common law exclusionary rules: relevance rules, rules of auxiliary policy and rules of extrinsic policy.[148] This kind of institutional taxonomy simply does not exist in civilian

142 Carlson Anyangwe *The magistracy and the bar in Cameroon* (CEPER: Yaoundé, 1989) 144, also 125–135 and 197–210; Nijboer "Common law tradition in evidence scholarship observed from a continental perspective," 316.

143 Thayer "Preliminary treatise on evidence," 47 and 266; Roger C. Park "An outsider's view of common law evidence" (1998) 96(6) *Michigan Law Review* 1468 at 1468 ('Others have thought of evidence law mainly as the child of the adversary system'); Maartens and Schwikkard "A juriless jurisdiction and the epistemic rules of evidence," 513–514; Zhuhao Wang "The fate of evidence law: Two paths of development" (2020) 24(3) *International Journal of Evidence & Proof* 329 at 329.

144 Turner and Weigend "The purposes and functions of exclusionary rules," 257.

145 Turner and Weigend "The purposes and functions of exclusionary rules," 258.

146 Turner and Weigend "The purposes and functions of exclusionary rules," 261.

147 *Caswell v Powell Duffryn Associated Collieries Ltd* [1939] 3 All ER 722 (HL) 733E–F; *Knoop NO v Gupta (Tayob Intervening)* 2021 (3) SA 88 (SCA) [19]; *Imperial Marine Company v The Motor Vessel Pasquale Della Gatta; Imperial Marine Company v The Motor Vessel Filippo Lembo* 2012 (1) SA 58 (SCA) [24]; *Gavrić v Refugee Status Determination Officer, Cape Town* 2019 (1) SA 21 (CC) [115].

148 Wigmore "Evidence in trials at common," 688; Damaška "Evidence law adrift," 47: 'An important source of the common law's penchant for exclusionary rules . . . is the environment of the divided court that facilitates their effective enforcement.'; Stephen C. Thaman 'Europe's new jury systems: The cases of Spain and Russia' (1999) 62(2) *Law and Contemporary Problems* 233 at 233: 'The classic separation of powers within the adversarial criminal process between a neutral judge, responsible for deciding questions of law and punishment,

processual doctrine. However, a closer look at civilian processual practices, particularly at the incidents and reasons for exclusion, suggests that a comparison in substance may be possible. Firstly, the exclusion of evidence on the ground that it lacks a sufficient degree of probative value is not something that civilian adjudicators are prepared to countenance.[149] Common law judges, by contrast, enforce an entrenched system of 'relevance rules'; for example, on opinion, character and similar-fact evidence, to exclude evidence that is irrelevant or lacking in a sufficient degree of probative value.[150] The belief of common law judges is that the *per se* exclusion of irrelevant evidence enhances the truth-seeking function of fact-finding. The practice in civilian jurisdictions generally would be not to bar the admission of such evidence before the end of the case, but to rather account for any probative deficiencies that the evidence may have in the weight given to it.[151] Secondly, common law jurisdictions adhere to a set of 'rules of auxiliary policy' as a basis for excluding evidence that is riddled with a degree of unreliability that outweighs its probative value.[152] A classic example of this is hearsay evidence. As Damaška says, the absence of rules that bar the reception of such evidence during the proceedings does not mean that civilian fact-finders are oblivious to the dangers associated with it, but its presentation rather communicates the following message to civilian adjudicators:

> Use original sources of information whenever they are reasonably available. When you feel you must rely on a derivative source, explain in a

---

and a panel of lay persons responsible for questions of fact and guilt, also gave rise to common law rules of evidence.'

149 Damaška "Evidence law adrift," 14–15; Jackson and Summers "The internationalization of criminal evidence: Beyond the common law and civil law traditions," 71 ('Intrinsic exclusionary rules, which exist primarily to enhance the accuracy of fact-finding, are not however commonly found in continental legal systems. Rules such as those found in most common law systems regulating the use of character or propensity evidence are extremely rare').

150 Wigmore "Evidence in trials at common," 688; Hock-Lai Ho *A philosophy of evidence law* (Oxford: Oxford University Press, 2008) 35: 'The law excludes evidence which it sees as only inviting illegitimate forms of reasoning and regulates deliberation by forbidding the fact-finder from engaging in those lines of objectionable reasoning.' See also Tshepo B. Mosaka "*Mpho le mphonyana*: Two iterations of admissibility in Africa" (2023) 67 *Journal of African Law* 391.

151 Damaška "Evidence law adrift," 17; Jackson and Summers "The internationalization of criminal evidence: Beyond the common law and civil law traditions," 71 ('The lack of such rules can be attributed in part to the 'unitary' character of the decision-making body in continental European jurisdictions, as opposed to the (mainly, but not solely) bifurcated structure of the courts in most common law systems. This makes it difficult to conceive of a role for concepts such as admissibility').

152 Wigmore "Evidence in trials at common," 689; Thayer "Preliminary treatise on evidence," 265.

written opinion the reasons that impelled you to give credence to information that is usually of inferior value.[153]

The closest analogue to common law exclusionary rules in the civilian context are doctrines of exclusion based on any prejudice that a reception of an item of evidence may bring upon one or more of the parties. This category of 'rules of extrinsic policy' excludes evidence that overrides or subverts the truth-seeking function of adjudication by prejudicing one or more of the parties.[154] Evidence obtained in breach of the legal privilege accorded to one of the parties is one such example that is familiar to both common law and civilian jurisdictions.[155] In any case, the civilian analogue of 'rules of extrinsic policy,' according to Damaška, is applied not as strict or peremptory bars against admission, but rather as a 'rule of thumb' to be dealt with at the end of the case in the evaluation of the evidence as a whole.[156]

3.5 Probative Criteria: Against Which Logical and Legal Criteria Are the Inferences to Be Evaluated?

Evidence that has been presented and accepted in accordance with the processual practices and rules of the appropriate lay or professional tribunal then has to be evaluated to determine whether the relevant disputed facts have been proven. The evaluation of evidence to prove a hate crime entails determining its probative effect on each one of the elements of the crime,[157] which are generalised in Chapter 2 to be the manifest isolation or discriminatory targeting of an individual or group (base offence), a prejudicial motivation and intention. According to orthodox processual doctrine, criminal cases in the common law context must be proven *beyond a reasonable doubt* (BARD),[158] whereas civilian fact-finders generally decide in accordance with their *intime conviction* (inner conviction).[159] Before the implementation of the common law BARD standard, Anglo-Saxon medieval fact-finders only convicted if they were 'certain.'[160] The civilian *intime conviction*, which some European jurisdictions have reframed to mean *conviction raisonnée* (reasoned conviction),[161]

153 Damaška "Evidence law adrift," 16.
154 Wigmore "Evidence in trials at common," 689.
155 Damaška "Evidence law adrift," 12–13.
156 Mirjan R. Damaška "Evidentiary barriers to conviction and two models of criminal procedure: A comparative study" (1973) 121(3) *University of Pennsylvania Law Review* 507 at 518.
157 Sarah Moss *Probabilistic knowledge* (Oxford: Oxford University Press, 2018) 203.
158 Wigmore "Evidence in trials at common," 363 ('All authorities agree that the burden is upon the State to make out its accusation . . . beyond all reasonable doubt'); Stephen "A Digest on the Law of Evidence," article 93.
159 Vuille "Forensic science evidence in non-adversary criminal justice systems," 354 at 365.
160 Larry Laudan "Is reasonable doubt reasonable?" (2003) 9 *Legal Theory* 295 at 297–298.
161 Damaška *Evaluation of evidence: Premodern and modern approaches*, 12; Damaška "Evidence law adrift," 20–24.

criterion originates from the work of Cesare Beccaria in the eighteenth century.[162] There are many differences between these two evaluation metrics, but foremost among these is that the one is an actual standard, while the other is not. The common law BARD standard sets a precise floor below which the probative value of the prosecution's evidence may not transcend for a successful conviction. However, no such probative minimum is prescribed in civilian jurisdictions.

Civilian jurisdictions generally adhere to a principle of 'freedom of evaluation of evidence,' or 'free proof' for short, that precludes them from affixing any precise rules or standards (*preuve légale, prueba legal/tasada, gesetzlicher Beweis*) in the evaluation of proof.[163] Therefore, it would be a mistake to use the language of evaluation 'rules' or 'standards' when theorising about the proof of hate crimes in most civilian jurisdictions. According to Taruffo, the effect of the free proof principle is a negative one, rather than a positive one: '[T]hese principles exclude the application of legal standards of proof but do not prescribe by themselves any positive standard of proof.'[164] Tuzet distinguishes between an 'assessment criteria' and a 'proof standard,' and places the civilian free proof principles in the former category.[165] Damaška similarly used the 'internal' and 'external' tropes to differentiate civil law and common law evaluation criteria.[166] The making and evaluation of probative judgements in the civilian context generally is left to the discretion of the fact-finder. This general position is representative of most civilian jurisdictions, but exceptions such as Germany,[167] Italy,[168]

162 See Cesare Beccaria *An essay on crimes and punishments* (Albany: WC Little & Co, 1872) (published originally in 1764).

163 Michele Taruffo "Rethinking the standards of proof" (2003) 51(3) *American Journal of Comparative Law* 659 at 666; Giovanni Tuzet "Evidence assessment and standards of proof: A messy issue" (2021) 2 *Quaestio facti: International Journal on Evidential Legal Reasoning* 87 at 95 ('Civil law countries usually have in their respective codes some basic rules about evidence and proof. Most of the time these rules set evidence assessment criteria instead of standards of proof. And nowadays these criteria are rather relaxed, leaving room to judicial discretion').

164 Taruffo "Rethinking the standards of proof," 666.

165 Tuzet "Evidence assessment and standards of proof: A messy issue," 89. See also Kai Ambos "Intime conviction in Germany: Conceptual foundations, historical development and current meaning" (2023) 4 *Quaestio facti: International Journal on Evidential Legal Reasoning* 167 at 168 (distinguishing between a 'standard' and a 'flexible method to assess available evidence').

166 Mirjan R. Damaška "Free proof and its detractors" (1995) 43(3) *The American Journal of Comparative Law* 343 at 347.

167 Taruffo "Rethinking the standards of proof," 669; Ambos "Intime conviction in Germany: Conceptual foundations, historical development and current meaning," 167.

168 See *Codice di procedura penale* (1988), article 533 (*oltre ogni ragionevole dubbio*).

Argentina[169] and China[170] represent a convergence in some respects between the common law and civilian traditions. However, the freedom afforded to civilian fact-finders, as Bohlander points out, does not mean 'a judicial-free-for-all'[171] that permits, for example, adjudication by the roll of a pair of dice. Fact-finders in civil law jurisdictions are nevertheless required to apply rational standards of logic and to ground their findings on comprehensible reasons.[172]

While a fixed standard of proof is prescribed among common law jurisdiction, and no such standard exists in civil law, this distinguishing feature should not be exaggerated because differing degrees of rule scepticism persist in both traditions. From the common law perspective, having a prescribed standard of proof has not been without problems. For example, the BARD standard has been held to be susceptible to confusion among jurors in England and Wales.[173] According to Spencer, the BARD standard is 'incapable of being precisely explained,' and English fact-finders have been discouraged by appellate judges from elaborating or explaining its meaning to jurors.[174] As a result, English jurors are currently instructed to convict only if they are 'sure' of the defendant's guilt.[175]

3.6 Conclusion

The term 'proof' designates a certain quality that a particular fact (e.g. an event, occurrence or state of affairs) bears after a set of conditions have been met. In the forensic context, these conditions are prescribed by law and extra-legal sources such as logic and epistemology. This chapter has explicated one of those conditions pertaining to the procedural and institutional practices of

169 Langer "Revolution in Latin American Criminal Procedure: Diffusion of legal ideas from the periphery," 630–631.

170 Yue "Chapter 2: The development of Chinese criminal procedure," 38.

171 Bohlander *Principles of German criminal procedure*, 31.

172 Jackson and Summers "The internationalization of criminal evidence: Beyond the common law and civil law traditions," 69–70.

173 *R v Kritz (Abraham Barnett)* [1950] 1. K.B 82 at 177 ('When once a Judge begins to use the words "reasonable doubt" and tries to explain what is a reasonable doubt and what is not, he is much more likely to confuse them').

174 John R. Spencer "Evidence," in *European criminal procedures*, ed. Mireille Delmas-Marty and John R. Spencer (revised by Alejandro Alvarez) (Cambridge: Cambridge University Press, 2002) 594 at 501.

175 *R v Hepworth (George Alfred)* [1955] 2 Q.B. 600). See also *R v Summers* [1952] 1 All ER 1059, CCA; *Walters v R* [1969] 2 AC 26, PC; *R v Yap Chuan Ching* (1976) 63 Cr App Rep 7; *Ferguson v R* [1979] 1 WLR 94, PC; *R v Bracewell* (1979) 68 Cr App R 44, CA; *R v Derek William Bentley* [2001] 1 Cr App R 326 (CA); *R v Alikor* [2004] EWCA Crim 1646; *R v Majid* [2009] EWCA Crim 2563; *R v Miah* (2018) EWCA Crim 563. See also Judicial College, The Crown Court compendium – Jury and trial management and summing up (July 2019) 5-1-5-3, available at: judiciary.uk (accessed: 20 September 2019).

instituting, processing and adjudicating a hate crime claim in a court of law. Chapter 3 has shown that there is more convergence around the world with respect to the processual condition than the material and probative conditions of proof. The primary reason for this is because of what has been referred to in this chapter as 'processual coloniality'; that is, the domination of two main traditions of processual law over much of the world's systems of fact-finding. The processual practices of most of the world, particularly in the Global South, are northbound gazing[176] towards the Anglo-American common law and European civil law traditions. Some of the problems associated with this phenomenon of coloniality, namely processual dualism and diffusion, are discussed briefly, but the chapter also leverages off this convergence in distilling the main questions that arise from the processual condition of proof into enquiries about: *Who is the fact-finder?* (jurisdiction). *Which evidentiary or extant facts may be relied upon (accepted or rejected) to draw inferential conclusions?* (admissibility). *Against which criteria or through which methods are these inferential conclusions to be evaluated?* (evaluative criteria). The main argument of the chapter is that the answers to these questions determine the meaning and outcomes of proof judgements about hate crimes. The next three chapters will turn to the third probative condition of the proof of hate crimes.

3.7 Bibliography

Books and Book Chapters

Adrian Bellengère et al *The law of evidence in South Africa* (Cape Town: Oxford University Press, 2013).
Alejandro Agüero "Latin American criminal law: A historical perspective," in *Göttingen handbook on Latin American public law and criminal justice*, eds. Kai Ambos and Jose Martinez (Baden-Baden: Nomos, 2023) 255.
Andrew A.F. Massawe *The burden of proof: How to defend yourself in criminal cases* (Mzumbe: Mzumbe University, 2000).
Ania Loomba *Colonialism/Postcolonialism* 3rd ed (London: Routledge, 2015).
Arthur T. Von Mehren and James R. Gordley *The civil law system: An introduction to the comparative study of law* 2nd ed (Boston: Little Brown & Company, 1977).
Bart Wauters and Marco de Benito *The history of law in Europe: An introduction* (Cheltenham: Elgar, 2017).
C. Eche Adah *The Nigerian law of evidence* (Lagos: Malthouse Press, 1997).
Carlson Anyangwe *The magistracy and the bar in Cameroon* (CEPER: Yaoundé, 1989).
Cesare Beccaria *An essay on crimes and punishments* (Albany: WC Little & Co, 1872) (published originally in 1764).
Charles F. Chamberlayne *A treatise on the modern law of evidence* vol 3 (London: Sweet & Maxwell, 1911).
Christine Boyle "A principled approach to relevance: The Cheshire Cat in Canada," in *Innovations in evidence and proof: Integrating theory, research and teaching*, eds. Paul Roberts and Mike Redmayne (Oxford: Hart, 2007) 87.

176 Mogobe B. Ramose "'African Renaissance': A northbound gaze," in *The African philosophy reader*, Pieter H. Coetzee and Abraham P.J. Roux 2nd ed (London: Routledge, 2002) 600.

Cliff Roberson and Dilip K. Das *An introduction to comparative legal models of criminal justice* 2nd ed (Boca Raton: CRC Press, 2016).
Craig M. Bradley "Overview," in *Criminal procedure: A worldwide study*, ed. Craig M. Bradley (Durham: Carolina Academic Press, 1999) xv.
David Schum *Evidential foundations of probabilistic reasoning* (Evanston, IL: Northwestern University Press, 1994).
David T. Johnson "Japan's lay judge system," in *Comparative criminal procedure*, eds. Jacqueline E. Ross and Stephen C. Thaman (Cheltenham: Elgar, 2016) 396.
Denis Salas "The role of the judge," in *European criminal procedures*, ed. Mireille Delmas-Marty and John R. Spencer (revised by Alejandro Alvarez) (Cambridge: Cambridge University Press, 2002) 488.
Ed Johnston and Tom Smith *Criminal procedure and punishment* 3rd ed (Saltford: Hall and Stitt, 2023).
Harold J. Berman *Law and revolution: The formation of the western legal tradition* (Cambridge: Harvard University Press, 1983).
Harry R. Dammer and Jay S. Albanese *Comparative criminal justice systems* 5th ed (Wadsworth Cengage Learning, 2014).
Henry F. Morris *Evidence in East Africa* (Lagos: African Universities Press, 1968).
Hock-Lai Ho *A philosophy of evidence law* (Oxford: Oxford University Press, 2008).
Jacqueline S. Hodgson *The metamorphosis of criminal justice: A comparative account* (New York: Oxford University Press, 2020).
James B. Thayer *A preliminary treatise on evidence at common law* (Boston: Little Brown and Co., 1898).
James F. Stephen *A digest on the law of evidence* (London: Macmillan, 1887).
James F. Stephen *The Indian Evidence Act (I of 1872): With an introduction on the principles of judicial evidence* (London: Macmillan, 1872).
James Q. Whitman *The origins of reasonable doubt: Theological roots of the criminal trial* (New Haven: Yale University Press, 2008).
Jeanmarie Fenrich et al "Introduction," in *The future of African customary law*, eds. Jeanmarie Fenrich et al (New York: Cambridge University Press, 2011) 1.
Jenia I. Turner and Thomas Weigend "The purposes and functions of exclusionary rules," in *Do exclusionary rules ensure a fair trial?* eds. Sabine Gless and Thomas Richter (Cham: Springer, 2019) 255.
Jeremy Bentham *Rationale of judicial evid*ence, ed. J.S. Mill vol 1 (London: Hunt & Clark, 1827).
Jeswald W. Salacuse *An introduction to law in French-speaking Africa* vol I (1969).
Joëlle Vuille "Forensic science evidence in non-adversary criminal justice systems," in *Forensic science evidence and expert witness testimony: Reliability through reform*, eds. Paul Roberts and Michael Stockdale (Cheltenham: Elgar, 2018) 354.
John D. Jackson "The case for a hybrid jury in Europe," in *Juries, lay judges and mixed courts: A global perspective*, eds. Sanja Ivković, Sanja K. Ivković, Shari S. Diamond, Valerie P. Hans and Nancy S. Marder (New York: Cambridge University Press, 2021) 304.
John D. Jackson "Managing uncertainty and finality: The function of the criminal trial in legal inquiry," in *Trial on trial: Truth and due process*, eds. R. Antony Duff et al vol 1 (Portland: Hart, 2004) 121.
John D. Jackson and Sarah J. Summers *The internationalization of criminal evidence: Beyond the common law and civil law traditions* (New York: Cambridge University Press, 2012).
John D. Jackson and Thomas Weigend "Witness evidence in pre-trial and trial procedure," in *Core concepts in criminal law and criminal justice*, eds. Kai Ambos et al (Cambridge: Cambridge University Press, 2022) 260.
John H. Langbein "Bifurcation and the bench: The influence of the jury on English conceptions of the judiciary," in *Judges and judging in the history of the common law*

and civil law: From antiquity to modern times, eds. Paul Brand and Joshua Getzler (Cambridge: Cambridge University Press, 2012) 67.

John H. Langbein *Prosecuting crime in the Renaissance: England, Germany, France* (Cambridge: Harvard University Press, 1974).

John H. Langbein, Renée L. Lerner and Bruce P. Smith *History of the common law: The development of Anglo-American legal institutions* (New York: Aspen, 2009).

John H. Merryman and Rogelio Pérez-Perdomo *The civil law tradition: An introduction to the legal systems of Europe and Latin America* 4th ed (Stanford: Stanford University Press, 2019).

John H. Wigmore *Evidence in trials at common* (revised Peter Tillers) vol 1 (Boston: Little Brown and Co., 1983).

John R. Spencer "Evidence," in *European criminal procedures*, eds. Mireille Delmas-Marty and John R. Spencer (revised by Alejandro Alvarez) (Cambridge: Cambridge University Press, 2002) 594.

Joshua C. Tate "Justice," in *A cultural history of law: In the middle ages*, eds. Emanuele Conte and Laurent Mayali vol 2 (London: Bloomsbury, 2019) 11.

Jospeter M. Mbuba "Introduction," in *Comparative criminal justice*, ed. Jospeter M. Mbuba (Lanham: Rowman & Littlefield, 2023) 1.

Kwame Nkrumah *Neo-colonialism: The last stage of imperialism* (Panaf Books Ltd, 1965).

Larry May *Ancient legal thought: Equity, justice and humaneness from Hammurabi and the pharaohs to Justinian and the Talmud* (New York: Cambridge University Press, 2019).

Liling Yue "Chapter 2: The development of Chinese criminal procedure," in *Four criminal procedure case studies in comparative perspective: China–Italy–Russia–U.S.A.*, ed. Marco Fabri (Baden-Baden: Nomos, 2016) 23.

Liz Campbell et al *The criminal process* 5th ed (Oxford: Oxford University Press, 2019).

Marco Fabri "Highlights of four case studies on criminal procedure," in *Four criminal procedure case studies in comparative perspective: China–Italy–Russia–U.S.A.*, ed. Marco Fabri (Baden-Baden: Nomos, 2016) 1.

Mathurin C. Tadonkeng "Land law and polygamy in the Bamiléké tribe in Cameroon," in *Property rights, land and territory in the European overseas empires*, ed. José V. Serrão (Lisbon: CEHC-IUL, 2014) 305.

Mauricio Duce J. and Claudio Fuentes M. "Trials and trial by jury in Latin America," in *Göttingen handbook on Latin American public law and criminal justice*, eds. Kai Ambos and Jose Martinez (Baden-Baden: Nomos, 2023) 517.

Máximo Langer "The long shadow of the adversarial and inquisitorial categories," in *The Oxford handbook of criminal law*, eds. Markus D. Dubber and Tatjana Hörnle (Oxford: Oxford University Press, 2014) 887.

Máximo Langer, Mike McConville and Luke Marsh, eds. *Research handbook on plea bargaining and criminal justice* (Cheltenham: Elgar, 2024).

Michael Bohlander *Principles of German criminal procedure* 2nd ed (Oxford: Hart, 2021).

Mirjan R. Damaška *Evaluation of evidence: Premodern and modern approaches* (Cambridge: Cambridge University Press, 2019).

Mirjan R. Damaška *Evidence law adrift* (New Haven: Yale University Press, 1997).

Mirjan R. Damaška *The faces of justice and state authority: A comparative approach to the legal process* (New Haven: Yale University Press, 1986).

Mogobe B. Ramose "'African Renaissance': A northbound gaze," in *The African philosophy reader*, Pieter H. Coetzee and Abraham P.J. Roux 2nd ed (London: Routledge, 2002) 600.

Neil Vidmar *World jury systems* (Oxford: Oxford University Press, 2000).

Pamela-Jane Schwikkard and Tshepo B. Mosaka *Principles of evidence* 5th ed (Claremont: Juta, 2023).
Paul Roberts, Jill Hunter, Simon N.M. Young and David Dixon "Introduction," in *The integrity of criminal process: From theory into practice*, eds. Jill Hunter, Paul Roberts, Simon N.M. Young and David Dixon (Oxford: Hart, 2016) 3.
Philip L. Reichel *Comparative criminal justice systems: A topical approach* 7th ed (New York: Pearson, 2018).
Randall Lesaffer *European legal history: A cultural and political perspective* (translated by Jan Arriens) (Cambridge: Cambridge University Press, 2009).
Renée L. Lerner *The jury: A very short introduction* (New York: Oxford University Press, 2023).
Richard Posner *The problems of jurisprudence* (Cambridge: Harvard University Press, 1990).
Richard Terrill *World criminal justice systems: A comparative survey* 9th ed (New York: Routledge, 2016).
Richard Vogler "Introduction," in *Criminal procedure in Europe*, eds. Richard Vogler and Barbara Huber (Berlin: Duncker & Humblot, 2008) 1.
Richard Vogler *A world view of criminal justice* (New York: Routledge, 2005).
Ronald J. Allen "Common sense, rationality and the legal process," in *The dynamics of judicial proof: Computation, logic and common sense*, eds. Marilyn MacCrimmon and Peter Tillers (New York: Springer, 2002) 43.
Ronald J. Allen, Joseph L. Hoffman, Debra A. Livingston, Andrew D. Leipold and Tracey L. Meares *Comprehensive criminal procedure* 5th ed (New York: Wolters Kluwer, 2020).
Sabelo J. Ndlovu-Gatsheni *Epistemic freedom in Africa: Deprovincialisation and decolonisation* (London: Routledge, 2018).
Sanja K. Ivković, Shari S. Diamond, Valerie P. Hans and Nancy S. Marder "Introduction," in *Juries, lay judges and mixed courts: A global perspective*, eds. Sanja Ivković, Sanja K. Ivković, Shari S. Diamond, Valerie P. Hans and Nancy S. Marder (New York: Cambridge University Press, 2021) 1.
Sanja K. Ivković and Valerie P. Hans "A worldwide perspective on lay participation," in *Juries, lay judges and mixed courts: A global perspective*, eds. Sanja K. Ivković, Shari S. Diamond, Valerie P. Hans and Nancy S. Marder (New York: Cambridge University Press, 2021) 323.
Sarah Moss *Probabilistic knowledge* (Oxford: Oxford University Press, 2018).
Simon Tabetabe "A look at preliminary inquiry under the Cameroon criminal procedure code," in *Readings in the Cameroon criminal procedure code*, ed. Andrew E. Sone (2007) 49.
Stephen E. Van der Merwe "A basic introduction to criminal procedure," in *Criminal procedure handbook*, ed. J. Johannes Joubert (Claremont: Juta, 2020) 3.
T. Akinola Aguda *The law of evidence in Nigeria* 3rd ed (London: Sweet & Maxwell, 1989).
Terence Anderson, William Twining and David Schum *Analysis of evidence* 2nd ed (Cambridge: Cambridge University Press, 2005).
Thomas Starkie *A practical treatise of the law of evidence* 3rd ed (Philadelphia: T & J.W Johnson & Co., 1842).
Upendra Baxi "The colonialist heritage," in *Comparative legal studies: Transitions and transitions*, eds. Pierre Legrand and Roderick Munday (Cambridge: Cambridge University Press, 2003) 46.
Valerie P. Hans, Hiroshi Fukurai, Sanja Kutnjak Ivković and Jaihyun Park "Global juries: A plan for research," in *The psychology of juries*, ed. Margaret B. Kovera (Washington: American Psychological Association, 2017) 131.

Vernon V. Palmer "Introduction to the mixed jurisdictions," in *Mixed jurisdictions worldwide: The third legal family*, ed. Vernon V. Palmer 2nd ed (New York: Cambridge University Press, 2012) 3.
Victor G. Hiemstra *Introduction to the law of criminal procedure* (Durban: Butterworths, 1977).
Walter D. Mignolo *The darker side of Renaissance: Literacy, territoriality and colonisation* 2nd ed (Ann Arbor: University of Michigan Press, 2003).
William Twining *Globalisation and legal theory* (New York: Cambridge University Press, 2000).
William Twining *Rethinking evidence: Exploratory essays* (Cambridge: Cambridge University Press, 2006) 227.
William Twining *Theories of evidence: Bentham and Wigmore* (London: Weidenfeld & Nicolson, 1985).
Yik Koon "Introduction to the criminal justice system in Malaysia," in *Comparative criminal justice*, ed. Jospeter M. Mbuba (Lanham: Rowman & Littlefield, 2023) 107.

Periodicals

Anibal Quijano "Coloniality of power and Eurocentricism in Latin America" (2000) 1(3) *Nepantla: Views from South* 533.
Anibal Quijano "Coloniality of power and Eurocentricism in Latin America" (2000) 15(2) *International Sociology* 215.
Anthony C. Diala "Legal pluralism and the future of personal family laws in Africa" (2021) 35(1) *International Journal of Law, Policy and the Family* 1.
Anton Wekerle "Modern African criminal law and procedure codes" (1978) 35(4) *The Quarterly Journal of the Library of Congress* 282.
Anyopeuh S. Munzu "Cameroon's search for a uniform legal system: The example of criminal justice" (1989) 1(1) *African Journal of International and Comparative Law* 46.
Berihun A. Gebeye "Decoding legal pluralism in Africa" (2017) 49(2) *Journal of Legal Pluralism and Unofficial Law* 228.
Buluma Bwire "Integration of African customary legal concepts into modern law: Restorative justice – A Kenyan example" (2019) 9(1) *Societies* 17.
Callie R. Snyman "The accusatorial and inquisitorial approaches to criminal procedure: Some points of comparison between the South African and the continental systems" (1975) 8(1) *Comparative and International Law Journal of Southern* Africa 100.
Christa Rautenbach "Therapeutic jurisprudence in the customary courts of South Africa: Traditional authority courts as therapeutic agents" (2005) 21(2) *South African Journal of Human Rights* 323.
Chukwunweike A. Ogbuabor "Inquisitorial and adversarial process in Nigeria's criminal justice system: The dilemma of a colonized state" (2015) 38(2) *University of Western Australia Law Review* 175.
David Pimentel "Legal pluralism in post-colonial Africa: Linking statutory and customary adjudication in Mozambique" (2011) 14 *Yale Human Rights & Development Law Journal* 59.
Eugene Cotran "The development and reform of the law in Kenya" (1983) 27(1) *Journal of African Law* 42.
Evode Kayitana "The accusatorial and inquisitorial models of criminal procedure: A historical and comparative approach" (2019) 3(2) *African Journal of Law and Human Rights* 187.
Francois du Bois and Danie Visser "The influence of foreign law in South Africa" (2003) 13 *Transnational Law & Contemporary Problems* 593.

Giovanni Tuzet "Evidence assessment and standards of proof: A messy issue" (2021) 2 *Quaestio Facti: International Journal on Evidential Legal Reasoning* 87.
Herbert Packer "The courts, the police and the rest of us" (1966) 57(3) *Journal of Criminal Law, Criminology and Police Science* 238.
Herbert Packer "Two models of the criminal process" (1964) 113(1) *University of Pennsylvania Law Review* 1.
Howard B. Miller "Beyond the law of evidence" (1966) 40(1) *Southern California Law Review* 1.
James B. Thayer "'Law' and 'fact' in jury trials" (1890) 4(4) *Harvard Law Review* 147.
James S. Read "Criminal law in the Africa of today and tomorrow" (1963) 7(1) *African Law Journal* 5.
Joachim Herrmann "Various models of criminal proceedings" (1978) 2(1) *South African Journal of Criminal Law and Criminology* 3.
Johannes F. Nijboer "Common law tradition in evidence scholarship observed from a Continental perspective" (1993) 41(2) *The American Journal of Comparative law* 399.
John D. Jackson "Making juries accountable" (2002) 50 *The American Journal of Comparative Law* 477.
John D. Jackson and Nikolay P. Kovalev "Lay adjudication and human rights in Europe" (2006) 13 *Columbia Journal of European Law* 83.
John H. Wigmore "The problem of proof" (1913) 8(2) *Illinois Law Review* 77.
Kai Ambos "Intime conviction in Germany: Conceptual foundations, historical development and current meaning" (2023) 4 *Quaestio Facti: International Journal on Evidential Legal Reasoning* 167.
L. Jonathan Cohen "The role of evidential weight in criminal proof" (1986) 66(4) *Boston University Law Review* 635.
Larry Laudan "Is reasonable doubt reasonable?" (2003) 9 *Legal Theory* 295.
Louis T.C. Harms "Demystification of the inquisitorial system" (2011) 14(5) *Potchefstroom Electronic Law Journal* 1.
Mahmood Mamdani "Indirect rule, civil society and ethnicity: The African dilemma" (1996) 23(1) *Social Justice* 145.
Marius Pieterse "It's a 'black thing': Upholding culture and customary law in a society founded on non-racialism" (2001) 17 *South African Journal of Human Rights* 364.
Máximo Langer "Revolution in Latin American criminal procedure: Diffusion of legal ideas from the periphery" (2007) 55 *The American Journal of Comparative* Law 617.
Michele Taruffo "Rethinking the standards of proof" (2003) 51(3) *American Journal of Comparative Law* 659.
Mirjan R. Damaška "Evidentiary barriers to conviction and two models of criminal procedure: A comparative study" (1973) 121(3) *University of Pennsylvania Law Review* 507.
Mirjan R. Damaška "Free proof and its detractors" (1995) 43(3) *The American Journal of Comparative Law* 343.
Nelson Maldonado-Torres "On the coloniality of being" (2007) 21(2–3) *Cultural Studies* 240.
Noah T. Fuashi "Statehood and the law-making process in Cameroon: From bifurcation to unification" (2012) 18(2) *Fundamina* 59.
Paul G. Mahoney "The common law and economic growth: Hayek might be right" (2001) 30(2) *Journal of Legal Studies* 503.
Paul Roberts "Five foundational fallacies of common law evidence" (translated by Ping Yang and Baosheng Zhang) (2018) 26 *Evidence Science* 93–108.
Peter W. Murphy "Some reflection on evidence and proof" (1999) 40 *Texas Law Review* 327.

Pieter J. Maartens and Pamela-Jane Schwikkard "A juryless jurisdiction and the epistemic rules of evidence" (2011) 128(3) *South African Law Journal* 513.
Richard D. Friedman "'E' is for eclectic: Multiple perspectives on evidence" (2001) 87 *Virginia Law Review* 2029.
Roger C. Park "Evidence scholarship, old and new" (1991) 75 *Minnesota Law Review* 849.
Roger C. Park "An outsider's view of common law evidence" (1998) 96(6) *Michigan Law Review* 1468.
Ronald J. Allen, Timothy Fry, Jessica Notebaert and Jeff and Van Dam "Reforming the law of evidence of Tanzania (Part one): The social and legal challenges" (2013) 31(1) *Boston University International Law Journal* 217.
Sandra F. Joireman "Inherited legal systems and effective rule of law: Africa and the colonial legacy" (2001) 39(4) *The Journal of Modern African Studies* 571.
Stephen C. Thaman "Europe's new jury systems: The cases of Spain and Russia" (1999) 62(2) *Law and Contemporary Problems* 233.
Stephen Humphreys "Laboratories of statehood: Legal intervention in colonial Africa and today" (2012) 75(4) *Modern Law Review* 475.
Thomas Gergen "The reception of the code civil (Napoléonic Code) of 1804: An example of "juridical migration"?" (2014) 1 *Journal of European History of Law* 26.
Thomas O. Main "The procedural foundation of substantive law" (2003) 78 *Washington University Law Review* 801.
Tshepo Bogosi Mosaka "Here is a table: A prolegomenon to a future new evidence scholarship in Africa" (2022) 26(2) *International Journal of Evidence & Proof* 178.
Tshepo Bogosi Mosaka "*Mpho le mphonyana*: Two iterations of admissibility in Africa" (2023) 67 *Journal of African Law* 391.
William Twining "Evidence as a multi-disciplinary subject" (2003) 2 *Law, Probability and Risk* 91.
William Twining "Narrative and generationalisations in argumentation about questions of fact" (1999) 40 *Texas Law Review* 351.
Zacchaeus Adangor "What is innovative in the Evidence Act, 2011?" (2015) 43 *Journal of Law, Policy and Globalisation* 34.
Zhuhao Wang "The fate of evidence law: Two paths of development" (2020) 24(3) *International Journal of Evidence & Proof* 329.

Online Resources

Judicial College *The Crown Court compendium – Jury and Trial Management and Summing Up* (July 2019), available at: www.judiciary.uk (accessed: 20 September 2019).

4 A Short History of Proof

4.1 Introduction

This chapter is the first of three chapters (the other two being Chapters 5 and 6) focusing on the probative condition of the evidential proof of hate crimes. The main argument asserted in this book is that the evidential proof of hate crimes is dependent on three material, processual and probative conditions. The first two of these conditions focusing on the legal meaning and elements of hate crimes, as well as the procedural practices of prosecuting hate crimes, were discussed in Chapters 2 and 3. The probative condition of evidential proof refers to the heuristics or models of drawing logical inferences from extant facts, which are processed in accordance with the relevant processual practices, to establishing the material facts that are in dispute. This chapter surveys the manner in which various historical communities around the world have developed and applied probative mechanisms in criminal adjudication. Having laid that historical foundation, the specific models of evidential proof that apply to hate crimes are developed and applied in Chapters 5 and 6.

Books on evidential proof are rare,[1] and that is largely because a 'law of proof' specialisation currently does not exist. Instead, proof is studied as part of several cognate subjects such as the law of evidence,[2] procedural law[3]

1 For example: Kevin M. Clermont *A general theory of evidence and proof: Forming beliefs in truth* (Cham: Springer, 2024); Christian Dahlman et al, eds. *Philosophical foundations of evidence law* (Oxford: Oxford University Press, 2021); Frederick Schauer *Uses of evidence in law, politics and everything else* (Cambridge: Harvard University Press, 2022); Donald Nicolson *Evidence and proof in Scotland: Context and critique* (Edinburgh: Edinburgh University Press, 2019); Chris Carey et al, eds. *Evidence and proof in ancient Greece* (Newcastle: Cambridge Scholars Publishing, 2024); Verena Klappstein and Maciej Dybowski, eds. *Theory of legal evidence – Evidence in legal theory* (Cham: Springer, 2021).

2 See James B. Thayer *A preliminary treatise on evidence at common law* (Boston: Little Brown, 1898) 1–2; William Twining *Rethinking evidence: Exploratory essays* (Evanston, IL: Northwestern University Press, 1994); William Twining *Rethinking evidence: Exploratory essays* (Cambridge: Cambridge University Press, 2006); Paul Roberts "Rethinking of the law of evidence: A twenty-first century agenda for teaching and research" (2002) 55(1) *Current Legal Problems* 297.

3 See generally, Jeremy Bentham *Rationale of judicial evidence* vol 1 (edited by J.S. Mill) (London: Hunt & Clark, 1827). For procedural law, see Joanna Gomula and Stephen Wittich, eds.

DOI: 10.4324/9781003493006-4

and, to a lesser extent, substantive law. Prior calls for a 'novum organum for the study of Judicial Evidence' by Wigmore[4] and a 'Bachelor of Facts' for the 'well-educated lawyer' by Twining[5] have not been heeded.[6] However, the phenomenon of proof, as this chapter and the next two chapters will show, is universal to any community with dispute resolution adjudicative mechanisms. Although it is theorised about and studied mostly by Euro-American scholars in the Global North,[7] adjudicators in some of the remotest parts of the world, for example indigenous courts in China[8] (the People's Mediation Committees) and Africa,[9] also have to grapple with evidential proof. One of the earliest English definitions of proof is from Best, who described it as 'a persuasion affirmative or disaffirmative of the existence or some other matter of fact.'[10] Wigmore regarded it as 'the ratiocinative process of contentious persuasion,

---

Research handbook on international procedural law (Cheltenham: Elgar, 2024); Koen Lenaerts et al *EU procedural law* 2nd ed (Oxford: Oxford University Press, 2023); Xiaobo Dong and Yafang Zhang *On contemporary Chinese legal system* (Gateway East: Springer, 2023) Ch 14; Michael D. Bayles *Procedural justice: Allocating to individuals* (Dordrecht: Kluwer, 1990); Jeremy Lever "Why procedure is more important than substantive law" (1999) 48(2) *International & Comparative Law Quarterly* 285. See also the *International Journal of Procedural Law* at: www.jurisquare.be (accessed: 15 May 2024). For substantive law, see Stephen J. Morse *Advanced introduction to substantive criminal law* (Cheltenham: Elgar, 2023); Elena Górriz Royo *Introduction to substantive criminal law* (Valencia: Tirant lo Blanch, 2019); Alan Reed and Michael Bohlander, eds. *Substantive issues in criminal law* (2014–2024) (five books), available at: www.routledge.com (accessed: 15 May 2024).

4 John H. Wigmore *The principles of judicial proof as given by logic, psychology and general experience and illustrated in judicial trials* (Boston: Little Brown Company, 1913) 1.

5 William Twining "Goodbye to Lewis Elliot: The academic lawyer as scholar" (1980) 15 *Journal of the Society of Public Teachers of Law* 2 at 14; William Twining "Taking facts seriously," in *Essays on Legal Education*, ed. Neil Gold (Toronto: Butterworths, 1982) 22 at 22–23 (on the hypothetical Xanadu Law School and the proposal of a 'Bachelor of Facts').

6 Twining would later regretfully acknowledge that his clarion call to 'take facts seriously' had 'failed to persuade,' see William Twining "Taking facts seriously – Again," in *Rethinking evidence: Exploratory essays*, ed. William Twining 2nd ed (Cambridge: Cambridge University Press, 2009) 417.

7 Tshepo B. Mosaka "Here is a table: A prolegomenon to a future new evidence scholarship in Africa" (2022) 26(2) *International Journal of Evidence & Proof* 178.

8 Nanning Zhang and Douglas Walton "Recent trends in evidence law in China and the new evidence scholarship" (2010) 9 *Law, Probability and Risk* 103 at 106 and 110; Valerie P. Hans et al "Global juries: A plan for research," in *The psychology of juries*, ed. Margaret B. Kovera (Washington: American Psychological Association, 2017) 131 at 135.

9 Digby S. Koyana "Traditional courts in South Africa in the twenty-first century," in *The future of African customary law*, Jeanmarie Fenrich et al (New York: Cambridge University Press, 2011) 227 at 234; John H. Soga *The Ama-Xosa* (New York: Cambridge University Press, 1937) 41 (on the procedure of councillors of a traditional court having to read a full reasoned judgement at the end of a fact-finding process).

10 William M.A. Best *Treatise on the principles of and practice as to proofs in courts of common law with rules for conducting the examination and of witnesses* (Philadelphia: T. & J.W. Johnson, 1849) 31. Cf. Twining *Rethinking evidence: Exploratory essays*, 179: 'Proof is the establishment of the existence or non-existence of some fact (a *factum probandum* or fact in issue).'

mind to mind, counsel to juror, each partisan seeking to move the mind of the tribunal.'[11] The word 'proof' derives from the Latin *probare*, which means 'to see out' or 'to trace by sight,'[12] thereby foregrounding a conception of evidence as a source of truth. More contemporary definitions emphasise concepts such as inference, argument and truth. For example, Ho argues that 'to prove something is to show that it is true' and that 'fact-finding,' therefore, is 'a search for the truth.'[13] According to Anderson, Schum and Twining, 'inferential reasoning and argument' are the process and 'proof or non-proof is the result,'[14] whereas Dennis characterises proof as being synonymous with 'the process of evaluating evidence' and that of 'drawing inferences from it.'[15] As such, proof, by virtue of consisting of 'inferential reasoning,'[16] is not only common to most jurisdictions but to most disciplines that share problems of evidence and inference.[17]

The core aim of this chapter is the historical exposition of seven different methods of proof in the context of criminal adjudication. These are ordeals, sworn witness testimony, rhetorical speeches, judicial battle, canonical confessions, electronic mechanisms and rational argumentation. Each of these methods is discussed as it emerged within its historical context. Therefore, it is not the purpose of the chapter to survey a general history of ideas, nor is it necessarily to discuss the history of a particular country or region. The focus rather will be on explicating the nature, legal effect and social context of each of the seven methods of proof in the context of criminal adjudication. For this purpose, the chapter is periodised into four eras: ***antiquity***, as spanning the period before the thirteenth century; the ***medieval period***, ranging from the thirteenth till the seventeenth centuries; the ***rationalist period***, beginning with the eighteenth century and ending in the 1980s; and the current era of New Evidence Scholarship that developed in the late twentieth century. Every attempt at periodisation is likely to attract controversies of, among others,

11 John H. Wigmore "The problem of proof" (1913) 8 *Illinois Law Review* 77 at 77.

12 Tshepo B. Mosaka "An introduction to proof in South Africa" (2022) 139(4) *South African Law Journal* 837 at 847; Thayer "A preliminary treatise on evidence at common law," 387; William Wills *An essay on the principles of circumstantial evidence* 3rd ed (Philadelphia: T. & J.W. Johnson, 1858) 2; James D. Williams *An introduction to classical rhetoric: Essential readings* (Chichester: John Wiley & Sons, 2009) 298 (on classical Greek forensic rhetoric having the three aims of *probare, delectare* and *flectere*); Cicero *De Oratore* II (translated by E.W. Sutton) (Cambridge: Harvard University Press, 1967) 331–334.

13 Hock-Lai Ho *A philosophy of evidence law* (Oxford: Oxford University Press, 2008) 51–52. See more generally, Hock-Lai Ho "Evidence and truth," in *Philosophical foundations of evidence law*, eds. Christian Dahlman et al (Oxford: Oxford University Press, 2021) 11.

14 Terence Anderson et al *Analysis of evidence* 2nd ed (Cambridge: Cambridge University Press, 2005) 94

15 Ian Dennis *The law of evidence* 6th ed (London: Sweet & Maxwell, 2017) 4.

16 Anderson et al *Analysis of evidence*, 46: 'Everyone draws inferences from evidence.'

17 William Twining "Evidence as a multi-disciplinary subject" (2003) 2 *Law, Probability and Risk* 91 at 97.

under-inclusion, unwarranted exclusion, essentialism, parochialism and imprecision.[18] For example, the three-part 'Antiquity-Medieval-Modernity' periodisation typically is characterised as the 'self-image and worldview of Renaissance and Modern Europe.'[19] Alternatively, colonial periodisations of African history demarcate three 'precolonial, colonial and post-colonial' periods,[20] whereas Marxian periodisations divide history into 'primitive communalism; slavery; feudalism; capitalism; and socialism (communism).'[21] Another alternative is Islamic periodisation, which divides history into six distinct periods: the 'Late Sâsânî Primitive Caliphal periods (c. 484–692)'; the 'High Caliphal period (c. 692–94)'; 'Earlier Middle Islamic Period (c. 945–1258)'; 'Later Middle Islamic Period (c. 1258–1503)'; 'Period of Gunpowder Empires (c. 1503–1789)'; 'Modern Technical Age (c. 1789 – present).'[22] A fifth example emanates from public international law scholars that periodise history into five different periods: 'antiquity (before 475 A.D.)'; the 'middle ages (476–1492)'; the 'sixteenth century (1493–1648)'; the 'seventeenth and eighteenth centuries (1649–1815)'; and '1815 to the present.'[23] Each of these was crafted to

18 See Randall Lesaffer *European legal history: A cultural and political perspective* (translated by Jan Arriens) (Cambridge: Cambridge University Press, 2009) 8; Barbara Mittler et al "Introduction: Periodisation in a global context," in *Chronologics: Periodisation in global context*, eds. Barbara Mittler, Thomas Maissen and Pierre Monnet (Heidelberg: Heidelberg University Publishing, 2022) 1 at 2 ('Accordingly, periodisations are never inert or innocent').

19 Lesaffer *European legal history: A cultural and political perspective*, 9. Alternative European periodisations break up the modern era into the early modern (1453–1789) and modern ages (1789–present) (at 8).

20 Kwesi K. Prah "Has Rhodes fallen? Decolonising the humanities in Africa and constructing intellectual sovereignty," *Academy of Science of South Africa Inaugural Humanities Lecture* (20 October 2016) 9, available at: www.hsrc.ac.za (accessed: 14 June 2024); Sabelo J. Ndlovu-Gatsheni "Ten challenges in reconfiguring African studies" (2023) *Review of African Political Economy* 1 at 9–10.

21 William E. Butler "Periodization and international law," in *Research handbook on the theory and history of international law*, ed. Alexander Orakhelashvili 2nd ed (Cheltenham: Elgar, 2020) 281 at 282.

22 Marshall G.S. Hodgson *The venture of Islam: Conscience and history in a world civilization* vol 1 (Chicago: University of Chicago Press, 1974) 96. Cf. Shelomo D. Goitein "A plea for the periodization of Islamic history" (1968) 88(2) *Journal of the American Oriental Society* 224 at 227–228 ('Arabism and Arabic Islam, 500–850 A.D.'; 'The intermediate civilization, 850–1250'; 'Institutionalised Islam, 1250–1800'; 'Transition to national cultures, 1800–'); Fred M. Donner "Periodisation as a tool of the historian with special reference to Islamic history" (2014) 91(1) *Der Islam* 20 at 34.

23 Butler "Periodization and international law," 282–283; Peter Macalister-Smith and Joachim Schwietzke "Literature and documentary sources relating to the history of public international law: An annotated bibliographical survey" (1999) 1 *Journal of the History of International Law* 136 at 145–148 (on the history of public international law). Cf. Wilhelm George Grewe *The epochs of international law* (translated by Michael Byers) (Berlin: Walter de Gruyter, 2000) Part I (*Ius gentium*: Middle Ages); Part II (*Ius inter gentes*: Spanish Age, 1494–1648); Part III (*Droit Public de l'Europe*: French Age, 1648–1815); Part IV (British Age, 1815–1919); Part V (League of Nations inter-war period, 1919–1944); Part VI (Age of American-Soviet rivalry and the rise of the Third World, 1945–1989).

suit the peculiar purpose of the crafter, and so is the case with the periodisation adopted in this chapter. To avoid any controversies associated with any of these forms of demarcation, this chapter will specifically focus on the seven methods of proof identified earlier, and their history for the limited purpose of locating their origins in time.

4.2 Proof in Antiquity

The most common methods of proof in antiquity were ordeals and the testimony of witnesses under oath.[24] Ordeals and testimony under oath were prevalent under ancient Mesopotamian[25] and Egyptian laws such as the Laws of Ur-Namma (ca. 2100 BCE); the Laws of Lipit-Ishtar (ca. 1930 BCE); the Laws of Eshnunna (ca. 1770 BCE); Code of Hammurabi (ca. 1754 BCE); the Middle Assyrian Laws (ca. 1076 BCE); and the Neo-Babylonian Laws (ca. 700 BCE).[26] These two methods of proof were deployed in territories across the world for more than a millennium until ordeals began their decline from the twelfth century.[27] The social and legal institutions of antiquity were marked by widespread polytheism,[28] divination[29] and superstition.[30] It was a 'world . . . full of gods and spirits who could influence the affairs of humans.'[31] Decision-making, it was believed, was the prerogative of the gods, who revealed their decisions to 'diviners,' 'exorcists' and 'lamentation priests.'[32] The ancient Roman

24 Larry May *Ancient legal thought: Equity, justice and humaneness from Hammurabi and the pharaohs to Justinian and the Talmud* (New York: Cambridge University Press, 2019) 43.

25 Mesopotamia, literally translated to mean 'between rivers,' refers to the civilisations that were located between the Tigris and Euphrates Rivers flowing from Turkey through to Syria and Iraq; see Barry Wimpfheimer "Codes," in *A cultural history of law: In antiquity*, ed. Julen Extabe (London: Bloomsbury, 2019) 59 at 60.

26 Kathryn Slanski "Justice," in *A cultural history of law: In antiquity*, ed. Julen Extabe (London: Bloomsbury, 2019) 21 at 24, n6; Martha T. Roth *Law collections from Mesopotamia and Asia Minor* 2nd ed (Atlanta: Scholars Press, 1997) ix (on the Sumerian dynasties of Ur (2112–2004 BCE), Larsa (2025–1763 BCE) and Isin (2017–1794 BCE); ancient Babylon (1894–1595 BCE); Assyria (ca. 1400–627 BCE); and Persia (538–331 BCE)).

27 John H. Langbein et al *History of the common law: The development of Anglo-American legal institutions* (New York: Aspen, 2009) 51.

28 May *Ancient legal thought: Equity, justice and humaneness from Hammurabi and the pharaohs to Justinian and the Talmud*, 5. For an account of ancient Egyptian polytheism, see Molefi K. Asante *African pyramids of knowledge: Kemet, Afrocentricity and Africology* (New York: Universal Write Publications, 2015) 77–78 (on the sun god, *Atum*; the god of the air, *Shu*; the god of moisture, *Tefnut*; the god of the earth, *Geb*; the god of the deserts, *Ausar*; and the sky goddess, *Nut*).

29 Marc Van de Mieroop *Philosophy before the Greeks: The pursuit of truth in ancient Babylonia* (Princeton: Princeton University Press, 2016) 87.

30 Sadakat Kadri *The trial: from Socrates to O.J. Simpson* (London: Harper Collins, 2005) 7.

31 May *Ancient legal thought: Equity, justice and humaneness from Hammurabi and the pharaohs to Justinian and the Talmud*, 5.

32 Van de Mieroop *Philosophy before the Greeks: The pursuit of truth in ancient Babylonia*, 53; May *Ancient legal thought: Equity, justice and humaneness from Hammurabi and the pharaohs to Justinian and the Talmud*, 53.

(400–600 BCE) *fas-nefas* dichotomy, for example, separated the world into the invisible world of gods and that of ordinary mortals in Roman society.[33] Other examples of religious influence are the ancient Greek belief that the King of Crete, Minos, climbed Mount Olympus every nine years to receive legal advice from Zeus to help him decide cases;[34] and King Hammurabi's claim that he had received the wisdom to write his code from Shamash, the sun god.[35] A third method of proof, in addition to ordeals and witness testimony under oath, that arose during this period of antiquity, in ancient Greece specifically, is classical rhetoric. The tribunals that deployed these methods of proof were constituted either by lay groups of assemblies, especially in ancient Greece,[36] or by sovereign rulers or priests in places like Babylon,[37] Assyria,[38] Egypt,[39] India[40] and China.[41]

An ordeal is a test of a litigant's guilt through the performance of an activity that required them to risk their lives.[42] Although the types of ordeals were almost endless,[43] they appear in the judicial history of virtually every

33 Bart Wauters and Marco de Benito *The history of law in Europe: An introduction* (Cheltenham: Elgar, 2017) 16.
34 Kadri *The trial: From Socrates to O.J. Simpson*, 1.
35 Percy Handcock *The Code of Hammurabi* (New York: Macmillan, 1920) 42.
36 Renée L. Lerner *The jury: A very short introduction* (New York: Oxford University Press, 2023) 5; Stephen C. Todd "Law and oratory at Athens," in *The Cambridge companion to ancient Greek law*, eds. Michael Gagarin and David Cohen (New York: Cambridge University Press, 2005) 97 at 100 ('Athenian lawcourts frowned on professionalism at all levels, as can be seen for instance in the way that the majority of cases were judged by a large body of *dikestai*'); Mogens H. Hansen *The Athenian democracy in the age of Demosthenes: Structure, principles and ideology* (translated by J.A. Crook) (Norman: University of Oklahoma Press, 1991) 180 ('The parties were required to carry their suits through in person, and it was actually a punishable offence to pay someone else to appear as your advocate in court'); Harvey Yunis "The rhetoric of law in fourth-century Athens," in *The Cambridge companion to ancient Greek law*, eds. Michael Gagarin and David Cohen (New York: Cambridge University Press, 2005) 191 at 195 ('A large portion of the citizen body, if not the bulk of it, was either barely literate or functionally illiterate. Because average citizens had to maintain access to the legal system and also had to represent themselves in court, a high degree of literacy could not be required just to participate in a trial and address a court').
37 May *Ancient legal thought: Equity, justice and humaneness from Hammurabi and the pharaohs to Justinian and the Talmud*, 52.
38 Godfrey R. Driver and John C. Miles *The Assyrian laws* (Oxford: Clarendon Press, 1935) 89.
39 May *Ancient legal thought: Equity, justice and humaneness from Hammurabi and the pharaohs to Justinian and the Talmud*, 52.
40 Richard W. Lariviere *The Nāradasmṛti* (New Delhi: Motilal Banarsidass Publishers, 2003) 269 (on the appointment of judges by the king in ancient Indian societies).
41 May *Ancient legal thought: Equity, justice and humaneness from Hammurabi and the pharaohs to Justinian and the Talmud*, 249.
42 Langbein et al *History of the common law: The development of Anglo-American legal institutions* 44.
43 John H. Wigmore *A kaleidoscope of justice: Containing authentic accounts of trial scenes from all times and climes* (Washington: Washington Law Book Co., 1941) 729.

nation in the world.[44] The types of ordeals varied regarding the degree of risk of harm they posed to the participating proband. They ranged from swallowing tests that entailed a litigant swallowing a dry portion of the Eucharist without choking to the proband walking on the hand of a corpse with the expectation that it does not bleed ('the test of the bier').[45] However, the most dangerous and infamous among these were those recognised by the Fourth Lateran Council: the ordeals of hot iron, cold water, hot water and fire.[46] The hot iron ordeal entailed a hot iron bar being pulled out of a fire and handed to the proband to carry using his hands and walking a distance of nine yards.[47] The proband's hands would then be wrapped in bandages for a few days and later they would be checked for any inculpatory signs of infection. A version of this type of ordeal was administered in ancient Egypt using a hot spoon being placed on the proband's tongue.[48] For example, a proband was acquitted in ancient Egypt on a charge of murdering a young boy from the Bedouin community near the Sinai desert.[49] A red hot spoon was placed on the proband's tongue and upon subsequent inspection, the tongue was 'perfectly healthy and normal in every way.'[50] The ordeals of boiling water and fire operated in a similar way as testing how the proband's skin will fare against the pressure of unbearable heat. Whereas it was the proband's hand that was subjected to intense heat in the boiling water ordeal (*aeneum, judicium acquae ferventis, cacabus,*

44 Wigmore *A kaleidoscope of justice: Containing authentic accounts of trial scenes from all times and climes*, 5; Langbein et al *History of the common law: The development of Anglo-American legal institutions*, 44 ('The ordeals predate Christianity, but the Church absorbed and ritualized them'); George Neilson *Trial by combat* (Glasgow: William Hodge & Co., 1890) 1–2 ('Ordeals of various kinds . . . once formed part of the judicial system of almost every nation, whether of the east or west. Trial by combat, on the contrary, in which the litigants were instruments in the appeal as well as subjects of it, had no such universality').

45 James Q. Whitman *The origins of reasonable doubt: Theological roots of the criminal trial* (New Haven: Yale University Press, 2008) 59.

46 Wigmore *A kaleidoscope of justice: Containing authentic accounts of trial scenes from all times and climes*, 5; Hock-Lai Ho "The legitimacy of medieval proof" (2004) 19(2) *Journal of Law and Religion* 259 at 261; Langbein et al *History of the common law: The development of Anglo-American legal institutions*, 44 ('Two main varieties were used in England; hot iron and cold water'); Whitman *The origins of reasonable doubt: Theological roots of the criminal trial*, 53 ('The most common forms used in Europe were the ordeal of the hot iron . . . and the ordeal of the cold water').

47 Wigmore *A kaleidoscope of justice: Containing authentic accounts of trial scenes from all times and climes*, 7 and 10; Langbein et al *History of the common law: The development of Anglo-American legal institutions*, 44.

48 Wigmore *A kaleidoscope of justice: Containing authentic accounts of trial scenes from all times and climes*, 246–247.

49 Wigmore *A kaleidoscope of justice: Containing authentic accounts of trial scenes from all times and climes*, 248–250.

50 Wigmore *A kaleidoscope of justice: Containing authentic accounts of trial scenes from all times and climes*, 250.

caldaria),[51] the fire ordeal required the proband to place his bare feet into an open wood fire.[52] In either case, the proband's skin showing any signs of infection, it was believed, meant that the gods had adjudged him guilty.[53] The fourth common type of ordeal involved a proband having his hands and feet bound with cords and lowered slowly into a river to see if he will drown (*judicium acquae frigidae*).[54] The drowning of the proband, it was believed, meant that the divine river-god had adjudged the proband guilty.[55] For example, the river ordeal was prescribed for the settlement of disputes about spousal accusations of adultery in ancient Sumeria[56] (ca. 2100 BCE) and for witchcraft-related matters under the Code of Hammurabi in ancient Babylon[57] (ca. 1750 BCE).

The charge towards the demise of ordeals was led principally by the European Church reformers of late antiquity. They criticised ordeals as 'tempting God' to induce a miracle or to give judgement at the beck and call of His subjects.[58] Secondly, they were known as 'judgements of blood' because it was believed that ordeals polluted the presiding officers, the witnesses and everybody else involved in an ordeal with the blood of the proband.[59] This culminated in canon 18 of the Fourth Lateran Council prohibiting all clerics from participating in 'judgements of blood.'[60]

51 Wigmore *A kaleidoscope of justice: Containing authentic accounts of trial scenes from all times and climes*, 10–11.

52 Wigmore *A kaleidoscope of justice: Containing authentic accounts of trial scenes from all times and climes*, 12.

53 Langbein et al *History of the common law: The development of Anglo-American legal institutions*, 45.

54 Langbein et al *History of the common law: The development of Anglo-American legal institutions*, 15; May *Ancient legal thought: Equity, justice and humaneness from Hammurabi and the pharaohs to Justinian and the Talmud*, 52 ('The Babylonian term for the river-god ordeal is *hursan*, and this test of truth was employed predominantly in property disputes as well as in the various assault cases we have been examining').

55 John Sassoon *Ancient laws and modern problems: The balance between justice and a legal system* (Bristol: Intellect, 2005) 53; May *Ancient legal thought: Equity, justice and humaneness from Hammurabi and the pharaohs to Justinian and the Talmud*, 47 ('The divine river-god ordeal seems to have been used in the most serious cases (perhaps corresponding to our criminal cases – although the categories of civil and criminal are not yet clearly separated), where getting to the truth was the most pressing').

56 See Law #14 of the (Ur)-Laws of Ur-Namma, as cited in Roth *Law collections from Mesopotamia and Asia Minor*, 18; May *Ancient legal thought: Equity, justice and humaneness from Hammurabi and the pharaohs to Justinian and the Talmud*, 45 ('[T]he river-god ordeal can be traced at least to these laws that were promulgated in approximately 2100 BCE').

57 Law #2 of the Code of Hammurabi, as cited in Roth *Law collections from Mesopotamia and Asia Minor*, 81. See also Law #24 of the ancient Assyrian laws of ca. 1076 BCE (at 161–162).

58 Whitman *The origins of reasonable doubt: Theological roots of the criminal trial*, 53.

59 Whitman *The origins of reasonable doubt: Theological roots of the criminal trial*, 53.

60 Fourth Lateran Council, Canon 18, cited in Henry J. Schroeder *Disciplinary decrees of the general councils, text, translation, and commentary* (St. Louis: B. Herder Book Co., 1937) 258.

Ordeals from antiquity would be resorted to as an alternative to sworn witness statements.[61] Sworn witness statements were in fact the standard mode of proof with ordeals being resorted to exceptionally where there was some deficiency with the testimony.[62] As Bartlett describes it, testimony given under oath was the 'corner-stone' of adjudication during this period.[63] A witness could testify orally or in writing.[64] For example, the practice in ancient Greece from the 370s BCE onwards was for witnesses to reduce their statements to writing and to have them read aloud in court by an officer of the court.[65] Once these statements were read, the only role of the witness would then be simply to confirm the contents thereof.[66] The epistemic warrant of sworn witness statements from antiquity rested on three pillars: the oath, the social status of a witness and the compurgation procedure.[67] The swearing of a witness upon designated holy relics was a form of confronting the gods in order to cleanse themselves of suspicion.[68] It was this religious connection to the gods that was believed to guarantee the epistemic warrant of witness testimony. In ancient Rome, for example, it was believed that a witness that gave false testimony attracted the harsh punishment of the gods.[69] A witness from ancient Ghana would swear that 'I shall speak what I know to be true, if I do not thus speak truthfully, may the gods kill me!'[70] The swearing of witnesses in the name of the gods, under threat of punishment, was also a practice in ancient Mesopotamia.[71] Secondly, the social status of a witness also contributed towards the probative value of their testimony.[72] It was believed that trustworthy statements could only be made by esteemed individuals with a 'relatively high social standing and unimpeached reputation,' whereas witnesses that were not oath worthy

61 Robert Bartlett *Trial by fire and water: The medieval judicial ordeal* (Oxford: Oxford University Press, 1986) 27.
62 Bartlett *Trial by fire and water: The medieval judicial ordeal*, 28.
63 Bartlett *Trial by fire and water: The medieval judicial ordeal*, 30.
64 Bartlett *Trial by fire and water: The medieval judicial ordeal*, 27.
65 David Mirhady "Arguments," in *A cultural history of law: In antiquity*, ed. Julen Extabe (London: Bloomsbury, 2019) 91 at 92–93; Gerhard Thür "The role of the witness in Athenian law," in *The Cambridge companion to ancient Greek law*, eds. Michael Gagarin and David Cohen (New York: Cambridge University Press, 2005) 146 at 148.
66 Todd "Law and oratory at Athens" 107.
67 Sanjeev Anand "The origins, early history and evolution of the English criminal trial jury" (2005) 43(2) *Alberta Law Review* 407 at 409.
68 Whitman *The origins of reasonable doubt: Theological roots of the criminal trial*, 62.
69 May *Ancient legal thought: Equity, justice and humaneness from Hammurabi and the pharaohs to Justinian and the Talmud*, 421.
70 Wigmore *A kaleidoscope of justice: Containing authentic accounts of trial scenes from all times and climes*, 422.
71 May *Ancient legal thought: Equity, justice and humaneness from Hammurabi and the pharaohs to Justinian and the Talmud*, 48.
72 Whitman *The origins of reasonable doubt: Theological roots of the criminal trial*, 62.

were compelled to resort to ordeals to prove their cases.[73] Oath-worthy witnesses of the early medieval period could even purge themselves by taking a 'purgative oath' that was the opposite of a confession, but equally dispositive of the dispute concerned.[74] The third pillar of epistemic warrant for witness testimony was the process of compurgation in terms of which a witness testified with the backing of a selection of his fellow oath-helpers or compurgators (variously known in medieval Europe as *juratores, conjuratores, sacramentales, collaundantes* or *compurgatores*).[75] The probative value of these compurgators paradoxically derived not from their witnessing of the facts that are in dispute, but from their 'strong familial ties' to the one of the litigants.[76] This is typical of small ancient communities where any knowledge about public incidents would not escape the eyes and ears of local relatives, friends and neighbours.[77]

The third method of proof from antiquity (in addition to ordeals and sworn testimony) originated in ancient Greece. The Greeks deployed rhetorical speeches to prove disputed facts in courts of law.[78] The term *rhêtor*, from which the word 'rhetoric' is derived, was used in the sixth and fifth centuries BCE to designate a politician who frequently made speeches in the Athenian assembly.[79] Aristotle traces the art of rhetoric to two Sicilians, Corax and his student Tisias, from Syracuse at around 467 BCE.[80] Corax, along with other Sophists, developed their teaching material from observing rhetorical speeches in several trials.[81] Rhetorical speeches within the forensic context were known

73 Whitman *The origins of reasonable doubt: Theological roots of the criminal trial*, 62–63; Bartlett *Trial by fire and water: The medieval judicial ordeal*, 27.
74 Whitman *The origins of reasonable doubt: Theological roots of the criminal trial*, 62.
75 Renata L. Mack *Comparative criminal procedure: History, processes and case studies* 2nd ed (New York: William S. Hein & Co, 2017) 6.
76 Mack *Comparative criminal procedure: History, processes and case studies*, 5.
77 Lerner *The jury: A very short introduction*, 14 ('Under these conditions, the king and his judges could expect that jurors would be self-informing'); Richard W. Lariviere *The Nāradasmṛti* (New Delhi: Motilal Banarsidass Publishers, 2003) 316 (on the requirement that 'witnesses must come from good families, be upright, pure of birth, deed and purpose, no less than three in number, unimpeachable, unsullied and intelligent' in ancient India).
78 William Twining "Goodbye to Lewis Elliot: The academic lawyer as scholar" (1980) 15 *Journal of the Society of Public Teachers of Law* 2 at 13; Solomon E. Salako *Evidence, proof and justice: Legal philosophy and the provable in English courts* (Ventus Publishing Apk, 2010) 9; William Twining "The Boston symposium: A comment" (1986) 66(3) *Boston University Law Review* 391 at 395–396; Cicero M.T. *De Oratore* (translated into English by E.W. Sutton and H. Rackham) (Cambridge: Harvard University Press, 1942) 191.
79 James D. Williams *An introduction to classical rhetoric: Essential readings* (Chichester: Wiley-Blackwell, 2009) 10.
80 Aristotle "Rhetoric and poetics," in *The complete works of Aristotle*, ed. Jonathan Barnes vol II (Princeton: Princeton University Press) 2430 at 2430; George A. Kennedy *A new history of classical rhetoric* (Princeton: Princeton University Press, 1994) 3.
81 Williams *An introduction to classical rhetoric: Essential readings*, 10.

as 'logography,'[82] and some of the classical logographers that Corax might have observed in forensic trials include Antiphon, Andocides, Lysias, Isocrates, Isaeus, Aeschines, Lycurgus, Demosthenes, Hyoerides and Dinarchus.[83] Greek adjudicative process was fluid, flexible and unconstrained by fixed rules about the range and types of information that may be submitted in popular court speeches.[84] The definition of the elements of a crime, rules about what types of evidence would be permitted or excluded, and the prescription of rules or standards of adjudication were simply absent in ancient Greek trial process.[85] As a result, evidential arguments traversed multiple areas, including 'law, politics, ideology, and the litigants' style and personality,'[86] and the types of evidence adduced ranged from lengthy rhetorical speeches from hired logographers to litigants even bringing weeping children for rhetorical effect.[87]

Rhetorical speeches were categorised by Aristotle into three genres: *ethos, pathos* and *logos*.[88] These three forms focused, respectively, on the personal character of the speaker,[89] the emotions of the audience[90] and the textual content of a speech.[91] Consistent with these three forms, the adjudicative aims of forensic oratory speeches was understood to be *probarem, delectare* and *flectere* (to prove, to delight and to persuade).[92] Although it began to wane after Greece was conquered after almost six decades of war with Rome, starting with the war against Macedonia in 200 BCE and culminating with the fall of Corinth in 147 BCE,[93] rhetoric continued to be studied and used in forensic courts in the Roman empire.[94]

82 David Mirhady "Arguments," in *A cultural history of law: In antiquity*, ed. Julen Extabe (London: Bloomsbury, 2019) 91 at 91.

83 Stephen C. Todd "Law and oratory at Athens," in *The Cambridge companion to ancient Greek law*, eds. Michael Gagarin and David Cohen (New York: Cambridge University Press, 2005) 97 at 99.

84 Adriaan Lanni "Relevance in Athenian courts," in *The Cambridge companion to ancient Greek law*, eds. Michael Gagarin and David Cohen (New York: Cambridge University Press, 2005) 112 at 113.

85 Lerner *The jury: A very short introduction*, 7–8. According to Lerner, '[t]he Athenian idea was that a wrong was whatever most people at the time thought it was' (at 9).

86 Harvey Yunis "The rhetoric of law in fourth-century Athens," in *The Cambridge companion to ancient Greek law*, eds. Michael Gagarin and David Cohen (New York: Cambridge University Press, 2005) 191 at 196.

87 Lerner *The jury: A very short introduction*, 7.

88 Aristotle "Rhetoric," in *The complete works of Aristotle*, ed. Jonathan Barnes vol II Book I (Princeton: Princeton University Press) 2152 at 2155, 1356a2–4; Williams *An introduction to classical rhetoric: Essential readings*, 36 (on Aristotle's *ethos, pathos and logos*).

89 Aristotle "Rhetoric," 2155, 1356a5.

90 Aristotle "Rhetoric," 2155, 1356a13–16.

91 Aristotle "Rhetoric," 2155, 1356a20.

92 Williams *An introduction to classical rhetoric: Essential readings*, 296.

93 John Briscoe "Rome and the class struggle in the Greek states 200–146 B.C." (1967) 36 *Past & Present* 3 at 3–4.

94 Williams *An introduction to classical rhetoric: Essential readings*, 296–297.

4.3 Medieval Period

The very long period from the thirteenth up until the seventeenth centuries is one in which a great number of methods of proof were deployed in various ways by communities around the world,[95] but two of these rose to prominence during this period. The focus of this section of the chapter will be on trial by battle and confessions under the Roman-canon system of proof. A trial by battle was a judicial duel between two litigants, or their proxies, in terms of which each engaged in physical combat to determine the verdict of the trial.[96] A confession, on the other hand, is the oral or written acknowledgement by a litigant of a criminal charge.[97] Confessions typically are unequivocal admissions of all the elements of a crime in the form: 'I admit that I murdered (intentionally and unlawfully) my spouse.'[98] Whereas confessions have been recognised and deployed in judicial proceedings since time immemorial,[99] trials by battle are traceable back to the sixth century in central Europe.[100] Judicial battle was unknown to most ancient societies, including Egypt, Rome, Greece and Mesopotamia, outside of Germania (western Europe) and its barbarian invaders from central Europe.[101] Confessions, by contrast, are more universal and their prevalence in judicial trials dates much further back. For example,

95 See Thayer "A preliminary treatise on evidence at common law," 8 and 16–46.

96 Neilson "Trial by combat," 1–3; Mack *Comparative criminal procedure: History, processes and case studies*, at 1 ('This ancient ritual seems then a natural starting point for exploring the origins of the adversarial system').

97 John H. Wigmore *Evidence in trials at common law* vol 3 (revised by James H. Chadbourn) (Boston: Little Brown and Company, 1970) 308; James F. Stephen *A digest on the law of evidence* 4th ed (London: Macmillan and Co., 1887) article 21; Lawrence S. Wrightsman and Saul M. Kassin *Confessions in the courtroom* (Newbury Park: SAGE, 1993) 3–4; Saul M. Kassin and Gisil H. Gudjohnsson "The psychology of confessions" (2004) 5(2) *Psychological Science in the Public Interest* 33 at 35. See also Joseph T. McCann "A conceptual framework for identifying various types of confessions" (1998) 16(4) *Behavioural Sciences & the Law* 391.

98 David Wolchover and Anthony Heaton-Armstrong *Wolchover and Heaton on confession evidence* (London: Sweet & Maxwell, 1996) 36; Peter Mirfield *Silence and improperly obtained evidence* (New York: Oxford University Press, 1997) 52–53 (a confession as any statement that is wholly or partially adverse to its maker); Susan Easton *Silence and confessions: The suspect as the source of evidence* (Basingstoke: Palgrave Macmillan, 2014) 144.

99 Kassin and Gudjohnsson "The psychology of confessions," 35.

100 Neilson "Trial by combat," 3; Edward L. Rubin "Trial by battle – Trial by argument" (2003) 56(2) *Arkansas Law Review* 261 at 264–265; Whitman *The origins of reasonable doubt: Theological roots of the criminal trial*, 53 ('Trial by battle is the earliest form of the "judgment of God" that is widely attested in Europe, dating back to the very early Middle Ages'); Bartlett *Trial by fire and water: The medieval judicial ordeal*, 103 ('[T]rial by battle is found in the early law codes of many Germanic peoples – the Burgundians, Lombards, Alamanni, Bavarians, Thuringians, Frisians, and Saxons. Moreover, although not mentioned in the most ancient version of Salic Law, battle was certainly employed as a proof by the Franks in the sixth century'); Wigmore *A kaleidoscope of justice: Containing authentic accounts of trial scenes from all times and climes*, 159 (on the prevalence of trials by battle in medieval Russia).

101 Neilson "Trial by combat," 1–3.

confessions were routinely recorded in the preliminary stage of Roman[102] and Babylonian[103] trials in the fifth and sixth centuries BCE, respectively. Moreover, the ancient Greeks also recognised confessions under torture (*basanoi*) as one of the five 'non-artistic proofs' (*atechnoi pisteis*).[104] However, confessions rose in prominence particularly during the formation of the Roman-canon system of proof in the twelfth and thirteenth centuries.[105] This rise in significance was driven and championed by the Catholic Church,[106] which transformed non-evidential penitential confessions that focused on the 'curing of souls' to the forensic method of proof that would reign all across Europe for the next four centuries.[107] Having grown its influence over several centuries, the Church attained various legislative, judicial and administrative functions in several territories across medieval Europe.[108]

Before proceedings to discuss the probative value of judicial battles and confessions under the Roman-canon system of proof, a brief sketch of the broader historiographic context within which these two methods of proof prevailed is useful to explicate the nature and evolution of these two institutions. The medieval period was marked by significant socio-political and legal change in many parts of the world. It is the period identified by Renaissance scholars as being a *medium aevum* between antiquity and modernity.[109] As such, the medieval period is characterised by widespread social, political, legal and cultural change since the polytheism of antiquity. From the perspective of western Europe, the change commences with the disintegration of ancient Mediterranean civilisations, as precipitated by the expansion of Islam in southern Arabia in 711 CE; the European transition from Greco-Roman domination to the amalgam of

102 James K. Gaynor "Law through the ages" (1972) 14(2) *South Texas Law Journal* 147 at 160.

103 Shalom E. Holtz *Neo-Babylonian trial records* (Atlanta: Society of Biblical Literature, 2014) 9–11.

104 Gerhard Thür "The role of the witness in Athenian Law," in *The Cambridge companion to ancient Greek law*, eds. Michael Gagarin and David Cohen (New York: Cambridge University Press, 2005) 146 at 146.

105 Ian Bryan *Interrogation and confession: A study of progress process and practice* (Aldershot: Ashgate, 1997) 11; Paul Roberts *Roberts & Zuckerman's Criminal Evidence* 3rd ed (Oxford: Oxford University Press, 2022) 581 ('The confession is a staple of the western literary canon, from the Confessions of Augustine, Montaigne, Rousseau, and De Quincey to . . . Confessions of a Window Cleaner and Confessions of a Shopaholic').

106 Mirjan R. Damaška *Evaluation of evidence: Premodern and modern approaches* (Cambridge: Cambridge University Press, 2019) 46.

107 John T. McNeill *A history of the cure of souls* (New York: Harper, 1951) vii and 288–289.

108 Heikki Pihlajamäki and Mia Korpiola "Medieval canon law: The origins of modern criminal law," in *The Oxford handbook of criminal law*, eds. Markus D. Dubber and Tatjana Hörnle (Oxford: Oxford University Press, 2014) 201 at 201–202; John C. Wei and Anders Winroth "Medieval canon law: Introduction," in *The Cambridge history of medieval canon law*, eds. Anders Winroth and John C. Wei (New York: Cambridge University Press, 2022) 1 at 3; Damaška *Evaluation of evidence: Premodern and modern approaches*, 25.

109 Julia M.H. Smith "Introduction: Regarding medievalists – Contexts and approaches," in *Companion to historiography*, ed. Michael Bentley (London: Routledge, 1997) 98.

Germanic, Celtic, Judaeo-Christian and Greco-Roman communities in the eastern and western parts of the Mediterranean; and the subsequent expansion of Europe into colonial territories in the Global South, such as Africa.[110] A related transition from the polytheism of ordeals and oaths in antiquity towards the centring of people (witnesses, legal representatives and adjudicators) as prominent sources, adducers and evaluators of evidence was also underway.[111] Roman-canonical confessions and judicial battles were early manifestations of this transition that placed a comparatively heavier load of the fate of trials on the shoulders of litigants and court officials than on anything else. This transition was facilitated, among others, by the emergence of the development and study of legal doctrine through the canonical collections written by John Gratian and his pupils in Bologna during the twelfth century,[112] as well as the establishment of specialised courts during the thirteenth century.[113] For example, the French monarch Louis IX (1226–1270) established the *Parlement de Paris*, which had jurisdiction to hear cases submitted to royal justice, in the middle of the thirteenth century;[114] the *Castile the Tribunal de Corte* (1274) and the *Real Audiencia de Aragón* (1274) were established and staffed with trained officials in Spain;[115] and the General Eyre (ca. 1176), the King's Court at Westminster (ca. 1176), the Common Bench (1190s) and the King's Bench (1230s) were established in England during the twelfth and thirteenth centuries.[116] As a result, the adjudicators that staffed these courts also gradually transitioned from lay feudal administrators, landowners, bishops and abbots[117] towards either professional judges who were trained under the Roman-canon system or lay juries.[118]

110 Lesaffer *European legal history: A cultural and political perspective*, 124; Roland Oliver and Anthony Atmore *Medieval Africa, 1250–1800* (Cambridge: Cambridge University Press, 2001) 228.

111 David Schum *Evidential foundations of probabilistic reasoning* (Evanston, IL: Northwestern University Press, 1994) 201; Susan Reynolds "Medieval law," in *The medieval world*, eds. Peter Linehan et al 2nd ed (London: Routledge, 2018) 568 at 569; Wigmore *A kaleidoscope of justice: Containing authentic accounts of trial scenes from all times and climes*, 729 ('The disappearance of the ordeals was due to the development of rationalism and the perceived inefficiency of ordeals').

112 Peter D. Clarke "Western canon law in the central and later middle ages," in *The Oxford handbook of European legal history*, eds. Heikki Pihlajamäki et al (Oxford: Oxford University Press, 2018) 265 at 266; Reynolds "Medieval law," 573. Gratian wrote the *Concordia discordantium canonum* ('Harmony of Contradictory Law'), which later came to be known as *Decretum Gratiani* ('Gratian's Decree') at around 1140 CE.

113 Wauters and de Benito *The history of law in Europe: An introduction*, 70–71.

114 Wauters and de Benito *The history of law in Europe: An introduction*, 70.

115 Wauters and de Benito *The history of law in Europe: An introduction*, 71.

116 Paul Brand "Judges and judging 1176–1307," in *Judges and judging in the history of the common law and civil law: From antiquity to modern times*, eds. Paul Brand and Joshua Getzler (Cambridge: Cambridge University Press, 2012) 3 at 4–7,

117 Lesaffer *European legal history: A cultural and political perspective*, 134; Arthur T. Von Mehren and James R. Gordley *The civil law system: An introduction to the comparative study of law* 2nd ed (Boston: Little Brown & Company, 1977) 4.

118 Langbein et al *History of the common law: The development of Anglo-American legal institutions*, 43; Cliff Roberson and Dilip K. Das *An introduction to comparative legal models of criminal justice* 2nd ed (Boca Raton: CRC Press, 2016) 36.

Before it eventually fell into disuse in the thirteenth and fourteenth centuries, the probative value of medieval judicial battle rested on three religious, status-based and punitive pillars. Firstly, the outcome of a trial by battle was believed to be a 'judgement of God' that punished the unsuccessful litigant while preserving the successful party.[119] It was for this reason that judicial battles were fought till the death of one of the litigants; that is, in order to showcase God's clearest and harshest judgement. Secondly, the probative value of trials by battle was justified on the basis of the status of a litigant. As it was in antiquity, the evidence of a litigant who had a higher social status generally was weighted higher than that of persons outside of this social class. The exclusion of women, minors, the elderly or maimed individuals from participating in judicial battles was a reflection of this general social belief.[120] Moreover, clerics, royalists and Jews, whose social status at the time rose alongside the rise of the Catholic Church in Europe, were entitled to hire and offer champions to battle on their behalf.[121] An example of this was when Queen Gundeberga, who was the wife of Lombard King Arioald (626–636), offered a champion to battle in her defence against treason charges in medieval Italy.[122] Thirdly, the probative weight of judicial duels was justified on deterrence grounds: that the fatal outcome of a battle (e.g. the unsuccessful litigant being castrated or having their eyes gouged out)[123] deterred any of the litigants from giving false testimony. For example, in an Anglo-Saxon case of the year 1219, an unsuccessful litigant, Simon of Duffield, who had been accused of breaking into the complainant's house and assaulting his daughter Hawisa, was hanged in front of his son and two daughters after losing a judicial battle.[124]

Confessions (*notoria*) under the Roman-canon system proof were regarded as 'the queen of proofs' (*regina probationum*[125] or *la reine des preuves*)[126] and thus placed at the very top of a formal hierarchy of proofs. As Figure 4.1 shows, the hierarchy consisted of two eyewitnesses (full proof); a single eyewitness (half proof); and circumstantial evidence at the very bottom.[127]

119 Whitman *The origins of reasonable doubt: Theological roots of the criminal trial*, 53; Ho "The legitimacy of medieval proof," 261; Lerner *The jury: A very short introduction*, 12; Bartlett *Trial by fire and water: The medieval judicial ordeal*, 115–116.

120 Bartlett *Trial by fire and water: The medieval judicial ordeal*, 110–112; Neilson "Trial by combat," 7–8 and 36–39; Whitman *The origins of reasonable doubt: Theological roots of the criminal trial*, 53; Langbein et al *History of the common law: The development of Anglo-American legal institutions*, 32 (most prosecutions in among Germanic tribes were brought by women who did not risk being compelled into battles).

121 Bartlett *Trial by fire and water: The medieval judicial ordeal*, 112.

122 Bartlett *Trial by fire and water: The medieval judicial ordeal*, 115.

123 Bartlett *Trial by fire and water: The medieval judicial ordeal*, 107.

124 Langbein et al *History of the common law: The development of Anglo-American legal institutions*, 30.

125 Damaška *Evaluation of evidence: Premodern and modern approaches*, 44.

126 Roberts *Roberts & Zuckerman's criminal evidence*, 581.

127 Damaška *Evaluation of evidence: Premodern and modern approaches*, 40; John H. Langbein *Torture and the law of proof: Europe and England in the ancien régime* (Chicago: University of Chicago Press, 1977) 4.

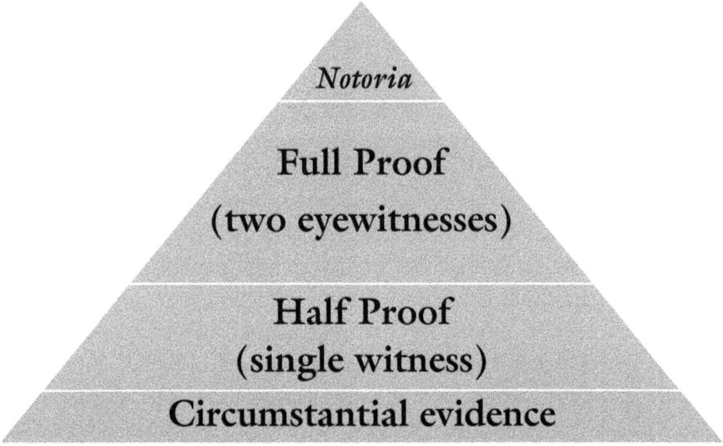

Figure 4.1 The hierarchy of proofs under the Roman-canon system

The esteemed ranking of confessions was also offered as a justification for the otherwise coercive methods of obtaining them. If litigants were not entrapped,[128] for example by being misled or deceived by investigators or by being additionally charged with a 'suspicion of heresy,'[129] they were tortured (*confessionem extorqueri*) using devices such as strappados, racks, thumbscrews and legscrews.[130] The high ranking of confessions on this hierarchy was explained by three reasons. The first of these rested on the unlikelihood that an innocent litigant would voluntarily make a statement that incriminates him or her, unless it is true.[131] Secondly, confessions gave cleric adjudicators, who were concerned with their own moral turpitude, moral comfort and a measure of protection against anybody that wanted to hold them accountable for their conviction and sentencing of adjudicators.[132] The third reason was that the relative limitations of investigative methods and the overall availability of evidence during the medieval period made dispute pieces of evidence such as confessions and eyewitness testimony rare and valuable.[133] Fourthly, the

128 Henry C. Lea *A history of the inquisition of the middle ages* vol I (London: Macmillan & Co., 1922) 408 and 433.

129 Mack *Comparative criminal procedure: History, processes and case studies*, 11.

130 Whitman *The origins of reasonable doubt: Theological roots of the criminal trial*, 61; Langbein *Torture and the law of proof: Europe and England in the ancien régime*, 15.

131 Thomas Starkie *A practical treatise of the law of evidence* 8th ed (Philadelphia: T. & J.W. Johnson & Co., 1860) 71.

132 Whitman *The origins of reasonable doubt: Theological roots of the criminal trial*, 11 ('[O]ur ancestors dreaded . . . the moral and spiritual responsibilities of judgment'); Damaška *Evaluation of evidence: Premodern and modern approaches*, 46.

133 Damaška *Evaluation of evidence: Premodern and modern approaches*, 45–46; Whitman *The origins of reasonable doubt: Theological roots of the criminal trial*, 11 ('In general, trustworthy

status of individual declarants once again played a role in the assessment of the probative value of confessions. Only litigants from upper social classes were permitted to give confessions, whereas minors, pregnant women, insane persons and the elderly were precluded.[134]

Confessions under the Roman-canon system were eventually abolished all across Europe in the eighteenth century.[135] One of the main reasons for this was that it was later realised in late medieval societies that coerced confessions were simply unreliable.[136] Furthermore, the emergence of the right to silence, among other human rights, in the seventeenth century also supported the move towards abolition.[137] Judicial battles, on the other hand, were in decline much earlier in the fifteenth century on account of the influence of the Church.[138] Members of the Church argued that judicial duels were susceptible to manipulation and unjust outcomes (e.g. where skilled fighters escape punishment for their crimes with impunity because nobody would dare challenge them to a battle),[139] and the second and fourth Lateran Councils consequentially banned trials by battle.[140]

---

oral declarations – whether accusations, witness testimony, confessions or oaths – were hard to come by'); Langbein *Torture and the law of proof: Europe and England in the ancien régime*, 8 ('The two-eyewitness rule left the Roman-canon system dependent upon the use of torture').

134 Damaška *Evaluation of evidence: Premodern and modern approaches*, 46. Cf. Langbein *Torture and the law of proof: Europe and England in the ancien régime*, 8 ('The status-based exemptions were widely disfavoured in the *ancien régime*. Neither in the German Carolina nor in French practice of the sixteenth and later centuries are they recognised').

135 See Langbein *Torture and the law of proof: Europe and England in the ancien régime*, 10; John H. Langbein "The legal history of torture," in *Torture: A collection*, ed. Sanford Levinson (New York: Oxford University Press, 2004) 93 at 95 ('Early in the nineteenth century, abolition reached the last corners of the Continent.').

136 Mirfield "Silence and improperly obtained evidence," 10; Langbein "The legal history of torture," 95 ('Alas, because torture tests endurance rather than veracity, innocent persons might (as one sixteenth-century handbook on criminal procedure warned) yield to "the pain and torment and confess things that they never did." For a variety of reasons, the safeguards never proved adequate.').

137 Hannah Quirk *The rise and fall of the right to silence* (New York: Routledge, 2017) 11; Wigmore *Evidence in trials at common law* vol 3 (revised by James H. Chadbourn) 286 ('The development of the principle of safeguarding the use of confessions was influenced . . . by the spirit of consideration for accused persons, which grew up during the latter half of the 1700s and the first part of the 1800s. It was generated as a natural reaction from the harshness and unjust severity prevailing in penal administration up to that time. We should consequently not expect to find the principle recognised outside the scope of criminal prosecutions').

138 Bartlett *Trial by fire and water: The medieval judicial ordeal*, 122 ('The "last judicial duel fought on English soil" took place in 1492').

139 Lerner *The jury: A very short introduction*, 12–13.

140 See Canon 14 of the Second Lateran Council and Canon 18 of the Fourth Lateran Council, cited in Henry J. Schroeder *Disciplinary decrees of the general councils, text, translation, and commentary* (St. Louis: B. Herder Book Co., 1937) 258.

4.4 The Rationalist Tradition

The transformation from the medieval era to the period of the Rationalist tradition represents the longest and most significant evolution of forensic methods of proof. The transition substituted *vox dei* (the voice of God) with *vox populi* (the voice of the people).[141] Human beings of this era had agency and were going to be held accountable for their participation in criminal adjudication. Their principal methodological tool for deciding disputes was their *reason*.[142] Unlike adjudicators of antiquity and the medieval period, Rationalist adjudicators would use their own reasoning as their method and justification for deciding disputes. Although litigants may permissibly differ with their reasons, but 'there is always a reason' given, as Wigmore says.[143] This reason is also generally humanly accessible, and not exclusively the privy of a sovereign ruler, cleric or deity. The popular sentiment was that 'the universe and nature could hold no secrets from the human mind' and that 'there were no mysteries or miracles' to be had in criminal adjudication.[144] For the purposes of evidential proof, which is defined in this book as *the property of a disputed fact* (P_m) *being established inferentially* (P_p) *from an extant fact (evidence)* (P_{proc}),[145] reason plays three important roles that distinguish this particular period from antiquity and the medieval era. Firstly, the exercise of drawing inferences (P_p) is undertaken by human beings themselves, and not by a deity or formal (canonical) numeric system. According to Anderson et al:

> Inferential reasoning, analyzing and weighing evidence, forming judgments about what has happened in the past or what is likely to happen in

141 Whitman *The origins of reasonable doubt: Theological roots of the criminal trial*, 54.

142 Michael Freeman *Lloyd's introduction to jurisprudence* 9th ed (London: Sweet & Maxwell, 2014) 1533; Michael S. Pardo "Judicial proof, evidence and pragmatic meaning: Towards evidentiary holism" (2000) 95(1) *Northwestern University Law Review* 399 at 399 ('The trial has developed into a condition of a decent society, and we cannot overemphasise its importance'); Ian Dennis *The law of evidence* 6th ed (London: Sweet & Maxwell, 2017) 28 ('The term "reasoned arguments" embodies the idea that the dispute is to be resolved within an institutional framework governed by rationality. In other words, the adjudicator is expected to decide the dispute by the exercise of reason in determining the relevant issues of fact and law. Personal prejudice and irrelevant reasons would not be acceptable grounds for decision'). Lon Fuller "The forms and limits of adjudication" (1978) 92(2) *Harvard Law Review* 353 at 357 and 364 ('[P]articipation through reasoned argument loses its meaning if the arbiter of the dispute is inaccessible to reason because he is insane, has been bribed, or is hopelessly prejudiced').

143 Wigmore *The principles of judicial proof as given by logic, psychology and general experience and illustrated in judicial trials*, viii. See also Joëlle Vuille "Forensic science evidence in non-adversary criminal justice systems," in *Forensic science evidence and expert witness testimony: Reliability through reform*, eds. Paul Roberts and Michael Stockdale (Cheltenham: Elgar, 2018) 354 at 365.

144 Wauters and de Benito *The history of law in Europe: An introduction*, 121–122.

145 See Pamela-Jane Schwikkard and Tshepo B. Mosaka *Principles of evidence* 5th ed (Claremont: Juta, 2023) 607.

> the future are a necessary part of coping with the problems of everyday living. They are basic human skills that form part of ordinary practical reasoning.[146]

Secondly, the reasoned findings or outcomes of adjudication was grounded on established or proven extant (evidentiary) facts that are investigated using rational means. Rationality, by definition, consists of the holding of a belief (cognitive), the performance of an action (practical), or the evaluation of an artefact (evaluative), on the basis of a *cogent* reason.[147] Therefore, the adjudication of a dispute without reliance on cogent reasons justifying the drawing of inferences from the extant facts is antithetical to this era in the evolution of methods of proof. Thirdly, the disputed facts are usually defined and promulgated through a democratic legislative process that involves the participation of human beings, and not always by unilateral sovereign or clerical decree.

The terms 'Enlightenment' (*Lumières, Aufklärung, Ilustración, Illuminismo*),[148] 'modernity'[149] and the 'Age of Reason'[150] are common descriptors of the Rationalist period that spans roughly from the eighteenth century to the present day. Twining described the homogeneity of ideas in Anglo-American evidence scholarship from Geoffrey Gilbert (1754)[151] to John Henry Wigmore (1905)[152] as falling within a 'Rationalist Tradition.'[153] For Kant, the Enlightenment period represents humankind developing the historical maturity and courage to make decisions relying on their own reasoning capacity without outsourcing this task to a deity, cleric or sovereign.[154] According to Kant, 'the motto of enlightenment' is *Sapere aude!*

146 Anderson et al *Analysis of evidence*, xvi; Schum *Evidential foundations of probabilistic reasoning*.

147 Nicholas Rescher *Rationality: A philosophical inquiry into the nature and the rationale of reason* (Oxford: Clarendon Press, 1988) 2–3; Frederick Schauer "Giving reasons" (1995) 47(4) *Stanford Law Review* 633 at 634 ('[G]iving reasons . . . [is] the practice of engaging in the linguistic act of providing a reason to justify what we do or what we decide'). See also Ralph H. Johnson *Manifest rationality* (Mahwah: Lawrence Erlbaum Associates, 2000) 14 and 161–162; Harold I. Brown *Rationality* (London: Routledge, 1988) 63.

148 Wauters and de Benito *The history of law in Europe: An introduction*, 121.

149 Lesaffer *European legal history: A cultural and political perspective*, 444.

150 Herbert A. Simon *Reason in human affairs* (Stanford: Stanford University Press, 1983) 3.

151 Geoffrey Gilbert *The law of evidence* (New York: Garland Publishers, 1754).

152 John H. Wigmore *A treatise on the system of evidence in trials at common law* vols 1–4 (Boston: Little, Brown and Company, 1905).

153 William Twining *Theories of evidence: Bentham and Wigmore* (London: Weidenfeld & Nicolson, 1985) 16 and 185; William Twining *Rethinking evidence: Exploratory essays* (Evanston, IL: Northwestern University Press, 1994) 185; William Twining *Rethinking evidence: Exploratory essays* 2nd ed (Cambridge: Cambridge University Press, 2006) 77–78.

154 Immanuel Kant "What is enlightenment?" in (1784) vol 4 December edition *Berlin Monthly* 481 at 481–494, see James Schmidt's translation at: Immanuel Kant "What is enlightenment?" in *What is enlightenment? Eighteenth century answers and twentieth-century questions*, ed. James Schmidt (Berkeley: University of California Press, 1996) 58 at 58–64.

That is, think for yourself.[155] As a consequence of this, each human being is accorded the freedom to make decisions in accordance with their own inferential reasoning process without adopting *holus-bolus* the procedures or outcomes of another non-human entity.[156] It is a function of this popular belief that principles such as the contemporary civilian 'free proof' system[157] and the common law 'freedom of proof' for jurors.[158] Coupled with this freedom was the responsibility of being accountable for one's own decisions. Unlike their medieval counterparts, who managed their moral risk of judging (i.e. the risk of convicting an innocent person or acquitting somebody that is guilty) by appealing to an external deity,[159] adjudicators of the Rationalist Tradition appealed either to their own reasoning capacity or the legitimate authority conferred upon them by an authorised legislative body to account for their decisions.[160]

Against this background, this chapter will focus specifically on two kinds of examples of methods of proof that define the fundamental tenets and popular beliefs of the Rationalist Tradition. Firstly, this was era in which various technological and electronic methods of proof emerged, such as x-ray machines, truth serums, polygraphs and fMRI machines. Given the illustrative aims of this discussion, as well as the space limitations of this chapter, the focus will be primarily on polygraphs. The second method of proof is the rational argumentation deployed by trained contemporary lawyers. These two methods of proof were inspired by two eighteenth-century revolutions that warrant a brief discussion by way of background. The first of these was the industrial revolution that commenced in the 1780s with the invention of the steam engine and various textile manufacturing technologies and lasted until the middle of the nineteenth century.[161] In the context of law, scientific innovation was pioneered in the nineteenth century by criminologists such as Hans Gross and Casare Lombrosso, who worked on various technologies that purported to improve the

155 Kant "What is enlightenment?" 494.

156 Kant "What is enlightenment?" 481. See also Jonathan I. Israel *Radical enlightenment: Philosophy and the making of modernity 1650–1750* (New York: Oxford University Press, 2001).

157 Mirjan R. Damaška "Free proof and its detractors" (1995) 43(3) *The American Journal of Comparative Law* 343.

158 William Twining "Freedom of proof and the reform of criminal evidence" (1997) 31 *Israel Law Review* 439 at 448; L. Jonathan Cohen "Freedom of proof," in *Facts in law, archives for philosophy of law and social philosophy*, ed. William Twining, Beiheft No. 16 (Wiesbaden: Franz Steiner Verlag, 1983) 1 at 1.

159 Whitman *The origins of reasonable doubt: Theological roots of the criminal trial*, 11.

160 Langbein *Torture and the law of proof: Europe and England in the ancien régime*, 6. Cf. David M. Better *Faith, force and reason: An armchair history of the rule of law* (Toronto: University of Toronto Press, 2022) 235 ('The rule of law is an idea that has been around in one form of another for at least four thousand years . . . Rulers governing by law, being bound by the law, and doing justice through the law has been the mantra for at least the last twenty-five hundred years').

161 Lesaffer *European legal history: A cultural and political perspective*, 376.

accuracy of witness testimony.[162] For example, Lombrosso developed a pulse monitor to register the heartbeat of a criminal suspect under interrogation,[163] while Hans Gross founded the first criminology institute (*Kriminalmuseum der Uni Graz*) that pioneered the scientific study of crime, which is known today as criminalistics.[164] Other early examples include the admission of x-ray reports in criminal proceedings for purposes of drawing inferences about various disputed facts commencing in 1898,[165] Vittorio Benussi developing a method of observing and measuring respiratory changes from witnesses that he associated with deception in 1914[166] and William Marston pioneering a novel procedure of testing the veracity of witness testimony by measuring their systolic blood pressure over the left brachial artery in 1917.[167] Furthermore, a Texas obstetrician developed a truth serum that would be given to a witness

162 Eugene B. Block *Lie detectors: Their history and use* (New York: David McKay Company, 1977) 11–12.

163 Eloise Keeler *The lie detector man: The career and cases of Leonarde Keeler* (Boston: Telshare Publishing Inc., 1984) 3; Block *Lie detectors: Their history and use*, 11 ('Lombroso based his answers on changes or lack of changes in blood pressure and heart beat of his subjects while they underwent intensive examination'); Stan Abrams *The complete polygraph handbook* (Lexington: Lexington Books, 1989) 2 ('The scientific approach to detecting deception began in the work of Cesare Lombroso in 1895'); David T. Lykken *A tremor in the blood: Uses and abuses of the lie detector* 2nd ed (New York: Plenum Trade, 1998) 24 ('Lombroso, the 19th-century Italian criminologist, and his student, Mosso, adapted the plethysmograph, a device for measuring changes in the volume of a limb, to produce continuous records of pulse and blood pressure changes in their subjects very similar to those obtained on the "cardio" channel of a modern interrogation polygraph').

164 See Hans Gross "Hans Gross museum of criminology," University of Graz website, available at: www.universitaetsmuseen.uni-graz.at (accessed: 7 October 2024).

165 Marshall Houts "Team testing will bring the polygraph safely into court," in *Legal admissibility of the polygraph*, ed. Normal Ansley (Springfield: Charles C. Thomas, 1975) 5 at 7. The adduction of evidence of magnetic resonance imaging and computed tomography scans would only be introduced later in the twentieth century; see Christine B. Lissitzyn and Marc W. Vallen *Forensic evidence in court: A case study approach* 2nd ed (Durham: Carolina Academic Press, 2018) 97. Moreover, the functional magnetic resource imaging (fMRI) technique is discussed at p. 100. See also Daniel D. Langleben et al "Telling truth from lie in individual subjects with fast event-related fMRI" (2005) 26 *Human Brain Mapping* 262 at 263 ('Several fMRI studies reported increased prefrontal and parietal activity during lie, with a subset reporting anterior cingulate cortex (ACC) activation or prolonged response time (RT) with lie'); Paul C. Giannelli *Scientific evidence* 6th ed vol 1 (New York: LexisNexis, 2020) 9–81.

166 Abrams *The complete polygraph handbook*, 2.

167 Abrams *The complete polygraph handbook*, 2; Curt R. Bartol and Anne M. Bartol *Introduction to forensic psychology: Research and applications* 5th ed (London: SAGE, 2019) 103 ('The first, crude lie-detection machine was invented by the psychologist William Marston . . . During its early beginnings in the United States, Marston's polygraph and others like it were used almost exclusively in criminal investigations'). Marston was a student of Harvard Psychology Professor, Hugo Münsterberg (1863–1916), who published Hugo Münsterberg *On the witness stand: Essays on psychology and crime* (New York: Doubleday, Page & Co., 1908) where he propounded the application of psychophysiological measurement techniques from experimental psychology to the forensic context (Gershon Ben-Shakhar and John J. Furedy

under questioning in the 1920s.[168] The measurement of the finger tremor and reaction time of criminal suspects under interrogation by a Soviet neuropsychologist called Alexander Luria in the 1930s was another significant example of technological innovation.[169] The first comprehensive publication summarising many of these technological methods of proof by a lawyer was Wigmore's *Principles of Judicial Proof* (1913), which was later renamed, for largely commercial reasons,[170] *The Science of Judicial Proof* in 1937.

Polygraphs, derived from the Greek words *poly* ('many') and *grapho* ('to write'),[171] are recording devices that accurately measure changes of different psychological parameters, including palm sweating, blood pressure and respiration.[172] This is done by a briefcase-sized machine that conducts measurements by attaching electric sensors to various parts of a litigant's or suspect's body and thereafter recording the measurements on a lengthy roll of paper using multiple digital pens.[173] The subject of a polygraph is placed under examination and subjected to a question-based test, while their physiological responses are measured and recorded.[174] The original sphygmomanometer (nicknamed

---

Theories and applications in detection of deception: A psychophysiological and international perspective (New York: Springer-Verlag, 1990) 3).

168 Block *Lie detectors: Their history and use*, 14; Giannelli *Scientific evidence*, 9–79 ('The so-called "truth serums" involve the use of drugs, such as scopolamine, sodium, amytal, sodium pentothal, and brevital sodium, that are central nervous system depressants. These drugs temporarily alter a person's psychological state in such a way as to "induce a relaxed state of mind in which the suspect becomes more talkative and has less emotional control."').

169 Lykken *A tremor in the blood: Uses and abuses of the lie detector*, 24. See Alexander Luria *The nature of human conflicts* (New York: Liveright Publishers, 1932).

170 Twining *Theories of evidence: Bentham and Wigmore*, viii and 119.

171 Adlert Vrij *Detecting lies and deceit: The psychology of lying and the implications for professional practice* (Chichester: John Wiley & Sons Ltd, 2000) 170; Giannelli *Scientific evidence*, 9–5 ('[T]he term "polygraph" simply means multiple writings').

172 Vrij *Detecting lies and deceit: The psychology of lying and the implications for professional practice*, 170.

173 Ewout H. Meijer and Peter J. Van Koppen "Lie detectors and the law: The use of the polygraph in Europe," in *Psychology and law: Bridging the gap*, ed. David Canter and Rita Žukauskienė (Aldershot: Ashgate, 2008) 31 at 32; Andrew Balmer *Lie detection and the law: Torture, technology and truth* (Abingdon: Routledge, 2018) 7 ('It usually comprises a heart rate monitor (to measure pulse), a pneumography (to measure respiration), an electric device (to measure perspiration, or "electrodermal response") and a sphygmomanometer (to measure blood pressure)'). Cf. Vrij *Detecting lies and deceit: The psychology of lying and the implications for professional practice*, 170 (In the typical use of the polygraph, four sensors are attached to the subject. Pneumatic tubes are stretched around the person's chest and stomach in order to measure changes in the depth and rate of breathing. A blood pressure cuff placed around the upper arm measures changes in blood pressure, and metal electrodes attached to the fingers measure palmar sweating).

174 Meijer and Van Koppen "Lie detectors and the law: The use of the polygraph in Europe," 32; Balmer *Lie detection and the law: Torture, technology and truth*, 7 ('The most frequently used technique for questioning subject is the Control Question Test (CQT)'). Cf. Petra van Kampen "Polygraphs in criminal justice systems: The effect of different legal cultures on the use of scientific evidence," in *Psychology and criminal justice: International review of*

'Shyggy'), which was the predecessor to the modern polygraph, was invented in 1921 by a graduate student named John Larson from the University of California, Berkeley.[175] Although rarely used for the purposes of adjudication, polygraphs are used in several countries, including Canada, Belgium, Japan, South Korea, Mexico, Pakistan, the Philippines and the United States, by police officers conducting criminal investigations.[176] Police officers in these jurisdictions use polygraphs mostly in the context of sexual offence cases.[177] However, the use of polygraphs in criminal investigations is by no means universal. In countries such as Spain, the Netherlands, the United Kingdom, Germany and Switzerland, the use of polygraphs is either prohibited or not part of common police investigative practices.[178] This sparse coverage of applications of polygraphs globally is partially on account of the controversies surrounding the epistemic credibility of this method of proof (investigation).[179] Firstly, while it is accepted that polygraphs are not 'lie detectors' in the strict sense of the phrase because they only detect physiological responses and not lies,[180] the connection between each physiological response to deception remains difficult to establish.[181] Put simply, there is 'no known physiological response or

---

theory and practice, eds. Janos Boros et al (Berlin: de Gruyter, 1998) 130 at 132–133. Vrij *Detecting lies and deceit: The psychology of lying and the implications for professional practice*, 173–174.

175 Keeler *The lie detector man: The career and cases of Leonarde Keeler*, 2; Block *Lie detectors: Their history and use*, 14, 15 ('Working together as a team, Vollmer, Larson and Keeler developed the version of the lie detector currently in use'); Ben-Shakhar and Furedy *Theories and applications in detection of deception: A psychophysiological and international perspective*, 2 (tracing psychophysiological methods of detecting guilt back to, among others: the Hindu practices of observing the physiological (facial vasodilation) changes of witnesses to determine guilt (ca. 900 BCE) and the heart monitoring practices of Alexander the Great's physician in the third century BCE); Lykken *A tremor in the blood: Uses and abuses of the lie detector*, 24 ('Marston not only invented modern lie detection but was among the first to appreciate its commercial possibilities').

176 Vrij *Detecting lies and deceit: The psychology of lying and the implications for professional practice*, 171.

177 Bartol and Bartol *Introduction to forensic psychology: Research and applications*, 106.

178 Meijer and Van Koppen "Lie detectors and the law: The use of the polygraph in Europe," 41–45; Petra van Kampen "Polygraphs in criminal justice systems: The effect of different legal cultures on the use of scientific evidence," in *Psychology and criminal justice: International review of theory and practice*, eds. Janos Boros et al (Berlin: de Gruyter, 1998) 130 at 146; Vrij *Detecting lies and deceit: The psychology of lying and the implications for professional practice*, 172.

179 van Kampen "Polygraphs in criminal justice systems: The effect of different legal cultures on the use of scientific evidence," 136.

180 Vrij *Detecting lies and deceit: The psychology of lying and the implications for professional practice*, 170.

181 van Kampen "Polygraphs in criminal justice systems: The effect of different legal cultures on the use of scientific evidence," 150; Giannelli *Scientific evidence*, 9–31 to 9–33 ('The principal argument against admissibility of polygraph evidence is lack of reliability'); Bartol and Bartol *Introduction to forensic psychology: Research and applications*, 105.

pattern of responses [that] is unique to deception.'[182] It is true that many of us experience an inner turmoil that generates a psychological response whenever we tell a lie, but Kleinmuntz and Szucko correctly point out that a similar response may be induced: 'when we are falsely accused of a crime, when we are anxious about having to defend ourselves against accusations, when we are questioned about sensitive topics – and, for that matter, when we are elated or otherwise emotionally stirred.'[183] Secondly, the introduction of countermeasures (e.g. through the taking of drugs, the biting of one's tongue, mental imagery, foot tensing, counting backwards or pressing one's toes against the floor) has the potential to alter a subject's physiological responses and thereby produce distorted results.[184] Thirdly, there are several immutable variables that could influence the result of the polygraph examination, including the number, frequency and form of questions; the cognitive capabilities of the examinee; the demeanour and bodily movements of the examiner, as observed by the examinee; and the ultimate interpretation of the results from the charts.[185]

The second revolution that precipitated forensic innovation in the context of the Rationalist Tradition emerged in France in the eighteenth century. The French Revolution was influenced principally by political frustrations towards the vagaries of feudalism, classism and royal absolutism under the ancien régime of Louis XVI (1774–1792).[186] It was further radicalised by the widespread starvation that was precipitated by the harsh winter and the bad harvest of 1788–1789.[187] The resulting civil unrest led to the infamous storming of the Bastille on 14 July 1789 and the capture and destruction of the Paris royal prison on 8 August 1789.[188] The revolution culminated in a coup d'etat and the crowing of Napoleon Bonaparte as the Emperor of France in 1804.[189] Napoleon's subsequent conquest of various territories, both in Europe and abroad, then widened the scope of influence of France's revolutionary reforms in the nineteenth and twentieth centuries.[190] Some of these reforms include Napoleon's codification of civil and criminal law (*Les Cinq Codes*), including the enactment of the *Code d'instruction criminelle* (1809)

182 *State of Connecticut v Porter* 241 Conn. 57, 698 A.2d 739 (1997) at 96.

183 Benjamin Kleinmuntz and Julian J. Szucko "On the fallibility of lie detection" (1983) 17(1) *Law & Society Review* 85 at 87.

184 Meijer and Van Koppen "Lie detectors and the law: The use of the polygraph in Europe," 35; Vrij *Detecting lies and deceit: The psychology of lying and the implications for professional practice*, 202.

185 van Kampen "Polygraphs in criminal justice systems: The effect of different legal cultures on the use of scientific evidence," 134; Lissitzyn and Vallen "Forensic evidence in court: A case study approach," 96 ('An examiner must use subjective judgment in interpreting the polygraph results. For this reason, most scientists would call polygraph "junk science."').

186 Lesaffer *European legal history: A cultural and political perspective*, 372.

187 Lesaffer *European legal history: A cultural and political perspective*, 405.

188 Lesaffer *European legal history: A cultural and political perspective*, 405.

189 Lesaffer *European legal history: A cultural and political perspective*, 411.

190 Lesaffer *European legal history: A cultural and political perspective*, 372.

and the *Code pénal* (1811);[191] the abolition of the death penalty, torture and corporal punishment;[192] and the adherence to the rule of law,[193] which includes the application of the principle of *nullum crimen, nulla poena sine lege* ('There may be no crime nor punishment without a previous law thereto appertaining').[194] Furthermore, it was also during this period that the transition began when judges gave reasoned decisions in criminal adjudication.[195] Reason-giving was particularly significant because it precipitated the second method of proof: rational argumentation, which is one of the hallmarks of the Rationalist Tradition.

Rational argumentation in the forensic context refers to the practice of professional lawyers and judges using logical reasons to justify their legal conclusions.[196] Argumentation, derived from the Latin verb *arguo*, which means 'to brighten' or 'to clarify,' denotes the proof or clarification of an ambiguity (e.g. a dispute) by advancing or relying on logical reasons.[197] According to Wigmore, forensic argumentation is the process of piecing together different pieces of evidence using the 'ordinary rules of logic and rhetoric.'[198] The use of arguments in the forensic context is not at all new or unique to the eighteenth-century Rationalist Tradition. For example, Roman and medieval lawyers were well known for their argumentative and oratory skill in secular and ecclesiastical courts. However, the claim here rather is that this method of proof matured and rose to prominence from the eighteenth century onwards. This claim will now be established with contrastive reference to the historical evolution of forensic proof.

The main factor that inhibited the flourishing of rational argumentation, in the form that it prevails today, during the antiquity and medieval periods was

191 Napoleon enacted five codes in total: the two already mentioned, the *Code Civile* (1804), the *Code de procédure civile* (1807) and the *Code de commerce* (1803); see Thomas Gergen "The reception of the Code Civil (Napoléonic Code) of 1804: An example of 'juridical migration'?" (2014) 1 *Journal of European History of Law* 26 at 27.

192 Wauters and de Benito *The history of law in Europe: An introduction*, 122–123.

193 Serge Dauchy "French law and its expansion in the early modern period," in *The Oxford handbook of European legal history*, eds. Heikki Pihlajamäki et al (Oxford: Oxford University Press, 2018) 760 at 777. See Charles-Louis Montesquieu *The spirit of laws* (translated by Thomas Nugent) (London: J. Nourse and P. Vaillant, 1750); John Locke *Two treatises of government* (London: Awnsham Churchill, 1690); Caesar Beccaria *On crimes and punishments* 5th ed (translated by Graeme R. Newman and Pietro Marongiu) (New Brunswick: Transaction Publishers, 2009) 22.

194 Wauters and de Benito *The history of law in Europe: An introduction*, 123.

195 John P. Dawson *The oracles of the law* (Ann Arbor: University of Michigan Law School, 1968) 380.

196 See Schauer "Giving reasons," 633–634.

197 Christian Kock "The reception of ancient rhetoric in modern argumentation theory and pedagogy," in *Brill's companion of the reception of ancient rhetoric*, eds. Sophia Papaioannou et al (Leiden: Brill, 2021) 489 at 489–490.

198 John H. Wigmore *Evidence in trials at common* vol 1 (revised by Peter Tillers) (Boston: Little Brown and Co., 1983) 6–7.

the lack or insufficiency of professionalisation of the legal profession. Firstly, the lack of professional training among lawyers and judges from antiquity meant that rational argumentation was not a feature of criminal adjudication.[199] For example, all of the participants of a criminal trial in ancient Greece – the litigants and adjudicators – were legal experts.[200] The same situation prevailed in Egypt and Mesopotamia.[201] Greek adjudicators (*dikastai*) decided cases by secret ballot[202] after hearing rhetorical speeches from logographers, who were not legally trained.[203] Furthermore, ancient Roman adjudicators similarly decided cases without any specialist training,[204] although specialist orators and jurists such as Cicero and Hortensius did attain legal training and practised in ecclesiastical and civil (secular) courts.[205] Roman adjudicators were not career professionals. They were appointed on an *ad hoc* basis for each individual case.[206]

The position evolved gradually during the medieval period when a 'recognisable legal profession began to emerge.'[207] Practitioners variously described as *advocati, causidici, iurisperiti, legis docti, iurisprudentes, notarii*, and *iudices* began to appear in ecclesiastical and civil (secular) courts from the twelfth century.[208] They were trained under the Roman-canon numeric system at some of the earliest law schools in Bologna and Paris during the middle of the twelfth century.[209] These early practitioners would later go on to be appointed

199 James A. Brundage *The medieval origins of the legal profession: Canonists, civilians and courts* (Chicago: Chicago University Press, 2008) 1; Wauters and de Benito *The history of law in Europe: An introduction*, 123–170.
200 Yunis "The rhetoric of law in fourth-century Athens" 194; May *Ancient legal thought: Equity, justice and humaneness from Hammurabi and the pharaohs to Justinian and the Talmud*, 249.
201 Kaius Tuori "Legal profession," in *A cultural history of law: In antiquity*, ed. Julen Extabe (London: Bloomsbury, 2019) 143 at 143.
202 Lerner *The jury: A very short introduction*, 8; Todd "Law and oratory at Athens" 94 ('Underlying the system of amateur prosecution is the assumption that every citizen is able to make use of his rights'); May *Ancient legal thought: Equity, justice and humaneness from Hammurabi and the pharaohs to Justinian and the Talmud*, 35 ('The ancient Mesopotamian judicial assembly seems to have grown out of the political assembly. In this sense justice is a matter initially of popular will, not of pronouncement from on high').
203 Tuori "Legal profession," 143; Brundage *The medieval origins of the legal profession: Canonists, civilians and courts*, 9 ('Lawyers never secured a stable foothold in the societies of ancient Greece').
204 Tuori "Legal profession," 143.
205 Brundage *The medieval origins of the legal profession: Canonists, civilians and courts*, 9 ('[T]he curriculum of the empire's law schools became standardized, at least in the East, toward the end of the fifth century. It comprised a four-year course of study, and would-be practitioners had to show certificates from their professors as evidence that they had completed it. They also had to pass an oral examination before they were admitted to practice') and 45.
206 Brundage *The medieval origins of the legal profession: Canonists, civilians and courts*, 15–16.
207 Brundage *The medieval origins of the legal profession: Canonists, civilians and courts*, 9.
208 Brundage *The medieval origins of the legal profession: Canonists, civilians and courts*, 61.
209 Brundage *The medieval origins of the legal profession: Canonists, civilians and courts*, 221.

as judges with law degrees.[210] However, there were at least four features of this period of criminal adjudication that still hindered the full flourishing of rational argumentation in the forensic context. Firstly, the Roman-canonical system of criminal adjudication left little room for judicial discretion and reasoned conclusions, and thus did not depend on highly trained lawyers.[211] One of the reasons for this was that the overwhelming reliance on torture by adjudicators under this regime left little or no room for rational argumentation.[212] Secondly, adjudicators were not required to give reasoned opinions for their findings.[213] Medieval inquisitions were shrouded in secrecy from the beginning till the end of a criminal trial.[214] Thirdly, lay litigants, who were not trained in forensic argumentation, had no right to legal representation.[215] This system of criminal litigation had spread all across Europe by the middle of the sixteenth century, owing to the enactment of seminal pieces of legislation such as the German *Constitutio Criminalis Carolina* of 1532; the French *Ordonnance royale* of 1539; and the Spanish *Ordonnance criminelle* of 1570.[216] The fourth feature is that although early medieval lawyers were professionally trained, the dominance of the Church, which originated the Roman-canon system of criminal adjudication, meant that the education of these early professionals had a heavy canonical focus for the purpose of training primarily clerics, and not lawyers in the modern sense.[217]

The practice of criminal adjudicators openly demonstrating the logical manner in which they arrived at their decisions reached its high point in the

210 Brundage *The medieval origins of the legal profession: Canonists, civilians and courts*, 4.

211 Brundage *The medieval origins of the legal profession: Canonists, civilians and courts*, 69; Langbein "The legal history of torture," 94.

212 Langbein *Torture and the law of proof: Europe and England in the ancien régime*, 8; John H. Langbein *Prosecuting crime in the Renaissance: England, Germany, France* (Cambridge: Harvard University Press, 1974) 180–182 (torture under articles 22–23 of the *Constitutio Criminalis Carolina* of 1532) and 238–239 (torture under articles 163–164 of the *Ordinance royale* of Villers-Cotterets (1539); Adhémar Esmein *A history of continental criminal procedure: With special reference to France* (translated by John Sampson) (Boston: Little Brown and Company, 1913) 251–271.

213 Dawson *The oracles of the law*, 376.

214 Dawson *The oracles of the law*, 376; Raoul C. Van Caenegem *Legal history: A European perspective* (London: The Hambledon Press, 1991) 82 ('The essentially public character of the debates also declines: secret investigations, depositions and deliberations in camera become frequent'); John R. Spencer "Adversarial vs inquisitorial systems: Is there still such a difference?" (2016) 20(5) *The International Journal of Human Rights* 601 at 608; John H. Merryman and Rogelio Pérez-Perdomo *The civil law tradition: An introduction to the legal systems of Europe and Latin America* 4th ed (Stanford: Stanford University Press, 2019) 130.

215 Merryman and Pérez-Perdomo *The civil law tradition: An introduction to the legal systems of Europe and Latin America*, 131.

216 Langbein *Prosecuting crime in the Renaissance: England, Germany, France*, 129.

217 Brundage *The medieval origins of the legal profession: Canonists, civilians and courts*, 69–70.

eighteenth and nineteenth centuries.[218] This process of reason-giving entails an adjudicator locating a specific result within a greater degree of generality, in the form of a 'rule, principle, maxim, standard or norm.'[219] This careful and logical interaction between the outcomes of specific cases and established legal doctrine is the hallmark of forensic argumentation in the Rationalist Tradition. Some of the eighteenth-century reforms that made room for the flourishing of this method of proof include the abolition of the Roman-canonical system, including judicial torture, in continental Europe;[220] the emergence of an orality principle that mandated open and oral criminal trials;[221] and the requirement of European adjudicators giving reasoned judgements in every criminal trial.[222] It was also during the same period that (continental) European jurisdictions began to introduce lay participation in the form of juries,[223] while the jury system in England had evolved to the point that a set of 'exclusionary rules' had emerged, among other things, to protect lay jurors against illegitimate patterns of reasoning.[224] Many of these reforms continue to obtain in many jurisdictions around the world.

4.5 New Evidence Scholarship

The evolution of rationalist methods of proof such as polygraphs and rational argumentation since the eighteenth and nineteenth centuries laid the foundations for a new scholarly movement that would later intensify the study of evidential proof within the forensic context. Richard Lempert coined the term 'New Evidence Scholarship' in the mid-1980s to describe this movement.[225]

218 John D. Jackson "Theories of truth finding in criminal procedure: An evolutionary approach" (1988) 10 *Cardozo Law Review* 475 at 496 and 563.

219 Schauer "Giving reasons," 642.

220 John H. Langbein "The English criminal trial jury on the eve of the French Revolution," in *The trial jury in England, France, Germany 1700–1900*, ed. Antonio P. Schioppa (Berlin: Duncker & Humblot, 1987) 7 at 33.

221 John D. Jackson and Thomas Weigend "Witness evidence in pre-trial and trial procedure," in *Core concepts in criminal law and criminal justice*, eds. Kai Ambos et al (Cambridge: Cambridge University Press, 2022) 260 at 262–263; Spencer "Adversarial vs inquisitorial systems: Is there still such a difference?" 608; Merryman and Pérez-Perdomo *The civil law tradition: An introduction to the legal systems of Europe and Latin America*, 131.

222 Dawson *The oracles of the law*, 374.

223 Merryman and Pérez-Perdomo *The civil law tradition: An introduction to the legal systems of Europe and Latin America*, 131.

224 Langbein "The English criminal trial jury on the eve of the French Revolution," 33; Lerner *The jury: A very short introduction*, 24 ('One of the strongest reasons for using the jury, and one that still exists today in some places, is to solve the problem of judicial bias . . . English judges were suspected because they were not independent . . . the judges were appointed by the Crown and served at the Crown's pleasure').

225 Richard Lempert "The new evidence scholarship: Analysing the process of proof" (1986) 66(3) *Boston University Law Review* 439; William Twining "The new evidence scholarship"

Lempert noticed a 'profound transformation'[226] in evidence scholarship from a focus on 'the articulation of rules' to a field concerned with 'the process of proof.'[227] Lempert coined the term at a symposium hosted by the Boston University School of Law in April 1986.[228] The meeting was convened by approximately 20 scholars from the United States, with the exception of Adrian Zuckerman, Jonathan Cohen and William Twining, all from Oxford in the United Kingdom.[229] For this reason, New Evidence Scholarship has earned a reputation for being a descriptor for debates about evidential proof and probabilistic in the United States following the promulgation of the American Federal Rules of Evidence in 1975.[230] The central theme was described by the host institution as focusing on the question, 'What does it mean to *prove* something so that a court will either order a person imprisoned or order a transfer of money or property?'[231] Twining, who was one of the attendees, reformulated the core question in similar terms: 'What constitute valid, cogent, and appropriate modes of reasoning about disputed questions of fact in adjudication?'[232]

Twelve papers were submitted to the symposium by four lawyers (Allan,[233] Zuckerman,[234] Nesson[235] and Tillers)[236] and six Bayesians (Lempert,[237]

(1999) 40 *South Texas Law Review* 351 at 352, n4 ('The term "New Evidence Scholarship" was coined by Richard Lempert').

226 Peter Tillers "Introduction" (1986) 66(3) *Boston University Law Review* 381 at 383.

227 Lempert "The new evidence scholarship: Analysing the process of proof," 439–440.

228 The conference proceedings were later published in the *Boston University Law Review* volume 66(3)–(4) of 1986; and again in Peter Tillers and Eric D. Green, eds. *Probability and inference in the law of evidence: The uses and limits of Bayesianism* (Dordrecht: Kluwer, 1988).

229 Adrian A.S. Zuckerman "Law, fact or justice?" (1986) 66(3) *Boston University Law Review* 487; L. Jonathan Cohen "The role of evidential weight in criminal proof" (1986) 66(3) *Boston University Law Review* 635; William Twining "The Boston symposium: A comment" (1986) 66(3) *Boston University Law Review* 391.

230 John D. Jackson "Modern trends in evidence scholarship: Is all rosy in the garden" (2003) 21 *Quinnipiac Law Review* 893 at 893–894; Susan Haack *Evidence matters: Science, proof, and truth in the law* (New York: Cambridge University Press 2014) 20, n91.

231 Eric D. Green "Foreword" (1986) 66(3) *Boston University Law Review* 377 at 377 and 379.

232 William Twining "The Boston symposium: A comment" (1986) 66(3) *Boston University Law Review* 391 at 391.

233 Ronald J. Allen "A reconceptualization of civil trials" (1986) 66(3) *Boston University Law Review* 401; Ronald J. Allen "Rationality, mythology and the 'acceptability of verdicts' thesis" (1986) 66(3) *Boston University Law Review* 541.

234 Adrian A.S. Zuckerman "Law, fact or justice?" (1986) 66(3) *Boston University Law Review* 487.

235 Charles Nesson "Agent orange meets blue bus: Factfinding at the frontiers of knowledge" (1986) 66(3) *Boston University Law Review* 521.

236 Tillers "Introduction," 381.

237 Richard Lempert "The new evidence scholarship: Analysing the process of proof" (1986) 66(3) *Boston University Law Review* 439.

Friedman,[238] Brilmayer,[239] Fienberg and Schervish,[240] and Schum).[241] This demarcation corresponded to the two substantive groupings that emerged during the symposium debates: the lawyers, led by Ronald J. Allen, who resisted the application of probability theories to the forensic context; and the Bayesians, led by Richard Lempert, who propounded Bayesian approaches to evidential proof.[242] This debate was triggered in earnest by the outcome of a California case from 1968.[243] The two defendants, Ms Janet Louis Collins and Mr Malcolm Ricardo Collins, in *People v Collins*,[244] were charged with robbing Mrs Juanita Brooks of her purse containing an amount ranging between $35 and $40 on 18 June 1964 at approximately 11:30 am in the southern neighbourhood of San Pedro in Los Angeles, California. The defendants denied 'any knowledge of or participation in the crime.'[245] In support of their defence that they were not present at the location of the crime scene at the time of the incident, the defendants called an alibi witness who testified that the two had visited her at an alternative location in Los Angeles, but she could not recall the precise date and time of the visit, except to say that it occurred 'in the middle of June.'[246] Therefore, the main issue concerned the identity of Mrs Brooks' robber, and whether it was the two defendants who had perpetrated it. The prosecution's case depended on the evidence of Mrs Brooks, an eyewitness named John Bass, Mrs Collins' employer, and the expert testimony of a state college mathematics instructor. Mrs Brooks testified that she noticed that her robber was a blonde woman with a ponytail.[247] The evidence of John Bass, who claimed to have observed the entire incident, was that he spotted the blonde robber running into a yellow car driven by a black person 'wearing

238 Richard D. Friedman "A diagrammatic approach to evidence" (1986) 66(3) *Boston University Law Review* 571; Richard D. Friedman "A close look at probative value" (1986) 66(3) *Boston University Law Review* 733.

239 Lea Brilmayer "Second-order evidence and Bayesian logic" (1986) 66(3) *Boston University Law Review* 673.

240 Stephen Fienberg and Mark J. Schervish "The relevance of Bayesian inference for the presentation of evidence and for legal decisionmaking" (1986) 66(3) *Boston University Law Review* 771.

241 David A. Schum "The construction of probability arguments" (1986) 66(3) *Boston University Law Review* 799; David A. Schum "Probability and the processes of discovery, proof and choice" (1986) 66(3) *Boston University Law Review* 825.

242 Twining "The Boston symposium: A comment," 393; Lempert "The new evidence scholarship: Analysing the process of proof," 440 ('The literature that relates theories of probability to theories of proof is largely a debate between those who advocate some role for Bayesian modes of inference in understanding or applying the law and those who criticize or reject this position').

243 Lempert "The new evidence scholarship: Analysing the process of proof," 441.

244 *People v Collins* 68 Cal. 2d 319 (1968).

245 *People v Collins*, at 326.

246 *People v Collins*, at 326.

247 *People v Collins*, at 319.

Table 4.1 An illustration of the characteristic ratios allocated in *People v Collins*

Characteristics	*Probability Ratios*
Owner of partly yellow car	1/10
Man with mustache	1/4
Black man with beard	1/10
Woman with ponytail	1/10
Woman with blond hair	1/3
Interracial couple in a car	1/1000

a mustache and beard.'[248] Mrs Collins' employer also testified that he spotted her with a ponytail on the day of the incident, and that she was picked up from work by a yellow car being driven by Mr Collins.[249] Incidentally, Mrs Collins was a white woman and Mr Collins was a black man, who owned a yellow car. The prosecution's evidence was concluded with the testimony of the state college mathematics instructor, who testified that assuming that the robbery was in fact committed by a white woman with a blond ponytail who left the scene in a yellow car in the company of a black man with a moustache and beard, 'there was an overwhelming probability that the crime was committed by any couple answering such distinctive characteristics.'[250] The prosecution illustrated this point by asking members of the jury to randomly assign various probability ratios to the relevant physical characteristics that were in dispute; for example, that 1 in 10 people owned a partly yellow car, that 1 in 4 men had moustaches, and that 1 in 10 black men had beards.[251] An illustration of this allocation of probability ratios is shown in Table 4.1.

The prosecutor then proceeded to ask jurors to apply the product rule, which, according to the expert witness, provides that the probability of the joint occurrence of a number of mutually independent events is equal to the product of the individual probabilities that each of the events will occur, to obtain an overall probability of the defendants being Mrs Brooks' robbers.[252] The prosecutor arrived at an answer of there being a 1 in 12 million chance that any couple matching the defined distinctive characteristics being innocent.[253] Therefore, on the illustrative ratios depicted in Table 4.1, the answer would be:

$$^{1}/_{10} \times {}^{1}/_{4} \times {}^{1}/_{10} \times {}^{1}/_{3} \times {}^{1}/_{10} \times {}^{1}/_{1000} = {}^{1}/_{(12 \times 10^{6})}.$$

248 *People v Collins*, at 319.
249 *People v Collins*, at 319.
250 *People v Collins*, at 325.
251 *People v Collins*, at 325.
252 *People v Collins*, at 325.
253 *People v Collins*, at 325.

The jury of the trial court in Los Angeles accepted this evidence and proceeded to convict the two defendants for the robbery of Mrs Brooks.[254] One of the defendants, Mr Collins, appealed his conviction to the California Supreme Court and impugned the admissibility of the mathematical probability evidence of the prosecutor's expert witness.[255] Sullivan J, on appeal, held that '[m]athematics, a veritable sorcerer in our computerized society, while assisting the trier of fact in the search for truth, must not cast a spell over him.'[256] The Supreme Court found that the prosecutor's expert testimony 'infected the case with fatal error' and proceeded to reverse the trial court's verdict on two grounds. Firstly, Sullivan J held that the assignment of probability ratios to individual characteristics (e.g. that there is a 1 in 10 chance of encountering an interracial couple in a car) was devoid of any mathematical foundation.[257] Secondly, there was inadequate proof of the statistical independence of the physical characteristics that were used for the application of the product rule.[258]

The outcome of the *Collins* case ignited a flurry of debate among probability theorists about the application of probabilistic analysis to the forensic context. This debate had already been brewing in the United States from much earlier in the twentieth century.[259] However, the criticism by Finkelstein and Fairley, a lawyer and a statistician, to the *Collins* judgement breathed new life into the discussion.[260] According Finkelstein and Fairley, the allocation and combination problems[261] discussed earlier from the *Collins* case could have been overcome by the application of Bayesian probability;[262] that is, by modifying our prior probability based on the initial probability ratios assigned to each characteristic with additional statistical evidence to obtain a posterior probability.[263] A detailed discussion of Bayesian probability is beyond the limited scope of this chapter, but it suffices to note that these initial debates gave rise to five waves of different bodies of scholarship

254 *People v Collins*, at 321.
255 *People v Collins*, at 321 and 326.
256 *People v Collins*, at 320.
257 *People v Collins*, at 327–328 and 330–331.
258 *People v Collins*, at 327–328. The court further explained in an appendix that the prosecutor's figures actually imply a likelihood of over 40% that the defendants' characteristics could be duplicated by at least one other couple who might equally have committed the robbery.
259 See *People v Risley*, 214 N.Y. 75 (1915); *People v Trujillo*, 32 Cal. 2d 105, cert. denied, 335 U.S. 887 (1948); *People v Jordan*, 45 Cal. 2d 697 (1955); *State v Sneed*, 76 N.M. 349 (1966); *Miller v State* 240 Ark. 340 (1966).
260 Michael O. Finkelstein and William B. Fairley "A Bayesian approach to identification evidence" (1970) 83(3) *Harvard Law Review* 489.
261 See generally, David H. Mellor *Probability: A philosophical introduction* (New York: Routledge, 2005) 14; William Twining "Debating probabilities" (1980) 2(1) *Liverpool Law Review* 51 at 52.
262 Finkelstein and Fairley "A Bayesian approach to identification evidence," 490.
263 Finkelstein and Fairley "A Bayesian approach to identification evidence," 496–502.

on evidence and proof under the broad banner of New Evidence Scholarship movement.[264] The first group of papers was by probability theorists contending for the application of probability theory,[265] particularly Bayes' theorem, to the forensic context.[266] Secondly, the initial probability proponents attracted a few sceptics to the application of probability theory to forensic questions of evidential proof.[267] Thirdly, Jonathan Cohen produced an alternative non-probabilistic inductive theory of probability that was inspired by the work of Francis Bacon.[268] The work of other epistemologists, who reflected on the structure and content of evidential proof, can also be added to this third wave of New Evidence Scholarship.[269] Fourthly, a group of American social scientists emerged in the late twentieth century and grounded their

264 Twining "The new evidence scholarship," 352–356. For an overview of the explosion of scholarship under the New Evidence Scholarship banner, see Roger Park et al "Bayes wars redivivus – An exchange" (2010) 8(1) *International Commentary on Evidence* 1; Michael S. Pardo "The nature and purpose of evidence theory" (2013) 2(3) *Vanderbilt Law Review* 547 at 553.

265 The initial debates occurred in the 1960s; see Vaughn C. Ball "The moment of truth: Probability theory and standards of proof" (1961) 14 *Vanderbilt Law Review* 807; John Kaplan "Decision theory and the factfinding process" (1968) 20 *Stanford Law Review* 1065; Alan D. Cullison "Probability analysis of judicial fact-finding: A preliminary outline of the subjective approach" (1969) 1 *University of Toledo Law Review* 538.

266 See David H. Kaye "Do we need a calculus of weight to understand proof beyond a reasonable doubt?" (1986) 66(4) *Boston University Law Review* 657; Lea Brilmayer "Second-order evidence and Bayesian logic" (1986) 66(4) *Boston University Law Review* 673; Richard D. Friedman "A closer look at probative value" (1986) 66(4) *Boston University Law Review* 733. See also David A. Schum "Alternative views on argument construction from a mass of evidence," in *The dynamics of judicial proof: Computation, logic and common sense*, eds. Marilyn MacCrimmon and Peter Tillers (Heidelberg: Physica-Verlag, 2002) 145 at 147 and 158–159; Vern R. Walker "Theories of uncertainty: Explaining the possible sources of error in inferences," in *The dynamics of judicial proof: Computation, logic and common sense*, eds. Marilyn MacCrimmon and Peter Tillers (Heidelberg: Physica-Verlag, 2002) 197 at 234; Dale A. Nance "The weights of evidence" (2008) 5 *Episteme* 267 at 268; Dale A. Nance *The burdens of proof: Discriminatory power, weight of evidence and tenacity of belief* (Cambridge: Cambridge University Press, 2016). Cf. L. Jonathan Cohen "The role of evidential weight in criminal proof" (1986) 66(4) *Boston University Law Review* 635 ('What is the legally correct way to judge proofs?').

267 See Laurence H. Tribe "Tribe by mathematics: Precision and ritual in the legal process" (1971) 84 *Harvard Law Review* 1329; Ronald J. Allen "A reconceptualization of civil trials" (1986) 66(3) *Boston University Law Review* 401.

268 See L. Jonathan Cohen *The probable and the provable* (Oxford: Oxford University Press, 1977).

269 See Haack *Evidence matters: Science, proof, and truth in the law*, 20–21, which was published originally as Susan Haack "Epistemology legalized: Or, truth, justice and the American way" (2004) 49 *American Journal of Jurisprudence* 43. See also, Susan Haack "Double-aspect of foundherentism: A new theory of empirical justification" (1993) 53(1) *Philosophy and Phenomenological Research* 113; Ernest Sosa "The raft and the pyramid: Coherence versus foundations in the theory of knowledge" (1980) 5(1) *Midwest Studies in Philosophy* 3.

theory of proof on the story model of juror decision-making.[270] The fifth wave consisted of 'explanatory' (non-probabilistic) theories, led principally by Allen and Pardo,[271] of evidential proof. A sixth wave that does not always self-identify with the New Evidence Scholarship movement was pioneered by argumentation theorists and informal logicians.[272] The multidisciplinarity of the New Evidence Scholarship movement suggests that this burgeoning

270 Lance W. Bennet and Martha S. Feldman *Reconstructing reality in the courtroom* (New Brunswick: Rutgers University Press, 1981); Reid Hastie et al *Inside the jury* (Cambridge: Harvard University Press, 1983); Nina Pennington and Reid Hastie "Evidence evaluation in complex decision making" (1986) 51(2) *Journal of Personality and Social Psychology* 242; Nina Pennington and Reid Hastie "A cognitive theory of juror decision making: The story model" (1991) (2–3) *Cardozo Law Review* 519; Nina Pennington and Reid Hastie "The story model for juror decision making," in *Inside the juror: The psychology of juror decision-making*, ed. Reid Hastie (Cambridge: Harvard University Press, 1993) 192. See also Willem A. Wagenaar et al *Anchored narratives: The psychology of criminal evidence* (New York: St Martin's Press, 1993); Willem A. Wagenaar "Anchored narratives: A theory of judicial reasoning and its consequences," in *Psychology, law and criminal justice: International developments in research and practice*, ed. Graham Davies et al (Berlin: de Gruyter, 1995) 267.

271 Ronald J. Allen "Rationality, algorithms and juridical proof: A preliminary inquiry" (1997) 1(5) *International Journal of Evidence and Proof* 254; Michael S. Pardo "Juridical proof, evidence, and pragmatic meaning: Toward evidentiary holism" (2000) 95 *Northwestern University Law Review* 399; Ronald R. Allen "Explanationism all the way down" (2008) 5(3) *Episteme* 320 at 321; Ronald J. Allen and Michael S. Pardo "The problematic value of mathematical models of evidence" (2007) 36(1) *The Journal of Legal Studies* 107; Ronald J. Allen and Michael S. Pardo "Judicial proof and the best explanation" (2008) 27 *Law and Philosophy* 223; Ronald J. Allen and Michael S. Pardo "Relative plausibility and its critics" (2019) 23 *International Journal of Evidence & Proof* 5.

272 Chaïm Perelman *The idea of justice and the problem of arguments* (translated by John Petrie) (1963); Chaïm Perelman and Lucie Olbrechts-Tyteca *The new rhetoric: A treatise on argumentation* (translated by John Wilkinson and Purcell Weaver) (Notre Dame: University of Notre Dame, 1969); Bart Verheij "Logic, context and valid inference or: Can there be a logic of law?" in *Legal knowledge based systems: JURIX 1999: The Twelfth Conference*, ed. Jaap van den Henrik (Nijmegen: Gerard Noodt Instituut, 1999) 109; Eveline E. Feteris *Fundamentals of legal argumentation: A survey of theories of theories on justification of judicial decisions* (Dordrecht: Springer, 1999); Douglas Walton *Legal argumentation and evidence* (University Park: Pennsylvania University Press, 2002); Floris J. Bex *Arguments, stories and criminal evidence: A formal hybrid theory* (Dordrecht: Springer, 2011); Douglas Walton *Burden of proof, presumption and argumentation* (New York: Cambridge University Press, 2014); Henrik Kaptein and Bastiaan van der Velden, eds. *Analogy and exemplary reasoning in legal discourse* (Amsterdam: Amsterdam University Press, 2017); Scott Brewer "Exemplary reasoning: Semantics, pragmatics, and the rational force of legal argument by analogy" (1996) 109 *Harvard Law Review* 923; Harm Kloosterhuis "Reconstructing complex analogy argumentation in judicial decisions: A pragma-dialectic perspective" (2005) 19 *Argumentation* 471; Giovanni Tuzet "Arguing on facts: Truth, trials and adversary procedures," in *Legal argumentation theory: Cross-disciplinary perspectives*, eds. Christian Dahlman and Eveline Feteris (Dordrecht: Springer, 2013) 207; Christian Dahlman "Unacceptable generalisations in arguments in legal evidence" (2017) 31 *Argumentation* 83; Richard D. Rieke "Investigating legal argument as a field," in *Dimensions of argument: Proceedings of the second summer conference on argumentation*, eds. Jack Rhodes and George Ziegelmueller (Annandale: Speech Communication Association, 1981) 152.

body of scholarship is likely to continue to grow the study of proof even further over the next few decades.

4.6 Conclusion

The historical evolution of forensic methods of proof essentially is a transition from the reliance on external to human sources of belief. This is so in three distinct senses. Firstly, this chapter has tracked the gradual increase in the participation of human beings, as litigators, fact-finders or legislators, from antiquity to the present day. Secondly, the role of human sources of evidence, mainly in the form of witness testimony, has also evolved and grown in significance since antiquity when the epistemic warrant of the testimony of a witness was tied up with superstition and religious doctrine (e.g. the swearing of an oath over holy relics). Modern adjudicators continue to hear and evaluate the testimony of witnesses to the present day, but the probative value thereof does not rest solely on whether or not the witness swore an oath. Thirdly, the professionalisation of trained lawyers precipitated the emergence of rational argumentation as a contemporary method of evidential proof in its own right. Therefore, to tell the story of the history of forensic methods of proof is to tell the story of human beings evolving to gain further trust in themselves to resolve disputed questions of fact in criminal adjudication.

This chapter advances the main argument of this book by grounding the third probative condition of the evidential proof of hate crimes in the correct historical context. The other two conditions, material and processual, were discussed in Chapters 2 and 3, respectively. The main purpose of this chapter has been to locate the main method of proof that is theorised about in the next two chapters, namely that of rational argumentation, within the relevant historical context. As shown in this chapter, rational argumentation, much like the phenomenon of hate crime prohibitions, is a product of the contemporary Rationalist Tradition of the very long history of forensic proof. This method of proof will now be explicated further in the next two chapters of this book.

4.7 Bibliography

Books and Book Chapters

Adhémar Esmein *A history of continental criminal procedure: With special reference to France* (translated by John Sampson) (Boston: Little Brown and Company, 1913).

Adlert Vrij *Detecting lies and deceit: The psychology of lying and the implications for professional practice* (Chichester: John Wiley & Sons Ltd, 2000).

Adriaan Lanni "Relevance in Athenian courts," in *The Cambridge companion to ancient Greek law*, eds. Michael Gagarin and David Cohen (New York: Cambridge University Press, 2005) 112.

Alexander Luria *The nature of human conflicts* (New York: Liveright Publishers, 1932).

Andrew Balmer *Lie detection and the law: Torture, technology and truth* (Abingdon: Routledge, 2018).

Aristotle "Rhetoric and Poetics," in *The complete works of Aristotle*, ed. Jonathan Barnes vol II (Princeton: Princeton University Press) 2430.
Aristotle "Rhetoric," in *The complete works of Aristotle*, ed. Jonathan Barnes vol II Book I (Princeton: Princeton University Press) 2152.
Arthur T. Von Mehren and James R. Gordley *The civil law system: An introduction to the comparative study of law* 2nd ed (Boston: Little Brown & Company, 1977).
Barbara Mittler et al "Introduction: Periodisation in a global context," in *Chronologics: Periodisation in global context*, eds. Barbara Mittler, Thomas Maissen and Pierre Monnet (Heidelberg: Heidelberg University Publishing, 2022) 1.
Barry Wimpfheimer "Codes," in *A cultural history of law: In antiquity*, ed. Julen Extabe (London: Bloomsbury, 2019) 59.
Bart Verheij "Logic, context and valid inference or: Can there be a logic of law?" in *Legal knowledge based systems: JURIX 1999: The Twelfth Conference*, eds. Jaap van den Henrik (Nijmegen: Gerard Noodt Instituut, 1999) 109.
Bart Wauters and Marco de Benito *The history of law in Europe: An introduction* (Cheltenham: Elgar, 2017).
Caesar Beccaria *On crimes and punishments* 5th ed (translated by Graeme R. Newman and Pietro Marongiu) (New Brunswick: Transaction Publishers, 2009).
Chaïm Perelman *The idea of justice and the problem of arguments* (translated by John Petrie) (London: Routledge, 1963).
Chaïm Perelman and Lucie Olbrechts-Tyteca *The new rhetoric: A treatise on argumentation* (translated by John Wilkinson and Purcell Weaver) (Notre Dame: University of Notre Dame, 1969).
Charles-Louis Montesquieu *The spirit of laws* (translated by Thomas Nugent) (London: J. Nourse and P. Vaillant, 1750).
Chris Carey, Mike Edwards and Brenda Grifith-Williams, eds. *Evidence and proof in ancient Greece* (Newcastle: Cambridge Scholars Publishing, 2024).
Christian Dahlman et al, eds. *Philosophical foundations of evidence law* (Oxford: Oxford University Press, 2021).
Christian Kock "The reception of ancient rhetoric in modern argumentation theory and pedagogy," in *Brill's companion of the reception of ancient rhetoric*, eds. Sophia Papaioannou et al (Leiden: Brill, 2021) 489.
Christine B. Lissitzyn and Marc W. Vallen *Forensic evidence in court: A case study approach* 2nd ed (Durham: Carolina Academic Press, 2018).
Cliff Roberson and Dilip K. Das *An introduction to comparative legal models of criminal justice* 2nd ed (Boca Raton: CRC Press, 2016).
Curt R. Bartol and Anne M. Bartol *Introduction to forensic psychology: Research and applications* 5th ed (London: SAGE, 2019).
Dale Nance *The Burdens of proof: Discriminatory power, weight of evidence and tenacity of belief* (Cambridge: Cambridge University Press, 2016).
David A. Schum "Alternative views on argument construction from a mass of evidence," in *The dynamics of judicial proof: Computation, logic and common sense*, eds. Marilyn MacCrimmon and Peter Tillers (Heidelberg: Physica-Verlag, 2002) 145.
David A. Schum *Evidential foundations of probabilistic reasoning* (Evanston, IL: Northwestern University Press, 1994).
David H. Mellor *Probability: A philosophical introduction* (New York: Routledge, 2005).
David M. Better *Faith, force and reason: An armchair history of the rule of law* (Toronto: University of Toronto Press, 2022).
David Mirhady "Arguments," in *A cultural history of law: In antiquity*, ed. Julen Extabe (London: Bloomsbury, 2019) 91.
David T. Lykken *A tremor in the blood: Uses and abuses of the lie detector* 2nd ed (New York: Plenum Trade, 1998).

David Wolchover and Anthony Heaton-Armstrong *Wolchover and Heaton on confession evidence* (London: Sweet & Maxwell, 1996).
Digby S. Koyana "Traditional courts in South Africa in the twenty-first century," in *The future of African customary law*, eds. Jeanmarie Fenrich et al (New York: Cambridge University Press, 2011) 227.
Donald Nicolson *Evidence and proof in Scotland: Context and critique* (Edinburgh: Edinburgh University Press, 2019).
Douglas N. Walton *Burden of proof, presumption and argumentation* (New York: Cambridge University Press, 2014).
Douglas N. Walton *Legal argumentation and evidence* (University Park: Pennsylvania University Press, 2002).
Elena Górriz Royo *Introduction to substantive criminal law* (Valencia: Tirant lo Blanch, 2019).
Eloise Keeler *The lie detector man: The career and cases of Leonarde Keeler* (Boston: Telshare Publishing Inc., 1984).
Eugene B. Block *Lie detectors: Their history and use* (New York: David McKay Company, 1977).
Eveline E. Feteris *Fundamentals of legal argumentation: A survey of theories of theories on justification of judicial decisions* (Dordrecht: Springer, 1999).
Ewout H. Meijer and Peter J. Van Koppen "Lie detectors and the law: The use of the polygraph in Europe," in *Psychology and Law: Bridging the gap*, eds. David Canter and Rita Žukauskienė (Aldershot: Ashgate, 2008) 31.
Floris J. Bex *Arguments, stories and criminal evidence: A formal hybrid theory* (Dordrecht: Springer, 2011).
Frederick Schauer *Uses of evidence in law, politics and everything else* (Cambridge: Harvard University Press, 2022).
Geoffrey Gilbert *The law of evidence* (New York: Garland Publishers, 1754).
George A. Kennedy *A new history of classical rhetoric* (Princeton: Princeton University Press, 1994).
George Neilson *Trial by combat* (Glasgow: William Hodge & Co., 1890).
Gerhard Thür "The role of the witness in Athenian law," in *The Cambridge companion to ancient Greek law*, eds. Michael Gagarin and David Cohen (New York: Cambridge University Press, 2005) 146.
Gershon Ben-Shakhar and John J. Furedy *Theories and applications in detection of deception: A psychophysiological and international perspective* (New York: Springer-Verlag, 1990).
Giovanni Tuzet "Arguing on facts: Truth, trials and adversary procedures," in *Legal argumentation theory: Cross-disciplinary perspectives*, eds. Christian Dahlman and Eveline Feteris (Dordrecht: Springer, 2013) 207.
Godfrey R. Driver and John C. Miles *The Assyrian laws* (Oxford: Clarendon Press, 1935).
Hannah Quirk *The rise and fall of the right to silence* (New York: Routledge, 2017).
Harold I. Brown *Rationality* (London: Routledge, 1988).
Harvey Yunis "The rhetoric of law in fourth-century Athens," in *The Cambridge companion to ancient Greek law*, eds. Michael Gagarin and David Cohen (New York: Cambridge University Press, 2005) 191.
Heikki Pihlajamäki and Mia Korpiola "Medieval canon law: The origins of modern criminal law," in *The Oxford handbook of criminal law*, eds. Markus D. Dubber and Tatjana Hörnle (Oxford: Oxford University Press, 2014) 201.
Henrik Kaptein and Bastiaan van der Velden, eds. *Analogy and exemplary reasoning in legal discourse* (Amsterdam: Amsterdam University Press, 2017).
Henry C. Lea *A history of the inquisition of the middle ages* vol I (London: Macmillan & Co., 1922).

Henry J. Schroeder *Disciplinary decrees of the general councils, text, translation, and commentary* (St. Louis: B. Herder Book Co., 1937).
Herbert A. Simon *Reason in human affairs* (Stanford: Stanford University Press, 1983).
Hock-Lai Ho "Evidence and truth," in *Philosophical foundations of evidence law*, eds. Christian Dahlman et al (Oxford: Oxford University Press, 2021).
Hock-Lai Ho *A philosophy of evidence* law (Oxford: Oxford University Press, 2008).
Hugo Münsterberg *On the witness stand: Essays on psychology and crime* (New York: Doubleday, Page & Co., 1908).
Ian Bryan *Interrogation and confession: A study of progress process and practice* (Aldershot: Ashgate, 1997).
Ian Dennis *The law of evidence* 6th ed (London: Sweet & Maxwell, 2017).
Immanuel Kant "What is enlightenment?" in *What is enlightenment? Eighteenth century answers and twentieth-century questions*, ed. James Schmidt (Berkeley: University of California Press, 1996) 58.
James A. Brundage *The medieval origins of the legal profession: Canonists, civilians and courts* (Chicago: Chicago University Press, 2008).
James B. Thayer *A preliminary treatise on evidence at common law* (Boston: Little Brown and Co., 1898).
James D. Williams *An introduction to classical rhetoric: Essential readings* (Chichester: John Wiley & Sons, 2009).
James F. Stephen *A digest on the law of evidence* 4th ed (London: Macmillan, 1887).
James Q. Whitman *The origins of reasonable doubt: Theological roots of the criminal trial* (New Haven: Yale University Press, 2008).
Jeremy Bentham *Rationale of judicial evidence* vol 1 (edited by J.S. Mill) (London: Hunt & Clark, 1827).
Joanna Gomula and Stephan Wittich, eds. *Research handbook on international procedural law* (Cheltenham: Elgar, 2024).
Joëlle Vuille "Forensic science evidence in non-adversary criminal justice systems," in *Forensic science evidence and expert witness testimony: Reliability through reform*, eds. Paul Roberts and Michael Stockdale (Cheltenham: Elgar, 2018) 354.
John C. Wei and Anders Winroth "Medieval canon law: Introduction," in *The Cambridge history of medieval canon law*, eds. Anders Winroth and John C. Wei (New York: Cambridge University Press, 2022) 1.
John D. Jackson and Thomas Weigend "Witness evidence in pre-trial and trial procedure," in *Core concepts in criminal law and criminal justice*, eds. Kai Ambos et al (Cambridge: Cambridge University Press, 2022) 260.
John H. Langbein "The English criminal trial jury on the eve of the French revolution," in *The trial jury in England, France, Germany 1700–1900*, ed. Antonio P. Schioppa (Berlin: Duncker & Humblot, 1987) 7.
John H. Langbein "The legal history of torture," in *Torture: A collection*, ed. Sanford Levinson (New York: Oxford University Press, 2004) 93.
John H. Langbein *Prosecuting crime in the Renaissance: England, Germany, France* (Cambridge: Harvard University Press, 1974).
John H. Langbein *Torture and the law of proof: Europe and England in the ancien régime* (Chicago: University of Chicago Press, 1977).
John H. Langbein, Renée L. Lerner and Bruce P. Smith *History of the common law: The development of Anglo-American legal institutions* (New York: Aspen, 2009).
John H. Merryman and Rogelio Pérez-Perdomo *The civil law tradition: An introduction to the legal systems of Europe and Latin America* 4th ed (Stanford: Stanford University Press, 2019).
John H. Soga *The Ama-Xosa* (New York: Cambridge University Press, 1937).
John H. Wigmore *Evidence in trials at common law* vol 1 (revised by Peter Tillers) (Boston: Little Brown, 1983).

John H. Wigmore *Evidence in trials at common law* vol 3 (revised by James H. Chadbourn) (Boston: Little Brown and Company, 1970).
John H. Wigmore *A kaleidoscope of justice: Containing authentic accounts of trial scenes from all times and climes* (Washington: Washington Law Book Co., 1941).
John H. Wigmore *The principles of judicial proof as given by logic, psychology and general experience and illustrated in judicial trials* (Boston: Little Brown Company, 1913).
John H. Wigmore *A treatise on the system of evidence in trials at common law* vols 1–4 (Boston: Little, Brown and Company, 1905).
John Locke *Two treatises of government* (London: Awnsham Churchill, 1690).
John P. Dawson *The oracles of the law* (Ann Arbor: University of Michigan Law School, 1968).
John T. McNeill *A history of the cure of souls* (New York: Harper, 1951).
Jonathan I. Israel *Radical enlightenment: Philosophy and the making of modernity 1650–1750* (New York: Oxford University Press, 2001).
Julia M.H. Smith "Introduction: Regarding medievalists – Contexts and approaches," in *Companion to historiography*, ed. Michael Bentley (London: Routledge, 1997) 98.
Kaius Tuori "Legal profession," in *A cultural history of law: In antiquity*, ed. Julen Extabe (London: Bloomsbury, 2019) 143.
Kathryn Slanski "Justice," in *A cultural history of law: In antiquity*, ed. Julen Extabe (London: Bloomsbury, 2019) 21.
Kevin M. Clermont *A general theory of evidence and proof: Forming beliefs in truth* (Cham: Springer, 2024).
Koen Lenaerts, Kathleen Gutman and Janek T. Nowak *EU procedural law* 2nd ed (Oxford: Oxford University Press, 2023).
L. Jonathan Cohen "Freedom of proof," in *Facts in law, archives for philosophy of law and social philosophy*, ed. William Twining, Beiheft No. 16 (Wiesbaden: Franz Steiner Verlag, 1983) 1.
Lance W. Bennet and Martha S. Feldman *Reconstructing reality in the courtroom* (New Brunswick: Rutgers University Press, 1981).
Larry May *Ancient legal thought: Equity, justice and humaneness from Hammurabi and the pharaohs to Justinian and the Talmud* (New York: Cambridge University Press, 2019).
Lawrence S. Wrightsman and Saul M. Kassin *Confessions in the courtroom* (Newbury Park: SAGE, 1993).
Marc Van de Mieroop *Philosophy before the Greeks: The pursuit of truth in ancient Babylonia* (Princeton: Princeton University Press, 2016).
Marcus T. Cicero *De Oratore I* (translated into English by E.W. Sutton and H. Rackham) (Cambridge: Harvard University Press, 1942).
Marcus T. Cicero *De Oratore II* (translated by E.W. Sutton) (Cambridge: Harvard University Press, 1967).
Marshall G.S. Hodgson *The venture of Islam: Conscience and history in a world civilization* vol 1 (Chicago: University of Chicago Press, 1974).
Marshall Houts "Team testing will bring the polygraph safely into court," in *Legal admissibility of the polygraph*, ed. Normal Ansley (Springfield: Charles C. Thomas, 1975) 5.
Martha T. Roth *Law collections from Mesopotamia and Asia Minor* 2nd ed (Atlanta: Scholars Press, 1997).
Michael D. Bayles *Procedural justice: Allocating to individuals* (Dordrecht: Kluwer, 1990).
Michael Freeman *Lloyd's introduction to jurisprudence* 9th ed (London: Sweet & Maxwell, 2014).
Mirjan R. Damaška *Evaluation of evidence: Premodern and modern approaches* (Cambridge: Cambridge University Press, 2019).

Mogens H. Hansen *The Athenian democracy in the age of Demosthenes: Structure, principles and ideology* (translated by J.A. Crook) (Norman: University of Oklahoma Press, 1991).

Molefi K. Asante *African pyramids of knowledge: Kemet, Afrocentricity and Africology* (New York: Universal Write Publications, 2015).

Nicholas Rescher *Rationality: A philosophical inquiry into the nature and the rationale of reason* (Oxford: Clarendon Press, 1988).

Nina Pennington and Reid Hastie "The story model for juror decision making," in *Inside the juror: The psychology of juror decision-making*, ed. Reid Hastie (Cambridge: Harvard University Press, 1993) 192.

Pamela-Jane Schwikkard and Tshepo B. Mosaka *Principles of evidence* 5th ed (Claremont: Juta, 2023).

Paul Brand "Judges and judging 1176–1307," in *Judges and judging in the history of the common law and civil law: From antiquity to modern times*, eds. Paul Brand and Joshua Getzler (Cambridge: Cambridge University Press, 2012) 3.

Paul C. Giannelli *Scientific evidence* 6th ed vol 1 (New York: LexisNexis, 2020).

Paul Roberts *Roberts & Zuckerman's criminal evidence* 3rd ed (Oxford: Oxford University Press, 2022).

Percy Handcock *The code of Hammurabi* (New York: Macmillan, 1920).

Peter D. Clarke "Western canon law in the central and later middle ages," in *The Oxford handbook of European legal history*, ed. Heikki Pihlajamäki et al (Oxford: Oxford University Press, 2018) 265.

Peter Mirfield *Silence and improperly obtained evidence* (New York: Oxford University Press, 1997).

Peter Tillers and Eric D. Green, eds. *Probability and inference in the law of evidence: The uses and limits of Bayesianism* (Dordrecht: Kluwer, 1988).

Petra van Kampen "Polygraphs in criminal justice systems: The effect of different legal cultures on the use of scientific evidence," in *Psychology and criminal justice: International review of theory and practice*, eds. Janos Boros et al (Berlin: de Gruyter, 1998) 130.

Ralph H. Johnson *Manifest rationality* (Mahwah: Lawrence Erlbaum Associates, 2000).

Randall Lesaffer *European legal history: A cultural and political perspective* (translated by Jan Arriens) (Cambridge: Cambridge University Press, 2009).

Raoul C. Van Caenegem *Legal history: A European perspective* (London: The Hambledon Press, 1991).

Reid Hastie, Steven D. Penrod and Nancy Pennington *Inside the jury* (Cambridge: Harvard University Press, 1983).

Renata L. Mack *Comparative criminal procedure: History, processes and case studies* 2nd ed (New York: William S. Hein & Co, 2017).

Renée L. Lerner *The jury: A very short introduction* (New York: Oxford University Press, 2023).

Richard D. Rieke. "Investigating legal argument as a field," in *Dimensions of argument: Proceedings of the second summer conference on argumentation*, eds. Jack Rhodes and George Ziegelmueller (Annandale: Speech Communication Association, 1981) 152.

Richard W. Lariviere *The Nāradasmṛti* (New Delhi: Motilal Banarsidass Publishers, 2003).

Robert Bartlett *Trial by fire and water: The medieval judicial ordeal* (Oxford: Oxford University Press, 1986).

Roland Oliver and Anthony Atmore *Medieval Africa, 1250–1800* (Cambridge: Cambridge University Press, 2001).

Sadakat Kadri *The trial: From Socrates to O.J. Simpson* (London: Harper Collins, 2005).

Serge Dauchy "French law and its expansion in the early modern period," in *The Oxford handbook of European legal history*, eds. Heikki Pihlajamäki et al (Oxford: Oxford University Press, 2018) 760.

Shalom E. Holtz *Neo-Babylonian trial records* (Atlanta: Society of Biblical Literature, 2014).

Solomon E. Salako *Evidence, proof and justice: Legal philosophy and the provable in English courts* (Ventus Publishing Apk, 2010).

Stan Abrams *The complete polygraph handbook* (Lexington: Lexington Books, 1989).

Stephen C. Todd "Law and oratory at Athens," in *The Cambridge companion to ancient Greek law*, eds. Michael Gagarin and David Cohen (New York: Cambridge University Press, 2005) 97.

Stephen J. Morse *Advanced introduction to substantive criminal law* (Cheltenham: Elgar, 2023).

Susan Easton *Silence and confessions: The suspect as the source of evidence* (Basingstoke: Palgrave Macmillan, 2014).

Susan Haack *Evidence matters: Science, proof, and truth in the law* (New York: Cambridge University Press, 2014).

Susan Reynolds "Medieval law," in *The medieval world*, eds. Peter Linehan et al 2nd ed (London: Routledge, 2018) 568.

Terence Anderson, William Twining and David Schum *Analysis of evidence* 2nd ed (Cambridge: Cambridge University Press, 2005).

Thomas Starkie *A practical treatise of the law of evidence* 8th ed (Philadelphia: T. & J.W. Johnson & Co., 1860).

Todd "Law and oratory at Athens," in *The Cambridge companion to ancient Greek law*, eds. Michael Gagarin and David Cohen (New York: Cambridge University Press, 2005) 97.

Valerie P. Hans, Hiroshi Fukurai, Sanja Kutnjak Ivković and Jaihyun Park "Global juries: A plan for research," in *The psychology of juries*, ed. Margaret B. Kovera (Washington: American Psychological Association, 2017) 131.

Verena Klappstein and Maciej Dybowski, eds. *Theory of legal evidence – Evidence in legal theory* (Cham: Springer, 2021).

Vern R. Walker "Theories of uncertainty: Explaining the possible sources of error in inferences," in *The dynamics of judicial proof: Computation, logic and common sense*, eds. Marilyn MacCrimmon and Peter Tillers (Heidelberg: Physica-Verlag, 2002) 197.

Wilhelm G. Grewe *The epochs of international law* (translated by Michael Byers) (Berlin: Walter de Gruyter, 2000).

Willem A. Wagenaar "Anchored narratives: A theory of judicial reasoning and its consequences," in *Psychology, law and criminal justice: International developments in research and practice*, ed. Graham Davies et al (Berlin: de Gruyter, 1995) 267.

Willem A. Wagenaar, Peter J. van Koppen and Henricus F.M. Crombag *Anchored narratives: The psychology of criminal evidence* (New York: St Martin's Press, 1993).

William E. Butler "Periodization and international law," in *Research handbook on the theory and history of international law*, ed. Alexander Orakhelashvili 2nd ed (Cheltenham: Elgar, 2020) 281.

William M.A. Best *Treatise on the principles of and practice as to proofs in courts of common law with rules for conducting the examination and of witnesses* (Philadelphia: T. & J.W. Johnson, 1849).

William Twining *Rethinking evidence: Exploratory essays* (Evanston, IL: Northwestern University Press, 1994).

William Twining *Rethinking evidence: Exploratory essays* 2nd ed (Cambridge: Cambridge University Press, 2006).

William Twining "Taking facts seriously – Again," in *Rethinking evidence: Exploratory essays*, ed. William Twining 2nd ed (Cambridge: Cambridge University Press, 2009) 417.

William Twining "Taking facts seriously," in *Essays on legal education*, ed. Neil Gold (Toronto: Butterworths, 1982) 22.
William Twining *Theories of evidence: Bentham and Wigmore* (London: Weidenfeld & Nicolson, 1985).
William Wills *An essay on the principles of circumstantial evidence* 3rd ed (Philadelphia: T. & J.W. Johnson, 1858).
Xiaobo Dong and Yafang Zhang *On contemporary Chinese legal system* (Gateway East: Springer, 2023).

Periodicals

Adrian A.S. Zuckerman "Law, fact or justice?" (1986) 66(3) *Boston University Law Review* 487.
Alan D. Cullison "Probability analysis of judicial fact-finding: A preliminary outline of the subjective approach" (1969) 1 *University of Toledo Law Review* 538.
Benjamin Kleinmuntz and Julian J. Szucko "On the fallibility of lie detection" (1983) 17(1) *Law & Society Review* 85.
Charles Nesson. "Agent orange meets blue bus: Factfinding at the frontiers of knowledge" (1986) 66(3) *Boston University Law Review* 521.
Christian Dahlman "Unacceptable generalisations in arguments in legal evidence" (2017) 31 *Argumentation* 83.
Dale A. Nance "The weights of evidence" (2008) 5 *Episteme* 267.
Daniel D. Langleben et al "Telling truth from lie in individual subjects with fast event-related fMRI" (2005) 26 *Human Brain Mapping* 262.
David A. Schum "The construction of probability arguments" (1986) 66(3) *Boston University Law Review* 799.
David A. Schum "Probability and the processes of discovery, proof and choice" (1986) 66(3) *Boston University Law Review* 825.
David. H. Kaye "Do we need a calculus of weight to understand proof beyond a reasonable doubt?" (1986) 66(4) *Boston University Law Review* 657.
Edward L. Rubin "Trial by battle – Trial by argument" (2003) 56(2) *Arkansas Law Review* 261.
Eric D. Green "Foreword" (1986) 66(3) *Boston University Law Review* 377.
Ernest Sosa "The raft and the pyramid: Coherence versus foundations in the theory of knowledge" (1980) 5(1) *Midwest Studies in Philosophy* 3.
Fred M. Donner "Periodisation as a tool of the historian with special reference to Islamic history" (2014) 91(1) *Der Islam* 20.
Frederick Schauer "Giving reasons" (1995) 47(4) *Stanford Law Review* 633.
Harm Kloosterhuis "Reconstructing complex analogy argumentation in judicial decisions: A pragma-dialectic perspective" (2005) 19 *Argumentation* 471.
Hock-Lai Ho "The legitimacy of medieval proof" (2004) 19(2) *Journal of Law and Religion* 259.
James K. Gaynor "Law through the ages" (1972) 14(2) *South Texas Law Journal* 147.
Jeremy Lever "Why procedure is more important than substantive law" (1999) 48(2) *International & Comparative Law Quarterly* 285.
John Briscoe "Rome and the class struggle in the Greek states 200–146 B.C." (1967) 36 *Past & Present* 3.
John D. Jackson "Modern trends in evidence scholarship: Is all rosy in the garden" (2003) 21 *Quinnipiac Law Review* 893.
John D. Jackson "Theories of truth finding in criminal procedure: An evolutionary approach" (1988) 10 *Cardozo Law Review* 475.
John H. Wigmore "The problem of proof" (1913) 8 *Illinois Law Review* 77.

John Kaplan "Decision theory and the factfinding process" (1968) 20 *Stanford Law Review* 1065.
John R. Spencer "Adversarial vs inquisitorial systems: Is there still such a difference?" (2016) 20(5) *The International Journal of Human Rights* 601.
Joseph T. McCann "A conceptual framework for identifying various types of confessions" (1998) 16(4) *Behavioural Sciences & the Law* 391.
L. Jonathan Cohen "The role of evidential weight in criminal proof" (1986) 66(3) *Boston University Law Review* 635.
Laurence H. Tribe "Tribe by mathematics: Precision and ritual in the legal process" (1971) 84 *Harvard Law Review* 1329.
Lea Brilmayer "Second-order evidence and Bayesian logic" (1986) 66(3) *Boston University Law Review* 673.
Lon Fuller "The forms and limits of adjudication" (1978) 92(2) *Harvard Law Review* 353.
Michael O. Finkelstein and William B. Fairley "A Bayesian approach to identification evidence" (1970) 83(3) *Harvard Law Review* 489.
Michael S. Pardo "Judicial proof, evidence and pragmatic meaning: Towards evidentiary holism" (2000) 95(1) *Northwestern University Law Review* 399.
Michael S. Pardo "The nature and purpose of evidence theory" (2013) 2(3) *Vanderbilt Law Review* 547.
Mirjan R. Damaška "Free proof and its detractors" (1995) 43(3) *The American Journal of Comparative Law* 343.
Nanning Zhang and Douglas N. Walton "Recent trends in evidence law in China and the new evidence scholarship" (2010) 9 *Law, Probability and Risk* 103.
Nina Pennington and Reid Hastie "A cognitive theory of juror decision making: The story model" (1991)(2–3) *Cardozo Law Review* 519.
Paul Roberts "Rethinking of the law of evidence: A twenty-first century agenda for teaching and research" (2002) 55(1) *Current Legal Problems* 297.
Peter Macalister-Smith and Joachim Schwietzke "Literature and documentary sources relating to the history of public international law: An annotated bibliographical survey" (1999) 1 *Journal of the History of International Law* 136.
Peter Tillers "Introduction" (1986) 66(3) *Boston University Law Review* 381.
Richard D. Friedman "A close look at probative value" (1986) 66(3) *Boston University Law Review* 733.
Richard D. Friedman "A diagrammatic approach to evidence" (1986) 66(3) *Boston University Law Review* 571.
Richard Lempert "The new evidence scholarship: Analysing the process of proof" (1986) 66(3) *Boston University Law Review* 439.
Roger Park, Peter Tillers, Frederick C. Moss, D. Michael Risinger, David H. Kaye, Ronald J. Allen, Samuel R. Gross, Bruce L. Hay, Michael S. Pardo and Paul F. Kirgis "Bayes wars redivivus – An exchange" (2010) 8(1) *International Commentary on Evidence* 1.
Ronald J. Allen "Rationality, mythology and the 'acceptability of verdicts' thesis" (1986) 66(3) *Boston University Law Review* 541.
Ronald J. Allen "A reconceptualization of civil trials" (1986) 66(3) *Boston University Law Review* 401.
Ronald J. Allen and Michael S. Pardo "Judicial proof and the best explanation" (2008) 27 *Law and Philosophy* 223.
Ronald J. Allen and Michael S. Pardo "The problematic value of mathematical models of evidence" (2007) 36(1) *The Journal of Legal Studies* 107.
Ronald J. Allen and Michael S. Pardo "Relative plausibility and its critics" (2019) 23 *International Journal of Evidence & Proof* 5.
Ronald R. Allen "Explanationism all the way down" (2008) 5(3) *Episteme* 320.

Sabelo J. Ndlovu-Gatsheni "Ten challenges in reconfiguring African studies" (2023) *Review of African Political Economy* 1.
Sanjeev Anand "The origins, early history and evolution of the English criminal trial jury" (2005) 43(2) *Alberta Law Review* 407.
Saul M. Kassin and Gisil H. Gudjohnsson "The psychology of confessions" (2004) 5(2) *Psychological Science in the Public Interest* 33.
Scott Brewer "Exemplary reasoning: Semantics, pragmatics, and the rational force of legal argument by analogy" (1996) 109 *Harvard Law Review* 923.
Shelomo D. Goitein "A plea for the periodization of Islamic history" (1968) 88(2) *Journal of the American Oriental Society* 224.
Stephen Fienberg and Mark J. Schervish "The relevance of Bayesian inference for the presentation of evidence and for legal decisionmaking" (1986) 66(3) *Boston University Law Review* 771.
Susan Haack "Double-aspect of foundherentism: A new theory of empirical justification" (1993) 53(1) *Philosophy and Phenomenological Research* 113.
Susan Haack "Epistemology legalized: Or, truth, justice and the American way" (2004) 49 *American Journal of Jurisprudence* 43.
Tshepo B. Mosaka "Here is a table: A prolegomenon to a future new evidence scholarship in Africa" (2022) 26(2) *International Journal of Evidence & Proof* 178.
Tshepo B. Mosaka "An introduction to proof in South Africa" (2022) 139(4) *South African Law Journal* 837.
Vaughn C. Ball "The moment of truth: Probability theory and standards of proof" (1961) 14 *Vanderbilt Law Review* 807.
William Twining "The Boston symposium: A comment" (1986) 66(3) *Boston University Law Review* 391.
William Twining "Debating probabilities" (1980) 2(1) *Liverpool Law Review* 51.
William Twining "Evidence as a multi-disciplinary subject" (2003) 2 *Law, Probability and Risk* 91.
William Twining "Freedom of proof and the reform of criminal evidence" (1997) 31 *Israel Law Review* 439.
William Twining "Goodbye to Lewis Elliot: The academic lawyer as scholar" (1980) 15 *Journal of the Society of Public Teachers of Law* 2.
William Twining "The new evidence scholarship" (1999) 40 *South Texas Law Review* 351.

Online Resources

Hans Gross. "Hans Gross museum of criminology," University of Graz website, available at: www.universitaetsmuseen.uni-graz.at (accessed: 7 October 2024).
The International Journal of Procedural Law, available at: www.jurisquare.be (accessed: 15 May 2024).
Kwesi K. Prah "Has Rhodes fallen? Decolonising the Humanities in Africa and constructing intellectual sovereignty," *Academy of Science of South Africa Inaugural Humanities Lecture* (20 October 2016), available at: www.hsrc.ac.za (accessed: 14 June 2024).

5 The Probative Condition I

5.1 An Introduction to Legal Argumentation

To prove hate crimes implies doing three things. Firstly, it entails establishing the defined elements of the specific type of hate crime, as discussed in Chapter 2. Secondly, it entails gathering, organising and presenting extant evidential facts in accordance with the relevant institutional processes described in Chapter 3. Thirdly, it also implies using inferential techniques that are logical and sound. The core question that this chapter, as well as the next, addresses pertains to the meaning of what this 'establishing' of hate crimes entails. For starters, the phenomenon of proof is neither peculiar to a particular country or a time in human history, nor to the discipline of law. The term derives originally from the Latin verb *probare*, which means to 'to test'[1] or 'to trace by sight,'[2] and it continues to retain its core meaning in several contemporary translations such as: *beweis* (German), *bewijs* (Dutch), *bevis* (Swedish) and *démonstration* (French).[3] Furthermore, the concept of proof also finds application within various disciplines. For example, a mathematician would define the term as the logical derivation of a statement from another basic *a priori* statement in accordance with an *a priori*–preserving rule of inference.[4]

1 Steven Schwartzman *The words of mathematics: An etymological dictionary of mathematical terms used in English* (Washington: Mathematical Association of America, 1994) 174.

2 Tshepo B. Mosaka "An introduction to proof in South Africa" (2022) 139(4) *South African Law Journal* 837 at 847; Thayer "A preliminary treatise on evidence at common law," 387; William Wills *An essay on the principles of circumstantial evidence* 3rd ed (Philadelphia: T. & J.W. Johnson, 1858) 2; James D Williams *An introduction to classical rhetoric: Essential readings* (Chichester: John Wiley & Sons, 2009) 298 (on classical Greek forensic rhetoric having the three aims of *probare, delectare* and *flectere*); Cicero *De Oratore* II (translated by E.W. Sutton) (Cambridge: Harvard University Press, 1967) 331–334.

3 Göran Sundholm "Proof-theoretical semantics and Fregean identity criteria for propositions" (1994) 77(3) *The Monist* 294 at 295–296.

4 Philip Kitcher *The nature of mathematical knowledge* (Oxford: Oxford University Press, 1984) 38; Bonnie Gold and Roger A. Simons *Proof and other dilemmas: Mathematics and philosophy* (Washington: Mathematical Association of America, 2008) 62–67; Alan Bundy et al "What is a proof?" (2005) 363 *Philosophical Transactions of the Royal Society* 2377; Steven G. Krantz *Handbook of logic and proof techniques for computer science* (Boston: Birkhäuser, 2002) 128.

DOI: 10.4324/9781003493006-5

For a computer scientist, the concept of proof denotes a belief that a program is *correct* and that the hardware to implement it is *reliable*.[5] An empirical scientist conceives of proof as the confirmation of a tested hypothesis with a sizeable mass of data.[6] The forensic conception of proof describes the quality of a *factum probandum* (disputed fact) being established inferentially by an extant (or admitted) fact or set of facts.[7]

Having located rational argumentation within the context of the historical evolution of forensic proof in the previous chapter, this chapter builds on that foundation by explicating this method of proof in greater detail. The concept of 'proof' has a lot in common with that of 'argumentation.' Firstly, they both operate within the context of an incomplete set of information. In other words, their 'ampliative' function suggests that they both involve the derivation of new information from information that we already possess.[8] The 'new' information in the forensic context represents the disputed facts (*facta probanda*) that the litigants are seeking to establish. Secondly, the inference of new information is always drawn from existing information that is either true or otherwise acceptable.[9] According to Kneale and Kneale, '[i]t is those types of discourse or inquiry in which *proof* is sought or demanded that naturally give rise to logical investigation; for to prove a proposition is to infer it validly from true premisses.'[10] Correspondingly, Wigmore poses two primary questions as conditions of proof within the forensic context: 'What is the Proposition desired to be proved?' and 'What is the Evidentiary Fact offered to prove it?'[11] This connection between proof and argumentation is the primary focus of this chapter. In particular, the main aim of this chapter is to discuss the

5 Dag Prawitz "Proof verifying programs and programs producing proofs: A conceptual analysis," in *Deduction, computation, experiment: Exploring the effectiveness of proof* (Milano: Springer, 2008) in 81 at 81 and 92–93; Donald Mackenzie *Mechanising proof: Computing, risk and trust* (Cambridge: MIT Press, 2001) 307.

6 Errol E. Harris *Hypothesis and perception: The roots of scientific method* (London: Routledge, 2013) 19; Roger F.G. Ormrod "Evidence and proof: Scientific and legal" (1972) 12(1) *Medicine, Science & the Law* 9 at 9; Hans Zeisel and David Kaye *Prove it with figures: Empirical methods in law and litigation* (New York: Springer, 1997); Lee Loevinger "Standards of proof in science and law" (1992) 32(3) *Jurimetrics* 323.

7 Pamela-Jane Schwikkard and Tshepo B. Mosaka *Principles of evidence* 5th ed (Claremont: Juta, 2023) 607.

8 Catarina Dutilh Novaes *The dialogical roots of deduction: Historical, cognitive and philosophical perspectives on reasoning* (Cambridge: Cambridge University Press, 2021) 17.

9 William C. Kneale and Martha Kneale, *Development of logic* (London: Oxford University Press, 1962) 1; Douglas Walton "Legal reasoning and argumentation," in *Handbook of legal reasoning and argumentation*, eds. Giorgio Bongiovanni et al (Dordrecht: Springer, 2018) 47 at 71.

10 Kneale and Kneale *Development of logic*, 1.

11 John H. Wigmore *The principles of judicial proof as given by logic, psychology and general experience and illustrated in judicial trials* (Boston: Little Brown & Company, 1913) 5; John H. Wigmore *Evidence in trials at common law* vol 1 (revised by Peter Tillers) (Boston: Little Brown & Company, 1983) 15.

general features and models of rational argumentation within the forensic context. The following section provides a broad overview of the basic features and history of legal argumentation, which encompasses all forms of rational argument within the forensic context, including probative argumentation. The remaining three sections outline *deductive, inductive* and *defeasible* models of argumentation. The next chapter will then proceed to apply these general models to the elements of hate crimes that were discussed earlier in Chapter 2.

5.2 A Brief History of Legal Argumentation

Argumentation, in the narrow and basic sense, consists of a set of propositions: the premisses and conclusion, which are joined by an inferential 'evidential link.'[12] On a wider definition, argumentation is defined to mean

> a communicative and interactional act complex aimed at resolving a difference of opinion with the addressee by putting forward a constellation of propositions the arguer can be held accountable for to make the standpoint at issue acceptable to a rational judge who judges reasonably.[13]

These contemporary definitions of argumentation are preceded by a very long history that is traceable to Aristotle, who is often credited with being 'the founder of the theory of argument.'[14] For the ancient Greeks, the Latin verb

12 John Woods and Douglas N. Walton *Argument: The logic of the fallacies* (Toronto: McGraw-Hill Ryerson, 1982) 1; John Woods et al *Argument: Critical thinking, logic and the fallacies* 2nd ed (Toronto: Prentice Hall, 2004) 2–3; Douglas N. Walton *Fundamentals of critical argumentation* (Cambridge: Cambridge University Press, 2006) 6; Martin P. Golding *Legal reasoning* (New York: Alfred A. Knopf, 1984) 35 ('[A]n argument, as we are using the term, consists minimally of at least two statements, of which one (the premise) is offered as a reason for accepting the other (the conclusion). Most actual arguments, of course, contain a number of premises that, taken together, are assumed to justify the conclusion.').

13 Frans H. van Eemeren et al *Handbook of argumentation theory* (Dordrecht: Springer, 2014) 7, as originally developed in Frans H. van Eemeren et al *Fundamentals of argumentation theory* (New York: Routledge, 1996) 5; Stephen Toulmin *The uses of argument* (Cambridge: Cambridge University Press, 1958) Ch III (on distinction between the 'gross anatomical' (wide) and the 'finer physiological' (narrow) structures of an argument); Robert Alexy *A theory of legal argumentation: The theory of rational discourse as theory of legal justification* (translated by Ruth Adler and Neil MacCormick) (Oxford: Oxford University Press, 1989) 221–286 (on the 'internal' and 'external' justifications of legal argumentation); Frans H. van Eemeren "The study of argumentation," in *The Sage handbook of rhetorical studies*, eds. Andrea A. Lunsford et al (Thousand Oaks: SAGE, 2009) 109 at 109; Frans H. Van Eemeren and Rob Grootendorst *A systematic theory of argumentation: The pragma-dialectical approach* (Cambridge: Cambridge University Press, 2004) 1; Ralph H. Johnson *Manifest rationality* (Mahwah: Lawrence Erlbaum Associates, 2000) 168; David Hitchcock "The practice of argumentative discussion" (2002) 16 *Argumentation* 287 at 289. See also Henry Prakken "Argumentation without arguments" (2011) 25 *Argumentation* 171.

14 Joseph Horowitz *Law and logic* (New York: Springer-Verlag, 1972) 1.

arguo meant 'to make clear, make known, show or prove.'[15] However, it is doubtful that the same term was used for what we mean by 'argument' today. Terms such as 'dialectic' (*dialektikos*),[16] 'analytic' and 'organon' were probably much closer in meaning than the more direct translation of *arguo*.[17]

The term 'legal argumentation,' however, is of much more recent origin. Although arguments and reasoning of all kinds have been used in courts since time immemorial, the specialist and scholarly study of 'legal argumentation' is traceable back to the 1970s, according to Feteris.[18] Before then, 'legal argumentation' scholarship appeared mainly under the guise of legal theory (jurisprudence) and legal philosophy. A distinction is being drawn here between the history of arguments being used in courts, which probably is as old as the discipline of law itself, and the specialist study of regular and/or peculiar arguments in forensic contexts.[19] For example, there is historical evidence of some form of argumentation, either in the narrow or broad sense, being deployed in ancient societies either in the form of the casuistic reasoning of Mesopotamian courts[20] or the rhetorical speeches of the Greek logographers.[21] The main difference between antiquity and the period after the 1970s is institutionalisation. According to Gabbay and Woods, the institutional domestication or

15 Christian Kock "The reception of ancient rhetoric in modern argumentation theory and pedagogy," in *Brill's companion of the reception of ancient rhetoric*, eds. Sophia Papaioannou et al (Leiden: Brill, 2021) 489 at 489–490.

16 Douglas Walton *Plausible argument in everyday conversation* (Albany: State University of New York Press, 1992) 4. Simply put, *dialektikos* for the Greeks meant 'to discuss' (at 4). See also Kneale and Kneale *Development of logic*, 7. For Aristotle, reasoning is 'dialectic' if its starting premisses are not 'demonstratively' (or 'analytically' true, but rather if they are 'generally accepted opinions' (*endoxa*); see Aristotle *Topics* (translated by W.A. Pickard-Cambridge) (Cambridge: NuVision Publications, 2005) Book 1, part 1; Aristotle *De Sophisticis Elenchis* (edited and translated by E.S. Forster) (Cambridge: Harvard University Press, 1955) 15. However, argumentation theorists commonly use the terms 'dialectic' and 'dialogue' interchangeably, see J. Anthony Blair "The limits of the dialogue model of argument" (1998) *Argumentation* 12(2) 325 at 337.

17 See Jan Woleński "Formal and informal in legal logic," in *Approaches to legal rationality*, eds. Dov M. Gabbay et al (Dordrecht: Springer, 2010) 73 at 74–75.

18 Eveline Feteris *Fundamentals of legal argumentation: A survey of theories on the justification of judicial decisions* 2nd ed (Dordrecht: Springer, 2017) 257; Eveline T. Feteris "A survey of 25 years of research on legal argumentation" (1997) 11 *Argumentation* 355.

19 See Kneale and Kneale *Development of logic*, 1, where a similar distinction is drawn with respect to the history of logic.

20 Samuel Greengus "Legal and social institutions of ancient Mesopotamia," in *Civilisations of the ancient Near East*, ed. Jack M. Sasson (New York: Simon & Schuster Macmillan, 1995) 469 at 472; John Sasson *Ancient laws and modern problems* (Bristol: Intellect, 2005) 32. Cf. Geoffrey Samuel "What is it to have knowledge of Roman legal methods," in *New developments in legal reasoning and logic: From ancient law to modern systems*, ed. Shahid Rahman et al (Dordrecht: Springer, 2022) 3 at 16.

21 Kaius Tuori "Legal profession," in *A cultural history of law: In antiquity*, ed. Julen Extabe (London: Bloomsbury, 2019) 143 at 143; James Gordley *The jurists: A critical history* (Oxford: Oxford University Press, 2013) especially Chs I, II and II.

fermentation of a specialisation is influenced by at least two primary *methodological* and *professional or administrative* factors.[22] Firstly, an institutionalised discipline's identity is defined by the commonality of research methods among scholars within that discipline (e.g. the textual analysis of the novel being synonymous with literary methodology). Secondly, institutionalisation is determined by the degree to which a discipline has been incorporated into the apparatus of a profession or administrative body (e.g. by the imposition of conditions of entry or the issuance of qualifications).[23] The second of these two factors also includes the publication of textbooks and journals, the convention of specialist conferences and the formation of educational or vocational courses and degree programmes.[24]

Legal argumentation scholars generally all use legal theory as their primary methodology for solving legal problems.[25] However, there is some debate about what precisely 'legal argumentation' means. According to Alexander and Sherwin, legal argumentation is nothing more than 'ordinary reasoning applied to legal problems.'[26] In other words, '[l]egal thinking is by no means special,' as it is 'no more special than problem-solving in other fields of reflection.'[27] On the other hand, some scholars consider that 'legal discourse is a special case of general practical discourse' because it 'occurs in the context of a number of limiting conditions,' particularly 'its involvement with doctrinal studies . . . [and] procedural ordinances and regulations.'[28] According to

22 Dov M. Gabbay and John Woods "Logic and the law: Crossing the lines of discipline," in *Approaches to legal rationality*, eds. Dov M. Gabbay et al (Dordrecht: Springer, 2010) 165 at 166.

23 Gabbay and Woods "Logic and the law: Crossing the lines of discipline," 166, n2.

24 Paul Roberts "The priority of procedure and the neglect of evidence and proof" (2015) 13 *Journal of International Criminal Justice* 479 at 480.

25 See William Twining "Evidence and legal theory," in *Law in context: Enlarging a discipline*, ed. William Twining (1997) 110 at 112–113; William Twining "Some jobs for jurisprudence" (1974) 1(2) *British Journal of Law and Society* 149 (five jobs of jurisprudence); Aleksander Peczenik *On law and reason* 2nd ed (Dordrecht: Springer, 2009) 13–14.

26 Larry Alexander and Emily Sherwin *Demystifying legal reasoning* (Cambridge: Cambridge University Press, 2008) 3; Arend Soeteman *Logic in law: Remarks on logic and rationality in normative reasoning, especially in law* (Dordrecht: Springer, 1989) 20–22.

27 Bartosz Brożek *The legal mind: A new introduction to legal epistemology* (New York: Cambridge University Press, 2020) 3–4.

28 Alexy "A theory of legal argumentation: The theory of rational discourse as theory of legal justification," 2 and 16; Feteris *Fundamentals of legal argumentation: A survey of theories on the justification of judicial decisions*, 2. See also Douglas Walton *Legal argumentation and evidence* (University Park: Pennsylvania University Press, 2002) 1 ('The first thing a person is struck by when beginning to study legal argumentation and comparing it to ordinary (non-legal) argumentation is the apparently quite impressive differences between the two'). This view is adopted with the caveat that recognises the distinction between 'argumentation' as a sub-species of the broader genus of 'legal reasoning'; see Douglas N. Walton "What is reasoning? What is an argument?" (1990) 87 *Journal of Philosophy* 339; Geoffrey Samuel *Rethinking legal reasoning* (Cheltenham: Elgar, 2018) 2.

Klappstein,[29] legal argumentation generally entails five distinguishing steps.[30] Firstly, legal arguers debate about the legal issues, as defined by established legal doctrine, that must be addressed. Secondly, the applicable legal rules that govern the dispute must be identified. Thirdly, the extant evidential facts to which the applicable legal rules must be applied must be ascertained and proven in their own right. Fourthly, legal arguments about the proof of these extant evidential facts must adhere to established institutional procedures. The fifth step is to conclude the application of the applicable legal rules to the facts and to persuade the forensic adjudicator about which legal outcome is appropriate in the circumstances. This debate about the precise meaning of 'legal argumentation' is beyond the scope of this chapter, but what is clear is that it includes the basic canons of logic at the minimum.

Reverting to the second *professional or administrative* factor of institutionalisation, legal argumentation has made significant progress over the past few decades, but there is still some way to go. For instance, Feteris traces the origins of legal argumentation scholarship to the 1970s on account of a seminal conference that was convened in Brussels between 30 August and 3 September 1971.[31] Under the chairmanship of Chaïm Perelman (1971–1975), the *Internationale Vereinigung für Rechts-und Sozialphilosophie* (IVR) ('International Association for Philosophy of Law and Social Philosophy') for the first time since its inception in 1910 convened its fifth World Congress for Legal and Social Philosophy with a focus on legal argumentation.[32] Legal argumentation continued to dominate the theme of several subsequent conferences organised by the IVR. These include the Munich *Argumentation und Recht* conference, which convened during 3–6 September 1978,[33] and the Graz *Argumentation and*

29 Verena Klappstein "Why does legal reasoning necessitate an interdisciplinary discourse and an examination from the point of theory of science," in *Theory of legal evidence – Evidence in legal theory*, eds. Verena Klappstein and Meciej Dybowski (Cham: Springer, 2021) 37 at 38–39.

30 For a contrastive account of 'four tasks undertaken by argumentation,' see Douglas Walton "Argumentation theory: A very short introduction," in *Argumentation in artificial intelligence*, eds. Iyad Rahwan and Guillermo R. Simari (Dordrecht: Springer, 2009) 1 at 2; Douglas N. Walton *Fundamentals of critical argumentation* (Cambridge: Cambridge University Press, 2006) 1; Frans H. van Eemeren et al *Fundamentals of argumentation theory* (New York: Routledge, 1996) 22.

31 Feteris *Fundamentals of legal argumentation: A survey of theories on the justification of judicial decisions*, 257.

32 The papers presented at this conference were subsequently published in *Die juristische Argumentation: Vorträge des Weltkongresses für Rechts- und Sozialphilosophie* (Legal argumentation: Proceedings of the World Congress for Legal and Social Philosophy) (Brussels: Franz Steiner Verlag, 1972).

33 See Winifried Hassemer, Arthur Kaufmann and Ulfrid Neumann, eds. *Argumentation und Recht: Vorträge auf der Tagung der Deutschen Sektion der Internationalen Vereinigung für Rechts und Sozialphilosophie* (Argumentation and law: Proceedings of the German section of the International Association for Philosophy of Law and Social Philosophy) (Munich: Franz Steiner Verlag, 1980.

Hermeneutics conference of 7–12 May 1978.[34] Moreover, several members of the IVR also organised smaller symposia on the same theme. The *International Symposium of Argumentation in Legal Science*, convened in Helsinki during 10–12 December 1979,[35] and the *Symposium On the Progress of Theory and Technology in Law and Ethics*, organised by Werner Krawitz and Robert Alexy and held on 27–28 October 1980,[36] are two notable examples. Furthermore, legal argumentation has also taken centre stage at a few of the World Congress for Legal and Social Philosophy meetings since the 1980s. For example, the 11th World Congress for Legal and Social Philosophy conference was organised by the IVR under the Chairmanship of Aulis Aarnio (1983–1987) in Helsinki during 14–20 August 1983. One of the seven themes of the conference was 'Models of Legal Reasoning.'[37] Legal argumentation has also featured among the themes of the 20th, 21st and 22nd World Congresses in Amsterdam (20–24 June 2001),[38] Lund (12–18 August 2003),[39] and Granada (24–29 May 2005), respectively.[40] In addition to these regular and seminal conferences by the IVR, the institutionalisation of legal argumentation is also promoted by institutions such as the International Society for the Study of Argumentation (ISSA), which has convened no fewer than 11 multidisciplinary conferences in Amsterdam since 1986;[41] and the Jurix Foundation for

34 See Werner Krawitz et al, eds. *Argumentation und Hermeneutik in der Jurisprudenz* (Argumentation and hermeneutics in jurisprudence) (Berlin: Duncker & Humblot, 1979).

35 Aulis Aarnio et al, eds. *Methodologie und Erkenntnis theorie der juristischen Argumentation: Beiträge des Internationalen Symposions* (Methodology and epistemology of legal argumentation: Proceedings of the International Symposium of Argumentation in Legal Science) (Berlin: Duncker & Humblot, 1981).

36 Werner Krawietz and Robert Alexy, eds. *Metatheorie juristischer Argumentation* (Metatheory of legal argumentation) (Berlin: Duncker & Humblot, 1983).

37 See generally, Neil MacCormick, Stavros Panou and Luigi Lombardi Vallauri, eds. "Conditions of validity and cognition in modern legal thought," in (*Geltungs- und Erkenntnisbedingungen im modernen Rechtsdenken*) (Proceedings of the 11th World Congress on Philosophy of Law and Social Philosophy) (Stuttgart: Franz Steiner Verlag, 1983).

38 Arend Soeteman, ed. *Pluralism and law* vol 4: Legal reasoning (Proceedings of the 20th World Congress for Legal and Social Philosophy) (Stuttgart: Franz Steiner Verlag, 2004). This conference was organised under the IVF presidency of Eugenio Bulygin (1999–2003).

39 Christian Dahlman and Werner Krawitcz, eds. *Values, rights and duties in legal and philosophical discourse* (Law and politics. In search of balance: Proceedings of the 21st World Congress for Legal and Social Philosophy) (Berlin: Duncker & Humblot, 2005). This conference was organised under the IVF presidency of Aleksander Peczenik (2003–2005).

40 Josep Aguiló-Regla, ed. *Lógica, argumentación e interpretación* (Logic, argumentation and interpretation: Proceedings of the 22nd World Congress for Legal and Social Philosophy) (Berlin: Duncker & Humblot, 2005). This was also under the IVF presidency of Aleksander Peczenik. Further Congresses were convened in 2007 (Kraków, Poland); 2009 (Beijing, China); 2011 (Frankfurt, Germany); 2013 (Belo Horizonte, Brazil); 2015 (Washington DC, United States); 2017 (Lisbon, Portugal); 2019 (Lucerne, Switzerland); 2022 (Bucharest, Romania); and 2024 (Seoul, South Korea).

41 See Bart Garssen et al, eds. *Proceedings of the Ninth Conference of the International Society for the Study of Argumentation* (Amsterdam: Sic Sat, 2019) preface. See also the International

Legal Knowledge Systems, which has organised at least 37 international conferences on the broad theme of the intersection of law, artificial intelligence and information systems.[42]

The institutional footprint of legal argumentation has not grown as quickly in the context of journals and teaching as it has with respect to conferences. A specialist journal focusing exclusively on legal argumentation is yet to appear. Publications in this area usually appear in generalist journals focusing on legal theory, argumentation theory or philosophy more generally.[43] Generalist journals, such as *Argumentation*; *Archiv für Rechts- und Sozialphilosophie* (Archives for Philosophy of Law and Social Philosophy); *Informal Logic*; the *International Journal for the Semotics of Law*; *Rechtstheorie* ('legal theory'); *Nederlands Tijdschrift voor Rechtsfilosofie en Rechtstheorie* ('Dutch journal for legal philosophy and theory'); and the *Quarterly Journal of Speech*, frequently publish legal argumentation articles. Moreover, a university course called Applied Legal Fundamentals, which has been taught by the University of Salzburg's Department of Legal Fundamentals since 1998, is a rarity.[44] Courses containing legal argumentation are usually taught as part of the vocational training of professional associations.

The institutionalisation of legal argumentation clearly is still gradually gaining a foothold. However, the intellectual foundation for this growth has by now already been laid. The remainder of the path of growth for this specialisation is now probably only a matter of time. Although the burgeoning of conferences around this theme is only traceable back to the 1970s, the intellectual foundation for the emergence of this brand of scholarship was laid much earlier than this. The historical roots of legal argumentation were inspired by two predominant scholarly revolts, under the guise of American Realism and Informal Logic, against legal and logical formalism in the twentieth century. These two revolts were preceded by an earlier turn towards formalism and mathematisation[45] in logic after the publication of Gottlob

---

Learned Institute of Argumentation Studies website: www.ilias-argumentation.com (accessed: 11 October 2024).

42 See Jurix website: www.jurix23.maastrichtlawtech.eu (accessed: 11 October 2024).

43 Feteris *Fundamentals of legal argumentation: A survey of theories on the justification of judicial decisions*, 257; Feteris "A survey of 25 years of research on legal argumentation," 356 ('The interest in legal argumentation started, of course, in legal theory').

44 See Günther Kreuzbauer "Teaching legal argumentation," in *Pluralism in law: Proceedings of the 20th World Congress for Legal and Social Philosophy*, ed. Arend Soeteman (Stuttgart: Franz Steiner Verlag, 2004) 79 at 79; Chad S. Carr "Using computer supported argument visualization to teach legal argumentation," in *Visualising argumentation: Software tools for collaborative and educational sense-making*, eds. Paul A. Kirschner et al (London: Springer-Verlag, 2003) 75.

45 Gabbay and Woods "Logic and the law: Crossing the lines of discipline," 168–169; Jan C. Joerden "Logik und Recht," in *Handbuch Rechtsphilosophie*, eds. Eric Hilgendorf and Jan C. Joerden (Berlin: Springer-Verlag, 2021) 244; Dieter Krimphove "A historical overview of the development of legal logic," in *Law and logic: Contemporary issues*, eds. Dieter Kimphove

Frege's *Begriffsschrift*[46] in 1879. The effect of this was to transform the focus of logic scholarship from being 'context-sensitive, agent-oriented, concretely realized, non-demonstrative, highly nuanced' to its contemporary iteration that is 'symbolic, formal, abstract, deductive, context-free, agent-insensitive, explicit and, most of all, mathematical.'[47] According to Gabbay and Woods, this fractured the historical relationship between logic and legal argumentation, which has retained its normative and context-sensitive aspects.[48] It is against this background that the American Realism movement, led by Oliver Wendell Holmes Jr,[49] Jerome Frank[50] and Karl Llewellyn,[51] emerged in the early twentieth century. The Realists rejected the Langdellian[52] 'scientism' and logical 'formalism' that had seeped into the study of law.[53] Their core contention was that 'there is more to the study of law than the study of rules' and that not every form of legal reasoning is reducible to logical syllogistic deduction.[54]

---

and Gabriel M. Lentner (Berlin: Duncker & Humblot, 2017) 11 at 30–34. For more on the 'logical-analytical approach to legal argumentation,' see Ulfrid Neumann *Juristische Argumentationstheorie* (Baden-Baden: Nomos, 2023) § 2 ('Legal argumentation theory').

46 Gottlob Frege *Begriffsschrift, eine der arithmetischen nachgebildete Formelsprache des reinen Denkens* ('Concept notation: A formula language of pure thought, modelled upon that of arithmetic') (Halle: Verlag von Louis Nerbert, 1879), translated by Stefan Bauer-Mengelberg "Concept script, a formal language of pure thought modelled upon that of arithmetic," in *From Frege to Gödel: A source book in mathematical logic, 1879–1931* (Cambridge: Harvard University Press, 1967) 1 at 1–82.

47 Gabbay and Woods "Logic and the law: Crossing the lines of discipline," 169–170.

48 Gabbay and Woods "Logic and the law: Crossing the lines of discipline," 170.

49 Oliver W. Holmes *The common law* (Boston: Little Brown, 1881) 1 ('The life of the law has not been logic: it has been experience').

50 Jerome Frank *Law and the modern mind* (New York: Brentano's, 1930); Jerome Frank "Why not a clinical lawyer-school?" (1933) 81(8) *University of Pennsylvania Law Review and American Law Register* 907.

51 Karl Llewellyn "A realistic jurisprudence – the next step" (1930) 3(4) *Columbia Law Review* 431; Karl Llewellyn "Some realism about realism – Responding to Dean Pound" (1931) 44 *Harvard Law Review* 1222.

52 See Christopher C. Langdell *A summary of the law of contracts* 2nd ed (Boston: Little Brown and Company, 1880) 19 (a syllogistic analysis of the acceptance of an offer in contract law). See also Richard Posner "Legal formalism, legal realism and the interpretation of statutes and the Constitution," in *The philosophy of legal reasoning: Precedents, statutes and analysis of legal concepts*, ed. Scott Brewer (New York: Routledge, 2011) 145.

53 William Twining *Karl Llewellyn and the realist movement* 2nd ed (New York: Cambridge University Press, 2012) 10. See also Dale A. Herbeck "Critical legal studies and argumentation theory" (1995) 9 *Argumentation* 719; Carla Faralli "The legacy of American legal realism" (2005) 48 *Scandinavian Studies in Law* 75; Brian Leiter "Legal formalism and legal realism: What is the issue?" (2010) 16 *Legal Theory* 111; Richard Posner "Realism about judges" (2011) 105(2) *Northwestern University Law Review* 577.

54 William Twining "Taking facts seriously," in *Law in context: Enlarging a discipline*, ed. William Twining (Oxford: Oxford University Press, 1997) 89 at 108; William Twining "The camel in the zoo," in *Law in context: Enlarging a discipline*, ed. William Twining (Oxford: Oxford University Press, 1997) 26 at 33; Ilmar Tammelo "Logic as an instrument of legal reasoning" (1970) 10(3) *Jurimetrics* 89 at 91.

Some of the earliest influential texts in legal argumentation that drew inspiration from this movement included Michael and Adler's *The Nature of Judicial Proof* (1931),[55] Levi's *An Introduction to Legal Reasoning* (1948)[56] and Stone's *The Province and Function of Law* (1946).[57] Furthermore, Golding's *Legal Reasoning* (1984),[58] Burton's *An Introduction to Law and Legal Reasoning* (1985)[59] and Weinreb's *Legal Reason* (2005)[60] are also contributors to this bourgeoning Realist response to legal formalism. Therefore, without the Realist turn away from an exclusive or overwhelming focus on legal doctrine, it is inconceivable that the specialist study of legal argumentation would have emerged.[61]

The second historical scholarly revolt that laid the intellectual foundations for the emergence of legal argumentation was by logicians, argumentation theorists and various other social scientists in the 1970s under the

55 Jerome Michael and Mortimer J. Adler *The nature of judicial proof: An inquiry into the logical, legal and empirical aspects of the law of evidence* (New York: Ad Press, 1931), especially Ch VII (set of lecture notes by two teachers of the law of evidence) (analysing trial proceedings as dialectical controversies where rhetorical arguments are presented).

56 Edward H. Levi "An introduction to legal reasoning" (1948) 15(3) *University of Chicago Law Review* 501, which was subsequently published as Edward H. Levi *An introduction to legal reasoning* (London: University of Chicago Press, 1949) (discussing what he calls 'reasoning by example' through various illustrative cases).

57 Julius Stone *The province and function of law: Law as logic, justice and social control* (Sydney: Associated General Publications, 1946), especially Chapters VI and VII (discussing the application of deductive and non-deductive logical forms to legal reasoning). See also Julius Stone *Legal systems and lawyers' reasoning* (London: Stevens & Sons, 1964), especially Chs 6 and 8; Otto C. Jensen *The nature of legal argument* (Oxford: Basil Blackwell, 1957).

58 Martin P. Golding *Legal reasoning* (New York: Alfred A. Knopf, 1984) (a case-based exposition of legal reasoning, including the logical forms and types of argumentation, especially appeals to precedent and argumentation by analogy (Ch III), that judges use in justification of their decisions).

59 Steven J. Burton *An introduction to law and legal reasoning* (Boston: Little Brown, 1985) (a textbook introducing law students to the forms of legal reasoning, including analogical (Ch 2) and deductive (Ch 3) forms, used by judges in deciding cases). The second and third editions of this text appeared in 1995 and 2007, respectively: Steven J. Burton *An introduction to law and legal reasoning* 2nd ed (Boston: Little Brown, 1995); Steven J. Burton *An introduction to law and legal reasoning* 3rd ed (New York: Aspen Publishers, 2007).

60 Lloyd Weinreb *Legal reason: The use of analogy in legal argument* (New York: Cambridge University Press, 2005) (addressed to both legal scholars and law students, this text distinguishes analogical reasoning from deductive and inductive forms and defends it as an appropriate form of 'everyday reasoning' for the forensic context). A second edition was published in 2016: Lloyd Weinreb *Legal reason: The use of analogy in legal argument* 2nd ed (New York: Cambridge University Press, 2016).

61 For other contemporary texts on legal argumentation, Scott Brewer, ed. *The philosophy of legal reasoning: Precedents, statutes and analysis of legal concepts* (New York: Routledge, 1998); Larry Alexander and Emily Sherwin *Demystifying legal reasoning* (New York: Cambridge University Press, 2008); Frederick Schauer *Thinking like a lawyer* (Cambridge, MA: Harvard University Press, 2009); Geoffrey Samuel *A short introduction to judging and to legal reasoning* (Cheltenham: Elgar, 2016); Geoffrey Samuel *Rethinking legal reasoning* (Cheltenham: Elgar, 2018).

broad banner of 'Informal Logic.' This group of scholars had generally grown dissatisfied with the capacity of formal deductive logic to operate in various context-sensitive areas, such as law, politics and religion, and they contended for the study of 'actual . . . real-life, ordinary, everyday' arguments 'in their native habitat of public discourse and persuasion.'[62] This alternative approach to logic produced scholarship that was characterised, among other things, by the adoption of dialectical approaches to the study of argumentation; a conviction about there being alternative forms and standards of logic other than the orthodox deductive and inductive variants;[63] a desire to expand the study of reasoning beyond argumentation to include 'critical thinking,' 'problem-solving' and 'decision-making' skills; and a propensity towards the study of fallacies as a legitimate basis for logical investigation and reasoning.[64] According to Johnson, the pioneering texts of the Informal Logic movement were Stephen Toulmin's *The Uses of Argument* (1958), Chaïm Perelman and Lucie Olbrechts-Tyteca's *La Nouvelle Rhétorique* [*The New Rhetoric*] (1958) and Charles Hamblin's *Fallacies* (1970).[65] Toulmin, who was a philosopher trained in Wittgensteinian formal logic, contended in context-sensitive areas such as law and politics the 'standards for judging the soundness, validity, cogency or strength of arguments' are not 'field-invariant,' as formal logicians would have it.[66] Quite the contrary, Toulmin had noticed that the 'procedures and rules of argument' in these practical areas had 'hardened into institutions.'[67] Toulmin contended that we should treat logic as a 'generalised jurisprudence' that served the purpose of 'testing our ideas against our actual practice of argument-assessment, rather than against a philosopher's ideal.'[68] Perelman and Olbrechts-Tyteca's text, which was published originally in French in 1958[69] and translated to English

62 Ralph H. Johnson *The rise of informal logic: Essays on argumentation, critical thinking, reasoning and politics* (Newport News: Vale Press, 1996) 13; Ralph H. Johnson and J. Anthony Blair "Informal logic in the twentieth century," in *Historical foundations of informal logic*, eds. Douglas Walton and Alan Brinton (New York: Routledge, 2016) Ch 12. See also Ralph H. Johnson and J. Antony Blair "The origins of informal logic," in *Handbook of the logic of argument and inference: The turn towards the practical*, eds. Dov M. Gabbay et al (Amsterdam: Elsevier, 2002) 339.

63 Cf. Aristotle "Rhetoric," in *The complete works of Aristotle*, ed. Jonathan Barnes vol II (Princeton: Princeton University Press) 2152 at 2156, 1356b7–9: '[E]veryone who proves anything at all is bound to use either deductions or inductions.'

64 See Johnson *The rise of informal logic: Essays on argumentation, critical thinking, reasoning and politics*, 10–11.

65 Johnson *The rise of informal logic: Essays on argumentation, critical thinking, reasoning and politics*, 13.

66 Stephen Toulmin *The uses of argument* (Cambridge: Cambridge University Press, 1958) 136–137.

67 Toulmin *The uses of argument*, 7.

68 Toulmin *The uses of argument*, 10.

69 Chaïm Perelman and Lucie Olbrechts-Tyteca *La Nouvelle Rhétorique: Traité de l'Argumentation* (Paris: *Presses universitaires de France*, 1958).

in 1969,[70] was titled *The New Rhetoric* because its authors purported to study 'the art of persuading and of convincing, the technique of deliberation and of discussion' in the 'dialectical' fashion, using 'everyday language,' as the ancient Greeks had done it before logic became mathematised in the nineteenth century.[71] For Hamblin, the core aim of his project was to resuscitate a subject that was widely considered at the time by formal logicians as 'an afterthought or adjunct to something else.'[72] This sentiment follows on the original treatment of fallacies as an appendix to Aristotle's *Topics*.[73]

These two revolts in American Realism and Informal Logic were influential in the eventual emergence of legal argumentation scholarship in the late twentieth century. Much of this scholarship, although not always overtly, resembles some of the features; for example, the consideration of contextual factors such as the everyday language and institutional implications of argumentation, discussed earlier in the context of Informal Logic and American Realism. Some of the most influential texts in this regard include Robert Alexy's *Theorie der juristischen Argumentation* ('A theory of legal argumentation') (1978),[74] Gerhard Struck's *Zur Theorie juristischer Argumentation* ('On the theory of legal reasoning') (1977),[75] *On Legal Reasoning* (1977) by the Finnish lawyer Aulis Aarnio,[76] and Neil MacCormick's seminal *Legal Reasoning and Legal Theory* (1978).[77] These early pioneering works in legal specialist triggered an eruption of further scholarship on legal argumentation from the 1980s onwards. Peczenik's *The Basis of Legal Justification* (1983)[78] and *On Law and Reason* (1989),[79] as well as Aarnio's *The Rational as Reasonable* (1987),[80] are notable examples.[81] However,

70 Chaïm Perelman and Lucie Olbrechts-Tyteca *The new rhetoric: A treatise on argumentation* (translated by John Wilkinson and Purcell Weaver) (Notre Dame: University of Notre Dame, 1969).
71 Perelman and Olbrechts-Tyteca *The new rhetoric: A treatise on argumentation*, 5.
72 Charles L. Hamblin *Fallacies* (Newport News: Vale Press, 1970) 10.
73 Aristotle *De Sophisticis Elenchis* (edited and translated by E.S. Forster) (Cambridge: Harvard University Press, 1955).
74 Originally published in German as Robert Alexy *Theorie der juristischen argumentation: die theorie des rationalen diskurses als theorie der juristischen begründung* (Frankfurt: Suhrkamp Verlag, 1978), but later translated into English as Robert Alexy, *A theory of legal argumentation: The theory of rational discourse as theory of legal justification* (translated by Ruth Adler and Neil MacCormick) (Oxford: Oxford University Press, 1989).
75 Gerhard Struck *Zur Theorie juristischer argumentation* (Berlin: Duncker & Humblot, 1977).
76 Aulis Aarnio *On legal reasoning* (Turun Yliopisto: Turku, 1977).
77 Neil MacCormick *Legal reasoning and legal theory* (Oxford: Clarendon Press, 1978).
78 Aleksander Peczenik *The basis of legal justification* (Förf: Lund, 1983).
79 Aleksander Peczenik *On law and reason* (Dordrecht: Kluwer, 1989) (2nd edition published in 2009).
80 Aulis Aarnio *The rational as reasonable: A treatise on legal justification* (Dordrecht: Reidel, 1987).
81 Other contemporary examples include Douglas Walton *Legal argumentation and evidence* (University Park: Pennsylvania University Press, 2002) 10; Neil MacCormick *Rhetoric and the rule of law: A theory of legal reasoning* (Oxford: Oxford University Press, 2005) 11; Douglas Walton *Argumentation methods for artificial intelligence in law* (Berlin: Kluwer, 2005) 12; Douglas Walton *Burden of proof, presumption and argumentation* (New York: Cambridge

not all scholars within legal argumentation scholarship have been influenced by the historical American Realist and Informal Logic movements. A small minority of scholars, led principally by Ulrich Klug,[82] have continued to apply modern mathematical techniques and symbolic notations of formal deductive logic to the legal context.[83] This book aims to contribute to this diverse body of legal scholarship that has continued to grow for several decades, but is yet to be fully institutionalised in the respects described earlier in this chapter.

5.3 Modelling Legal Argumentation

The primary purpose of legal argumentation is the development of criteria for distinguishing between 'a good or bad, an acceptable or an unacceptable type of argument in the law.'[84] These criteria will depend largely on the degree to which they are able to persuade[85] judges, jurors, lawyers, prosecutors, investigators and all other participants in the adjudicative process. Legal argumentation scholarship generally fulfils this overarching purpose by performing three argumentative tasks concerning the ***identification, analysis*** and ***evaluation*** of legal arguments.[86] The first task for legal argumentation scholars is to identify the logical forms of the types of arguments that occur frequently in the forensic context (e.g. appeals to authority, arguments by analogy, arguments from an established rule, and evidential arguments). The second task is to analyse the specified forms of arguments while taking into account the relevant contextual factors, including the application of any institutional norms, that may affect the overall persuasiveness of the arguments. The third task is to evaluate the persuasive effect of legal arguments in justification of the conclusion that is sought to be reached.

The function of legal argumentation can be illustrated by considering a basic problem that confronts all forms of forensic adjudication, namely the mapping

---

University Press, 2014) 13; Douglas Walton et al *Statutory interpretation: Pragmatics and argumentation* (New York: Cambridge University Press, 2021). A summary of the history of legal argumentation scholarship is also tracked in Feteris *Fundamentals of legal argumentation: A survey of theories on the justification of judicial decisions* (first published in 1999, and a second edition appeared in 2017).

82 Ulrich Klug *Juristische Logik* (Berlin: Springer-Verlag, 1958) 3 ('It should therefore be noted that within the investigations to be carried out here, wherever there is talk of logic in general, what is meant is what was defined above as formal logic'); Joseph Horovitz "Ulrich Klug's legal logic: A critical account" (1966) 9(33) *Logique et Analyse* 78 at 78.

83 See generally, Ulrich Klug *Juristische Logik* (Oxford: Clarendon Press, 1978) 2; Arend Soeteman *Logic in law: Remarks on logic and rationality in normative reasoning, especially in law* (Dordrecht: Springer, 1989) 3; Joseph Horovitz *Law and logic: A critical legal account* (New York: Springer-Verlag, 1972) 4; Henry Prakken *Logical tools for modelling legal argument* (Dordrecht: Kluwer Academic Publishers, 1997).

84 MacCormick *Legal reasoning and legal theory*, 12–13; Feteris *Fundamentals of legal argumentation: A survey of theories on the justification of judicial decisions*, 24–25.

85 MacCormick *Legal reasoning and legal theory*, 14.

86 Cf. the four argumentation tasks referred to in note 30 earlier in this chapter.

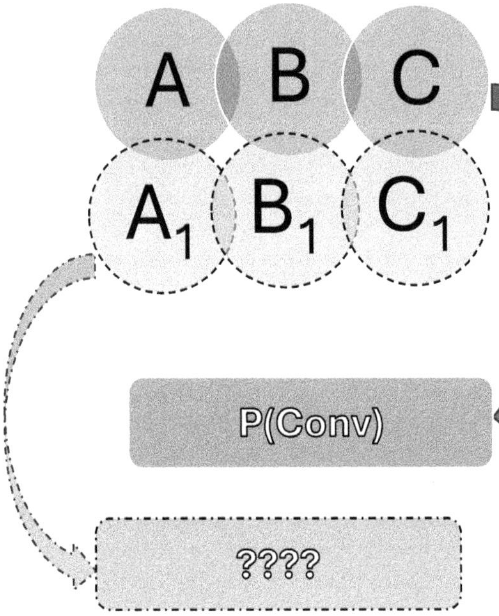

Figure 5.1 A flow chart mapping existing legal doctrine to novel cases

of general rules (*genus*) onto specific cases (*species*). A juridical asymmetry always obtains between existing legal doctrine and novel disputes and cases. The problem arises, as Figure 5.1 shows, when an existing legal rule provides that A + B + C = P_{conv}, whereas the facts of a live case are that $A_1 + B_1 + C_1$.[87]

Another way to frame this basic problem is to contrast between a factual scenario in which A + B + C establish X, whereas D + E establish not-X. As Wigmore says, 'there is no law (yet known) of logical thought which tells us that (A + B + C) + (D + E) must equal X, or must equal Not-X.'[88] The variations in the premisses, on either of the two framings of the problem, render the drawing of the conclusion doubtful, as illustrated in the flow chart in Figure 5.2.

This problem is also illustrated by Hart's examples of what he calls 'problems of the penumbra'[89] and by Dworkin's Herculean 'hard cases.'[90] For example,

87 Alexy "A theory of legal argumentation: The theory of rational discourse as theory of legal justification," 2; Peczenik *On law and reason*, 14–15; Feteris *Fundamentals of legal argumentation: A survey of theories on the justification of judicial decisions*, 3–5.

88 John H. Wigmore "The problem of proof" (1913) 8 *Illinois Law Review* 77 at 82.

89 Herbert L.A. Hart "Positivism and the separation of Law and morals" (1958) 71(4) *Harvard Law Review* 593 at 606–615 (on 'problems of the penumbra'); Lon L. Fuller "Positivism and fidelity to law – A replay to Professor Hart" (1957) 71(4) *Harvard Law Review* 630 at 666.

90 Ronald Dworkin *Taking rights seriously* (Cambridge, MA: Harvard University Press, 1978) Ch 4 (on 'hard cases'); MacCormick *Legal reasoning and legal theory*, VIII (on 'clear cases and hard cases').

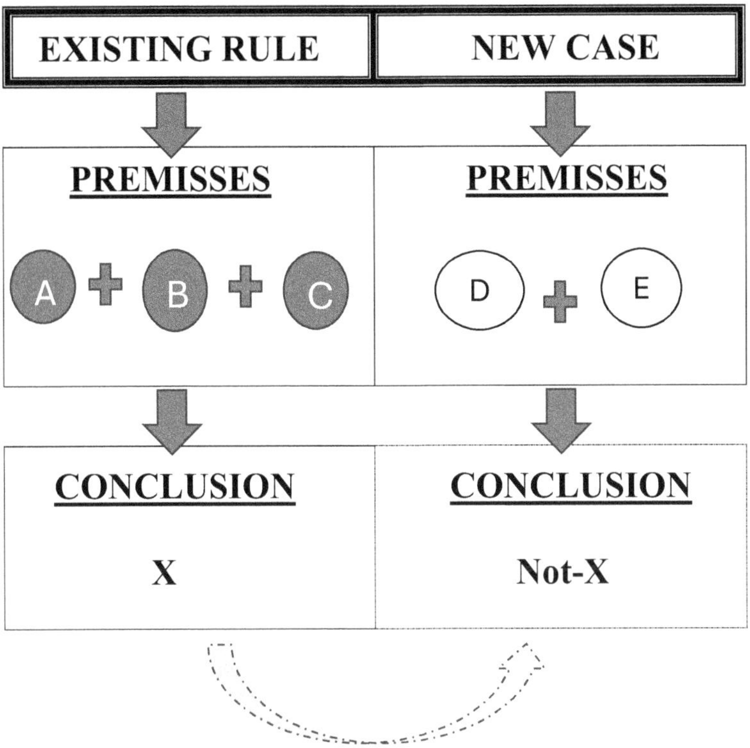

Figure 5.2 A flow chart distinguishing between arguing from existing legal doctrine to novel cases

Hart postulates the following scenario: a rule forbids the entry of *vehicles* into a public park, yet a litigant drives her roller skates, bicycle, private plane or toy vehicle into the park.[91] The question is whether the rule applies to this litigant. Similarly, a rule prohibits any person from kidnapping another person against their will, yet a litigant persuades a religious victim to run away with him by deceiving her into believing that her resistance against fleeing will be followed by severe religious sanction.[92] This juridical asymmetry, in all these examples and illustrations, is filled by legal argumentation.[93]

The remainder of this section will now consider some of the common forms of legal arguments that are used in the forensic context. This is by no means a closed list. There is an infinite amount of forms of argumentation that recur in forensic adjudication, ranging from 'open-ended moral reasoning [and]

91 Hart "Positivism and the separation of law and morals," 607.
92 Adapted from Dworkin "Taking rights seriously," 107.
93 See Frederick Schauer "Giving reasons" (1995) 47(4) *Stanford Law Review* 633 at 642.

empirical reasoning' to more standard forms of 'deduction from authoritative rules.'[94] For example, Demele lists 17 different categories of 'classic legal arguments,' including the *argumentum a contrario* (argument from the contrary), the *argumentum ab absurdo* (argument from absurdity), the *a simili* argument (analogical argument), the *a fortiori* argument (argument from strength) and the *argumentum ab exemplo* (argument by way of example).[95] Owing to the limited scope of this chapter, only four of these common forms will be discussed briefly: the *argumentum ad verecundiam* (appeal to authority), the *argumentum ad analogia legis* (analogical argument), the *argumentum ad opinion doctorum* (argument from established rule) and the evidential argument (argument towards a hypothesis).

The appeal to authority (*argumentum ad verecundiam*) is one of the oldest forms of argument to be used in forensic adjudication. Various authorities, such as the Fathers of the Church, religious scriptures, the gods, the prophets, scientists, doctrine, general opinion and philosophers, have been invoked since antiquity to bolster the probative force of arguments made in the forensic context.[96] The standard form of the basic argument takes a deductive (membership of a reference class) form:

(1) God says all X's are prohibited.
(2) A is an X.
(3) Therefore, A is prohibited.[97]

A similar example takes the following epistemic form.

(1) Everything X says is true.
(2) X said that P.
(3) Therefore, P.[98]

94 Alexander and Sherwin "Demystifying legal reasoning," 3; Vincent A. Wellman "Practical reasoning and judicial justification: Toward an adequate theory" (1985) 57(1) *University of Colorado Law Review* 45 (discussing deductive, analogical and practical reasoning as 'dominant theories of judicial reasoning'); Tammelo "Logic as an instrument of legal reasoning," 89 (discussing deductive, inductive and 'paraductive' forms of legal reasoning); Jan Woleński "Formal and informal in legal logic," in *Approaches to legal rationality*, eds. Dov M. Gabbay et al (Dordrecht: Springer, 2010) 74 ('[C]haracteristic patterns of legal arguments, like argumentum a *majori ad minus, argumentum a minori ad majus, argumentum a contrario, argumentum a fortiori, argumentum a simile, analogia legis, analogia iuris* or various kinds of presumptions (for example, that persons died in an aircraft catastrophe, died at the same moment)').

95 Giovanni Damele "Analogia legis and analogia iuris: An apparent distinction," in *Systematic approaches to argument by analogy*, eds. Henrique J. Ribeiro (Cham: Springer, 2014) 243 at 250, n8, citing Giovanni Tarello *Diritto, enunciati, usi* (Bologna: Il Mulino, 1974); Giovanni Tarello *L'interpretazione della legge* (Milano: Giuffré, 1974) for a fuller taxonomy of variants of legal argumentation.

96 Perelman and Olbrechts-Tyteca *The new rhetoric: A treatise on argumentation*, 307.

97 Douglas Walton *Appeal to expert opinion: Arguments from authority* (University Park: Pennsylvania State University Press, 1992) 93.

98 Hamblin *Fallacies*, 218.

In general terms, the second (minor) premise holds because it is a member of the general class that depends for its truth on the authority appealed to in the first (major) premise. Furthermore, true to its deductive form, the authoritative claim in the first premise is framed in absolutist terms without any room for exceptions to the general rule.

(1) All As are B.
(2) X is an A.
(3) Therefore, X is a B.[99]

This form of argumentation was common and especially popular in antique societies that generally believed that 'the power to adjudicate breaches of the law rested in the hands of the gods.'[100]

The second common form of argument is the argument by analogy (*argumentum ad analogia legis*). The concept of analogy (ἀναλογία), which derives from the Greek words *ana* ('according to') and *logon* ('ratios'),[101] referred originally to the mathematical concept of proportion or ratios of two sets of numbers (e.g. the ratio of 8 and 2, which is 4, was considered to be *analogical* to that of 4 and 1, which is also 4).[102] The form of this type of argument represents a relationship between a 'theme' (source) and a *phoros* (target).[103]

99 Walton "Appeal to expert opinion: Arguments from authority," 93.

100 Sadakat Kadri *The trial: From Socrates to O.J. Simpson* (London: Harper Perennial, 2005) 1. For later positivistic versions ('law as command') of the *argumentum ad verecundiam*, see Thomas Hobbes *Leviathan* (Oxford: Clarendon Press, 1909); Jeremy Bentham "What a law is," in *Bentham's political thought*, ed. Bhikhu Parekh (London: Croom Helm, 1973) 146–156; Jeremy Bentham *Of laws in general* (edited by H.L.A. Hart) (London: Athlone Press, 1970); John Austin *Province of jurisprudence determined* (London: Weidenfeld & Nicolson, 1971).

101 Fabrizio Macagno and Douglas Walton "Argument from analogy in law, the classical tradition, and recent theories" (2009) 42(2) *Philosophy & Rhetoric* 154 at 168; Bartosz Brożek "Analogical arguments," in *Handbook of legal reasoning and argumentation*, eds. Giorgio Bongiovanni et al (Dordrecht: Springer, 2018) 365 at 365–368 (on the Greek analogia and the Latin *proportionalitas*); Clifford Ando "Exemplum, analogy and precedent in Roman law," in *Exemplarity and singularity: Thinking through particulars in philosophy, literature and law*, eds. Michèle Lowrie and Susanne Lüdemann (London: Routledge, 2015) 88 at 90–92 (on the Roman *exemplum* and *ad similia*).

102 Scott Brewer "Exemplary reasoning: Semantics, pragmatics and the rational force of legal argument by analogy" (1996) 109 *Harvard Law Review* 923 at 949–950; Perelman and Olbrechts-Tyteca *The new rhetoric: A treatise on argumentation*, 372–373.

103 Perelman and Olbrechts-Tyteca *The new rhetoric: A treatise on argumentation*, 372. Perelman and Olbrechts-Tyteca add that '[a]lthough the typical analogy comprises four terms,' analogous arguments may also be illustrated using three terms, namely: 'B is to A as C is to B' (at 375). According to Ribeiro, 'It was not until the twentieth century and, in particular, Perelman and Olbrechts-Tyteca's (1969) pioneering research that this argument was granted due relevance in the context of a new conception of rationality and argumentation in general. (Note, in this respect, that even Toulmin (1958) apparently does not present a conception of analogy or analogical reasoning in general' (Henrique J. Ribeiro "Introduction,"

(1) Generally, case C_1 (source) is similar to case C_2 (target).
(2) Proposition A is true (false) in case C_1.
(3) Therefore, Proposition A is true (false) in case C_2.[104]

Analogical argumentation by definition is an argument in which 'from the fact that two entities are alike in some respect(s), it is concluded that they are also alike in some other respect(s).'[105]

(1) *a* has features $f_1, f_2 \ldots f_n$.
(2) *b* has features $f_1, f_2 \ldots f_n$.
(3) Therefore, *a* and *b* should be treated or classified in the same way with respect to f_{n+1}.[106]

The claim here is that if a case, evidentiary fact, action, entity or state of affairs (*a*) has the same features (f_1 till f_n) as another (*b*), then the two should be treated in the same way on account of this similarity. The reason for the inclusion of f_{n+1} in the conclusion is to indicate that similarity likewise applies to any additional features within the *f* category of attributes.[107] Analogical arguments are common to most systems of legal adjudication; for example, the Chinese *Tui Lei* ('extended variant or sort'),[108] the Islamic *qiyās* ('analogy' or 'correlational inference')[109] and the Roman *exemplum* or *ex facto ius ortur*[110] are variations of analogical reasoning.

---

in *Systematic approaches to argument by analogy*, ed. Henrique J. Ribeiro (Cham: Springer, 2014) 1 at 1–2)).

104 Douglas Walton *Argumentation schemes for presumptive reasoning* (Mahwah: Lawrence Erlbaum Association, 1996) 77; Douglas Walton et al *Argumentation schemes* (New York: Cambridge University Press, 2008) 56; Walton *Legal argumentation and evidence*, 327. See also Claudio Michelon "The uses of precedent and legal argument," in *Philosophical foundations of precedent*, eds. Timothy Endicott et al (Oxford: Oxford University Press, 2023) 117 at 123–126 (on analogical applications of the argument from precedent); Cass R. Sunstein "Analogical reasoning and precedent," in *Philosophical foundations of precedent*, eds. Timothy Endicott et al (Oxford: Oxford University Press, 2023) 217.

105 Irving M. Copi et al *Introduction to logic* 15th ed (New York: Routledge, 2019) 500. See also Patrick J. Hurley *A concise introduction to logic* 14th ed (Boston: Wadsworth, 2024) 448.

106 Marcello Guarini "A defence of non-deductive reconstructions of analogical arguments" (2004) 24(2) *Informal Logic* 153 at 161.

107 Guarini "A defence of non-deductive reconstructions of analogical arguments," 161–162.

108 Yun Xie "Argument by analogy in ancient China" (2019) 33 *Argumentation* 323.

109 Walter E. Young "The formal evolution of Islamic juridical dialectic: A brief glimpse," in *New developments in legal reasoning and logic: From ancient law to modern systems*, ed. Shahid Rahman et al (Dordrecht: Springer, 2022) 83 at 88.

110 Geoffrey Samuel "What is it to have knowledge of Roman legal methods," in *New developments in legal reasoning and logic: From ancient law to modern systems*, eds. Shahid Rahman et al (Dordrecht: Springer, 2022) 3 at 38; James Gordley *The jurists: A critical history* (Oxford: Oxford University Press, 2013) 7–12; Geoffrey Samuel *Rethinking historical jurisprudence* (Cheltenham: Elgar, 2022) Chs 3 and 4; Clifford Ando "*Exemplum*, analogy and precedent in Roman law," in *Exemplarity and singularity: Thinking through particulars in*

The third common form of legal argumentation is the argument from established rule (*argumentum ad opinion doctorum*). At the core of this argument is a claim of fit between a particular case and an established rule.

(1) Generally, if Case_n fits established Rule_R, then the outcome of this case should follow what is stated by Rule_R.
(2) Case_1 fits Rule_R.
(3) Therefore, the outcome of Case_1 should follow what is stated by Rule_R.[111]

For example:

(1) As a rule, if X commits a base offence under a bias motivation, then X has committed a hate crime.
(2) X has committed a base offence under a bias motivation.
(3) Therefore, X has committed a hate crime.

Arguments of this sort derive their legitimacy from the authority of the first (major) premise, which usually emanates from a combination of a legislative decree (Rule_R) and an authoritative interpretation of the meaning of the rule, particularly the outcome it requires.[112] There might also be some debate about whether or not the disputed case (Case_1) actually fits the parameters of the rule.

The fourth common type of legal argument is the evidential argument (argument towards a hypothesis). According to Bex, this type of argument consists of an '*e* is evidence for *p*' evidential generalisation.[113] The claim here is an empirical one, namely that the hypothesis is *confirmed* by the evidence or data. This type of argument can be structured in a variety of ways, including in the form of an argument from positive (or negative) verification.

(1) If A (a hypothesis) is true, then B (a proposition reporting an event) will be observed to be true.
(2) B has been observed to be true, in a given instance.
(3) Therefore, A is true.[114]

---

philosophy, literature and law, eds. Michèle Lowrie and Susanne Lüdemann (London: Routledge, 2015) Ch 9.

111 Walton *Legal argumentation and evidence*, 328; Walton *Burden of proof, presumption and argumentation*, 87; Walton *Argumentation schemes for presumptive reasoning*, 90; Walton et al *Argumentation schemes*, 343.

112 Samuel "What is it to have knowledge of Roman legal methods," 22–23.

113 Floris J. Bex *Arguments, stories and criminal evidence: A formal hybrid theory* (Dordrecht: Springer, 2011) 36.

114 Walton et al *Argumentation schemes*, 331. The negative version of the argument (from falsification) entails the following: (1) if A (hypothesis) is true, then B (a proposition reporting an event) will be observed to be true; (2) B has been observed to be false, in a given instance; (3) therefore, A is false (at 331–332). See also Walton *Argumentation schemes for presumptive reasoning*, 67; Walton *Legal argumentation and evidence*, 325–326; David Schum *Evidential*

The second (minor) premise in the forensic context will usually emanate from the usual sources of evidence: witness testimony, real evidence and documentary evidence. For example, the claim will be that (1) if X committed a hate crime in a dense marketplace, an eyewitness would have observed this to be true; (2) Y (an eyewitness) observed and testified that X committed a hate crime in a dense marketplace; (3) therefore, X committed a hate crime in a dense marketplace.[115] Arguments of this form are applicable to disputes of fact, and less so in the context of disputes about the existence, content (meaning), application and validity of established legal rules.[116] The discussion in this chapter is limited to a brief outline of the common forms of legal argumentation without evaluating the logical strengths and weaknesses of each argument. The evaluation of these arguments will be undertaken in Chapter 6 that focuses on their application to the context of hate crimes.

5.4 Deductive Probative Models

A deductive argument is identifiable by a conclusion that follows 'by necessity' because its truth is guaranteed by the truth of the premise(s) from which it is drawn.[117] The word 'deduction' is a modern translation of the much older technical word 'syllogism,' which refers to a specific form of valid argument that was formulated originally by Aristotle.[118] The ancient Greeks used the verb *syllogizesthai* (*συλλογίζεσθαι*) to mean 'to add up' or 'to compute,'[119] whereas in the noun sense *syllogismos* (συλλογισμός), the ordinary meaning was a 'computation' or 'reckoning.'[120] Aristotle himself gave a more technical definition.

> A 'syllogismos' is an argument (logos) in which, (i) certain things being posited (*tethentôn*), (ii) something other than what was laid down

foundations of probabilistic reasoning (New York: Wiley, 1994) 77–83; Arthur C. Hastings *A reformulation of the modes of reasoning in argumentation* (Northwestern University: unpublished PhD thesis, 1962) 78–92.

115 See Bex "Arguments, stories and criminal evidence: A formal hybrid theory," 36. Cf. Walton *Legal argumentation and evidence*, 330, where a similar argument relying on witness testimony can be structured in the form of an argument from position to know: (1) source *a* is in a position to know about things in a certain subject domain S containing proposition A; (2) *a* asserts that A is true (false); (3) A is true (false).

116 On the distinction between argumentation about disputes of fact and those of law, see Walton "Legal reasoning and argumentation," 47; Giovanni Tuzet "Arguing on facts: Truth, trials and adversary procedures," in *Legal argumentation theory: Cross-disciplinary perspectives*, eds. Christian Dahlman and Eveline Feteris (Dordrecht: Springer, 2013) 207.

117 Catarina Dutilh Novaes *The dialogical roots of deduction: Historical, cognitive and philosophical perspectives on reasoning* (Cambridge: Cambridge University Press, 2021) 3.

118 Robin Smith "Logic," in *The Cambridge companion to Aristotle*, ed. Jonathan Barnes (Cambridge: Cambridge University Press, 1995) 27 at 30.

119 Gisela Striker *Aristotle: Prior analytics* Book I (translated by Gisela Striker) (Oxford: Oxford University Press, 2009) 79.

120 Smith "Logic" 30.

> (*keimenôn*) (iii) results by necessity (*eks anagkês sumbainei*) (iv) because these things are so. By 'because these things are so' I mean that it results through these, and by 'resulting through these' I mean that no term is required from outside for the necessity to come about.[121]

Although the ordinary word pre-dates Aristotle, his conception of a syllogism as a valid logical argument in these terms was pioneering.[122] According to Novaes, Aristotle's *Prior Analytics*, where deductive arguments are discussed, was influenced by developments both in mathematics and dialectics at the time.[123]

There are three basic features that distinguish deductive arguments from other types of argumentation.[124] Deductive arguments are first and foremost necessarily truth preserving.[125] This means that the truth contained in the premisses is retained in the conclusion because the conclusion cannot be false if the premisses are true.[126] This is achieved by a recombining and restating in the conclusion information that is already, categorically or implicitly, contained in the premisses. Accordingly, deductive arguments are non-ampliative. For example, the conclusion that 'Z has no wife' is already contained in the premise that 'Z is a bachelor.'[127] If the premise is true, then the conclusion follows by necessary implication. Another way that the truth of the premisses

121 Aristotle "The prior analytics," in *The complete works of Aristotle*, ed. Jonathan Barnes vol I (Princeton: Princeton University Press) 39 at 40, 24b18–22; Catarina Dutilh Novaes "The syllogism as defined by Aristotle, Ockham, and Buridan," in *The language of thought in late medieval philosophy: Essays in honor of Claude Panacio*, eds. Jenny Pelletier and Magali Roques (Cham: Springer, 2017) 217 at 219. See also Aristotle "Topics," in *The complete works of Aristotle*, ed. Jonathan Barnes vol I (Princeton: Princeton University Press) 167 at 167, 100a25.

122 Novaes *The dialogical roots of deduction: Historical, cognitive and philosophical perspectives on reasoning*, 108 ('[H]e really seems to have been the first to systematize the concept of deduction') and 109 ('Aristotle was the first to formulate a precise theory of implication: the theory of syllogistic as presented in Prior Analytics').

123 Novaes *The dialogical roots of deduction: Historical, cognitive and philosophical perspectives on reasoning*, 107. Novaes further added that: '[T]he first fully-fledged theory of deductive reasoning [lies] in Aristotle's syllogistic' (at 98). Marko Malink "The beginnings of formal logic: Deduction in Aristotle's topics vs. prior analytics" (2015) 60(3) *Phronesis* 267 at 267 ('It is widely agreed that Aristotle's Prior Analytics marks the beginning of formal logic. Aristotle's main concern in this treatise is with deductions (*syllogismoi*)').

124 Novaes *The dialogical roots of deduction: Historical, cognitive and philosophical perspectives on reasoning*, 4–5.

125 Novaes *The dialogical roots of deduction: Historical, cognitive and philosophical perspectives on reasoning*, 5; Antonino Rotolo and Giovanni Sartor "Deductive and deontic reasoning," in *Handbook of legal reasoning and argumentation*, eds. Giorgio Bongiovanni et al (Dordrecht: Springer, 2018) 243 at 250 ('[A]n argument is deductively valid if there is no interpretation (in the semantics) in which its premisses are all true and its conclusion false').

126 Merilee H. Salmon *Introduction to logic and critical thinking* 6th ed (Boston: Clark Baxter, 2013) 81.

127 Salmon *Introduction to logic and critical thinking*, 80.

of a deductive argument is preserved is through arguments based on class membership, which was the main preoccupation of Aristotle in the Prior Analytics.[128] The truth of the premisses is preserved by attributing a property that recurs in a general class to a member of that general class by sheer virtue of this membership. For example:

(1) No athletes are vegetarians.
(2) All football players are athletes.
(3) Therefore, no football players are vegetarians.[129]

A similar example is the claim that (1) all dogs are animals; (2) Y is a dog; (3) therefore, Y is an animal.[130] Provided that all dogs are in fact animals, and that Y is a dog (in other words, that the premisses are true), the conclusion that Y is animal cannot be false. Deductive arguments can also appear in the form of the statement of a general principle and a stated implication of that principle. For example:

(1) All deliberate killing of helpless persons is wrong.
(2) Euthanasia (mercy killing) is a deliberate killing of a helpless person.
(3) Therefore, euthanasia is wrong.[131]

The truth of the general principle, namely that deliberately killing helpless persons is wrong, is preserved in the conclusion pertaining to euthanasia, which the second premise claims to be an example of 'a deliberate killing of a helpless person.' The epistemic truth of the general principle (premise (1)) or the second premise is another matter altogether that is beyond the scope of deductive logic. Similarly, the conclusion that '3 + 4' = '4 + 3' necessarily follows from the general principle that 'addition is commutative.'[132] A further feature of deductive arguments is that the addition of an additional premise, such as '5 + 4' = '4 + 5,' does not affect the validity of the overall argument. This is because deductive arguments are *monotonic*,[133] which is to say that a truth-preserving conclusion that follows necessarily from a true premise will remain valid irrespective of how many subsets or iterations of the same premise are added.

The second feature of deductive arguments is that they follow a perspicuous stepwise structure. This means that the move from premisses to conclusion

128 Aristotle "The prior analytics," 41, 26a1 ('If A is predicated of every B, and B of every C, A must be predicated of every C'); Copi et al "Introduction to logic," 151.
129 Copi et al "Introduction to logic," 151.
130 Novaes *The dialogical roots of deduction: Historical, cognitive and philosophical perspectives on reasoning*, 3.
131 Salmon *Introduction to logic and critical thinking*, 83–84.
132 Salmon *Introduction to logic and critical thinking*, 80.
133 Novaes *The dialogical roots of deduction: Historical, cognitive and philosophical perspectives on reasoning*, 5.

must be made openly, demonstrably and in a step-by-step manner.[134] Therefore, the preservation of the truth of the premisses must be undertaken in a number of clear steps, and 'not "mentally" by a given individual' where one or more intermediate steps are missing from the premise to the conclusion.[135] The third feature of deductive argumentation is that it requires the bracketing of one's belief with respect to the epistemic truth of the content of the premisses.[136] The premisses are to be approached on a 'topic-neutral' and 'formal' basis;[137] that is, they are taken at face value and as contingent upon the separate verification of their epistemic warrant. Therefore, the focus of deductive logic is on the *validity* of arguments as determined by the structural relationship, such as in the form of class membership or as general principle and stated example, between the premisses and conclusion.[138]

Turning now to consider the basic form of a deductive argument, one of the oldest examples derives probably from the Enlightenment period.[139]

(1) All men are mortal.
(2) Socrates is a man.
(3) Socrates is mortal.[140]

The membership of Socrates in the general class of men (second premise) licences the attribution of a property (i.e. mortality) that is germane to all men (first premise) to him as well. As a result of its non-ampliative nature, the conclusion to this argument does not contain any new information (on either men being mortal or Socrates being a man) that is not already contained in the premisses. Another example of a deductive argument is the following claim:

(1) All Mondays are days on which there is a ferry to Mombasa.
(2) Today is Monday.
(3) Therefore, today is a day on which there is a ferry to Mombasa.[141]

134 Novaes *The dialogical roots of deduction: Historical, cognitive and philosophical perspectives on reasoning*, 7.
135 Novaes *The dialogical roots of deduction: Historical, cognitive and philosophical perspectives on reasoning*, 6–7.
136 Novaes *The dialogical roots of deduction: Historical, cognitive and philosophical perspectives on reasoning*, 8.
137 Rotolo and Giovanni Sartor "Deductive and deontic reasoning," 247.
138 Copi et al "Introduction to logic," 192.
139 See John S. Mill *A system of logic: Ratiocinative and inductive, being a connected view of the principles of evidence, and the methods of scientific investigation* 2nd ed (London: John W. Parker, 1846) Ch III, p. 113. First edition published in 1843.
140 Salmon *Introduction to logic and critical thinking*, 80–81. Aristotle "The prior analytics," 41, 32b38–39 ('Whenever A may belong to every B, and B to every C, there will be a perfect deduction that A may belong to every C'). See also Rotolo and Giovanni Sartor "Deductive and deontic reasoning," 53: '(1) All Ps are Qs; and (2) *a* is a P; (3) therefore, *a* is a Q.'
141 See also Rotolo and Giovanni Sartor "Deductive and deontic reasoning," 50.

In addition to this original form, focusing on class membership, that was developed by Aristotle, a further set of well-known deductive forms was developed by the post-Aristotelian Stoic philosophers led by Zeno of Citium from approximately 300 till 130 BCE.[142] These include the *modus ponendo ponens* (the mood that affirms the consequent by affirming the antecedent); the *modus tollendo tollens* (the mood that denies the antecedent by denying the consequent); the *modus ponendo tollens* (the mood that denies the consequent by affirming the antecedent); and the *modus tollendo ponens* (the mood that affirms the consequent by denying the antecedent).[143]

Some of the main shortcomings of deductive forms of argumentation pertain to their limited application in the number of contexts in which they can apply (e.g. in mathematics),[144] given that they require a sufficient amount of information available to verify the epistemic content of their premisses. As a result, as Novaes argues, 'deductive reasoning is usually quite "costly,"' particularly because we do not always need 'absolute certainty' in everyday contexts of reasoning.[145] This is also the case in the forensic context where the information (evidence) available is always incomplete,[146] and where adjudicators decide cases on the basis of non-absolute metrics such as 'common sense'[147] and their 'inner convictions.' Deductive models may find application in deontic debates about the content (prohibitive, permissive, peremptory) of legal obligations,[148] and MacCormick classically used a deductive *modus ponens* model to explain the factual and legal aspects of legal argumentation: (1)

142 van Eemeren et al *Handbook of argumentation theory*, 105.

143 van Eemeren et al *Handbook of argumentation theory*, 113–114. See also Susanne Bobzien "Stoic syllogistic," in *Oxford studies in ancient philosophy*, ed. Christopher C.W. Taylor vol XIV (New York: Oxford University Press, 1996) 133 (on the Stoic 'indemonstrable arguments (anapodeiktoi)'); Susanne Bobzien "Logic," in *The Cambridge companion to the Stoics*, ed. Brad Inwood (Cambridge: Cambridge University Press, 2003) 85; Cf. Copi et al "Introduction to logic," 214–223 (on 15 valid forms of categorical syllogism, including the well-known *Barbara, Celarent, Darii, Ferio, Camestres, Cesare, Boroko* and *Festino* scholastic forms).

144 Novaes *The dialogical roots of deduction: Historical, cognitive and philosophical perspectives on reasoning*, 12; Ikka Niiniluoto "Induction," in *Handbook of epistemology*, eds. Ikka Niiniluoto et al (Dordrecht: Springer, 2004) 521 at 522 ('This idea is prominent in the "metamathematical" study of formal systems, where the acceptable premises are axioms of logic or some mathematical theory').

145 Novaes *The dialogical roots of deduction: Historical, cognitive and philosophical perspectives on reasoning*, 19.

146 Ronald J. Allen and Michael S. Pardo "Juridical proof and the best explanation" (2007) 27(3) *Law and Philosophy* 223 at 227–228; Walton *Legal argumentation and evidence*, 209–210; Floris Bex et al "Towards a formal account of reasoning about evidence: Argumentation schemes and generalisations" (2003) 11 *Artificial Intelligence and Law* 125 at 133.

147 Paul Roberts *Roberts & Zuckerman's criminal evidence* 3rd ed (Oxford: Oxford University Press, 2022) 175.

148 Rotolo and Giovanni Sartor "Deductive and deontic reasoning," 243; Giovanni Sartor *Legal reasoning: a cognitive approach to the law* (Dordrecht: Springer, 2007) 453 ('the term *deontic* derives from the Greek verb *deomai* which means being due or obligatory').

in any case, if *p* then *q*; (2) in the instant case, *p*; (3) therefore, in the instant case, *q*.[149] The second shortcoming of deductive arguments is that they are non-ampliative,[150] whereas much of the value of proof and argumentation, as indicated earlier this chapter, lies in the fact that they can generate new information from facts that are known. The third shortcoming is that deductive arguments are not particularly useful in verifying the starting evidential premisses that are often the subject of dispute in the forensic context.[151]

5.5 Inductive Probative Models

An inductive argument consists of a logical conclusion drawn from a build-up of prior 'patterns, resemblances or other kinds of regularities in our experiences.'[152] The etymology of the word is traceable to the Latin *inductio*,[153] which in turn derives from the Greek word *epagoge* (ἐπάγειν), which means 'to bring or lead in, or on.'[154] Cicero defined *inductio* to mean something akin to an analogical argument:

> a form of argument which *leads* the person with whom one is arguing to give assent to certain undisputed facts, through this assent it wins his

149 MacCormick *Legal reasoning and legal theory*, 24. See also Neil MacCormick *Rhetoric and the rule of law: A theory of legal reasoning* (Oxford: Oxford University Press, 2005) Ch 3; Anthony G. Guest "Logic in the law," in *Oxford essays in jurisprudence*, ed. Anthony G. Guest (London: Oxford University Press, 1961) 176; Steven J. Burton *An introduction to law and legal reasoning* (Boston: Little, Brown and Company, 1985) Ch 3. Cf. Jerome Michael and Mortimer J. Adler "The trial of an issue of fact (part 1)" (1934) 34(7) *Columbia Law Review* 1224 at 1241–1242; Terence Anderson et al *Analysis of evidence* 2nd ed (Cambridge: Cambridge University Press, 2005) 60–61, where *q* is regarded as the legal conclusion or verdict (on the merits) and *p* as the *ultimate probandum*.

150 Novaes *The dialogical roots of deduction: Historical, cognitive and philosophical perspectives on reasoning*, 21.

151 Michael and Adler "The trial of an issue of fact (part 1)," 1272. For the reason that deductive conclusions are analytically implied in, and therefore, do not they add anything new to the premisses, Reichenbach comments that '[s]uch emptiness is the very essence of deductive inference and represents the price which we pay for the necessary truth of the conclusion,' see Hans Reichenbach *Rise of scientific philosophy* (Berkeley: University of California Press, 1968) 81. Schum points out that '[w]hat we require in our daily lives are inferences whose conclusions go beyond evidential premises' (Schum "Evidential foundations of probabilistic reasoning," 23).

152 Alan Hausman et al *Logic and philosophy: A modern introduction* 13th ed (Indianapolis: Hackett Publishing Company, 2021) 5; Brian Skyrms *Choice and chance: An introduction to inductive logic* 4th ed (Belmont: Wadsworth, 2000) 17; Alex Stein "The refoundation of evidence law" (1996) 9 *Canadian Journal of Law & Jurisprudence* 279 at 307 ('Such arguments also build up generalizations about the regular course of events, as attested to by the uniformities assembled from individual evidential sources').

153 John R. Milton "Induction before Hume," in *Handbook of the history of logic*, eds. Dov M. Gabbay et al (Amsterdam: Elsevier, 2011) 1 at 1.

154 Milton "Induction before Hume" 2; Moreover, Miller further adds that '*epagoge* was translated as *istiqrá*, a word whose root meaning was investigation or examination' (at 14).

approval of a doubtful proposition because this resembles the facts to which he has assented.[155]

For Boethius, the *argumentum inductio* 'is discourse by means of which there is a progression from particulars to universals.'[156] Aristotle similarly defined the Greek term *epagoge* in the language of 'a passage from particulars to universals.'[157] In particular, Aristotle conceived the role of inductive arguments as being to supplement his deductive forms (*syllogismos*) by establishing their epistemic veracity.[158] Furthermore, British empiricists such as Mill later defined inductive argumentation as consisting of 'the operation of discovering and proving general propositions.'[159] However, Sinnott-Armstrong and Fogelin sound a necessary caution about this 'particulars to universals' trope because inductive arguments, depending on how they are framed, may well proceed from universal propositions to individual conclusions.[160] For example, the inductive argument that (1) a person's fixed designs are probably carried out; (2) X planned to kill Y; (3) therefore, X probably did kill Y can be framed in this way or by substituting the first and second premisses, namely: (1) X planned to kill Y; (2) a person's fixed designs are probably carried out; and (3) therefore, X probably did kill Y.[161] Another example of inductive argumentation

155 Cicero *De Inventione* Book I (translated by Harry M. Hubbel) (Cambridge: Harvard University Press, 1949) 93, para 51; Niiniluoto "Induction," 523 (defining analogy as 'a species of induction').

156 Boethius *De topicis differentiis* Book II (translated by Eleonor Stump) (Ithaca: Cornell University Press, 1978) 44/1183B, para 25–39.

157 Aristotle "Topics," 174, 105a10–18; Aristotle "Posterior analytics," in *The complete works of Aristotle*, ed. Jonathan Barnes vol I (Princeton: Princeton University Press) 114 at 132, 81b1 ('[D]emonstration depends on universals and induction on particulars, and it is impossible to consider universals except through induction').

158 See also Milton "Induction before Hume" 5–6 (Aristotle is interested in using induction (epagoge) to justify the premisses of his deductive syllogisms); Niiniluoto "Induction," 522 ('Aristotle required that the theorems of special sciences have to be demonstrated by deductive syllogisms which start from axioms or "the first premises." Aristotle thought that such axioms have to be necessarily true, but he realised that – due to the problem of circularity – they cannot be established in the same demonstrative way. The process of reaching these general axioms was called epagoge by Aristotle. This term was translated as *inductio* by the Latin commentators').

159 Mill "A system of logic: Ratiocinative and inductive, being a connected view of the principles of evidence, and the methods of scientific investigation," 347; Francis Bacon *Novum organum* Book I (translated and edited by Peter Urbach and John Gibson) (IL: Open Court, 1994) 111, para 105. Cf. David Hume *A treatise on human nature* Book I Part III (London: Clarendon Press, 1888) 86–94/Section VI.

160 Walter Sinnott-Armstrong and Robert Fogelin *Understanding arguments: An introduction to informal logic* 9th ed (Stamford: Cengage Learning, 2015) 182.

161 See Wigmore *The principles of judicial proof as given by logic, psychology and general experience and illustrated in judicial trials*, 5; John H. Wigmore *Evidence in trials at common law* vol 1A (revised by Peter Tillers) (Boston: Little Brown & Company, 1983) 984; George F. James "Relevancy, Probability and the Law" (1941) 29(6) *California Law Review* 689 at 694–700; Anderson et al "Analysis of Evidence," 100 (on the convertibility of induction to deduction).

that proceeds from universals to particulars arises in the context of empirical researchers who begin with a hypothesis about the causes of the extinction of dinosaurs and then proceed to look for data to confirm or refute this.[162]

Niiniluoto identifies three types of induction: *enumerative, statistical* and *singular*.[163] Enumerative induction consists of a generalisation that proceeds from a part to a whole or a finite sample to a whole population. For example, the claim that all the ravens observed until now have been black (sample), therefore, all ravens are black (population) is a form of enumerative induction.[164] The second variant of inductive argumentation draws a statistical conclusion about a population from a defined sample. The claim that 3 in 4 people in a randomised sample are female, therefore, 75% of the whole population is female is an example of statistical induction.[165] Thirdly, inductive arguments can take the form of an inference from a sample to a likely new individual from the population. An example of this type of singular inductive inference is the claim that all of the swans observed so far have been white, therefore, the next swan to be observed will also likely be white.[166] Furthermore, inductive arguments generally have three primary features in common. Firstly, the premisses of inductive arguments, unlike those of deductive arguments, provide only partial support to the conclusion.[167] This is because inductive arguments are 'ampliative,'[168] which is to say that the information contained in the conclusion goes beyond that contained in the premisses. Secondly, the evaluative strength or soundness of inductive arguments is measured in degrees (more probable or not) and not in kind or validity.[169] It is this particular feature of inductive argumentation that has made it attractive to so many lawyers and theorists over the years.[170] Thirdly, inductive arguments are non-monotonic,[171] which

162 Sinnott-Armstrong and Fogelin *Understanding arguments: An introduction to informal logic*, 182.
163 Niiniluoto "Induction," 523.
164 Niiniluoto "Induction," 523.
165 See Niiniluoto "Induction," 523.
166 Niiniluoto "Induction," 523.
167 Sinnott-Armstrong and Fogelin *Understanding arguments: An introduction to informal logic*, 181.
168 Salmon *Introduction to logic and critical thinking*, 91; Skyrms *Choice and chance: An introduction to inductive logic*, 19; Niiniluoto "Induction," 522.
169 Sinnott-Armstrong and Fogelin *Understanding arguments: An introduction to informal logic*, 181.
170 See Richard Eggleston *Evidence, proof and probability* (London: Weidenfeld and Nicolson, 1978) 130; James F. Stephen *A digest on the law of evidence* 4th ed (London: Macmillan and Co., 1887) article 1; James B. Thayer "Presumptions and the law of evidence" (1889) 3(4) *Harvard Law Review* 141 at 165; Wigmore *The principles of judicial proof as given by logic, psychology and general experience and illustrated in judicial trials*, 20; Michael and Adler "The trial of an issue of fact (part 1)," 1278, n82; Paul Roberts "From theory into practice: Introducing the reference class problem" (2007) 11 *International Journal of Evidence & Proof* 243 at 244–245.
171 Sinnott-Armstrong and Fogelin *Understanding arguments: An introduction to informal logic*, 180–181.

means that their premisses are sensitive to information changes. For example, the strength of the claim that 'all swans that have been observed thus far are white (sample), therefore, the next swan to be observed is likely to be white,' is affected by the discovery of a black swan.[172]

As observed from all the examples used thus far, the basic model of an inductive argument takes the form: (1) statement about a sample, therefore, (2) statement about the entire population or about a new sample.[173] For example, the claim that (1) the sun has always risen every morning so far (sample), therefore, (2) the sun will rise tomorrow (or every morning), is a commonplace inductive form of reasoning that we encounter 'so frequently in everyday life.'[174] According to Walton, the basic model of an enumerative inductive argument takes the following form:

(1) For most (or a certain proportion of *x*), if *x* is an F then *x* is a G; and
(2) *a* is an F.
(3) *a* is a G.[175]

Statistical forms of inductive arguments often are a lot more robust than other variants. For example, the specific indication of a precise percentage in the following example provides a fairly accurate picture of evaluative strength:

(1) At least 90% (or 54) of the oranges in the box are good.
(2) These four oranges are taken randomly from the box.
(3) Therefore, oranges are probably (90% chance) good.[176]

Inductive reasoning, including the use of Bayes' theorem,[177] is commonly used in the various forensic science specialisms, such as crime scene examination; DNA profiling, fingerprinting, trace examination and drug analysis.[178]

172 Sinnott-Armstrong and Fogelin *Understanding arguments: An introduction to informal logic*, 181.
173 Cf. Ian Hacking *An introduction to probability and inductive logic* (New York: Cambridge University Press, 2001) 13.
174 Alan Hausman et al *Logic and philosophy: A modern introduction* 13th ed (Indianapolis: Hackett Publishing Company, 2021) 5.
175 Walton *Legal argumentation and evidence*, 109.
176 Hacking *An introduction to probability and inductive logic*, 13. For other similar examples, see Salmon *Introduction to logic and critical thinking*, 218.
177 See Thomas Bayes *An essay towards solving a problem in the doctrine of chances* (London: C. Davis, 1763).
178 Paul Roberts "Making sense of forensic science evidence," in *Forensic science evidence and expert witness testimony: Reliability through reform*, eds. Paul Roberts and Michael Stockdale (Cheltenham: Elgar, 2018) 27 at 62. Michael J. Saks "Forensic identification: From a faith-based 'science' to a scientific science" (2010) (1–3) *Forensic Science International* 14. Other examples of statistical evidence and inductive logic are cases of paternity, immigration and employment discrimination cases; see Colin G.G. Aitken and Franco Taroni *Statistics*

Furthermore, inductive analysis also finds application in the context of the character and recidivism propensity of criminal offenders, particularly in sexual offence cases.[179] In general, inductive arguments are vulnerable to counter-arguments on the basis of (1) the (epistemic or otherwise) acceptability of the premisses, (2) the size of the sample relied upon and (3) the randomisation of the sample.[180]

5.6 Defeasible Probative Models

A defeasible argument consists of a conclusion that is tentatively accepted, subject to the possibility of revision on account of new information being available.[181] For this reason, defeasibility is non-monotonic,[182] which means that the evaluative strength of defeasible arguments is sensitive to the addition of new premisses. For example, the claim that (1) X's hat and coat are missing from the hanger, therefore, (2) X has left the house,[183] is subject to revision upon new information emanating about X's whereabouts. Similarly, the strength of the argument that (1) X can hear loud sounds of rain from inside the tin roof, therefore, (2) it is raining outside,[184] is also sensitive to the introduction of new information about the observed weather conditions outside. Therefore, defeasibility operates as 'a framework of belief revision'[185] to cater for the many everyday instances of decision-making in the midst of limited information, time and resources.

The term 'defeasible' is traceable to medieval English contract law,[186] but the origins of the concept or model of reasoning probably go back even

---

and the evaluation of evidence for forensic scientists 2nd ed (Chichester: John Wiley & Sons Ltd, 2004) 312–328; Bernard Robertson et al *Interpreting evidence: Evaluating forensic science in the courtroom* (Wiley, 2016) 35–38; Ronald J. Allen "Factual ambiguity and a theory of evidence" (1994) 88(2) *Northwestern University Law Review* 604 at 634–640.

179 See Mike Redmayne "The relevance of bad character" (2002) 61(3) *The Cambridge Law Journal* 684 at 691; Roger C. Park "Character at the crossroads" (1998) 49 *Hastings Law Journal* 717 at 758–772; Edward J. Imwinkelried "Undertaking the task of reforming the American character evidence prohibition: The importance of getting the experiment off on the right foot" (1995) 22 *Fordham Urban Law Journal* 285; Katherine K. Baker "Once a rapist? Motivational evidence and relevancy in rape law" (1997) 110 *Harvard Law Review* 563; John Monahan et al *Rethinking risk assessment: The MacArthur study of mental disorder and violence* (New York: Oxford University Press, 2001) 44–45.

180 Sinnott-Armstrong and Fogelin *Understanding arguments: An introduction to informal logic*, 188.

181 Douglas Walton *Argument evaluation and evidence* (Cham: Springer, 2016) 10.

182 Walton *Argument evaluation and evidence*, 225.

183 Walton *Argumentation schemes for presumptive reasoning*, 17.

184 See Douglas N. Walton *Arguments from ignorance* (University Park: Pennsylvania University Press, 1996) 1–2.

185 Douglas Walton "Defeasible reasoning and informal fallacies" (2011) *Synthese* 179 at 386.

186 Walton "Defeasible reasoning and informal fallacies," 385; Walton "Legal reasoning and argumentation," 49.

further than that.[187] Hart used the term to describe the status of a contract that has met the formal requirements (e.g. an offer, acceptance and compliance with any legal requirements) of validity, but was still subject to exceptions in the form of defences (e.g. duress, mistake or fraud) that could be relied upon to vitiate the contract.[188] A contract that has met the first set of formal requirements of validity, Hart argues, should be accepted as being 'defeasible' *unless* any of the latter exceptions have been raised to assail it. Therefore, the contractual defeasible argument would take the form that 'if $a + b + c$ exist, then a contract ought to be recognized to exist, unless x, y or z exists.'[189] MacCormick extended this analysis to all kinds of 'legal arrangements' (e.g. contracts, wills, decisions or rules) by arguing that the fulfilment of conditions C_1 C_2 C_3 activates the operation of Rule_R *unless* 'some kind of invalidating intervention' or exceptional condition e_1 exists.[190] According to Governatori et al, this openness to possible exceptions is a characteristic feature of all legal norms.[191] In moral philosophy, defeasible reasoning is tracks back to the introduction of '*prima facie* duties' by David Ross in 1930 as a deflation of Kant's absolute duties.[192] Pollock contends that the concept

187 Elsewhere, the concept of defeasible reasoning has been traced back to Plato's dialogues, see Frederick Schauer "Is defeasibility an essential property of law?" in *The logic of legal requirements: Essays on defeasibility*, eds. Jordi Ferrer Beltrán and Giovanni Battista Ratti (Oxford: Oxford University Press, 2012) 77 at 77; Donald Nute "Preface," in *Defeasible deontic logic*, ed. Donald Nute (Dordrecht: Springer, 1997) vii. See also Robert Koons "Defeasible reasoning," in *The Stanford encyclopedia of philosophy*, ed. Edward N. Zalta (2022), available at: www.plato.stanford.edu (accessed: 17 April 2024) (where defeasible reasoning is traced back to Aristotle).

188 Herbert L.A. Hart "The ascription of responsibility and rights" (1948–1949) 49 *Proceedings of the Aristotelian Society* 171 at 174–175, reprinted in Herbert L.A. Hart "The ascription of responsibility and rights," in *Logic and language*, ed. Antony Flew (New York: Doubleday & Company, 1965) 151 at 154–155; Ronald P. Loui "Hart's critics on defeasible concepts and ascriptivism," in *Proceedings of the Fifth International Conference on Artificial Intelligence and Law* (New York: ACM Press, 1995) 21 at 21 ('Hart's "Ascription of Responsibility and Rights" is where we find perhaps the first clear pronouncement of defeasibility and the technical introduction of the term'); Walton "Defeasible reasoning and informal fallacies," 385 ('[T]he origin of the term in modern philosophy and law is a paper called 'The Ascription of Responsibility and Rights' by Hart').

189 Richard H.S. Tur "Defeasibilism" (2001) 21(2) *Oxford Journal of Legal Studies* 355 at 359.

190 Neil MacCormick "Defeasibility in law and logic," in *Informatics and the foundations of legal reasoning*, eds. Zenon Bankwoski et al (Dordrecht: Springer, 1995) 99 at 99–100.

191 Guido Governatori et al "Logic and the law: Philosophical foundations, deontics, and defeasible reasoning," in *Handbook of deontic logic and normative systems*, eds. Dov M. Gabbay et al vol 2 (College Publications, 2021) 657 at 686.

192 Jordi Ferrer Beltrán and Giovanni Battista Ratti "Defeasibility and legality: A survey," in *The logic of legal requirements: Essays on defeasibility*, eds. Jordi Ferrer Beltrán and Giovanni Battista Ratti (Oxford: Oxford University Press, 2012) 11 at 22. Cf. William D. Ross *The right and the good* (Oxford: Clarendon Press, 1930) 19ff.

of defeasibility in artificial intelligence emanates from the work of Roderick Chisholm in the mid to late twentieth century.[193] According to Pollock, defeasibility in this context refers to epistemic and practical reasoning that entails preliminary conclusions being drawn that are subject to retraction if new information arises.[194]

The basic model of a defeasible argument is identifiable usually by the ⇒ symbol to indicate that the metric of evaluation is something other than deduction (⊃) or induction (→) that falls within a third category that is variously named as 'abductive, presumptive, defeasible, or plausibilistic.'[195] For example:

(1) W (witness) asserts that proposition A is true.
(2) W is in a position to know whether A is true or not.
(3) Therefore, A *plausibly* is true.[196]

Another way to frame a defeasible argument is to say:

(1) Generally E, but subject to future possible exceptions (F).
(2) E.
(3) In this case there is no exception known yet to the general rule that if E then F.
(4) Therefore, F.[197]

193 John L. Pollock *Cognitive carpentry: A blueprint for how to build a person* (Cambridge: Massachusetts Institute of Technology Press, 1995) 40, n24. See generally, Roderick M. Chisholm *Theory of knowledge* 3rd ed (Englewood Cliffs: Prentice-Hall, 1989) 53–60; Roderick M. Chisholm *Perceiving: A philosophical study* (Ithaca: Cornell University Press, 1957).

194 Pollock *Cognitive carpentry: A blueprint for how to build a person*, 40; John L. Pollock "Defeasible reasoning" (1987) 11(4) *Cognitive Science* 481 at 481–482. See generally, Drew McDermott and John Doyle "Non-monotonic logic I" (1980) 13 *Artificial Intelligence* 41; John McCarthy "Circumspection – A form of non-monotonic reasoning" (1980) 13 *Artificial Intelligence* 27; Ray Reiter "A logic for default reasoning" (1980) 13 *Artificial Intelligence* 81; David Makinson *Bridges from classical to nonmonotonic logic* (London: College Publications, 2005); Donald Nute "Defeasible reasoning," in *Handbook of logic in artificial intelligence and logic programming*, eds. Dov M. Gabbay vol 3 (Oxford: Clarendon Press, 1994) 353.

195 Walton *Argument evaluation and evidence*, 1–2. Cf. Charles S. Peirce "The proper treatment of hypotheses: A preliminary chapter, toward an examination of Hume's argument against miracles, in its logic and in its history," in *Historical perspectives on Peirce's logic of science*, ed. Carolyn Eisele vol 2 (Berlin: Mouton Publishers, 1985); Charles Hartshorne and Paul Weiss, eds. *The collected articles of Charles Sanders Peirce* vol 1 (Cambridge: Harvard University Press, 1931–1935).

196 Walton *Argument evaluation and evidence*, 46.

197 Douglas N. Walton *Abductive reasoning* (Tuscaloosa: University of Alabama Press, 2005) 151. Cf. Walton *Legal argumentation and evidence*, 44.

The *non-excipiens* clause is a common feature of many defeasible forms of argumentation. The model in general terms is that:

(1) (Rule *n*:) $B_x \Rightarrow F_x$.
(2) B_x.
(3) Rule *n* ought not to apply to the present case.
(4) Therefore, $\sim F_x$.[198]

Rule *n* provides that if B has the property *x*, then F generally will also bear property *x*. The second premise establishes that B in fact does have property *x*, thereby rendering Rule *n* defeasibly applicable and the conclusion F_x tentatively acceptable. However, the *non-excipiens* clause in the third premise introduces the possibility that there may be other contextual grounds (e.g. the existence of normative rules; the absurdity of the outcome of Rule *n* under the circumstances; or existence of institutional practices that militate against drawing the F_x conclusion on these facts) on which it may be unwarranted to apply Rule *n*. In the circumstances, the raising of the *non-excipiens* clause in the third premise warrants an $\sim F_x$ conclusion.[199]

5.7 Conclusion

The evidential proof of a fact by way of argumentation in the forensic context by definition is to infer a conclusion about that fact from an established extant (accepted) fact. This chapter has undertaken a comprehensive analysis of the structure and content of this form of argumentation. In the first instance, legal argumentation generally addresses the judicial asymmetry that arises between established legal doctrine and a disputed novel case or fact. An established legal rule provides that certain consequences (e.g. that a person should be found guilty) should follow under one or more conditions. A dispute about at least one of these conditions temporarily halts the application of the rule and gives to the probative chasm that warrants legal argumentation. Therefore, legal argumentation not only fulfils the epistemic function of generating new knowledge about the disputed fact(s), but it also brings the two disputants together.

The chapter discusses not only the common forms of argument – the appeal to authority (*argumentum ad verecundiam*), the analogical argument (*argumentum ad analogia legis*), the argument from an established rule (*argumentum ad opinion doctorum*) and the evidential argument (the argument towards a

198 This example is adapted from the very different example crafted in Douglas N. Walton and Erik C.W. Krabbe *Commitment in dialogue: Basic concepts of interpersonal reasoning* (Albany: State University of New York Press, 1995) 180.

199 Cf. Bart Verheij "Logic, context and valid inference or: Can there be a logic of law?" in *Legal knowledge based systems: JURIX 1999: The Twelfth Conference*, eds. Jaap van den Henrik et al (Nijmegen: Gerard Noodt Instituut, 1999) 109 at 110.

hypothesis) – but it also outlines the three basic *deductive, inductive* and *defeasible* models of general argumentation. In so doing, the chapter has built a robust and comprehensive theoretical foundation on which the next chapter can build. The general models of argumentation that have been developed in this chapter will now be applied to the context of hate crimes in the next chapter.

5.8 Bibliography

Books and Book Chapters

Alan Hausman, Frank Boardman and Howard Kahane *Logic and philosophy: A modern introduction* 13th ed (Indianapolis: Hackett Publishing Company, 2021).

Aleksander Peczenik *The basis of legal justification* (Förf: Lund, 1983).

Aleksander Peczenik *On law and reason* 2nd ed (Dordrecht: Springer, 2009).

Anthony G. Guest "Logic in the law," in *Oxford essays in jurisprudence*, ed. Anthony G. Guest (London: Oxford University Press, 1961) 176.

Antonino Rotolo and Giovanni Sartor "Deductive and deontic reasoning," in *Handbook of legal reasoning and argumentation*, eds. Giorgio Bongiovanni, Gerald Postema, Antonino Rotolo, Giovanni Sartor, Chiara Valentini and Douglas N. Walton (Dordrecht: Springer, 2018) 243.

Arend Soeteman *Logic in law: Remarks on logic and rationality in normative reasoning, especially in law* (Dordrecht: Springer, 1989).

Arend Soeteman, ed. *Pluralism and law vol 4: Legal reasoning* (Proceedings of the 20th world congress for legal and social philosophy) (Stuttgart: Franz Steiner Verlag, 2004).

Aristotle *De Sophisticis Elenchis* (edited and translated by E.S. Forster) (Cambridge: Harvard University Press, 1955).

Aristotle "Posterior analytics," in *The complete works of Aristotle*, ed. Jonathan Barnes vol I (Princeton: Princeton University Press) 114.

Aristotle "The prior analytics," in *The complete works of Aristotle*, ed. Jonathan Barnes vol I (Princeton: Princeton University Press) 39.

Aristotle "Rhetoric," in *The complete works of Aristotle*, ed. Jonathan Barnes vol II (Princeton: Princeton University Press) 2152.

Aristotle "Topics," in *The complete works of Aristotle*, ed. Jonathan Barnes vol I (Princeton: Princeton University Press) 167.

Aristotle *Topics* (translated by W.A. Pickard-Cambridge) (Cambridge: NuVision Publications, 2005).

Arthur C. Hastings *A reformulation of the modes of reasoning in argumentation* (Northwestern University: unpublished PhD thesis, 1962).

Aulis Aarnio *On legal reasoning* (Turun Yliopisto: Turku, 1977).

Aulis Aarnio *The rational as reasonable: A treatise on legal justification* (Dordrecht: Reidel, 1987).

Aulis Aarnio, Ikka Niiniluoto and Jyrki Uusitalo, eds. *Methodologie und Erkenntnis theorie der juristischen Argumentation: Beiträge des Internationalen Symposions* (Methodology and epistemology of legal argumentation: Proceedings of the International Symposium of Argumentation in Legal Science) (Berlin: Duncker & Humblot, 1981).

Bart Garssen, David Godden, Gordon Mitchell and Jean Wagemans, eds. *Proceedings of the Ninth Conference of the International Society for the Study of Argumentation* (Amsterdam: Sic Sat, 2019).

Bart Verheij "Logic, context and valid inference or: Can there be a logic of law?" in *Legal knowledge based systems: JURIX 1999: The Twelfth Conference*, eds. Jaap van den

Henrik, Marie-Francine Moens, Jon Bing, Bea van Buggenhout, John Zeleznikow and Carolus Grütters (Nijmegen: Gerard Noodt Instituut, 1999) 109,
Bartosz Brożek "Analogical arguments," in *Handbook of legal reasoning and argumentation*, eds. Giorgio Bongiovanni, Gerald Postema, Antonino Rotolo, Giovanni Sartor, Chiara Valentini and Douglas N. Walton (Dordrecht: Springer, 2018) 365.
Bartosz Brożek *The legal mind: A new introduction to legal epistemology* (New York: Cambridge University Press, 2020).
Bernard Robertson, G. Anthony Vignaux and Charles E.H. Berger *Interpreting evidence: Evaluating forensic science in the courtroom* (Wiley, 2016).
Boethius *De topicis differentiis* Book II (translated by Eleonor Stump) (Ithaca: Cornell University Press, 1978).
Bonnie Gold and Roger A. Simons *Proof and other dilemmas: Mathematics and philosophy* (Washington: Mathematical Association of America, 2008).
Brian Skyrms *Choice and chance: An introduction to inductive logic* 4th ed (Belmont: Wadsworth, 2000).
Cass R. Sunstein "Analogical reasoning and precedent," in *Philosophical foundations of precedent*, eds. Timothy Endicott et al (Oxford: Oxford University Press, 2023) 217.
Catarina Dutilh Novaes *The dialogical roots of deduction: Historical, cognitive and philosophical perspectives on reasoning* (Cambridge: Cambridge University Press, 2021).
Catarina Dutilh Novaes "The syllogism as defined by Aristotle, Ockham, and Buridan," in *The language of thought in late medieval philosophy: Essays in honor of Claude Panacio*, eds. Jenny Pelletier and Magali Roques (Cham: Springer, 2017) 217.
Chad S. Carr "Using computer supported argument visualization to teach legal argumentation," in *Visualising argumentation: Software tools for collaborative and educational sense-making*, eds. Paul A. Kirschner, Simon J.B. Schum and Chad S. Carr (London: Springer-Verlag, 2003) 75.
Chaïm Perelman and Lucie Olbrechts-Tyteca *La Nouvelle Rhétorique: Traité de l'Argumentation* (Paris: Presses universitaires de France, 1958).
Chaïm Perelman and Lucie Olbrechts-Tyteca *The new rhetoric: A treatise on argumentation* (translated by John Wilkinson and Purcell Weaver) (Notre Dame: University of Notre Dame, 1969).
Charles Hartshorne and Paul Weiss, eds. *The collected articles of Charles Sanders Peirce* vol 1 (Cambridge: Harvard University Press, 1931–1935).
Charles L. Hamblin *Fallacies* (Newport News: Vale Press, 1970).
Charles S. Peirce "The proper treatment of hypotheses: A preliminary chapter, toward an examination of Hume's argument against miracles, in its logic and in its history," in *Historical perspectives on Peirce's logic of science*, ed. Carolyn Eisele vol 2 (Berlin: Mouton Publishers, 1985).
Christian Dahlman and Werner Krawitez, eds. *Values, rights and duties in legal and philosophical discourse* (Law and politics. In search of balance: Proceedings of the 21st World Congress for Legal and Social Philosophy) (Berlin: Duncker & Humblot, 2005).
Christian Kock "The reception of ancient rhetoric in modern argumentation theory and pedagogy," in *Brill's companion of the reception of ancient rhetoric*, eds. Sophia Papaioannou, Andreas Serafin and Michael Edwards (Leiden: Brill, 2021) 489.
Christopher C. Langdell *A summary of the law of contracts* 2nd ed (Boston: Little Brown and Company, 1880).
Claudio Michelon "The uses of precedent and legal argument," in *Philosophical foundations of precedent*, eds. Timothy Endicott et al (Oxford: Oxford University Press, 2023) 117.
Clifford Ando "Exemplum, analogy and precedent in Roman law," in *Exemplarity and singularity: Thinking through particulars in philosophy, literature and law*, ed. Michèle Lowrie and Susanne Lüdemann (London: Routledge, 2015) 88.

Colin G.G. Aitken and Franco Taroni *Statistics and the evaluation of evidence for forensic scientists* 2nd ed (Chichester: John Wiley & Sons Ltd, 2004).

Dag Prawitz "Proof verifying programs and programs producing proofs: A conceptual analysis," in *Deduction, computation, experiment: Exploring the effectiveness of proof*, eds. Rosella Lupacchini and Giovanni Corsi (Milano: Springer, 2008) 81.

David Hume *A treatise on human nature* Book I Part III (London: Clarendon Press, 1888).

David Makinson *Bridges from classical to nonmonotonic logic* (London: College Publications, 2005).

David Schum *Evidential foundations of probabilistic reasoning* (Evanston, IL: Northwestern University Press, 1994).

Dieter Krimphove "A historical overview of the development of legal logic," in *Law and logic: contemporary issues*, eds. Dieter Kimphove and Gabriel M. Lentner (Berlin: Duncker & Humblot, 2017) 11.

Donald Mackenzie *Mechanising proof: Computing, risk and trust* (Cambridge: MIT Press, 2001).

Donald Nute "Defeasible reasoning," in *Handbook of logic in artificial intelligence and logic programming*, eds. Dov. M. Gabbay, Christopher J. Hogger and John A. Robinson vol 3 (Oxford: Clarendon Press, 1994) 353.

Donald Nute "Preface," in *Defeasible deontic logic*, ed. Donald Nute (Dordrecht: Springer, 1997) vii.

Douglas N. Walton *Abductive reasoning* (Tuscaloosa: University of Alabama Press, 2005).

Douglas N. Walton *Appeal to expert opinion: Arguments from authority* (University Park: Pennsylvania State University Press, 1992).

Douglas N. Walton *Argument evaluation and evidence* (Cham: Springer, 2016).

Douglas N. Walton *Argumentation methods for artificial intelligence in law* (Berlin: Kluwer, 2005).

Douglas N. Walton *Argumentation schemes for presumptive reasoning* (Mahwah: Lawrence Erlbaum Association, 1996).

Douglas N. Walton "Argumentation theory: A very short introduction," in *Argumentation in artificial intelligence*, eds. Iyad Rahwan and Guillermo R. Simari (Dordrecht: Springer, 2009) 1.

Douglas N. Walton *Arguments from ignorance* (University Park: Pennsylvania University Press, 1996).

Douglas N. Walton *Burden of proof, presumption and argumentation* (New York: Cambridge University Press, 2014).

Douglas N. Walton *Fundamentals of critical argumentation* (Cambridge: Cambridge University Press, 2006).

Douglas N. Walton *Legal argumentation and evidence* (University Park: Pennsylvania University Press, 2002).

Douglas N. Walton "Legal reasoning and argumentation," in *Handbook of legal reasoning and argumentation*, eds. Giorgio Bongiovanni, Gerald Postema, Antonino Rotolo, Giovanni Sartor, Chiara Valentini and Douglas N. Walton (Dordrecht: Springer, 2018) 47.

Douglas N. Walton *Plausible argument in everyday conversation* (Albany: State University of New York Press, 1992).

Douglas N. Walton, Christopher Reed and Fabrizio Macagno *Argumentation schemes* (New York: Cambridge University Press, 2008).

Douglas N. Walton and Erik C.W. Krabbe *Commitment in dialogue: Basic concepts of interpersonal reasoning* (Albany: State University of New York Press, 1995).

Douglas N. Walton, Fabrizio Macagno and Giovanni Sartor, *Statutory interpretation: Pragmatics and argumentation* (New York: Cambridge University Press, 2021).

Dov M. Gabbay and John Woods "Logic and the law: Crossing the lines of discipline," in *Approaches to legal rationality*, eds. Dov M. Gabbay, Patrice Canivez, Shahid Rahman and Alexandre Theircelin (Dordrecht: Springer, 2010) 165.

Edward H. Levi *An introduction to legal reasoning* (London: University of Chicago Press, 1949).

Errol E. Harris *Hypothesis and perception: The roots of scientific method* (London: Routledge, 2013).

Eveline E. Feteris *Fundamentals of legal argumentation: A survey of theories of theories on justification of judicial decisions* (Dordrecht: Springer, 1999).

Eveline E. Feteris *Fundamentals of legal argumentation: A survey of theories of theories on justification of judicial decisions* 2nd ed (Dordrecht: Springer, 2017).

Floris J. Bex *Arguments, stories and criminal evidence: A formal hybrid theory* (Dordrecht: Springer, 2011).

Francis Bacon *Novum organum* Book I (translated and edited by Peter Urbach and John Gibson) (IL: Open Court, 1994).

Frans H. van Eemeren "The study of argumentation," in *The SAGE handbook of rhetorical studies*, eds. Andrea A. Lunsford et al (Thousand Oaks: SAGE, 2009) 109.

Frans H. van Eemeren, Bart Garssen, Erik C.W. Krabbe, A. Francisca S. Henkemans, Bart Verheij and Jean H.M. Wagemans *Handbook of argumentation theory* (Dordrecht: Springer, 2014).

Frans H. van Eemeren and Rob Grootendorst *A systematic theory of argumentation: The pragma-dialectical approach* (Cambridge: Cambridge University Press, 2004).

Frans H. van Eemeren, Rob Grootendorst, Ralph H. Johnson, Christian Plantin and Charles A. Willard *Fundamentals of argumentation theory* (New York: Routledge, 1996).

Frederick Schauer "Is defeasibility an essential property of law?" in *The logic of legal requirements: Essays on defeasibility*, eds. Jordi Ferrer Beltrán and Giovanni Battista Ratti (Oxford: Oxford University Press, 2012) 77.

Frederick Schauer *Thinking like a lawyer* (Cambridge, MA: Harvard University Press, 2009).

Geoffrey Samuel *Rethinking legal reasoning* (Cheltenham: Elgar, 2018).

Geoffrey Samuel *A short introduction to judging and to legal reasoning* (Cheltenham: Elgar, 2016).

Geoffrey Samuel "What is it to have knowledge of Roman legal methods," in *New developments in legal reasoning and logic: From ancient law to modern systems*, eds. Shahid Rahman, Matthias Armgardt and Hans C.N. Kvernenes (Dordrecht: Springer, 2022) 3.

Gerhard Struck *Zur Theorie juristischer argumentation* (Berlin: Duncker & Humblot, 1977).

Giovanni Damele "Analogia legis and analogia iuris: An apparent distinction," in *Systematic approaches to argument by analogy*, eds. Henrique J. Ribeiro (Cham: Springer, 2014) 243.

Giovanni Sartor *Legal reasoning: A cognitive approach to the law* (Dordrecht: Springer, 2007).

Giovanni Tarello *Diritto, enunciati, usi* (Bologna: Il Mulino, 1974).

Giovanni Tarello *L'interpretazione della legge* (Milano: Giuffré, 1974).

Giovanni Tuzet "Arguing on facts: Truth, trials and adversary procedures," in *Legal argumentation theory: Cross-disciplinary perspectives*, eds. Christian Dahlman and Eveline Feteris (Dordrecht: Springer, 2013) 207.

Gisela Striker *Aristotle: Prior analytics* Book I (translated by Gisela Striker) (Oxford: Oxford University Press, 2009).

Gottlob Frege *Begriffsschrift, eine der arithmetischen nachgebildete Formelsprache des reinen Denkens* ('Concept notation: A formula language of pure thought, modelled upon that of arithmetic') (Halle: Verlag von Louis Nerbert, 1879), translated by

Stefan Bauer-Mengelberg "Concept script, a formal language of pure thought modelled upon that of arithmetic," in *From Frege to Gödel: A source book in mathematical logic, 1879–1931* (Cambridge: Harvard University Press, 1967) 1.

Guido Governatori, Antonino Rotolo and Giovanni Sartor "Logic and the law: Philosophical foundations, deontics, and defeasible reasoning," in *Handbook of deontic logic and normative systems*, eds. Dov Gabbay, John Horty, Xavier Parent, Ron van der Meyden and Leendert van der Torre vol 2 (College Publications, 2021) 657.

Günther Kreuzbauer "Teaching legal argumentation," in *Pluralism in law: Proceedings of the 20th World Congress for Legal and Social Philosophy*, ed. Arend Soeteman (Stuttgart: Franz Steiner Verlag, 2004) 79.

Hans Zeisel and David Kaye *Prove it with figures: Empirical methods in law and litigation* (New York: Springer, 1997).

Henrique J. Ribeiro "Introduction," in *Systematic approaches to argument by analogy*, ed. Henrique J. Ribeiro (Cham: Springer, 2014) 1.

Henry Prakken *Logical tools for modelling legal argument* (Dordrecht: Kluwer Academic Publishers, 1997).

Herbert L.A. Hart "The ascription of responsibility and rights," in *Logic and language*, ed. Antony Flew (New York: Doubleday & Company, 1965) 151.

Ian Hacking *An introduction to probability and inductive logic* (New York: Cambridge University Press, 2001).

Ikka Niiniluoto "Induction," in *Handbook of epistemology*, eds. Ikka Niiniluoto, Matti Sintonen and Jan Woleński (Dordrecht: Springer, 2004) 521.

Irving M. Copi, Carl Cohen and Victor Rodych *Introduction to logic* 15th ed (New York: Routledge, 2019).

James D. Williams *An introduction to classical rhetoric: Essential readings* (Chichester: John Wiley & Sons, 2009).

James F. Stephen *A digest on the law of evidence* 4th ed (London: Macmillan & Co., 1887).

James Gordley *The jurists: A critical history* (Oxford: Oxford University Press, 2013).

Jan C. Joerden "Logik und Recht," in *Handbuch Rechtsphilosophie*, eds. Eric Hilgendorf and Jan C. Joerden (Berlin: Springer-Verlag, 2021) 244.

Jan Woleński "Formal and informal in legal logic," in *Approaches to legal rationality*, eds. Dov M. Gabbay, Patrice Canivez, Shahid Rahman and Alexandre Theircelin (Dordrecht: Springer, 2010) 73.

Jeremy Bentham *Of laws in general* (edited by H.L.A. Hart) (London: Athlone Press, 1970).

Jeremy Bentham "What a law is," in *Bentham's political thought*, ed. Bhikhu Parekh (London: Croom Helm, 1973) 146.

Jerome Frank *Law and the modern mind* (New York: Brentano's, 1930).

Jerome Michael and Mortimer J. Adler *The nature of judicial proof: An inquiry into the logical, legal and empirical aspects of the law of evidence* (New York: Ad Press, 1931).

John Austin *Province of jurisprudence determined* (London: Weidenfeld & Nicolson, 1971).

John H. Wigmore *Evidence in trials at common law* vol 1 (revised by Peter Tillers) (Boston: Little Brown, 1983).

John H. Wigmore *The principles of judicial proof as given by logic, psychology and general experience and illustrated in judicial trials* (Boston: Little Brown & Company, 1913).

John L. Pollock *Cognitive carpentry: A blueprint for how to build a person* (Cambridge: Massachusetts Institute of Technology Press, 1995).

John Monahan, Henry J. Steadman, Eric Silver, Paul S. Applebaum, Pamela C. Robbins, Edward P. Mulvey, Loren H. Roth, Thomas Grisso and Steven Banks *Rethinking risk assessment: The MacArthur study of mental disorder and violence* (New York: Oxford University Press, 2001).

John R. Milton "Induction before Hume," in *Handbook of the history of logic*, eds. Dov M. Gabbay, John Woods and Akihiro Kanamori (Amsterdam: Elsevier, 2011) 1.

John S. Mill *A system of logic: Ratiocinative and inductive, being a connected view of the principles of evidence, and the methods of scientific investigation* 2nd ed (London: John W. Parker, 1846).

John Sasson *Ancient laws and modern problems* (Bristol: Intellect, 2005).

John Woods, Andrew D. Irvine and Douglas N. Walton *Argument: Critical thinking, logic and the fallacies* 2nd ed (Toronto: Prentice Hall, 2004).

John Woods and Douglas N. Walton *Argument: The logic of the fallacies* (Toronto: McGraw-Hill Ryerson, 1982).

Jordi Ferrer Beltrán and Giovanni Battista Ratti "Defeasibility and legality: A survey," in *The logic of legal requirements: Essays on defeasibility*, eds. Jordi Ferrer Beltrán and Giovanni Battista Ratti (Oxford: Oxford University Press, 2012) 11.

Josep Aguiló-Regla, ed. *Lógica, argumentación e interpretación* (Logic, argumentation and interpretation: Proceedings of the 22nd World Congress for Legal and Social Philosophy) (Berlin: Duncker & Humblot, 2005).

Joseph Horowitz *Law and logic* (New York: Springer-Verlag, 1972).

Julius Stone *Legal systems and lawyers' reasoning* (London: Stevens & Sons, 1964).

Julius Stone *The province and function of law: Law as logic, justice and social control* (Sydney: Associated General Publications, 1946).

Kaius Tuori "Legal profession," in *A cultural history of law: In antiquity*, ed. Julen Extabe (London: Bloomsbury, 2019) 143.

Larry Alexander and Emily Sherwin *Demystifying legal reasoning* (Cambridge: Cambridge University Press, 2008).

Lloyd Weinreb *Legal reason: The use of analogy in legal argument* (New York: Cambridge University Press, 2005).

Lloyd Weinreb *Legal reason: The use of analogy in legal argument* 2nd ed (New York: Cambridge University Press, 2016).

Marcus T. Cicero *De Inventione* I (translated by Harry M. Hubbel) (Cambridge: Harvard University Press, 1949).

Marcus T. Cicero *De Oratore* II (translated by E.W. Sutton) (Cambridge: Harvard University Press, 1967).

Martin P. Golding *Legal reasoning* (New York: Alfred A. Knopf, 1984).

Merilee H. Salmon *Introduction to logic and critical thinking* 6th ed (Boston: Clark Baxter, 2013).

Neil MacCormick "Defeasibility in law and logic," in *Informatics and the foundations of legal reasoning*, eds. Zenon Bankwoski et al (Dordrecht: Springer, 1995) 99.

Neil MacCormick *Legal reasoning and legal theory* (Oxford: Clarendon Press, 1978).

Neil MacCormick *Rhetoric and the rule of law: A theory of legal reasoning* (Oxford: Oxford University Press, 2005).

Neil MacCormick, Stavros Panou and Luigi Lombardi Vallauri, eds. "Conditions of validity and cognition in modern legal thought" (*Geltungs- und Erkenntnisbedingungen im modernen Rechtsdenken*) (*Proceedings of the 11th World Congress on Philosophy of Law and Social Philosophy*) (Stuttgart: Franz Steiner Verlag, 1983).

Oliver W. Holmes *The common law* (Boston: Little Brown, 1881).

Otto C. Jensen *The nature of legal argument* (Oxford: Basil Blackwell, 1957).

Pamela-Jane Schwikkard and Tshepo B. Mosaka *Principles of evidence* 5th ed (Claremont: Juta, 2023).

Patrick J. Hurley *A concise introduction to logic* 14th ed (Boston: Wadsworth, 2024).

Paul Roberts "Making sense of forensic science evidence," in *Forensic science evidence and expert witness testimony: Reliability through reform*, eds. Paul Roberts and Michael Stockdale (Cheltenham: Elgar, 2018) 27.

Paul Roberts *Roberts & Zuckerman's criminal evidence* 3rd ed (Oxford: Oxford University Press, 2022).

Philip Kitcher *The nature of mathematical knowledge* (Oxford: Oxford University Press, 1984).
Ralph H. Johnson *Manifest rationality* (Mahwah: Lawrence Erlbaum Associates, 2000).
Ralph H. Johnson *The rise of informal logic: Essays on argumentation, critical thinking, reasoning and politics* (Newport News: Vale Press, 1996).
Ralph H. Johnson and J. Anthony Blair "Informal logic in the twentieth century," in *Historical foundations of informal logic*, eds. Douglas N. Walton and Alan Brinton (New York: Routledge, 2016).
Ralph H. Johnson and J. Antony Blair "The origins of informal logic," in *Handbook of the logic of argument and inference: The turn towards the practical*, eds. Dov M. Gabbay et al (Amsterdam: Elsevier, 2002) 339.
Richard Eggleston *Evidence, proof and probability* (London: Weidenfeld and Nicolson, 1978).
Richard Posner "Legal formalism, legal realism and the interpretation of statutes and the Constitution," in *The philosophy of legal reasoning: Precedents, statutes and analysis of legal concepts*, ed. Scott Brewer (New York: Routledge, 2011) 145.
Robert Alexy *Theorie der juristischen argumentation: die theorie des rationalen diskurses als theorie der juristischen begründung* (Frankfurt: Suhrkamp Verlag, 1978).
Robert Alexy *A theory of legal argumentation: The theory of rational discourse as theory of legal justification* (translated by Ruth Adler and Neil MacCormick) (Oxford: Oxford University Press, 1989).
Robin Smith "Logic," in *The Cambridge companion to Aristotle*, ed. Jonathan Barnes (Cambridge: Cambridge University Press, 1995) 27.
Roderick M. Chisholm *Perceiving: A philosophical study* (Ithaca: Cornell University Press, 1957).
Roderick M. Chisholm *Theory of knowledge* 3rd ed (Englewood Cliffs: Prentice-Hall, 1989).
Ronald Dworkin *Taking rights seriously* (Cambridge, MA: Harvard University Press, 1978).
Ronald P. Loui "Hart's critics on defeasible concepts and ascriptivism," in *Proceedings of the fifth international conference on artificial intelligence and law* (New York: ACM Press, 1995) 21.
Sadakat Kadri *The trial: From Socrates to O.J. Simpson* (London: Harper Collins, 2005).
Samuel Greengus "Legal and social institutions of ancient Mesopotamia," in *Civilisations of the ancient Near East*, ed. Jack M. Sasson (New York: Simon & Schuster Macmillan, 1995) 469.
Scott Brewer, ed. *The philosophy of legal reasoning: Precedents, statutes and analysis of legal concepts* (New York: Routledge, 1998).
Stephen Toulmin *The uses of argument* (Cambridge: Cambridge University Press, 1958).
Steven G. Krantz *Handbook of logic and proof techniques for computer science* (Boston: Birkhäuser, 2002).
Steven J. Burton *An introduction to law and legal reasoning* (Boston: Little Brown, 1985).
Steven J. Burton *An introduction to law and legal reasoning* 2nd ed (Boston: Little Brown, 1995).
Steven J. Burton *An introduction to law and legal reasoning* 3rd ed (New York: Aspen Publishers, 2007).
Steven Schwartzman *The words of mathematics: An etymological dictionary of mathematical terms used in English* (Washington: Mathematical Association of America, 1994).
Susanne Bobzien "Logic," in *The Cambridge companion to the Stoics*, ed. Brad Inwood (Cambridge: Cambridge University Press, 2003) 85.

Susanne Bobzien "Stoic syllogistic," in *Oxford studies in ancient philosophy*, ed. Christopher C.W. Taylor vol XIV (New York: Oxford University Press, 1996) 133.

Terence Anderson, William Twining and David Schum *Analysis of evidence* 2nd ed (Cambridge: Cambridge University Press, 2005).

Thomas Bayes *An essay towards solving a problem in the doctrine of chances* (London: C. Davis, 1763).

Thomas Hobbes *Leviathan* (Oxford: Clarendon Press, 1909).

Ulfrid Neumann *Juristische Argumentationstheorie* (Baden-Baden: Nomos, 2023).

Ulrich Klug *Juristische Logik* (Berlin: Springer-Verlag, 1958).

Ulrich Klug *Juristische Logik* (Oxford: Clarendon Press, 1978).

Verena Klappstein "Why does legal reasoning necessitate an interdisciplinary discourse and an examination from the point of theory of science," in *Theory of legal evidence – Evidence in legal theory*, eds. Verena Klappstein and Meciej Dybowski (Cham: Springer, 2021) 37.

Walter E. Young "The formal evolution of Islamic juridical dialectic: A brief glimpse," in *New developments in legal reasoning and logic: From ancient law to modern systems*, ed. Shahid Rahman et al (Dordrecht: Springer, 2022) 83.

Walter Sinnott-Armstrong and Robert Fogelin *Understanding arguments: An introduction to informal logic* 9th ed (Stamford: Cengage Learning, 2015).

Werner Krawitz, Kasimierz Opalek, Aleksander Peczenik and Alfred Schramm, eds. *Argumentation und Hermeneutik in der Jurisprudenz* (Argumentation and Hermeneutics in Jurisprudence) (Berlin: Duncker & Humblot, 1979).

Werner Krawietz and Robert Alexy, eds. *Metatheorie juristischer Argumentation* (Metatheory of Legal Argumentation) (Berlin: Duncker & Humblot, 1983).

William C. Kneale and Martha Kneale, *Development of logic* (London: Oxford University Press, 1962).

William D. Ross *The right and the good* (Oxford: Clarendon Press, 1930).

William Twining "The camel in the zoo," in *Law in context: Enlarging a discipline*, ed. William Twining (Oxford: Oxford University Press, 1997) 26.

William Twining "Evidence and legal theory," in *Law in context: Enlarging a discipline*, ed. Williams Twining (Oxford: Oxford University Press, 1997) 110.

William Twining *Karl Llewellyn and the realist movement* 2nd ed (New York: Cambridge University Press, 2012).

William Twining "Taking facts seriously," in *Law in context: Enlarging a discipline*, ed. William Twining (Oxford: Oxford University Press, 1997) 89.

William Wills *An essay on the principles of circumstantial evidence* 3rd ed (Philadelphia: T. & J.W. Johnson, 1858).

Winifried Hassemer, Arthur Kaufmann and Ulfrid Neumann, eds. *Argumentation und Recht: Vorträge auf der Tagung der Deutschen Sektion der Internationalen Vereinigung für Rechts und Sozialphilosophie* (Argumentation and law: Proceedings of the German section of the International Association for Philosophy of Law and Social Philosophy) (Munich: Franz Steiner Verlag, 1980).

Periodicals

Alan Bundy et al "What is a proof?" (2005) 363 *Philosophical Transactions of the Royal Society* 2377.

Alex Stein "The refoundation of evidence law" (1996) 9 *Canadian Journal of Law & Jurisprudence* 279.

Brian Leiter "Legal formalism and legal realism: What is the issue?" (2010) 16 *Legal Theory* 111.

Carla Faralli "The legacy of American legal realism" (2005) 48 *Scandinavian Studies in Law* 75.

Dale A. Herbeck "Critical legal studies and argumentation theory" (1995) 9 *Argumentation* 719.
David Hitchcock "The practice of argumentative discussion" (2002) 16 *Argumentation* 287.
Douglas N. Walton "Defeasible reasoning and informal fallacies" (2011) *Synthese* 179.
Douglas N. Walton "What is reasoning? What is an argument?" (1990) 87 *Journal of Philosophy* 339.
Drew McDermott and John Doyle "Non-monotonic logic I" (1980) 13 *Artificial Intelligence* 41.
Edward H. Levi "An introduction to legal reasoning" (1948) 15(3) *University of Chicago Law Review* 501.
Edward J. Imwinkelried "Undertaking the task of reforming the American character evidence prohibition: The importance of getting the experiment off on the right foot" (1995) 22 *Fordham Urban Law Journal* 285.
Floris Bex, Henry Prakken, Chris Reed and Douglas N. Walton "Towards a formal account of reasoning about evidence: Argumentation schemes and generalisations" (2003) 11 *Artificial Intelligence and Law* 125.
Frederick Schauer "Giving reasons" (1995) 47(4) *Stanford Law Review* 633.
George F. James "Relevancy, probability and the law" (1941) 29(6) *California Law Review* 689.
Göran Sundholm "Proof-theoretical semantics and Fregean identity criteria for propositions" (1994) 77(3) *The Monist* 294.
Henry Prakken "Argumentation without arguments," (2011) 25 *Argumentation* 171.
Herbert L.A. Hart "The ascription of responsibility and rights" (1948–1949) 49 *Proceedings of the Aristotelian Society* 171.
Herbert L.A. Hart "Positivism and the separation of law and morals" (1958) 71(4) *Harvard Law Review* 593.
Ilmar Tammelo "Logic as an instrument of legal reasoning" (1970) 10(3) *Jurimetrics* 89.
J. Anthony Blair "The limits of the dialogue model of argument" (1998) *Argumentation* 12(2) 325.
James B. Thayer "Presumptions and the law of evidence" (1889) 3(4) *Harvard Law Review* 141.
Jerome Frank "Why not a clinical lawyer-school?" (1933) 81(8) *University of Pennsylvania Law Review and American Law Register* 907.
Jerome Michael and Mortimer J. Adler "The trial of an issue of fact (part 1)" (1934) 34(7) *Columbia Law Review* 1224.
John H. Wigmore "The problem of proof" (1913) 8 *Illinois Law Review* 77.
John L. Pollock "Defeasible reasoning" (1987) 11(4) *Cognitive Science* 481.
John McCarthy "Circumspection – A form of non-monotonic reasoning" (1980) 13 *Artificial Intelligence* 27.
Karl Llewellyn "A realistic jurisprudence – The next step" (1930) 3(4) *Columbia Law Review* 431.
Karl Llewellyn "Some realism about realism – Responding to Dean Pound" (1931) 44 *Harvard Law Review* 1222.
Katherine K. Baker "Once a rapist? Motivational evidence and relevancy in rape law" (1997) 110 *Harvard Law Review* 563.
Lee Loevinger "Standards of proof in science and law" (1992) 32(3) *Jurimetrics* 323.
Lon L. Fuller "Positivism and fidelity to law – A replay to Professor Hart" (1957) 71(4) *Harvard Law Review* 630.
Marcello Guarini "A defence of non-deductive reconstructions of analogical arguments" (2004) 24(2) *Informal Logic* 153.
Marko Malink "The beginnings of formal logic: Deduction in Aristotle's topics vs. prior analytics" (2015) 60(3) *Phronesis* 267.

Michael J. Saks "Forensic identification: From a faith-based 'science' to a scientific science" (2010) (1–3) *Forensic Science International* 14.
Mike Redmayne "The relevance of bad character" (2002) 61(3) *The Cambridge Law Journal* 684.
Paul Roberts "From theory into practice: Introducing the reference class problem" (2007) 11 *International Journal of Evidence & Proof* 243.
Ray Reiter "A logic for default reasoning" (1980) 13 *Artificial Intelligence* 81.
Richard H.S. Tur "Defeasibilism" (2001) 21(2) *Oxford Journal of Legal Studies* 355.
Richard Posner "Realism about judges" (2011) 105(2) *Northwestern University Law Review* 577.
Roger C. Park "Character at the crossroads" (1998) 49 *Hastings Law Journal* 717.
Roger F.G. Ormrod "Evidence and proof: Scientific and legal" (1972) 12(1) *Medicine, Science & the Law* 9.
Ronald J. Allen "Factual ambiguity and a theory of evidence" (1994) 88(2) *Northwestern University Law Review* 604.
Ronald J. Allen and Michael S. Pardo "Juridical proof and the best explanation" (2007) 27(3) *Law and Philosophy* 223.
Scott Brewer "Exemplary reasoning: Semantics, pragmatics and the rational force of legal argument by analogy" (1996) 109 *Harvard Law Review* 923.
Tshepo B. Mosaka "An introduction to proof in South Africa" (2022) 139(4) *South African Law Journal* 837.
Vincent A. Wellman "Practical reasoning and judicial justification: Toward an adequate theory" (1985) 57(1) *University of Colorado Law Review* 45.
William Twining "Some jobs for jurisprudence" (1974) 1(2) *British Journal of Law and Society* 149.
Yun Xie "Argument by analogy in ancient China" (2019) 33 *Argumentation* 323.

Online Resources

Jurix, available at: www.jurix23.maastrichtlawtech.eu (accessed: 11 October 2024).
Learned Institute of Argumentation Studies, available at: www.ilias-argumentation.com (accessed: 11 October 2024).

6 The Probative Condition II

6.1 Introduction

The main question that this book has sought to answer is *how to prove hate crimes in the forensic context*. The answer given in this book has been delivered through three conditions of evidential proof that consist of a general legal definition of hate crimes (*materiality* condition), the institutional rules and procedures through which extant evidential facts are presented and processed (*processual* condition) and the heuristics and methods through which probative judgements are arrived at from the extant evidential facts (*probative* condition). Chapters 4 and 5, respectively, have sketched the historical evolution and theoretical foundations of various methods of proof. The chapter now aims to apply one of these methods, legal argumentation, to the context of hate crimes.

The aim of this chapter is fulfilled in three ways. Firstly, by developing a basic taxonomy of propositions of fact and outlining the two most basic patterns of inferences in the first two sections of the chapter. Secondly, the bulk of the chapter is taken up by a discussion of three core probative arguments of hate crimes from *wrongness*, *prejudice* and *responsibility*. These three sets of arguments correspond to the four general elements of hate crimes that were identified in Chapter 2. The first two of these elements, consisting of the manifest isolation or discriminatory targeting of an individual or group, as well as the victim being a member of a protected social group, are combined and discussed under the broad argument from wrongness for purposes of this chapter. Furthermore, the argument from responsibility will consider the element of fault in the form of intention, as explained later in the chapter. The last section of the chapter will proceed to develop evaluation criteria, drawing from dialectical argumentation theory, for the three main arguments from *wrongness*, *prejudice* and *responsibility*.

6.2 A Taxonomy of Propositions of Fact

The objects of evidential proof in the forensic context are what are known as 'propositions of fact,' which are variously named '*facta probanda*,' 'facts

DOI: 10.4324/9781003493006-6

in issue,' 'disputed facts,' 'ultimate *probandum*,' or 'legal issues.'[1] A 'proposition' is a statement or assertion containing a factual predicate;[2] for example, 10 + 10 = 2, X murdered Y, hate is a strong word, pineapples are yellow, it is raining outside, and a bachelor is unmarried are all examples of propositions[3] because each asserts that something, *x*, is the case or not.[4] Propositions appear in the form of lawyers' assertions, adjudicative findings, witness statements, submissions from the litigants and official remarks from bailiffs and other court staff, all throughout legal proceedings. Each of these make truth claims about forensic facts of various kinds concerning events, states of affairs or even the existence and/or content of legal provisions.[5]

The phrase 'proposition of fact' is reserved in the forensic context for disputed facts that are the objects of proof. For example, in the context of hate crimes, these would be the general requirements discussed in Chapter 2: the

1 John H. Wigmore *The principles of judicial proof as given by logic, psychology and general experience and illustrated in judicial trials* (Boston: Little Brown & Company, 1913) 27; John H. Wigmore *Evidence in trials at common law* vol 1 (revised by Peter Tillers) (Boston: Little Brown & Company, 1983) 13–20.

2 Paul Roberts and Colin Aitken *The logic of forensic proof: Inferential reasoning in criminal evidence and forensic science* (Practitioner Guide No. 3) (London: Royal Statistical Society, 2014) 30. For contemporary purposes, the usage of propositions, at least under the name in its modern meaning, is traced back to Gottlob Frege; see Gottlob Frege "The thought: A logical inquiry," in *Philosophical Logic*, ed. Peter F. Strawson (London: Oxford University Press, 1967) 20. See also Gottlob Frege "*Begriffsschrift*," in *Translations from the philosophical writings of Gottlob Frege*, eds. Peter Geach and Max Black (New York: Philosophical Library, 1952) 1–21. More recently, see Daniel Vanderveken *Meaning and speech acts* vol 1 (Cambridge: Cambridge University Press, 1990) 78 ('propositions have truth values because they represent states of affairs which either exist or do not exist in the world'); Irving M. Copi et al *Introduction to logic* 15th ed (New York: Routledge, 2019) 2; John Woods and Douglas Walton *Argument: The logic of the fallacies* (Toronto: McGraw-Hill Ryerson, 1982) 1–2 (the premisses and conclusion of an argument are two variants of propositions).

3 See Roberts and Aitken *The logic of forensic proof: Inferential reasoning in criminal evidence and forensic science*, 30. On Montrose's elementary distinction between 'general' (related to 'scientific laws') and 'particular' propositions of fact, these propositions all fall into the latter category; see James L. Montrose "Basic concepts of the law of evidence" (1954) 70 *Law Quarterly Review* 527 at 529. However, not all human communication necessarily is propositional, as some forms of human communication such as 'a smile, a touch, a sigh, a screech of pain,' as Roberts and Aitken point out, 'are too 'primitive' (at 31). The propositions typically used in criminal trials, according to Roberts and Aitken, are either of the 'empirical type' and 'institutional type.'

4 Roberts and Aitken *The logic of forensic proof: Inferential reasoning in criminal evidence and forensic science* 30.

5 See Jeremy Bentham *Rationale of judicial evidence* vol 1 (edited by J.S. Mill) (London: Hunt & Clark, 1827) 21; David Schum *Evidential foundations of probabilistic reasoning* (New York: Wiley, 1994) 18 (on 'fact' as an 'event'); Montrose "Basic concepts of the law of evidence," 534 (on 'facts' as 'discriminated parts of the totality of existence,' 'sections of history' or 'empirical phenomena'). For a very wide definition of 'facts,' see Jaap Hage "Of norms," in *Handbook of legal reasoning and argumentation*, ed. Giorgio Bongiovanni et al (Dordrecht: Springer, 2018) loc 3581 at loc 3839 (Kindle numbering). Legal norms are types of fact that 'motivate or guide behaviour.'

base offence,[6] a bias or prejudicial motivation, and responsibility in the form of intention. Montrose draws a useful distinction between this category of facts with what he calls 'brute facts.'[7] These are the extant facts from which inferences about the disputed facts are drawn. For example, a blood-stained knife, a bullet cartridge, fingerprints, cell phone images or videos, and footprints are all 'brute facts' from which disputed facts can be drawn. What converts them into propositions of fact are the fact-based assertions that are made about them (e.g. that 'the blood-stained knife belongs to litigant X' or that 'the fingerprints show the litigant's guilt'). The application of probative judgements to disputed facts requires that these propositions of fact be organised into a coherent taxonomy.[8]

There are various ways through which propositions of fact can be organised. For example, they may be organised into three *source*, *activity* and *offence* categories.[9] Propositions of fact about the location and origins of evidential items are pitched generally at source-level in the form, for example: 'the fibres at the crime scene match those of the clothes belonging to litigant Y,' 'litigant Z's semen was found on victim W's clothes' or 'the flammable materials that burnt down victim V's house were found at litigant S' house.'[10] Activity-level propositions pertain to the kinds of actions that one or more litigants performed. These include propositions such as 'litigant Y punched victim U in the face,' 'litigant Z had intercourse with victim W' or 'litigant S burnt down victim V's house.'[11] Typical examples of propositions of fact that are pitched at offence-level are 'litigant Y acted intentionally against victim U,' 'victim W did not consent to the intercourse with litigant Z,' and 'litigant S's actions against victim V's house was without justification.'[12] Furthermore, Wigmore developed a taxonomy that operates at two analytical dimensions. On the one hand, he classifies general *facta probanda* into four groups pertaining to (1) 'events, qualities, or conditions of physical (inanimate) nature' (external conditions), (2) 'the identity of a thing or person' (identity), (3) 'a quality or condition

6 The term 'base offence' is used here as a shorthand for the two requirements of (1) the manifest isolation or discriminatory targeting of an individual or group and (2) the target or victim being a member of the protected social group.

7 Montrose "Basic concepts of the law of evidence," 534.

8 See David Schum "Marshalling thoughts and evidence during fact investigation" (1999) 40(2) *South Texas Law Review* 401; Terence Anderson et al *Analysis of evidence* 2nd ed (Cambridge: Cambridge University Press, 2005) 112–114.

9 Richard Cook et al "A hierarchy of propositions: Deciding which level to address in casework" (1998) 38(4) *Scientific & Justice* 231 at 232. Aitken et al add 'sub-source' propositions to this hierarchy: Colin Aitken et al *Fundamentals of probability and statistical evidence in criminal proceedings* (Practitioner guide no. 1) (London: Royal Statistical Society, 2010) 55.

10 See Aitken et al *Fundamentals of probability and statistical evidence in criminal proceedings*, 55.

11 See Aitken et al *Fundamentals of probability and statistical evidence in criminal proceedings*, 57.

12 See Aitken et al *Fundamentals of probability and statistical evidence in criminal proceedings*, 58.

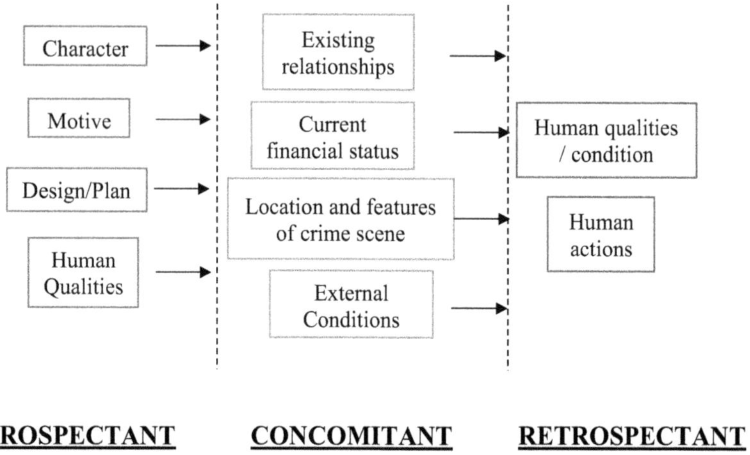

Figure 6.1 A diagram of Wigmore's taxonomy of propositions of fact

of a human being' (human quality or condition) and 'the doing of a human act (human action).'[13] Wigmore simultaneously conceives of each category of these propositions of fact as operating at three temporal perspectives. From the *prospectant* perspective (i.e. before the occurrence of a crime), 'the evidentiary facts of character, plan or design, motive (human qualities or conditions), point forward to a future act.'[14] The second perspective is *concomitant* with the time at which the crime occurred, where 'evidentiary circumstances such as family relationships, the need of money, and the like' (external conditions)[15] and 'outward exhibitions of conduct' may be used as 'a priori indications' of the relevant *facta probanda*.[16] From the third perspective, the *retrospectant* perspective (i.e. after the crime has occurred), propositions falling into the categories of human actions (e.g. 'hiding or running away after the event'), external conditions (e.g. possession of items connected with the crime) and human qualities or conditions (e.g. 'consciousness of guilt') have '*a posteriori* value' as showing 'the probable sources' of the relevant *facta probanda*.[17] A diagram of Wigmore's elaborate taxonomy is captured in Figure 6.1.

13 Wigmore *The principles of judicial proof as given by logic, psychology and general experience and illustrated in judicial trials*, 30. Cf. Wigmore *Evidence in trials at common law*, 1139, where Wigmore initially had made a three-fold classification: 'I. A Human Act; II. A Human Quality, Condition, or State; III. A fact or condition of External Nature.'

14 Wigmore *Evidence in trials at common law*, 1140. Cf. Wigmore *The principles of judicial proof as given by logic, psychology and general experience and illustrated in judicial trials*, 30.

15 Wigmore also offers examples of 'conditions of an external nature' such as the physical properties and geographic location of crime scenes, see Wigmore *Evidence in trials at common law*, 1140–1141.

16 Wigmore *Evidence in trials at common law*, 1140–1141.

17 Wigmore *Evidence in trials at common law*, 1140–1141; Wigmore *The principles of judicial proof as given by logic, psychology and general experience and illustrated in judicial trials*, 30.

6.3 Two Basic Patterns of Inferential Reasoning

The propositions of fact in any given case, as the taxonomy above shows, are 'actually a jumbled mixture of matters of unequal ontological status with an unequal degree of accessibility to our cognitive apparatus.'[18] It is no different with respect to hate crimes, which generally consist of the intentional perpetration of a base offence under a prejudicial motivation.[19] The wrongdoing component of the office (i.e. the base offence) is a depersonalised, objective and standard-setting proposition of fact. It is a general prohibition against the perpetration of the base offence *by anybody*, unless one relies on a recognised ground of justification. The prejudice and intention requirements change the focus of the enquiry towards the idiosyncratic capacities, attributes and overall disposition of the *individual perpetrator*. This conceptual variation warrants a corresponding distinction between the kinds of logical inferences that are required to establish these two facts.

The first inferential pattern proceeds from a norm to a disputed fact (N-to-F), whereas the second is from an extant fact to a disputed fact (F-to-F). To claim that 'perpetrating violence against a human being is unlawful, therefore, X's act of stabbing Y is unlawful' or that 'firing a gun at an unarmed person is unreasonable, therefore, adult Z firing a gun at minor child W is unreasonable' is to argue from a norm to a disputed fact (N-to-F).[20] This pattern of inferential reasoning is *evaluative* in so far as it measures the disputed fact referred to in the conclusion against the standard set in the norm that is stated in the premise. Conversely, claims such as 'alibi witness W testified that litigant *V* was not present at the scene at the time of the crime, therefore, litigant *V* did not commit the crime' and 'litigant T's blood test revealed traces of prohibited drugs, therefore, litigant T consumed prohibited drugs' follow a fact-to-fact (F-to-F) inferential pattern. F-to-F inferences are *existential* in that a disputed fact is inferred from an extant 'brute' fact. Existential F-to-F generalisations reflect a world-to-world direction of fit (from one brute fact or occurrence to another), whereas justificatory N-to-F inferences take on a word-to-world direction (a fictional or normative standard is used to measure the justification of an action).[21] Furthermore, another distinguishing feature

18 Mirjan R. Damaška "Truth in adjudication" (1998) 49 *Hastings Law Journal* 289 at 299; Kevin M. Clermont "A theory of factfinding: The logic for processing evidence" (2020) 104(2) *Marquette Law Review* 351 at 353–354, n10.

19 Joanna Botha and Avinash Govindjee "Regulating cases of 'extreme hate speech' in South Africa: A suggested framework for a legislated criminal sanction" (2014) 27(2) *South African Journal of Criminal Justice* 117 at 119; Office for Democratic Institutions and Human Rights *Hate crime laws: A practical guide* 2nd ed (2022) 1. Available at: www.osce.org (accessed: 2 January 2023).

20 Ronald J. Allen and Michael S. Pardo "Facts in law and facts of law" (2003) 7 *The International Journal of Evidence & Proof* 153 at 157.

21 Cf. Gertrude E.M. Anscombe *Intention* 2nd ed (Cambridge: Cambridge University Press, 1976) 56; John Searle *Expression and meaning: Studies in the theory of speech acts* (Cambridge: Cambridge University Press, 1979) 1–27; Hage "Of norms," 3839 (ebook numbering).

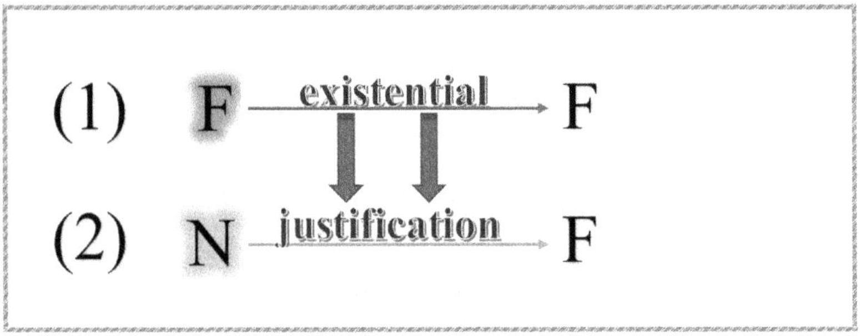

Figure 6.2 A graphical representation of two patterns of existential and justificatory inferences

between these two patterns of reasoning is that existential reasoning generally addresses *ex post facto* empirical questions about '*what* happened,' while justificatory reasoning responds to *ex ante* normative questions about '*why* a particular standard or norm has been contravened or not.'[22] The distinction between these two patterns of inferential reasoning is captured in Figure 6.2.

It is not claimed in this chapter that existential F-to-F and justificatory N-to-F inferences are the only patterns of reasoning in criminal adjudication, nor that a neat distinction between the two is always attainable. For example, propositions such as 'X acted reasonably,' 'X acted in accordance with the reasonable person' or 'X's actions were justified' are compounds that combine normative and factual features.[23] The claim rather is that these two basic patterns of inference feature in most of the argumentation models discussed in the next section of this chapter.

6.4 An Argument From Wrongness

Probative arguments that establish the wrongness of a crime usually take the form of an evaluative N-to-F inference. The antecedent refers to a norm or standard (e.g. the reasonable person of ordinary intelligence would not drive under the influence of alcohol) and the consequent is factual scenario (e.g. the breathalyser test revealed traces of alcohol from the breath of a driver of a vehicle) that is being evaluated.[24] The arguer's main purpose then is a justificatory one for either complying or failing to meet the antecedent standard. The antecedent may take the form of a *duty*, a (legal or moral) *norm*, or some form

22 See Damaška "Truth in adjudication," 299–300.
23 See James Grant "The double life of unlawfulness: Fact and law" (2007) 20 *South African Journal of Criminal Justice* 1 at 4–5.
24 Grant "The double life of unlawfulness: Fact and law," 4–5; *S v Basson* 2005 (1) SA 171 (CC) [50]–[51].

of *harm*.[25] The claims that 'X had a duty to respond in a proportionate manner to his attack, therefore, X breached his duty by using a nuclear bomb against Y's verbal threat';[26] 'a doctor disclosing a patient's confidential information without their consent is prohibited, therefore, doctor W telling his friend T about patient Z's medical condition is unlawful';[27] and 'corruption is harmful to the deserved beneficiaries of transactional goods, therefore, X diverting a tender award towards an undeserving bidder harms the interests of deserving bidders,'[28] are three examples of evaluative inferences that proceed from a

25 George P. Fletcher *The grammar of criminal law: American, comparative and international* vol 1 (Oxford: Oxford University Press, 2007) 37.

26 Fletcher *The grammar of criminal law: American, comparative and international*, 37; Immanuel Kant *Grounding for the metaphysics of morals* (translated by J.W. Ellington) [1785] (Indianapolis: Hackett, 1998) 12 ('An action done from duty has its moral worth') and 13 ('Duty is the necessity of an action done out of respect for the law'). See R. Antony Duff and Sandra E. Marshall "Criminalising hate?" in *Hate, politics, law: Critical perspectives on combating hate*, eds. Thomas Brudholm and Birgitte S. Johansen (New York: Oxford University Press, 2018) 115 at 121 ('To hate any fellow citizen is thus already to lack civic virtue . . . If I then enact that hatred in my conduct toward the other person, I violate my civic duty to her').

27 Fletcher *The grammar of criminal law: American, comparative and international*, 41–41; Herbert L.A. Hart *Punishment and Responsibility: Essays in the philosophy of law* 2nd ed (Oxford: Oxford University Press, 2008) 6 ('Why are certain kinds of action forbidden by law and so made crimes or offences? The answer is: To announce to society that these actions are not to be done and to secure that fewer of them are done. These are the common immediate aims of making any conduct a criminal offence and until we have laws made with these primary aims we shall lack the notion of a "crime" and so of a "criminal"'); Paul Roberts "On the preconditions and possibilities of criminal law theory" (1998) 11(3) *South African Journal of Criminal Justice* 285 at 302 ('For legal positivists, law is to be identified by its institutional pedigree as a political fact emanating from the right kinds of sources, typically (for Anglo-American lawyers) the work product of legislatures (statutes) and judges (common law precedents). Criminal laws on this view are simply laws with the right sort of institutional history, and crimes are the prohibitions they specify.').

28 Fletcher *The grammar of criminal law: American, comparative and international*, 39–40; Andrew P. Simester and Anthony T.H. Smith "Criminalisation and the role of theory," in *Harm and culpability*, eds. in Andrew P. Simester and Anthony T.H. Smith (Oxford: Clarendon Press, 1996) 1 at 4. See John S. Mill *On liberty* (edited by D. Bromwich and G. Kateb) (New Haven: Yale University Press, 2003) 76; Herbert L.A. Hart *Law, liberty and morality* (Stanford: Stanford University Press, 1963) 4–5; Cf. Steven D. Smith "Is the harm principle illiberal?" (2006) 51 *American Journal of Jurisprudence* 1; Arthur Ripstein "Beyond the harm principle" (1999) 34 *Philosophy and Public Affairs* 215; Bernard E. Harcourt "The collapse of the harm principle" (1999) 90 *Journal of Criminal Law and Criminology* 109 at 113; Meir Dan-Cohen "Defending dignity," in *Harmful thoughts: Essays on law, self and morality*, ed. Meir Dan-Cohen (Princeton: Princeton University Press, 2002) 150; Markus D. Dubber *Victims in the war on crime* (New York: New York University Press, 2002). The harm principle has since been extended further to cover 'remote harm' (or 'long term risks of harm'); see Andrew von Hirsh "Extending the harm principle: 'Remote' harms and fair imputation," in *Harm and culpability*, eds. in Andrew P. Simester and Anthony T.H. Smith (Oxford: Clarendon Press, 1996) 259; Andrew J. Ashworth "Criminal attempts and the role of resulting harm" (1988) 19(3) *Rutgers Law Journal* 725 at 733–734 (on extending the harm principle to cover inchoate and preventive crimes). Functional equivalents deployed by continental jurists include

duty, a norm and the stipulation of harm to a factual conclusion. The probative argument for the wrongness of a hate crime, which consists of the manifest discriminatory targeting of a victim who is a member of a protected demographic, also takes the form of one or more of these three inferential patterns.

The first argument from wrongness in the context of hate crimes takes the form of an appeal to authority (*argumentum ad verecundiam*). The basic form of this type of argumentation is framed as an appeal to opinion of an expert.

(1) E is an expert in domain D.
(2) E asserts that A is known to be true.
(3) A is within D.
(4) Therefore, A may (*plausibly*) be taken to be true.[29]

The argument in the context of hate crimes is a positivistic one.

(1) The legislature is authorised to outlaw wrongful conduct.
(2) The legislature has outlawed hateful conduct (base offence).
(3) Hateful conduct falls within the legislature's authority.
(4) Therefore, hateful conduct *plausibly* is wrongful.[30]

This form of argumentation is applicable especially to the kinds of hate crimes that consist of an underlying predicate or base offence, such as murder, assault or arson.[31] However, as argued in Chapter 2, the scope of the arguments

---

the notion of 'legal goods' (*Rechtsgüter*), the principle of legality, the ultimo ratio doctrine and the 'proscribed consequence' principle, see Nina Peršak *Criminalising harmful conduct: The harm principle, its limits and continental counterparts* (New York: Springer, 2007) Ch V; Johannes Keiler and David Roef "Principles of criminalisation and the limits of criminal law," in *Comparative concepts of criminal law*, eds. Johannes Keiler and David Roef 3rd ed (Cambridge: Intersentia, 2019) Ch II.

29 Douglas N. Walton *Informal logic: A handbook for critical argumentation* (Cambridge: Cambridge University Press, 1989) 193; Douglas Walton *Argumentation schemes for presumptive reasoning* (Mahwah: Lawrence Erlbaum Association, 1996) 64; Douglas Walton *Appeal to expert opinion: Arguments from authority* (University Park: Pennsylvania State University Press, 1992) 200–201. Cf. Douglas Walton *Legal argumentation and evidence* (University Park: Pennsylvania University Press, 2002) 330; Douglas Walton et al *Argumentation schemes* (New York: Cambridge University Press, 2008) 310; Trudy Govier *A practical study of argument* 7th ed (Boston: Cengage Learning, 2014) 125–126.

30 For more on classic legal positivism, see Herbert L.A. Hart *Concept of law* 3 ed (Oxford: Oxford University Press, 2012) Ch IV; Herbert L.A. Hart *Punishment and responsibility: Essays in the philosophy of law* 2nd ed (Oxford: Oxford University Press, 2008) 22; Joseph Raz "Authority, law and morality" (1985) 68 *The Monist* 295; Joseph Raz *The authority of law: Essays on law and morality* 2nd ed (Oxford: Oxford University Press, 2009).

31 Thomas Brudholm "Conceptualising hatred globally: Is hate crime a human rights violation?" in *The globalization of hate: Internationalising hate crime*, eds. Jennifer Schweppe and Mark A. Walters (Oxford: Oxford University Press, 2016) 31 at 34; Randy Blazak "Isn't every crime a hate crime? The case for hate crime laws" (2011) 5(4) *Sociology Compass* 244 at 245–246; Barbara Perry *In the name of hate: Understanding hate crimes* (New York:

developed in this book are framed widely to be of application to a number of contexts and jurisdictions that do not all precondition the sanctioning of hateful conduct on the basis of a criminal law violation. Secondly, international law instruments that sanction hateful conduct are framed widely as to encompasses both criminal and non-criminal violations using language that covers 'all dissemination of ideas based on racial superiority or hatred, incitement to racial discrimination' and 'all acts of violence or incitement to such acts against any race or group of persons of another colour or ethnic origin.'[32] Thirdly, there are breaches of non-criminal constitutional and statutory prohibitions against hateful conduct that may justify an *ad verecundiam* argument in some jurisdictions.[33] For example, the dissemination of racist slurs on posters or T-shirts,[34] the burning of crosses and wearing Nazi or Confederate uniforms at a fraternity meeting,[35] the mailing of derogatory letters or fliers to homosexuals[36] or the placement of a noose or dead animal on somebody's desk at a workplace[37] are all pertinent examples in this regard.

Furthermore, there are two additional probative arguments for the wrongness of hate crimes that may be advanced. They both take the form of an orthodox *argumentum ad consequentiam* (argument from good/bad consequences): for example, 'If A is brought about, then bad (good) consequences may plausibly occur, therefore, A should not (should) be brought about.'[38] Consequential arguments are traditionally considered to be fallacious because they 'affirm the consequent.'[39] However, if reconsidered in the dialectical

Routledge, 2001) 8; Office for Democratic Institutions and Human Rights "Hate crime laws: A practical guide," 15.

32 International Convention on the Elimination of all forms of Racial Discrimination of 1965, article 4 (182 parties), International Covenant on Civil and Political Rights of 1966, article 20(1): 'Any advocacy of national, racial or religious hatred that constitutes incitement to discrimination, hostility or violence shall be prohibited by law' (ratified by 173 countries).

33 See Perry *In the name of hate: Understanding hate crimes*, 8.

34 Howard J. Ehrlich "Campus ethnoviolence," in *Race and ethnic conflict: Contending views on prejudice, discrimination and ethnoviolence*, eds. Fred J. Pincus and Howard J. Ehrlich 2nd ed (New York: Westview Press, 1999) 271 at 271; Jeremy Waldron *The harm in hate speech* (Cambridge: Harvard University Press, 2012) 34: 'So it is with the phenomenon that we in America call "hate speech," a term that can cover things as diverse as Islamophobic blogs, cross-burnings, racial epithets, bestial depictions of members of racial minorities, genocidal radio broadcasts in Rwanda in 1994, and swastika-blazoned Nazis marching in Skokie, Illinois, with placards saying "Hitler should have finished the job."'

35 Ehrlich "Campus ethnoviolence," 280.

36 Ehrlich "Campus ethnoviolence," 280.

37 Mari J. Matsuda "Public response to racist speech: Considering the victim's story," in *Words that wound: Critical race theory, assaultive speech and the first amendment*, eds. Mari J. Matsuda et al (New York: Westview Press, 1999) 17 at 20–21.

38 Walton *Argumentation schemes for presumptive reasoning*, 75; Walton et al *Argumentation schemes*, 332.

39 Merilee H. Salmon *Introduction to logic and critical thinking* 6th ed (Boston: Clark Baxter, 2013) 313. For a historical overview, see Douglas Walton "Historical origins of *Argumentum ad consequentiam*" (1999) 13 *Argumentation* 251.

terms as a form of practical reasoning (e.g. as a form of 'advice-giving dialogue'), then consequential arguments can be legitimate forms of reasoning.[40] Therefore, the first of the two consequential arguments in the context of hate crimes takes the following form:

(1) If vulnerable minorities are the subject of hateful actions, then they may plausibly suffer alienation and terror.
(2) Therefore, vulnerable minorities should not be the subject of hateful actions.

The harmful effects of hateful actions in the messages they communicate to their victims are captured poignantly by Jeremy Waldron:

> Don't be fooled into thinking you are welcome here. The society around you may seem hospitable and nondiscriminatory, but the truth is that you are not wanted, and you and your families will be shunned, excluded, beaten, and driven out, whenever we can get away with it. We may have to keep a low profile right now. But don't get too comfortable. Remember what has happened to you and your kind in the past. Be afraid.[41]

According to Duff and Marshall, the distinctive wrong of hate speech is 'a genuine threat of exclusion or oppression' as 'a plausible prospect.'[42] The kind of exclusion being contemplated here is their 'membership of the polity – their civic status.'[43] Therefore, '[t]o hate is to exclude from fellowship and recognition' because '[w]hat I hate is what I would like to destroy, or to push right away from me . . . it is something unworthy of my respect, concern, or even attention . . . it has no place in my life.'[44] These effects are particularly acute on statistical, economic or political minority groups because of their 'vulnerability, social marginality and invisibility.'[45]

The second consequential argument operates more at macro societal level, namely:

(1) If vulnerable minorities are the subject of hateful actions, then patterns of structural societal inequality will be reinforced.
(2) Therefore, vulnerable minorities should not be the subject of hateful actions.

40 Douglas Walton *Scare tactics: Arguments that appeal to fear and threats* (Dordrecht: Springer, 2000) 132 and 136.
41 Waldron *The harm in hate speech*, 1–2.
42 Duff and Marshall "Criminalising hate?" 122.
43 Duff and Marshall "Criminalising hate?" 122.
44 Duff and Marshall "Criminalising hate?" 120.
45 Ryken Grattet and Valerie Jenness "Examining the boundaries of hate crime law: Disabilities and the 'dilemma of difference'" (2001) 91(3) *Journal of Criminal Law and Criminology* 653 at 653–654.

The effects of hate crimes far exceed a single individual or physical or financial damage.[46] They have the potential of fostering widespread fear, hostility and suspicion across an entire community. This is particularly because, unlike most other crimes, hate crimes 'enact domination by reinstating and reinforcing the subordinate position of the individuals and [groups] being addressed.'[47] They reinforce the hegemony of the perpetrator's demographic, while simultaneously subordinating the identity of the victim's group.[48] According to Perry, the individual victim of a hate crime is almost immaterial on this score because 'the victims are [*demographically*] interchangeable' and the hateful actions are more 'symbolic' than idiosyncratic.[49] It is for this reason that proving actual harm to a specific individual often is not required in most jurisdictions.[50]

6.5 An Argument From Prejudice

Hateful actions are punished if they are motivated by prejudice towards the victim.[51] This invocation of a motivation has little to do with the perpetrator's hatred or ill feelings, which may well, and often do, exist, towards the victim.[52] As a matter of fact, a perpetrator of a hateful action may be genuinely 'well-intentioned' in aiming, for example, 'to rid the world of evil' (mission hate crimes),[53] 'to blame others for their loss' (resentful or

46 Perry *In the name of hate: Understanding hate crimes*, 10.
47 Caitlin R. Carlson "Hate speech as a structural phenomenon" (2020) 54(2) *First Amendment Studies* 217 at 219.
48 Perry *In the name of hate: Understanding hate crimes*, 10; Neil Chakraborti and Jon Garland *Hate crime: Impact, causes and responses* 2nd ed (London: Sage, 2015) 4; Mari J. Matsuda "Public response to racist speech: Considering the victim's story," in *Words that wound: Critical race theory, assaultive speech and the first amendment*, eds. Mari J. Matsuda et al (New York: Westview Press, 1999) 17 at 23 ('Racism, as used here, comprises the ideology of racial supremacy and the mechanisms for keeping selected victim groups in subordinated positions.').
49 Perry *In the name of hate: Understanding hate crimes*, 10.
50 Frederick M. Lawrence *Punishing hate: Bias crimes under American law* (Cambridge: Harvard University Press, 1999) 67.
51 Brudholm "Conceptualising hatred globally: Is hate crime a human rights violation?" 34; Botha and Govindjee "Regulating cases of 'extreme hate speech' in South Africa: A suggested framework for a legislated criminal sanction," 119; Joanna Botha "The selection of victim groups in hate-crime legislation" (2019) 136 *South African Law Journal* 781 at 784 ('The bias motive against the victim's group status distinguishes the hate crime from an ordinary crime.').
52 Lawrence *Punishing hate: Bias crimes under American law*, 9; Botha and Govindjee "Regulating cases of 'extreme hate speech' in South Africa: A suggested framework for a legislated criminal sanction," 119; James B. Jacobs and Kimberly Potter *Hate crimes: Criminal law & identity politics* (New York: Oxford University Press, 1998) 11.
53 Jack Levin and Jack McDevitt *Hate crimes: The rising tide of bigotry and bloodshed* (New York: Plenum Press, 1993) Ch 7; Jack Levin and Jack McDevitt *Hate crimes revisited: America's war on those who are different* (Boulder, CO: Westview Press, 2002) Ch 7.

retaliatory hate crimes),[54] 'to protect themselves against [perceived] outsiders' (defensive hate crimes)[55] and 'for the thrill of it' (thrill-seeking hate crimes).[56] However, none of these motivations would save the perpetrator from criminal sanction. What would be required is that the perpetrator was not motivated by bias or prejudice. A prejudice is a naked preference that comes into being without much rational deliberation or selection in a human being. Prejudices often, as Jacobs and Potter say, 'are passed down to us by family, friends, school, religion and culture.'[57] Some of these preferences are good (e.g. in respect of careers, schools and food), and others are innocuous (e.g. in respect of weather conditions, sports teams or music).[58] Therefore, this begs the question as to what kind of prejudice is 'bad' for purposes of hate crimes.

The bad kind of prejudice is one that is based solely on the victim's membership of a protected demographic, such as religion, gender, sexual orientation, race or ethnicity.[59] This type of demographic-based preference is grounded on a separation between 'us' and 'them,' rather than just 'me' and 'you,' or between 'in-groups' and 'out-groups.'[60] Moreover, the perpetrator enforces these bigoted demarcations by excluding the victim from his own hegemonic demographic group and placing them into a subordinated and marginalised group.[61] The probative argument for this type of motivation takes the form of a hasty generalisation that is best illustrated through an orthodox Barbara syllogism.

54 Levin and McDevitt *Hate crimes: The rising tide of bigotry and bloodshed*, Ch 4; Levin and McDevitt *Hate crimes revisited: America's war on those who are different*, Ch 4.
55 Levin and McDevitt *Hate crimes: The rising tide of bigotry and bloodshed*, Ch 6; Levin and McDevitt *Hate crimes revisited: America's war on those who are different*, Ch 6.
56 Levin and McDevitt *Hate crimes: The rising tide of bigotry and bloodshed*, Ch 5; Levin and McDevitt *Hate crimes revisited: America's war on those who are different*, Ch 5.
57 Jacobs and Potter *Hate crimes: Criminal law & identity politics*, 12.
58 Jacobs and Potter *Hate crimes: Criminal law & identity politics*, 11–12.
59 Heidi M. Hurd "Why liberals should hate 'hate crime legislation'" (2001) 20(2) *Law & Philosophy* 215 at 219; Lawrence *Punishing hate: Bias crimes under American law*, 29–39 and appendices B and C (on the 'animus' and 'discriminatory selection' models). Cf. Paul H. Robinson "Hate crimes: Crimes of motive, character or group terror" (1992) *Annual Survey of American Law* 605 (on the plausibility of the recklessness model to capture the motivational requirement of hate crimes). See generally, Michael D. Bayles "Character, purpose and criminal responsibility" (1982) 1 *Law & Philosophy* 5; R. Antony Duff "Choice, character and criminal liability" (1993) 12 *Law & Philosophy* 345.
60 Jon Garland and Corinne Funnell "Defining hate crime internationally: Issues and conundrums," in *The globalization of hate: Internationalising hate crime*, eds. Jennifer Schweppe and Mark A. Walters (Oxford: Oxford University Press, 2016) 15 at 17; Jonathan O. Chimakonam and L. Uchenna Ogbonnaya *African metaphysics, epistemology, and a new logic: A decolonial approach to philosophy* (Cham: Palgrave Macmillan, 2021) 2.
61 Perry *In the name of hate: Understanding hate crimes*, 10.

(1) A → B.
(2) C → B.
(3) C → A.[62]

Coined by the medieval scholastic philosophers as a mnemonic chant to indicate one of Aristotle's three figures, namely: AAA-I,[63] the Barbara is valid no matter which terms are substituted for the letters A, B and C.

(1) All Africans are humans.
(2) All Batswana are Africans.
(3) Therefore, all Batswana are humans.[64]

In the context of hate crimes, the basic probative argument for the prejudice requirement consists of the following hasty generalisation:

(1) Members of Protected Group A generally (or all) are B (generalisation).
(2) Victim C is a member of Protected Group A (membership).
(3) Therefore, Victim C is B.

Once the perpetrator has excluded the victim from the 'in-group' and placed them into the 'out-group' their reasoning is similar, namely (1) outgroups are dangerous; (2) X is a member of an outgroup; (3) therefore, X is dangerous.[65] The first premise not only reflects on a particular demographic group in overly general or absolutist terms, but it also casts aspersions against it. This founding generalisation often is derived by the perpetrator either from their own idiosyncratic experience with members of the demographic concerned or from second-hand information about the group. For example, the perpetrator may begin with generalisations, which may be grounded in fact (partially or wholly) or not, such as 'Yesterday's mosque bombing was committed by a Muslim' or 'Honduras is the most dangerous country in the world.' The perpetrator's next step then is to accord the victim membership of this group on the ground of religion, nationality, gender, ethnicity or any such demographic

62 Irving M. Copi et al *Introduction to logic* 14th ed (London: Routledge, 2014) 192; Aristotle "The prior analytics," in *The complete works of Aristotle*, ed. Jonathan Barnes vol I (Princeton: Princeton University Press) 39 at 41, 26a1 ('If *A* is predicated of every *B*, and *B* of every *C*, *A* must be predicated of every *C*'); Gisela Striker *Aristotle: Prior analytics* Book I (translated by Gisela Striker) (Oxford: Oxford University Press, 2009) 68 and 82–83.

63 Alan Hausman et al *Logic and philosophy: A modern introduction* 13th ed (Indianapolis: Hackett Publishing Company, 2021) 344, n8.

64 See Copi et al *Introduction to logic*, 192.

65 See Jack Levin and Gordana Rabrenovic "Hate as cultural justification for violence," in *Hate crimes: Understanding and defining hate crime*, ed. Brian Levin vol 1 (Westport: Praeger Publishers, 2009) 41 at 47; Garland and Funnell "Defining hate crime internationally: Issues and conundrums," 17.

(e.g. 'X is a Muslim' or 'Y is a citizen of Honduras'). The conclusion thereafter transposes the aspersion cast against the group as a whole in the first premise to the individual victim as a member of that demographic (e.g. 'X committed yesterday's bombing' or 'Y is dangerous').

6.6 An Argument From Responsibility

Criminal responsibility turns its focus towards the perpetrator, and not the action, as with the wrongdoing requirement. The enquiry focuses on the 'general capacities and opportunities'[66] possessed by the perpetrator at the time of the incident. The degree of blameworthiness with which the perpetrator is adjudged corresponds to the degree of 'choices and control'[67] that were available to her. A specific fault requirement often is not expressly articulated in hate crime statutes in most jurisdictions. However, as argued in Chapter 2, the fault requirement is discussed as a recognition of the operation of the general principles of criminal law that provide that a fault requirement generally applies *ex lege*, unless expressly excluded by the legislature.[68] Therefore, the kind of fault that will be discussed is the intention variant. The basic probative argument for the direct or deliberate form of intention draws on the concepts of 'knowledge' and 'desire.'

(1) Consequences that are *Known* and *Desired plausibly* are Intended.
(2) Consequence X was *Known* and *Desired.*
(3) Therefore, Consequence X *plausibly* was intended.[69]

The first knowledge antecedent is grounded of the further claim that 'evidential facts that form part of a perpetrator's general experience plausibly will be known by him.'[70] For the second desire antecedent, the additional claim is that 'consequences that have the potential to advance the interests of the perpetrator plausibly will be desired by him.'[71]

66 Michael S. Moore *Placing blame: A theory of the criminal law* (Oxford: Oxford University Press, 1997) 404; Victor Tadros *Criminal responsibility* (Oxford: Oxford University Press, 2005) 100 ('[A]n agent is criminally responsible for his action only insofar as that action reflects on him *qua* agent'); Andrew P. Simester "A disintegrated theory of culpability," in *The sanctity of life and the criminal law: The legacy of Glanville Williams*, eds. Dennis J. Baker and Jeremy Horder (Cambridge: Cambridge University Press, 2013) 178 at 179.
67 Andrew Ashworth "Belief, intent and criminal liability," in *Oxford essays in jurisprudence*, eds. John Eekelaar and John Bell (Oxford: Clarendon Press, 1987) 1 at 17.
68 The full set of reasons and references for this point are provided in full in Chapter 2 and will not be repeated here.
69 Tshepo B. Mosaka "A probative argument of intention" (2023) 87(5–6) *Journal of Criminal Law* 329 at 342.
70 Mosaka "A probative argument of intention," 341.
71 Mosaka "A probative argument of intention," 341–342.

For purposes of hate crimes, the probative argument for the perpetrator that acts with deliberate intention rests on the ***knowledge*** of the exclusion of the victim from the perpetrator's civic polity, coupled with the ***desire*** to marginalise or subordinate the victim.

(1) Consequences that are *Known* and *Desired plausibly* are Intended.
(2) The social exclusion and subordination of the victim was known and desired by the perpetrator.
(3) Therefore, the social exclusion and subordination of the victim *plausibly* was intended by the perpetrator.

Most jurisdictions[72] also have an expanded non-deliberate form of intention that can be modelled along the following lines of probative argument.

(1) Consequences that are *Known* and *Controlled plausibly* are Intended.
(2) Consequence X was *Known* and *Controlled.*
(3) Therefore, Consequence X *plausibly* was Intended.[73]

The probative argument of non-deliberate forms of intention for purposes of hate crimes is also conditions upon the antecedents of knowledge and control.

(1) Consequences that are *Known* and *Controlled plausibly* are Intended.
(2) The social exclusion and subordination of the victim was known and controlled by the perpetrator.
(3) Therefore, the social exclusion and subordination of the victim *plausibly* was intended by the perpetrator.

It is clear that knowledge forms the basis not only of deliberate and non-deliberate forms of intention, but of all forms of criminal responsibility more generally. Therefore, the main difference between the two basic models is that the more exacting antecedent of 'desire' is applicable to the deliberate

72 See generally, Herbert L.A. Hart *Punishment and responsibility: Essays in the philosophy of law* 2nd ed (Oxford: Oxford University Press, 2008) 114; Glanville Williams "Oblique intention" (1987) 46(3) *Cambridge Law Journal* 417 at 418; Jeremy Bentham *Introduction to the principles of morals and legislation* (edited by J.H. Burns and H.L.A. Hart) [1789] (London: Methuen, 1970) 86–87 (where the term 'oblique' intention was coined); Itzhak Kugler *Direct and oblique intention in the criminal law* (Aldershot: Ashgate, 2002) (*direct* and *oblique* intention); R. Antony Duff *Intention, agency and criminal liability: Philosophy of action and the criminal law* (Oxford: Blackwell, 1990) 43. In Francophone jurisdictions, a distinction is made between *dol direct* and *dol indirect*, see John A. Spencer "Intentional killings in French law," in *Homicide law in comparative perspective*, ed. Jeremy Horder (Portland: Hart, 2007) 39 at 43; Catherine Elliot *French criminal law* (New York: Routledge, 2001) 66–67. For an African perspective, see Carlson Anyangwe *Criminal law: The general part* (Bamenda: Langaa, 2015) 186; Francis D.P. Situma *Criminal law in Kenya* (Kluwer, 2012) 43.

73 Mosaka "A probative argument of intention," 342.

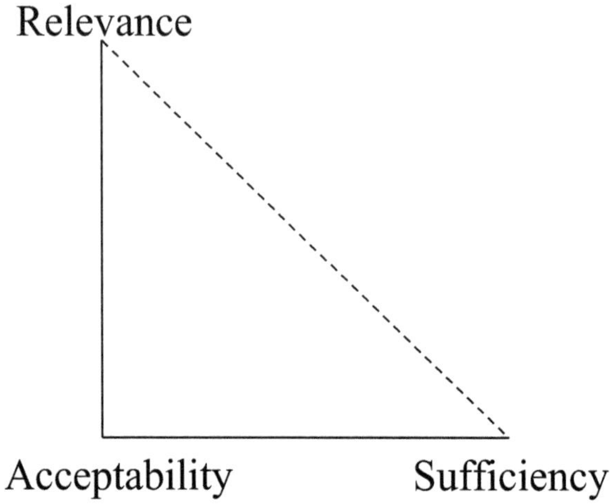

Figure 6.3 RAS triangle of argumentation evaluation

form of intention, which usually attracts a harsher punishment for that reason, whereas the lesser 'control' requirement is reserved for non-deliberate forms of intention. These general forms of argumentation also find application to the hate crime context in their current form.

6.7 Evaluation of Argumentation Models

Aside from the identification and analysis of the forms of arguments, the evaluation of the cogency of arguments is also a primary goal of argumentation theory.[74] To evaluate an argument is to determine its cogency or logical soundness by, among other things, ascertaining the epistemic warrant of its premisses, the degree to which it can withstand criticism and whether or not it meets any prescribed normative standard or goal of probative sufficiency.[75] The arguments discussed in this chapter will be evaluated according to Blair and Johnson's RAS criteria of *relevance*, *acceptability* and *sufficiency*, as shown in the triangle captured in Figure 6.3.[76] These three criteria correspond to

74 Douglas N. Walton *Fundamentals of critical argumentation* (Cambridge: Cambridge University Press, 2006) 1; Nicholas Capaldi and Miles Smit *The art of deception: An introduction to critical thinking* (revised) (New York: Prometheus Books, 2007) 23; Frans H. van Emeren et al *Fundamentals of argumentation theory: A handbook of historical backgrounds and contemporary developments* (New York: Routledge, 1996) 12.

75 See Trudy Govier *A practical study of argument* 7th ed (Boston: Cengage Learning, 2014) 108; Ralph H. Johnson and J. Anthony Blair *Logical self-defense* (New York: International Debate Education Association, 2006) 50 ('A logically good argument . . . is one whose premises supply strong grounds for any reasonable person to accept the conclusion. In other words, a reasonable person would accept its conclusion, based on its premises, and would be justified in so doing').

76 Johnson and Blair *Logical self-defense*, 54–55; J. Anthony Blair "Relevance, acceptability and sufficiency today" (2007) 8(1–2) *Anthropology & Philosophy* 33 at 33–34; Douglas Walton and

the three basic moves that an arguer generally makes, namely to assert the premisses as being true or otherwise acceptable, to assert that there is a connection between the premisses and the conclusion, and to assert the conclusion.[77]

Firstly, the criterion of relevance entails testing the relationship between premisses and the conclusion to ascertain whether the premisses have some bearing on the truth or merit of the conclusion.[78] A premise that bears little or no probative connection to the conclusion is irrelevant. Some common examples of fallacies of irrelevance include the *ignoration elenchi* ('missing the point') (alternatively known as a *non-sequitur*), the straw man, the red herring, the *ad hominem* attack, the *argumentum ad populum* (appeal to the populace), the *argumentum ad baculum* (appeal to force) and the *argumentum ad misericordiam* (appeal to pity).[79] The second criterion is that the premisses must be acceptable to a rational person.[80] According to Govier, there are seven potential bases upon which a premise may be acceptable,[81] including if it is supported by a cogent subargument (e.g. it may be argued by analogy that a similar argument was accepted on a separate occasion),[82] if it is a matter of common knowledge, if it is known *a priori* to be true (e.g. that 17 is a prime number),[83] if it is supported by reliable testimony, or if it is backed by the opinion of an expert. Furthermore, an argument may be found to be acceptable if it is supported elsewhere by the arguer or another person, or it may be provisionally acceptable, without independent knowledge of it being rationally acceptable, for the sake of argument.[84]

Thirdly, the relevant and acceptable premisses are tested to ascertain their logical sufficiency in establishing the conclusion. The determination here is whether or not the premisses 'considered together'[85] are 'sufficient in number

---

Thomas F. Gordon "Formalising informal logic" (2015) 35(4) *Informal Logic* 508 at 529–527; Govier *A practical study of argument*, 87–88. Cf. Edward T. Damer *Attacking faulty reasoning: A practical guide to fallacy-free arguments* (Boston: Cengage Learning, 2013) 31 (five criteria, including relevance, acceptability and sufficiency). For a critical discussion, see Frans H. van Eemeren et al *Handbook of argumentation theory* (Dordrecht: Springer, 2014) 381–383.

77 Govier *A practical study of argument*, 104.

78 Damer *Attacking faulty reasoning: A practical guide to fallacy-free arguments*, 33.

79 Copi et al *Introduction to logic*, 101–118; Walter Sinnott-Armstrong and Robert Fogelin *Understanding arguments: An introduction to informal logic* 9th ed (Stamford: Cengage Learning, 2015) Ch 15. For an analogous relevance criterion in law, see Mirjan R. Damaška "Evidentiary barriers to conviction and two models of criminal procedure: A comparative study" (1973) 121(3) *University of Pennsylvania Law Review* 507 at 518; Joëlle Vuille "Admissibility and appraisal of scientific evidence in continental European criminal justice systems: Past, present and future" (2013) 45(4) *Australian Journal of Forensic Sciences* 389 at 390.

80 Damer *Attacking faulty reasoning: A practical guide to fallacy-free arguments*, 35.

81 Govier *A practical study of argument*, 128. Cf. Damer *Attacking faulty reasoning: A practical guide to fallacy-free arguments*, 36 (for six 'Standards of Premise Acceptability') and 37 (for six 'Conditions of Premise Unacceptability').

82 Govier *A practical study of argument*, 117–118.

83 Govier *A practical study of argument*, 118.

84 Govier *A practical study of argument*, 128.

85 Govier *A practical study of argument*, 87.

and strength' to justify the acceptance of the conclusion.[86] There are varying criteria of sufficiency depending on the model of argumentation one adopts. For example, the sufficiency of *deductive* arguments is determined in accordance with a criterion of entailment, namely where it is impossible for premisses that are relevant and true not to entail, of necessity, the conclusion.[87] According to Blair, deductive logic is not easily applicable to 'contexts of practical reasoning,' such as 'morality, law, business, politics, engineering, medicine, the skilled trades, crafts.'[88] Another example of a system of evaluation is the determination of sufficiency using predetermined dialogical decision rules that both parties agree to in a *pragma-dialectic model* of argumentation.[89] Some of the rules that the parties affix before their dialogue begins include the imposition of burdens of proof, the prescription of a goal for the dialogue and specifying the level and kind of support an argument must have to succeed.[90] According to Walton, criminal trials are best modelled as persuasion dialogues under the pragma-dialectic system of argumentation evaluation.[91] Some of the reasons for this comparison pertain to the application of pragma-dialectic features such as 'decision rules,' 'error preference presumptions' and fixed 'standards [or criteria] of proof'[92] (e.g. the common law 'beyond a reasonable doubt' standard[93] and the civilian *conviction raisonnée* criterion)[94] in the forensic context.[95]

86 Govier *A practical study of argument*, 38.
87 J. Anthony Blair *Groundwork in the theory of argumentation* (Dordrecht: Springer, 2012) 51–52.
88 Blair *Groundwork in the theory of argumentation*, 53.
89 Blair *Groundwork in the theory of argumentation*, 55.
90 Douglas Walton *The new dialectic: Conversational contexts of argument* (Toronto: University of Toronto Press, 1998) 246.
91 Walton *The new dialectic: Conversational contexts of argument*, 234–235; Douglas Walton *Dialog theory for critical argumentation* (Amsterdam: John Benjamins, 2007) 94.
92 For a comparative discussion, see Mirjan R. Damaška "Free proof and its detractors" (1995) 43(3) *The American Journal of Comparative Law* 343 at 347; Kevin M. Clermont and Emily Sherwin "A comparative view of standards of proof" (2002) 50 *American Journal of Comparative Law* 243; Kevin M. Clermont "Standards of proof revisited" (2009) 33(3) *Vermont Law Review* 469; Michele Taruffo "Rethinking standards of proof" (2003) 51(3) *American Journal of Comparative Law* 659; Giovanni Tuzet "Assessment criteria or standards of proof? An effort in clarification" (2018) 28 *Artificial Intelligence and Law* 91.
93 John H. Wigmore *Evidence in trials at common* vol IV (revised by James H. Chadbourn) (Boston: Little Brown and Company, 1970) § 2497; James B. Thayer *A preliminary treatise on evidence at common law* (Boston: Little Brown and Co., 1898) 363; James F. Stephen *A digest on the law of evidence* (London: Macmillan, 1887) article 93; *Woolmington v Director of Public Prosecutions* [1935] AC 462 (HL).
94 Mirjan R. Damaška "Evidentiary barriers to conviction and two models of criminal procedure: A comparative study" (1973) 121(3) *University of Pennsylvania Law Review* 506 at 344; Christopher Champod and Joëlle Vuille "Scientific evidence in Europe: Admissibility, evaluation and equality of arms" (2011) 9(1) *International Commentary on Evidence* 1 at 17; Joëlle Vuille "Forensic science evidence in non-adversary criminal justice systems," in *Forensic science evidence and expert witness testimony: Reliability through reform*, eds. Paul Roberts and Michael Stockdale (Cheltenham: Elgar, 2018) 354 at 365.
95 John D. Jackson "Managing uncertainty and finality: The function of the criminal trial in legal inquiry," in *Trial on trial: Truth and due process*, eds. R. Antony Duff et al vol 1 (Portland: Hart, 2004) 121 at 127; Alex Stein "The refoundation of evidence law" (1996) 9 *Canadian*

The evaluation of legal arguments from a pragma-dialectic perspective also requires a consideration of these and other applicable institutional features in determining the cogency of the arguments of the arguers.

The mechanism of testing arguments under the pragma-dialectic scheme, on the influence of the ancient Greek 'dialectic' (*dialektikos*),[96] relies on alternative or oppositional critical questioning.[97] A successful argument in this regard is one that is able to withstand critical questioning from the co-arguer.[98] In general, there are at least four categories of critical questions or points of attack to any given argument: to challenge the premisses, the relationship between the premisses and conclusion, the conclusion, or the any applicable *non-excipiens* clause.[99] The challenge against the premisses is mainly an epistemic or practical one, namely whether the premisses are true or otherwise well supported,[100] while impugning the connection between the premisses and conclusion is to challenge the relevance of the premisses.[101] Furthermore, the conclusion of an argument generally can be challenged by way of a counterargument (i.e. the claim that a different conclusion has or can be reached on the same premisses).[102] Finally, to challenge the *non-excipiens* clause is to contend that there are other reasons beyond the logic of that particular argument that the conclusion should not be drawn from the premisses (e.g. if it

---

Journal of Law & Jurisprudence 279 at 294; Ronald. J. Allen "How presumptions should be allocated: Burdens of proof, uncertainty and ambiguity in modern legal discourse" (1994) 17(3) *Harvard Journal of Law and Public Policy* 627 at 629; Douglas Walton *Burden of proof, presumption and argumentation* (New York: Cambridge University Press, 2014) Ch 2.

96 Douglas Walton *Plausible argument in everyday conversation* (Albany: State University of New York Press, 1992) 4 (simply put, *dialektikos* for the Greeks meant 'to discuss'); William C. Kneale and Martha Kneale, *Development of logic* (London: Oxford University Press, 1962) 7. For Aristotle, reasoning is 'dialectic' if its starting premisses are not 'demonstratively' (or 'analytically' true, but rather if they are 'generally accepted opinions' (*endoxa*), see Aristotle *Topics* (translated by W.A. Pickard-Cambridge) (Cambridge: NuVision Publications, 2005) Book 1, part 1; Aristotle *De Sophisticis Elenchis* (edited and translated by E.S. Forster) (Cambridge: Harvard University Press, 1955) 15.

97 Walton et al *Argumentation schemes*, 16–17; Ralph H. Johnson *Manifest rationality* (Mahwah: Lawrence Erlbaum Associates, 2000) 206; David Hitchcock "Good reasoning on the Toulmin model" (2005) 19 *Argumentation* 373 at 388 (modern critical questioning was pioneered by Arthur Hastings in 1963).

98 Blair *Groundwork in the theory of argumentation*, 54. See also Frans H. van Eemeren and Rob Grootendorst *A systematic theory of argumentation: The pragma-dialectical approach* (New York: Cambridge University Press, 2004) Ch 6 (15 rules for a critical discussion).

99 Bart Verheij "Dialectical argumentation with argumentation schemes" (2003) 11(2) *Artificial Intelligence and Law* 167 at 183. Cf. Bart Verheij "Evaluating arguments based on Toulmin's scheme," in *Arguing on the Toulmin model: New essays in argument analysis and evaluation*, eds. David Hitchcock and Bart Verheij (Dordrecht: Springer, 2006) 181 at 194–195 (five types of rebuttals on the Toulmin model). Cf. Stephen Toulmin *The uses of argument* (Cambridge: Cambridge University Press, 1958) 93–94. Toulmin's 'data' and 'claims' are equivalent to 'premisses' and 'conclusions,' whereas 'warrants' are synonymous with 'major premisses' (generalisations or conditionals) (at 90–91).

100 Verheij "Dialectical argumentation with argumentation schemes," 182.

101 Verheij "Dialectical argumentation with argumentation schemes," 183.

102 Verheij "Dialectical argumentation with argumentation schemes," 183.

normatively or legally prohibited to draw such a conclusion within a particular context).[103] The remainder of this section will now discuss the sets of critical questions that are applicable to each of the arguments identified earlier from *wrongness, prejudice* and *responsibility*.

There are two kinds of arguments from wrongness: the appeal to authority (*argumentum ad verecundiam*) and the argument from bad consequences (*argumentum ad consequentiam*). By way of recollection, the following positivistic *ad verecundiam* argument was discussed earlier:

(1) The legislature is authorised to outlaw wrongful conduct.
(2) The legislature has outlawed hateful conduct (base offence).
(3) Hateful conduct falls within the legislature's authority.
(4) Therefore, hateful conduct *plausibly* is wrongful.

This standard appeal to authority can be subjected to no fewer than five critical questions challenging the credibility and authority of the legislature, the legitimacy and legal compliance of the legislation, and the internal composition and procedural compliance of the legislature.

CQ_1: Whether the legislature is authorised to pass legislation on hate crimes.
CQ_2: Whether the hate crime legislation compliance with other legal and constitutional provisions (e.g. the right to freedom of expression).
CQ_3: Whether the legislature was properly constituted.
CQ_4: Whether the process followed to pass and promulgate the hate crimes legislation was lawful.
CQ_5: Whether the legislature relied on rational reasons and supporting evidence to justify the need for hate crime legislation within a particular community.[104]

The second set of arguments from wrongness took the form of a consequential argument in which it was claimed that (1) if vulnerable minorities are the subject of hateful actions, then they may plausibly suffer alienation and terror, (2) therefore, vulnerable minorities should not be the subject of hateful actions. A similar, yet additional, argument operating at a macro-societal level was also discussed. The claim here was that (1) if vulnerable minorities are the subject of hateful actions, then patterns of structural societal inequality will be reinforced, (2) therefore, vulnerable minorities should not be the subject of hateful actions. Both these consequential arguments are based on the potential

103 Verheij "Dialectical argumentation with argumentation schemes," 182–183.
104 Cf. Walton et al *Argumentation schemes*, 310; Walton *Legal argumentation and evidence*, 330; Walton *Argumentation schemes for presumptive reasoning*, 64–65; Walton *Appeal to expert opinion: Arguments from authority*, 200–201.

harm of hateful actions against the victims concerned. The critical questions for both arguments are the same.

CQ$_1$: How strong is the likelihood that the cited consequences (i.e. alienation, terror and structural societal inequality) will or may occur?
CQ$_2$: What is the sufficiency of the evidence tendered in support of the contended likelihood of the adverse consequences?
CQ$_3$: Are there any potential good consequences that may arise from the hateful actions to account for?
CQ$_4$: Do any precautionary or preventative measures exist, or have any been taken to avert the adverse consequences from ensuing?[105]

A prosecutor will have succeeded in defending the arguments from wrongness (i.e. the appeal to authority and the consequential arguments) if she can properly respond to the perpetrator's critical questions. The degree to which the prosecutor is able to respond to critical questioning corresponds to the sufficiency of her arguments from wrongness in the hate crime prosecution.

The argument from prejudice was next to be discussed earlier in this chapter. It takes the form of a hasty generalisation (*secundum quid*).

(1) Members of Protected Group A generally (or all) are B (generalisation).
(2) Victim C is a member of Protected Group A (membership).
(3) Therefore, Victim C is B.

There are at least three potential critical questions that the perpetrator of hate crimes may raise in response to this argument.

CQ$_1$: How many exceptions are there to the generalisation of members with the characteristic B?
CQ$_2$: How did the perpetrator obtain the information about the characteristics of members of the protected group?
CQ$_3$: What evidence was relied upon to establish Victim C's membership of the protected group?

The hasty generalisation was first identified as a fallacy by Aristotle in his text, *De Sophisticis Elenchis* ('On Sophistical Refutations').[106] This form of argument

105 Cf. Walton *Argumentation schemes for presumptive reasoning*, 75–76; Walton et al *Argumentation schemes*, 332–333.

106 John Woods *The death of argument: Fallacies in agent-based reasoning* (Dordrecht: Springer, 2004) 301; Aristotle *De Sophisticis Elenchis* (translated by E.S. Forster) (Cambridge: Harvard University Press, 1955) 25/166b30: 'Fallacies connected with Accident occur when it is claimed that some attribute belongs similarly to the thing and to its

is characterised generally by three logical failures: it neglects or overlooks qualifications or exceptions in its generalisations (presumptive failure), it usually applies incorrect sampling procedures (e.g. arguing from a sample size that is too small or unrepresentative) and it fails to account for the adequacy of existing evidence or the availability of new information.[107] In sum, 'when a conclusion is attractive to us,' as Salmon argues, 'laziness, prejudice, fear, hope, or some other strong psychological motivation tempts us to accept it without evidence.'[108]

Finally, the sets of argument from responsibility were framed to suit the deliberate and non-deliberate forms of intention. The deliberate form of probative argument was grounded, by recollection, on the concepts of 'knowledge' and 'desire' as well as the perpetrator's motive to exclude and subordinate the victim of a hate crime.

(1) Consequences that are *Known* and *Desired plausibly* are Intended.[109]
(2) The social exclusion and subordination of the victim was known and desired by the perpetrator.
(3) Therefore, the social exclusion and subordination of the victim *plausibly* was intended by the perpetrator.

On the other hand, the non-deliberate form of probative argument was structured using the concepts of 'knowledge' and 'control.'

(1) Consequences that are *Known* and *Controlled plausibly* are Intended.
(2) The social exclusion and subordination of the victim was known and controlled by the perpetrator.
(3) Therefore, the social exclusion and subordination of the victim plausibly was intended by the perpetrator.

---

accident'; Aristotle *The art of rhetoric* (translated by J.H. Freese) (Cambridge: Harvard University Press, 1926) 331/1401b6. See also Aníbal A. Bueno "Aristotle, the fallacy of accident, and the nature of predication: A historical inquiry" (1988) 26(1) *Journal of the History of Philosophy* 5; Douglas Walton "Ignoring qualifications (*secondum quid*) as a subfallacy of hasty generalisations" (1990) 33(129–130) *Logique & Analyse* 113 at 131–135.

107 Walton "Ignoring qualifications (*secondum quid*) as a subfallacy of hasty generalisations," 114–115; Copi et al *Introduction to logic*, 71–73; Aristotle *De Sophisticis Elenchis*, 25/166b30: '[S]ince the same thing has many accidents, it does not necessarily follow that all the same attributes belong to all the predicates of a thing and to that of which they are predicated.'

108 Salmon *Introduction to logic and critical thinking*, 204.

109 It was explained earlier that the epistemic warrant of the knowledge and desire antecedents in turn would be established the claims 'evidential facts that form part of a perpetrator's general experience plausibly will be known by him' and 'consequences that have the potential to advance the interests of the perpetrator plausibly will be desired by him,' respectively.

There are three epistemic, volitional and attitudinal critical questions that the perpetrator may pose in response to these kinds of deliberate and non-deliberate forms of probative argumentation.

CQ_1: Was the perpetrator aware of all the surrounding or contributing facts?
CQ_2: Was the perpetrator's achievement of their goals (i.e. the exclusion and subordination of the victim) interrupted by an intervening event?
CQ_3: Are the consequences consistent with what the agent desired?[110]

In the event that the prosecutor, who is making the deliberate and/or non-deliberate probative arguments from responsibility, is unable to adequately respond to these questions, then she will have failed to prove the intention requirement of the hate crime concerned. However, as indicated several times both in this chapter and Chapter 2, not all jurisdictions expressly recognise an intention requirement.

6.8 Conclusion: The Argument From Hate

The overall probative argument from hate consists of the wrongful and intentional perpetration of a hateful action under a prejudicial motivation. It is made up of three separate probative arguments from wrongness, prejudice and responsibility in the form of intention. Therefore, as a matter of evidential proof, is to wrong them by intentionally targeting them for subordination and exclusion from within a defined civic polity. This chapter has identified, analysed and evaluated the logical forms of these arguments. However, it remains an open question, which possibly is the subject of a separate book, as to whether the critical questions posed in evaluation of the arguments adequately meet the institutionally imposed standards or criteria of proof within the forensic context. Each argument is tested through a handful of critical questions, and it is clear enough that the prosecutor's success will depend on the degree to which she is able to adequately respond. As to how many precise questions guarantee success, the standard against which the quality of the perpetrator's questions is to be measured (some are surely better or more difficult than others), and the number of questions it takes to comply with any personal or institutional standards or criteria of logical persuasion, these are all open

110 The third of these questions is derived from Duff's 'failure test': if the perpetrator's action does not preclude an expected consequence, will it be a failure? If so, that consequence is one that the perpetrator intended to bring about. If not, 'it is merely a foreseen side-effect' of the perpetrator's action. See R. Antony Duff *Intention, agency and criminal liability: Philosophy of action and the criminal law* (Oxford: Blackwell, 1990) 61. Cf Cathleen M. Kaveny "Inferring intention from foresight" (2004) 120 *Law Quarterly Review* 81 at 88–94, where the distinction between 'intention' and 'foresight' is criticised. Kaveny prefers that we stick with intention, as purpose, and then distinguish between remote, intermediate and immediate purposes.

questions that reveal a potential shortcoming of the pragma-dialectic method of argumentation evaluation. This takes nothing away from the contribution made by the chapter in identifying the logical forms of hate crime argumentation as well as a basic mechanism of testing them.

6.9 Bibliography

Books and Book Chapters

Alan Hausman, Frank Boardman and Howard Kahane *Logic and philosophy: A modern introduction* 13th ed (Indianapolis: Hackett Publishing Company, 2021).

Andrew Ashworth "Belief, intent and criminal liability," in *Oxford essays in jurisprudence*, eds. John Eekelaar and John Bell (Oxford: Clarendon Press, 1987) 1.

Andrew P. Simester "A disintegrated theory of culpability," in *The sanctity of life and the criminal law: The legacy of Glanville Williams*, eds. Dennis J. Baker and Jeremy Horder (Cambridge: Cambridge University Press, 2013) 178.

Andrew P. Simester and Anthony T.H. Smith "Criminalisation and the role of theory," in *Harm and culpability*, eds. in Andrew P. Simester and Anthony T.H. Smith (Oxford: Clarendon Press, 1996) 1.

Andrew von Hirsh "Extending the harm principle: 'Remote' harms and fair imputation," in *Harm and culpability*, eds. in Andrew P. Simester and Anthony T.H. Smith (Oxford: Clarendon Press, 1996) 259.

Aristotle *The art of rhetoric* (translated by J.H. Freese) (Cambridge: Harvard University Press, 1926).

Aristotle *De Sophisticis Elenchis* (edited and translated by E.S. Forster) (Cambridge: Harvard University Press, 1955).

Aristotle "The prior analytics," in *The complete works of Aristotle*, ed. Jonathan Barnes vol I (Princeton: Princeton University Press) 39.

Aristotle *Topics* (translated by W.A. Pickard-Cambridge) (Cambridge: NuVision Publications, 2005).

Barbara Perry *In the name of hate: Understanding hate crimes* (New York: Routledge, 2001).

Bart Verheij "Evaluating arguments based on Toulmin's scheme," in *Arguing on the Toulmin model: New essays in argument analysis and evaluation*, eds. David Hitchcock and Bart Verheij (Dordrecht: Springer, 2006) 181.

Carlson Anyangwe *Criminal law: The general part* (Bamenda: Langaa, 2015).

Catherine Elliot *French criminal law* (New York: Routledge, 2001).

Colin Aitken, Paul Roberts and Graham Jackson *Fundamentals of probability and statistical evidence in criminal proceedings* (Practitioner guide no. 1) (London: Royal Statistical Society, 2010).

Daniel Vanderveken *Meaning and speech acts* vol 1 (Cambridge: Cambridge University Press, 1990).

David Schum *Evidential foundations of probabilistic reasoning* (Evanston, IL: Northwestern University Press, 1994).

Douglas N. Walton *Appeal to expert opinion: Arguments from authority* (University Park: Pennsylvania State University Press, 1992).

Douglas N. Walton *Argumentation schemes for presumptive reasoning* (Mahwah: Lawrence Erlbaum Association, 1996).

Douglas N. Walton *Burden of proof, presumption and argumentation* (New York: Cambridge University Press, 2014).

Douglas N. Walton *Dialog theory for critical argumentation* (Amsterdam: John Benjamins, 2007).

Douglas N. Walton *Fundamentals of critical argumentation* (Cambridge: Cambridge University Press, 2006).
Douglas N. Walton *Informal logic: A handbook for critical argumentation* (Cambridge: Cambridge University Press, 1989).
Douglas N. Walton *Legal argumentation and evidence* (University Park: Pennsylvania University Press, 2002).
Douglas N. Walton *The new dialectic: Conversational contexts of argument* (Toronto: University of Toronto Press, 1998).
Douglas N. Walton *Plausible argument in everyday conversation* (Albany: State University of New York Press, 1992).
Douglas N. Walton *Scare tactics: Arguments that appeal to fear and threats* (Dordrecht: Springer, 2000).
Douglas N. Walton, Christopher Reed and Fabrizio Macagno *Argumentation schemes* (New York: Cambridge University Press, 2008).
Edward T. Damer *Attacking faulty reasoning: A practical guide to fallacy-free arguments* (Boston: Cengage Learning, 2013).
Francis D.P. Situma *Criminal law in Kenya* (Kluwer, 2012).
Frans H. van Eemeren, Bart Garssen, Erik C.W. Krabbe, A. Francisca S. Henkemans, Bart Verheij and Jean H.M. Wagemans *Handbook of argumentation theory* (Dordrecht: Springer, 2014).
Frans H. van Eemeren and Rob Grootendorst *A systematic theory of argumentation: The pragma-dialectical approach* (New York: Cambridge University Press, 2004).
Frans H. van Eemeren, Rob Grootendorst, Ralph H. Johnson, Christian Plantin and Charles A. Willard *Fundamentals of argumentation theory* (New York: Routledge, 1996).
Frederick M. Lawrence *Punishing hate: Bias crimes under American law* (Cambridge: Harvard University Press, 1999).
George P. Fletcher *The grammar of criminal law: American, comparative and international* vol 1 (Oxford: Oxford University Press, 2007).
Gertrude E.M. Anscombe *Intention* 2nd ed (Cambridge: Cambridge University Press, 1976).
Gisela Striker *Aristotle: Prior analytics* Book I (translated by Gisela Striker) (Oxford: Oxford University Press, 2009).
Gottlob Frege "Begriffsschrift," in *Translations from the philosophical writings of Gottlob Frege*, eds. Peter Geach and Max Black (New York: Philosophical Library, 1952) 1.
Gottlob Frege "The thought: A logical inquiry," in *Philosophical logic*, ed. Peter F. Strawson (London: Oxford University Press, 1967) 20.
Herbert L.A. Hart *Concept of law* 3rd ed (Oxford: Oxford University Press, 2012).
Herbert L.A. Hart *Law, liberty and morality* (Stanford: Stanford University Press, 1963).
Herbert L.A. Hart *Punishment and responsibility: Essays in the philosophy of law* 2nd ed (Oxford: Oxford University Press, 2008).
Howard J. Ehrlich "Campus ethnoviolence," in *Race and ethnic conflict: Contending views on prejudice, discrimination and ethnoviolence*, eds. Fred J. Pincus and Howard J. Ehrlich 2nd ed (New York: Westview Press, 1999) 271.
Immanuel Kant *Grounding for the metaphysics of morals* (translated by J.W. Ellington) [1785] (Indianapolis: Hackett, 1998).
Irving M. Copi, Carl Cohen and Victor Rodych *Introduction to logic* 15th ed (New York: Routledge, 2019).
Itzhak Kugler *Direct and oblique intention in the criminal law* (Aldershot: Ashgate, 2002).
J. Anthony Blair *Groundwork in the theory of argumentation* (Dordrecht: Springer, 2012).

Jaap Hage "Of norms," in *Handbook of legal reasoning and argumentation*, eds. Giorgio Bongiovanni, Gerald Postema, Antonino Rotolo, Giovanni Sartor, Chiara Valentini and Douglas N. Walton (Dordrecht: Springer, 2018) loc 3581 (Kindle numbering).

Jack Levin and Gordana Rabrenovic "Hate as cultural justification for violence," in *Hate crimes: Understanding and defining hate crime*, ed. Brian Levin vol 1 (Westport: Praeger Publishers, 2009) 41.

Jack Levin and Jack McDevitt *Hate crimes revisited: America's war on those who are different* (Boulder: Westview Press, 2002).

Jack Levin and Jack McDevitt *Hate crimes: The rising tide of bigotry and bloodshed* (New York: Plenum Press, 1993).

James B. Jacobs and Kimberly Potter *Hate crimes: Criminal law & identity politics* (New York: Oxford University Press, 1998).

James B. Thayer *A preliminary treatise on evidence at common law* (Boston: Little Brown and Co., 1898).

James F. Stephen *A digest on the law of evidence* (London: Macmillan, 1887).

Jeremy Bentham *Introduction to the principles of morals and legislation* (edited by J.H. Burns and H.L.A. Hart) [1789] (London: Methuen, 1970).

Jeremy Bentham *Rationale of judicial evid*ence vol 1 (edited by J.S. Mill) (London: Hunt & Clark, 1827).

Jeremy Waldron *The harm in hate speech* (Cambridge: Harvard University Press, 2012).

Johannes Keiler and David Roef "Principles of criminalisation and the limits of criminal law," in *Comparative concepts of criminal law*, eds. Johannes Keiler and David Roef 3rd ed (Cambridge: Intersentia, 2019).

John A. Spencer "Intentional killings in French law," in *Homicide law in comparative perspective*, ed. Jeremy Horder (Portland: Hart, 2007) 39.

John D. Jackson "Managing uncertainty and finality: The function of the criminal trial in legal inquiry," in *Trial on trial: Truth and due process*, eds. R. Antony Duff et al vol 1 (Portland: Hart, 2004) 121.

John H. Wigmore *Evidence in trials at common law* vol 1 (revised by Peter Tillers) (Boston: Little Brown, 1983).

John H. Wigmore *The principles of judicial proof as given by logic, psychology and general experience and illustrated in judicial trials* (Boston: Little Brown & Company, 1913).

John S. Mill *On liberty* (edited by D. Bromwich and G. Kateb) (New Haven: Yale University Press, 2003).

John Searle *Expression and meaning: Studies in the theory of speech acts* (Cambridge: Cambridge University Press, 1979).

John Woods *The death of argument: Fallacies in agent-based reasoning* (Dordrecht: Springer, 2004).

John Woods and Douglas N. Walton *Argument: The logic of the fallacies* (Toronto: McGraw-Hill Ryerson, 1982).

Jon Garland and Corinne Funnell "Defining hate crime internationally: Issues and conundrums," in *The globalization of hate: Internationalising hate crime*, eds. Jennifer Schweppe and Mark A. Walters (Oxford: Oxford University Press, 2016) 15.

Jonathan O. Chimakonam and L. Uchenna Ogbonnaya *African metaphysics, epistemology, and a new logic: A decolonial approach to philosophy* (Cham: Palgrave Macmillan, 2021).

Joseph Raz *The authority of law: Essays on law and morality* 2nd ed (Oxford: Oxford University Press, 2009).

Mari J. Matsuda "Public response to racist speech: Considering the victim's story," in *Words that wound: Critical race theory, assaultive speech and the first amendment*, eds. Mari J. Matsuda, Charles R. Lawrence, Richard Delgado and Kimberlé W. Crenshaw (New York: Westview Press, 1999) 17.

Markus D. Dubber *Victims in the war on crime* (New York: New York University Press, 2002).
Meir Dan-Cohen "Defending dignity," in *Harmful thoughts: Essays on law, self and morality*, ed. Meir Dan-Cohen (Princeton: Princeton University Press, 2002) 150.
Merilee H. Salmon *Introduction to logic and critical thinking* 6th ed (Boston: Clark Baxter, 2013).
Michael S. Moore *Placing blame: A theory of the criminal law* (Oxford: Oxford University Press, 1997).
Neil Chakraborti and Jon Garland *Hate crime: Impact, causes and responses* 2nd ed (London: Sage, 2015).
Nicholas Capaldi and Miles Smit *The art of deception: An introduction to critical thinking* (revised) (New York: Prometheus Books, 2007).
Nina Peršak *Criminalising harmful conduct: The harm principle, its limits and continental counterparts* (New York: Springer, 2007).
Paul Roberts and Colin Aitken *The logic of forensic proof: Inferential reasoning in criminal evidence and forensic science* (Practitioner Guide No. 3) (London: Royal Statistical Society, 2014).
R. Antony Duff *Intention, agency and criminal liability: Philosophy of action and the criminal law* (Oxford: Blackwell, 1990).
R. Antony Duff and Sandra E. Marshall "Criminalising hate?" in *Hate, politics, law: Critical perspectives on combating hate*, eds. Thomas Brudholm and Birgitte S. Johansen (New York: Oxford University Press, 2018) 115.
Ralph H. Johnson *Manifest rationality* (Mahwah: Lawrence Erlbaum Associates, 2000).
Ralph H. Johnson and J. Anthony Blair *Logical self-defense* (New York: International Debate Education Association, 2006).
Stephen Toulmin *The uses of argument* (Cambridge: Cambridge University Press, 1958).
Terence Anderson, William Twining and David Schum *Analysis of evidence* 2nd ed (Cambridge: Cambridge University Press, 2005).
Thomas Brudholm "Conceptualising hatred globally: Is hate crime a human rights violation?" in *The globalization of hate: Internationalising hate crime*, eds. Jennifer Schweppe and Mark A. Walters (Oxford: Oxford University Press, 2016) 31.
Trudy Govier *A practical study of argument* 7th ed (Boston: Cengage Learning, 2014).
Victor Tadros *Criminal responsibility* (Oxford: Oxford University Press, 2005).
Walter Sinnott-Armstrong and Robert Fogelin *Understanding arguments: An introduction to informal logic* 9th ed (Stamford: Cengage Learning, 2015).
William C. Kneale and Martha Kneale *Development of logic* (London: Oxford University Press, 1962).

Periodicals

Alex Stein "The refoundation of evidence law" (1996) 9 *Canadian Journal of Law & Jurisprudence* 279.
Andrew J. Ashworth "Criminal attempts and the role of resulting harm" (1988) 19(3) *Rutgers Law Journal* 725.
Aníbal A. Bueno "Aristotle, the fallacy of accident, and the nature of predication: A historical inquiry" (1988) 26(1) *Journal of the History of Philosophy* 5.
Arthur Ripstein "Beyond the harm principle" (1999) 34 *Philosophy and Public Affairs* 215.
Bart Verheij "Dialectical argumentation with argumentation schemes" (2003) 11(2) *Artificial Intelligence and Law* 167.

Bernard E. Harcourt "The collapse of the harm principle" (1999) 90 *Journal of Criminal Law and Criminology* 109.
Caitlin R. Carlson "Hate speech as a structural phenomenon" (2020) 54(2) *First Amendment Studies* 217.
Cathleen M. Kaveny "Inferring intention from foresight" (2004) 120 *Law Quarterly Review* 81.
Christopher Champod and Joëlle Vuille "Scientific evidence in Europe: Admissibility, evaluation and equality of arms" (2011) 9(1) *International Commentary on Evidence* 1.
David Hitchcock "Good reasoning on the Toulmin model" (2005) 19 *Argumentation* 373.
David Schum "Marshalling thoughts and evidence during fact investigation" (1999) 40(2) *South Texas Law Review* 401.
Douglas N. Walton "Historical origins of *Argumentum ad consequentiam*" (1999) 13 *Argumentation* 251.
Douglas N. Walton "Ignoring qualifications (*secondum quid*) as a subfallacy of hasty generalisations" (1990) 33(129–130) *Logique & Analyse* 113.
Douglas N. Walton and Thomas F. Gordon "Formalising informal logic" (2015) 35(4) *Informal Logic* 508.
Giovanni Tuzet "Assessment criteria or standards of proof? An effort in clarification" (2018) 28 *Artificial Intelligence and Law* 91.
Glanville Williams "Oblique intention" (1987) 46(3) *Cambridge Law Journal* 417.
Heidi M. Hurd "Why liberals should hate 'hate crime legislation'" (2001) 20(2) *Law & Philosophy* 215.
J. Anthony Blair "Relevance, acceptability and sufficiency today" (2007) 8(1–2) *Anthropology & Philosophy* 33.
James Grant "The double life of unlawfulness: Fact and law" (2007) 20 *South African Journal of Criminal Justice* 1.
James L. Montrose "Basic concepts of the law of evidence" (1954) 70 *Law Quarterly Review* 527.
Joanna Botha "The selection of victim groups in hate-crime legislation" (2019) 136 *South African Law Journal* 781.
Joanna Botha and Avinash Govindjee "Regulating cases of 'extreme hate speech' in South Africa: A suggested framework for a legislated criminal sanction" (2014) 27(2) *South African Journal of Criminal Justice* 117.
Joëlle Vuille "Admissibility and appraisal of scientific evidence in continental European criminal justice systems: Past, present and future" (2013) 45(4) *Australian Journal of Forensic Sciences* 389.
Joseph Raz "Authority, law and morality" (1985) 68 *The Monist* 295.
Kevin M. Clermont "Standards of proof revisited" (2009) 33(3) *Vermont Law Review* 469.
Kevin M. Clermont "A theory of factfinding: The logic for processing evidence" (2020) 104(2) *Marquette Law Review* 351.
Kevin M. Clermont and Emily Sherwin "A comparative view of standards of proof" (2002) 50 *American Journal of Comparative Law* 243.
Michael D. Bayles "Character, purpose and criminal responsibility" (1982) 1 *Law & Philosophy* 5.
Michele Taruffo "Rethinking standards of proof" (2003) 51(3) *American Journal of Comparative Law* 659.
Mirjan R. Damaška "Evidentiary barriers to conviction and two models of criminal procedure: A comparative study" (1973) 121(3) *University of Pennsylvania Law Review* 506.
Mirjan R. Damaška "Free proof and its detractors" (1995) 43(3) *The American Journal of Comparative Law* 343.

Mirjan R. Damaška "Truth in adjudication" (1998) 49 *Hastings Law Journal* 289.
Paul H. Robinson "Hate crimes: Crimes of motive, character or group terror" (1992) *Annual Survey of American Law* 605.
Paul Roberts "On the preconditions and possibilities of criminal law theory" (1998) 11(3) *South African Journal of Criminal Justice* 285.
R. Antony Duff "Choice, character and criminal liability" (1993) 12 *Law & Philosophy* 345.
Randy Blazak "Isn't every crime a hate crime? The case for hate crime laws" (2011) 5(4) *Sociology Compass* 244.
Richard Cook, Ian W. Evett, Graham Jackson, John P. Jones and James A. Lambert "A hierarchy of propositions: Deciding which level to address in casework" (1998) 38(4) *Scientific & Justice* 231.
Ronald J. Allen "How presumptions should be allocated: Burdens of proof, uncertainty and ambiguity in modern legal discourse" (1994) 17(3) *Harvard Journal of Law and Public Policy* 627.
Ronald J. Allen and Michael S. Pardo "Facts in law and facts of law" (2003) 7 *The International Journal of Evidence & Proof* 153.
Ryken Grattet and Valerie Jenness "Examining the boundaries of hate crime law: Disabilities and the 'dilemma of difference'" (2001) 91(3) *Journal of Criminal Law and Criminology* 653.
Steven D. Smith "Is the harm principle illiberal?" (2006) 51 *American Journal of Jurisprudence* 1.
Tshepo B. Mosaka "A probative argument of intention" (2023) 87(5–6) *Journal of Criminal Law* 329.

Online Resources

Office for Democratic Institutions and Human Rights *Hate crime laws: A practical guide* 2nd ed (2022), available at: www.osce.org (accessed: 2 January 2023).

7 The Study of Applied Proof

7.1 The Relativistic Proof of Hate Crimes: Three Main Conclusions

A specialised 'law of proof,' never mind that of 'applied proof,'[1] currently does not exist. Such a specialisation would focus on 'proof in the general sense,' that is, 'the part concerned with the ratiocinative process of contentious persuasion, mind to mind, counsel to juror.'[2] There is a comparatively small, but growing, group of scholars that study 'issues of probabilistic and mathematical proof in court'[3] and, more generally, '[w]hat constitute[s] valid, cogent, and appropriate modes of reasoning about disputed questions of fact in adjudication.'[4] Furthermore, there are also scholars that focus on more discrete aspects of the evaluation of evidence, such as burdens and standards of proof, beginning with James Fitzjames Stephen in 1872.[5] Stephen's section on 'the proof of facts' is potentially misleading until one reads the substance of the 34 articles discussed under this heading.[6] The focus of the discussion in this section is on judicial notice and various forms of presenting evidence (i.e. through oral testimony and documents). Elsewhere in a section titled 'Production and Effect of Evidence,' Stephen focuses on doctrinal rules regulating burdens of proof, presumptions, estoppel and the competency and presentation of witness

1 On Twining's 'middle-order theorising,' see William Twining "Evidence and legal theory," in *Law in context: Enlarging a discipline*, ed. William Twining (Oxford: Oxford University Press, 1997) 110 at 112–113; William Twining "Some jobs for jurisprudence" (1974) 1(2) *British Journal of Law and Society* 149 (five jobs of jurisprudence); Aleksander Peczenik *On law and reason* 2nd ed (Dordrecht: Springer, 2009) 13–14.

2 John H. Wigmore "The problem of proof" (1913) 8 *Illinois Law Review* 77 at 77.

3 Eric D. Green "Foreword" (1986) 66(3) *Boston University Law Review* 377 at 379.

4 William Twining "The Boston symposium: A comment" (1986) 66(3) *Boston University Law Review* 391 at 391.

5 James F. Stephen *The Indian Evidence Act (I of 1872): With an introduction on the principles of judicial evidence* (London: Macmillan, 1872); James F. Stephen *A digest on the law of evidence* 12th ed (London: Macmillan & Co., 1876–1948).

6 Stephen *A digest on the law of evidence*, articles 58–92; Stephen *The Indian Evidence Act (I of 1872): With an introduction on the principles of judicial evidence*, 9.

DOI: 10.4324/9781003493006-7

testimony.[7] While contemporary scholarship on the related topics of burdens and standards of proof abounds,[8] research that focuses pointedly and exclusively (i.e. without an over-reliance on doctrinal rules) on evidential proof rarely appears. This book's contribution pertains overwhelmingly on the heuristics and models of forensic proof, and to a lesser extent on any incidental doctrinal rules that govern the adjudicative evaluation of evidence.

Furthermore, the book's primary focus on evidential proof is directed towards the context of hate crimes, thereby rendering the overall project as a study in *applied* forensic proof. It is through this contextual application that the structure and content of evidential proof in the forensic context is examined and developed. Therefore, the book departs from the Benthamist orthodoxy of separating substantive and procedural law.[9] The view rather is that substantive law is 'neither a procedural nor trans-procedural' and that it is 'constructed with a specific procedural apparatus in mind to vindicate the rights created or the responsibilities assigned by that substantive law.'[10] The contention with respect to evidential proof, by parity of reasoning, is that a study in *applied* proof is one that does not segregate heuristic of proof with their substantive objects. Moreover, the project undertaken in this book goes a step further than this by also integrating the procedural aspects, especially

7 Stephen *A digest on the law of evidence*, articles 93–143. Compare this to modern inheritors of Stephen's model, see Nicola Monaghan *Law of evidence* (Cambridge: Cambridge University Press, 2015) Chs 3 and 10–11; Ratanlal Ranchhoddas and Dhirajlal K. Thakore *Law of evidence (PB)* 27th ed (New Delhi: LexisNexis, 2020) Chs VII–X; Charanjit Singh *Unlocking the law of evidence* 4th ed (London: Routledge, 2023) Chs 2 and 14; Ian Dennis *The law of evidence* 8th ed (London: Sweet & Maxwell, 2024) Chs 10–14; Richard D. Friedman *An advanced introduction to evidence* (Cheltenham: Elgar, 2024) Chs 15 and 17.

8 For example, Dale A. Nance *The burdens of proof: Discriminatory power, weight of evidence and tenacity of belief* (Cambridge: Cambridge University Press, 2016); Jean-Francois Blanchette *Burdens of proof: Cryptographic culture and evidence law in the age of electronic documents* (Cambridge, MA: MIT Press, 2012); Douglas Walton *Burden of proof, presumption and argumentation* (New York: Cambridge University Press, 2014); Henry Prakken and Giovanni Sartor "A logical analysis of burdens of proof," in *Legal evidence and proof*, eds. Henry Prakken et al (Farnham: Ashgate, 2009) Ch 9. See also Kevin Clermont *Standards of decision in law: Psychological and logical bases for the standard of proof, here and abroad* (Durham: California Academic Press, 2013); Robert J. MacCoun "Standards of proof: Theories and evidence," in *Research handbook on law and psychology*, ed. Rebecca Hollander-Blumoff (Cheltenham: Elgar, 2024) Ch 10.

9 Jeremy Bentham *Rationale of judicial evidence* vol 1 (edited by J.S. Mill) (London: Hunt & Clark, 1827) 24–25; Thomas Starkie *Practical treatise of the law of evidence and digest of proofs in civil and criminal proceedings* vol 1 3rd ed (Philadelphia: T. & J.W. Johnson, 1842) 1; James F. Stephen *A digest on the law of evidence* (London: Macmillan & Co., 1876) ix; James B. Thayer *A preliminary treatise on evidence at common law* (Boston: Little Brown and Co., 1898) 530; John H. Wigmore *A treatise on the system of evidence in trials at common law* vol 1 (Boston: Little Brown, 1905), xi and 41; Charles F. Chamberlayne *A treatise on the modern law of evidence* vol 3 (London: Sweet & Maxwell, 1911) 2230–2235.

10 Thomas O. Main "The procedural foundation of substantive law" (2003) 78 *Washington University Law Review* 801 at 822.

in relation to the identity and competence of the fact-finder, the rules governing which extant facts are acceptable, and the logical and legal standards or criteria against which probative inferences are evaluated, in so far as these have an influence on the structure and/or content of probative judgements. This three-way – ***material*** (Chapter 2), ***processual*** (Chapter 3) and ***probative*** (Chapters 4, 5 and 6) – integration of theory characterises the kind of study in applied proof that this book is propounding.

The six chapters of this book together respond to the main question about how the global phenomenon of hate crimes can be proven in the forensic context. After introducing the core problem, as it arises in both the areas of evidential proof and the criminal law of hate, the second chapter begins the response by defining and tracing the history of hate crimes around the world. Chapter 2 lays the groundwork by responding to the first question anybody would ask about the relatively unknown phenomenon of hate crimes: what precisely are hate crimes? A legal definition is given that encompasses all three penalty-enhancing, sentence aggravating, and substantive variants of hate crime offences.[11] Furthermore, the history of hate crimes statutes is traced to the late twentieth-century post-war era of identity politics and human rights. The chapter concludes the discussion by identifying four general elements of hate crimes pertaining to the (1) intentional and (2) manifest isolation or discriminatory targeting of an individual or group (3) for the prejudicial reason (4) that they belong to a protected social demographic group.

The third chapter focuses on the ***processual*** aspects of probative reasoning. In particular, once the legal meaning and elements of hate crimes have been identified in Chapter 2, the next question pertains to the processing of the extant facts from which inferential conclusions about the substantive elements of hate crimes can be drawn. Chapter 3 pays particular attention towards three distinct questions: (1) By whom (adjudicator) are these facts to be processed? (2) Under which rules or practices are acceptable facts to be distinguished from those that are not? (3) Against which logical and legal standards and criteria are the inferences from the extant facts to establishing the substantive elements of hate crimes to be measured? These three areas of focus all revolve around the processing of the extant facts that are the foundation of all forms of probative judgements. The main focus of the chapter may be on procedural aspects, but the discussion is framed in such a way that it reveals the role of these processual practices in the founding and processing of the extant facts that are the basis of probative inferences.

The remaining three chapters complete the comprehensive response to the main question by turning the focus towards the logical methods and heuristics

11 Gail Mason "Legislating against hate," in *The Routledge international handbook on hate crime*, eds. Nathan Hall et al (New York: Routledge, 2015) 59 at 60; James B. Jacobs and Kimberly Potter *Hate crimes: Criminal law & identity politics* (New York: Oxford University Press, 1998) 29.

of proving hate crimes. Chapter 4 begins the discussion by tracing the historical evolution of methods of proof from *antiquity*, focusing on ordeals and sworn testimony under religious relics, and the *medieval period*, foregrounding judicial battle and confessions under the Roman-canon system; up until the contemporary *rationalist period* that has extended into the emergence of the New Evidence Scholarship movement. The discussion in the third of these three periods focuses mainly on the methods of rational argumentation and electronic methods such as polygraphs. The chapter that follows picks up on this discussion by extending the analysis of the rational argumentation method of evidential proof. The discussion in Chapter 5, 'The Probative Condition I,' serves a foundational and theory-building purpose. Its connection to Chapter 6, 'The Probative Condition II,' is that it develops the foundation theory and generic arguments that are applied to the hate crime context in the next chapter. Chapter 5 tracks the brief history of legal argumentation scholarship to the 1970s and proceeds to explicate the deductive, inductive and defeasible models as standard forms of legal and non-legal argumentation.

Building on the historical and theoretical foundation laid by Chapters 4 and 5, respectively, Chapter 6 applies all of the theorising that has occurred up to that point to the context of hate crimes. The chapter ultimately develops three sets of probative arguments from *wrongness*, *prejudice* and *responsibility*. These arguments correspond to the four general elements of hate crimes identified in Chapter 2. Furthermore, the chapter also relies on the processual aspects that were discussed in Chapter 3 to develop a basic taxonomy of propositions of fact and to guide the evaluation of the three arguments towards the end of the chapter. The arguments from wrongness are based on two generic models of the conventional appeal to authority (*argumentum ad verecundiam*) and the argument from consequences (*argumentum ad consequentiam*). The argument from prejudice is characterised as a hasty generalisation (*secundum quid*) and illustrated through the classic Barbara AAA-I syllogism. The form of responsibility considered is in the form of intention in its deliberate (by design) and expanded non-deliberate forms. Both arguments take the form of a defeasible *modus ponens* (affirming the antecedent).

The answer to the main question of this book is given in the form of three *material* (Chapter 2), *processual* (Chapter 3) and *probative* (Chapters 4, 5 and 6) conditions. This manner of answer aims to offer an integrated conception of evidential proof that advances the kind of study of applied proof that this book propounds. Overall, there are three main conclusions that can be drawn from the theorising about evidential proof in this book as a relativistic and applied concept. Firstly, the development of a grand and all-compassing 'general theory of proof' is impeded by the kind of methodological pluralism that is adopted in this book.[12] Specific theories are likely to achieve more

12 Peter Tillers "Mapping inferential domains" (1986) 66(4) *Boston University Law Review* 883 at 894–895. Cf. Douglas Walton *Legal argumentation and evidence* (University Park:

in discrete areas of criminal process; for example, the application of abductive reasoning in the pre-trial investigative context,[13] the reliance on statistical analysis to support the bad character evidence of a repeat offender's recidivism probability at sentencing stage,[14] and the application of various deductive,[15] inductive (Bayesian)[16] and defeasible[17] theories to the trial context. Secondly, forensic proof is relativistic, and not substance blind, in so far as its structure and content are determined and/or influenced by various *material* (the elements of crimes or causes of actions that are the objects of proof) and *processual* (the rules and practices that govern the acceptance and processing of the

---

Pennsylvania University Press, 2002) 200–201, 291 and 321–322 (on his 'Plausibilistic theory'); L. Jonathan Cohen *The probable and the provable* (Oxford: Oxford University Press, 1977) 56–57 and 246 (on his 'Baconian Inductivism'); Terence Anderson et al *Analysis of evidence* 2nd ed (Cambridge: Cambridge University Press, 2005) 114–115 (on their 'seven step protocol'); Joseph B. Kadane and David A. Schum *A probabilistic analysis of the Sacco and Vanzetti evidence* (New York: Wiley, 1996) 33 (on their holistic modelling of the facts of the Sacco and Vanzetti case).

13 Floris J. Bex *Arguments, stories and criminal evidence: A formal hybrid theory* (Dordrecht: Springer, 2011) 22, 83 and 141.

14 Mike Redmayne "The relevance of bad character" (2002) 61(3) *The Cambridge Law Journal* 684 at 691; Roger C. Park "Character at the crossroads" (1998) 49 *Hastings Law Journal* 717 at 758–772; Edward J. Imwinkelried "Undertaking the task of reforming the American character evidence prohibition: The importance of getting the experiment off on the right foot" (1995) 22 *Fordham Urban Law Journal* 285; Katherine K. Baker "Once a rapist? Motivational evidence and relevancy in rape law" (1997) 110 *Harvard Law Review* 563; John Monahan et al *Rethinking risk assessment: The MacArthur study of mental disorder and violence* (New York: Oxford University Press, 2001) 44–45.

15 Neil MacCormick *Legal reasoning and legal theory* (Oxford: Clarendon Press, 1978) 24; Neil MacCormick *Rhetoric and the rule of law: A theory of legal reasoning* (Oxford: Oxford University Press, 2005) Ch 3; Anthony G. Guest "Logic in the law," in *Oxford essays in jurisprudence*, ed. Anthony G. Guest (London: Oxford University Press, 1961) 176; Steven J. Burton *An introduction to law and legal reasoning* (Boston: Little, Brown and Company, 1985) Ch 3. Cf. Jerome Michael and Mortimer J. Adler "The trial of an issue of fact (part 1)" (1934) 34(7) *Columbia Law Review* 1224 at 1241–1242; Terence Anderson et al *Analysis of evidence* 2nd ed (Cambridge: Cambridge University Press, 2005) 60–61, where q is regarded as the legal conclusion or verdict (on the merits) and p as the *ultimate probandum*.

16 See Ronald Meester and Lonneke Stevens "Bayesian reasoning and the prior in court: Not legally normative but unavoidable" (2024) 23(1) *Law, Probability and Risk* 1; Franco Taroni et al "The logic of inference and decision for scientific evidence," in *Philosophical foundations of evidence law*, eds. Christian Dahlman et al (Oxford: Oxford University Press, 2021) 251; Norman Fenton and David Lagnado "Bayesianism: Objections and rebuttals," in *Philosophical foundations of evidence law*, eds. Christian Dahlman et al (Oxford: Oxford University Press, 2021) 267; Christian Dahlman and Eivind Kolflaath "The problem of the prior in criminal trials," in *Philosophical foundations of evidence law*, eds. Christian Dahlman et al (Oxford: Oxford University Press, 2021) 287.

17 Ronald J. Allen and Michael S. Pardo "Relative plausibility and its critics" (2019) 23 *International Journal of Evidence & Proof* 5; Susan Haack "Epistemology legalized: Or, truth, justice and the American way" (2004) 49 *American Journal of Jurisprudence* 43; Walton *Legal argumentation and evidence*, 200–201.

extant facts on which probative inferences are based) factors.[18] This probative relativism is party and standpoint dependent. In criminal cases, the burden and meaning of proof is impacted by the institutional asymmetry between the prosecution, who bears the heavier burden of proving all three of the ***material, processual*** and ***probative*** conditions of proof ($P_{conv} = P_m \wedge P_{proc} \wedge P_p$), whereas the defence only has to disprove at least one of these conditions, namely $P_{acq} = P_{conv} - [P_m \vee P_{proc} \vee P_p]$. Furthermore, the content and structure of probative judgement is determined, from a standpoint perspective, by the number (the more facts are being denied, the heavier the burden for the prosecution) and quality (e.g. the denial of ***mens rea*** as opposed to a challenge against the credibility of a witness) of disputed facts that are denied. Proof judgements are sensitive to these nuances.

The third overall conclusion is that notwithstanding which probative model one uses, standards or criteria of proof are notoriously difficult to define with any measure of precision. Civilian jurisdictions that remain associated with that tradition are generally sceptical about affixing any strict proof standards. The ***intime conviction*** trope is understood as an 'assessment criterion' rather than a standard against which to evaluate probative arguments.[19] Moreover, owing to perennial problems of definition, the 'beyond a reasonable doubt' standard has been dispensed with in England and Wales in preference for juries being instructed to be 'sure.'[20]

7.2 Legal Contributions

This project makes at least three contributions to legal scholarship. The first of these is with respect to substantive criminal law doctrine. The meaning, history, general elements and typology of hate crimes are discussed in Chapter 2. The broad style of theorising adopted in the book will enable scholars to have

18 Tshepo B. Mosaka "Here is a table: A prolegomenon to a future new evidence scholarship in Africa" (2022) 26(2) *International Journal of Evidence & Proof* 178 at 182–183. Cf. William Twining "Evidence as a multi-disciplinary subject" (2003) 2 *Law, Probability and Risk* 91 at 97.

19 Michele Taruffo "Rethinking the standards of proof" (2003) 51(3) *American Journal of Comparative Law* 659 at 666; Giovanni Tuzet "Evidence assessment and standards of proof: A messy issue" (2021) 2 *Quaestio facti: International Journal on Evidential Legal Reasoning* 87 at 95; Kai Ambos "Intime conviction in Germany: Conceptual foundations, historical development and current meaning" (2023) 4 *Quaestio facti: International Journal on Evidential Legal Reasoning* 167 at 168 (distinguishing between a 'standard' and a 'flexible method to assess available evidence').

20 See *R v Hepworth (George Alfred)* [1955] 2 Q.B. 600. See also, see *R v Summers* [1952] 1 All ER 1059, CCA; *Walters v R* [1969] 2 AC 26, PC; *R v Yap Chuan Ching* (1976) 63 Cr App Rep 7; *Ferguson v R* [1979] 1 WLR 94, PC; *R v Bracewell* (1979) 68 Cr App R 44, CA; *R v Derek William Bentley* [2001] 1 Cr App R 326 (CA); *R v Alikor* [2004] EWCA Crim 1646; *R v Majid* [2009] EWCA Crim 2563; *R v Miah* (2018) EWCA Crim 563. See also Judicial College, *The Crown Court compendium – Jury and trial management and summing up* (July 2019) 5-1 to 5-3, available at: judiciary.uk (accessed: 20 September 2019).

a global perspective about the law of hate crimes across several jurisdictions around the world. Furthermore, the chapter also makes substantive arguments about the operation of an implicit intention requirement; also most statutes around the world do not expressly provide for this requirement. These arguments will assist lawyers, adjudicators, policy makers and legislators to be able to read in this particular requirement in their hate crime statutes. Furthermore, the criminal law theorising in Chapter 2 may also be found to be useful by countries that have recently promulgated hate crime legislation, such as Scotland in 2021[21] and South Africa in 2023.[22]

The second contribution here is to procedural law doctrine, and ongoing debates about processual coloniality especially. The current situation is that the processual systems of the Euro-American regions where less than 7% (approximately 530 million people) of the world's population lives domineers over the rest of the world, where about 7.5 billion people live.[23] Chapter 3 applies decolonial theory to identify and explain the problems of *processual dualism* (where the colonial variant of legal pluralism involves indigenous legal regimes being subordinate to the legal systems that were inherited during the colonial period) and *diffusion* (the post-colonial legal practices in the Global South being debased and peripheral versions of those in the Euro-American centre). There are gradual signs of widespread legal reform around the global in places like Japan[24] and much of South America,[25] but the world has not moved much

21 Hate Crime and Public Order (Scotland) Act of 2021.

22 Prevention and Combatting of Hate Crimes and Hate Speech Act 13 of 2023.

23 Evode Kayitana "The accusatorial and inquisitorial models of criminal procedure: A historical and comparative approach" (2019) 3(2) *African Journal of Law and Human Rights* 187 at 187; Callie R. Snyman "The accusatorial and inquisitorial approaches to criminal procedure: Some points of comparison between the South African and the continental systems" (1975) 8(1) *Comparative and International Law Journal of Southern Africa* 100; Joachim Herrmann "Various models of criminal proceedings" 2(1) *South African Journal of Criminal Law and Criminology* (1978) 3; Sandra F. Joireman "Inherited legal systems and effective rule of law: Africa and the colonial legacy" (2001) 39(4) *The Journal of Modern African Studies* 571; Louis T.C. Harms "Demystification of the inquisitorial system" (2011) 14(5) *Potchefstroom Electronic Law Journal* 1; Chukwunweike A. Ogbuabor "Inquisitorial and adversarial process in Nigeria's criminal justice system: The dilemma of a colonised state" (2015) 38(2) *University of Western Australia Law Review* 175.

24 See David T. Johnson "Japan's lay judge system," in *Comparative criminal procedure*, eds. Jacqueline E. Ross and Stephen C. Thaman (Cheltenham: Elgar, 2016) 396.

25 Mauricio Duce J. and Claudio Fuentes M. "Trials and trial by jury in Latin America," in *Göttingen handbook on Latin American public law and criminal justice*, eds. Kai Ambos and Jose Martinez (Baden-Baden: Nomos, 2023) 517; Richard Vogler "Introduction," in *Criminal procedure in Europe*, eds. Richard Vogler and Barbara Huber (Berlin: Duncker & Humblot, 2008) 1 at 12: '[W]here 80% of all countries, including Nicaragua, Guatamala, and Chile have abandoned inquisitorial for more adversarial procedures in the last decade.' Máximo Langer "Revolution in Latin American criminal procedure: Diffusion of legal ideas from the periphery" (2007) 55 *The American Journal of Comparative Law* 617 at 631: '[D]uring the

from holistic common law–civil law domination. Ultimately, the problem of coloniality, as Chimakonam and Ogbonnaya say, is one of divisive artificial borders, between 'superiority and inferiority,' 'in-groups and out-groups,' 'the self and other,' and 'the world and the rest of it.'[26] These borders, above all, are intellectual or psychological in so far as to halt the fostering of bridges and the mending of fences where there is processual, political and social division or difference.

The third contribution that this book makes to legal scholarship is to the area of evidence law. In the first instance, the book introduces the study of forensic proof in the *applied* sense that investigates the structure and content of evidential proof from the perspective of the substantive disputed facts that are sought to be established. As indicated earlier in this chapter, evidence and proof scholarship commonly focuses exclusively on proof-related aspects such as burdens and standards of proof and to a lesser extent on the substantive law crimes or causes of action to which probative judgements apply. Furthermore, the applied method of studying forensic proof that this book propounds is precondition on a relativistic and integrated conception of proof that is not solely 'epistemological'[27] but that also incorporates the *material* (Chapter 2) and *processual* (Chapter 3) aspects that determine or influence the structure and content of probative judgements. Chapter 6 specifically makes a contribution by developing three models of argumentation from *wrongness, prejudice* and *responsibility* for the purpose of proving hate crimes.

7.3 Theoretical and Interdisciplinary Contributions

The specific areas with which this book engages – hate crimes, argumentation theory and New Evidence Scholarship – are all multidisciplinary and global in their coverage. Firstly, hate crimes are a global phenomenon.[28] They appear on the statute books of several countries around the world, including in several

---

last 15 years . . .14 Latin American countries . . . and a number of Latin American province and state jurisdictions replaced their inquisitorial codes with accusatorial ones.'

26 Jonathan O. Chimakonam and L. Uchenna Ogbonnaya *African metaphysics, epistemology, and a new logic: A decolonial approach to philosophy* (Cham: Palgrave Macmillan, 2021) 2.

27 See Larry Laudan *Truth, error and criminal law: An essay in legal epistemology* (New York: Cambridge University Press, 2006) 2; Michael S. Pardo "The field of evidence and the field of knowledge" (2005) 24(5) *Law and Philosophy* 321 at 321; Haack "Epistemology legalized: Or, truth, justice and the American way," 43; Jeremy Bentham "An introductory view of the rationale of evidence," in *The works of Jeremy Bentham*, ed. John Bowring vol 6 (London: Simpkin, Marshall & Co., 1843) 5: 'The field of evidence is no other than the field of knowledge.'

28 Jennifer Schweppe and Mark A. Walters, eds. *The globalisation of hate: Internationalising hate crime?* (New York: Oxford University Press, 2016); Paul Iganski and Jack Levin *Hate crime: A global perspective* (New York: Routledge, 2015).

African[29] and South American[30] jurisdictions. Moreover, over 182 countries have ratified the International Convention on the Elimination of all forms of Racial Discrimination that binds them to criminally punish, among others, 'all acts of violence or incitement to such acts against any race or group of persons of another colour or ethnic origin.'[31] Furthermore, the burgeoning field of hate studies has been described by the editor of the first issue of the *Journal of Hate Studies* as adopting a 'comprehensive, integrated, multi-disciplinary approach to the study of the phenomenon of "hate" itself' and that attracts a variety of scholars from fields such as 'psychology, religious studies, information science and technology, human rights activism, and law.'[32]

Secondly, argumentation theory is also a multidisciplinary field with a very wide scholarly coverage. Scholars in this area generally focus on the identification, analysis and evaluation of arguments in varying ordinary contexts such as 'philosophy, logic, linguistics, discourse analysis, rhetoric, speech communication, education, psychology, sociology, political science, law and many other disciplines.'[33] To the extent that this group of scholars focuses on the context of law, and forensic adjudication in particular, this project engages with them too. There generally are two forms of legal argumentation: those that focus on factual (evidential) disputes and those that focus on the existence, meaning and application of legal rules.[34] Thirdly, the emerging area of New Evidence Scholarship is also multidisciplinary in focus in so far as it concerns the 'shared

29 Constitution of the Arabic Republic of Egypt, article 53; Law Determining Offences and Penalties in General no. 68 of 2018, article 163; *Constitution de la Niger République*, 2010, article 4; *Constitution de la République du Sénégal*, 2001, article 5; *Constituição da República de Moçambique*, 2004, article 39; *Constitution de la République de Guinée*, 2010, article 4; *La Constitution de la Guinée équatoriale*, 1991, article 15(1). Cf. Constitution of the of Namibia, 1990, article 23(1). See also the Prevention and Combatting of Hate Crimes and Hate Speech Act 13 of 2023 (South Africa); *Mbatha v Van Staden* (1982) (2) SA 260 (N) (on the commission of the crime of criminal *iniuria* by a person expressing racial epithets to another).

30 *Decreto-Lei No 2.848, De 7 de Dezembro de 1940, Código Penal*, article 140(3) (Brazil); *Ley contra el racism y toda forma de discriminacion* no. 045 (2010) article 23, read with article 281 of *Código Penal decreto ley 10426 de 23 Agosto de 1972* (Bolivia).

31 International Convention on the Elimination of all forms of Racial Discrimination of 1965, article 4. See also International Covenant on Civil and Political Rights of 1966, article 20(1): 'Any advocacy of national, racial or religious hatred that constitutes incitement to discrimination, hostility or violence shall be prohibited by law' (ratified by 173 countries). See also African Charter on Human and People's Rights of 1986, articles 2 and 18(3) (ratified by 54 countries); European Union Charter of Fundamental Rights of 2000, article 21; Additional Protocol to the Convention on Cybercrime, Concerning the Criminalisation of Acts of a Racist and Xenophobic Nature Committed through Computer Systems of 2003.

32 See George A. Critchlow "Preface" (2002) 1(1) *Journal of Hate Studies* 1 at 2.

33 Frans H. van Eemeren et al *Fundamentals of argumentation theory* (New York: Routledge, 1996) ix; Douglas Walton et al *Argumentation schemes* (New York: Cambridge University Press, 2008) 1.

34 Douglas Walton "Legal reasoning and argumentation," in *Handbook of legal reasoning and argumentation*, eds. Giorgio Bongiovanni et al (Dordrecht: Springer, 2018) 47 at 47.

family of problems about evidence and inference.'[35] This book is written by an author who is predominantly trained in law, but this engagement with scholars in these wide-ranging fields significantly widens the scope and intended reach of the book. Put simply, it is a book for everyone.

7.4 Future Research Directions

The main argument of the book – that the evidential proof of hate crimes can be answered through three sets of arguments from *wrongness, prejudice* and *responsibility* that are considered within a broader, and more integrated and relativistic, conception of proof that is conditioned upon the *material* (Chapter 2), *processual* (Chapter 3) and *probative* (Chapters 4, 5 and 6) aspects of forensic adjudication – has responded to the core question. However, there are at least four aspects in the book's theorising that have been bracketed for further reflection. Firstly, it is the question as to whether the theoretical mechanisms of evaluating arguments sufficient correspond or comply with the normative prescriptions on the degree of persuasiveness that should be achieved for a successful prosecution. Chapter 6 of the book evaluates the three arguments from wrongness, prejudice and responsibility using the RAS Triangle (on the relevance, acceptability and sufficiency of arguments) developed by Blair and Johnson,[36] as well as the pragma-dialectic method of posing critical questions that was pioneered by Arthur Hastings in 1962.[37] The determination of argumentative success under these metrics is determined by whether or not an argument is able to withstand oppositional critical questions. It is not entirely clear whether this criterion adequately approximates normative criteria such as 'beyond a reasonable doubt' or the '*intime conviction*.' The question is ripe for further research.

Secondly, it has been argued in Chapter 2 of the book that on the basis of the general principles of criminal law, the kind of responsibility required is

35 William Twining "Evidence as a multi-disciplinary subject" (2003) 2 *Law, Probability and Risk* 91 at 97.

36 Ralph H. Johnson and J. Anthony Blair *Logical self-defense* (New York: International Debate Education Association, 2006) 54–55; J. Anthony Blair "Relevance, acceptability and sufficiency today" (2007) 8(1–2) *Anthropology & Philosophy* 33 at 33–34; Douglas Walton and Thomas F. Gordon "Formalising informal logic" (2015) 35(4) *Informal Logic* 508 at 529–527; Trudy Govier *A practical study of argument* 7th ed (Boston: Cengage Learning, 2014) 87–88. Cf. Edward T. Damer *Attacking faulty reasoning: A practical guide to fallacy-free arguments* (Boston: Cengage Learning, 2013) 31 (five criteria, including: relevance, acceptability and sufficiency). For a critical discussion, see Frans H. van Eemeren et al *Handbook of argumentation theory* (Dordrecht: Springer, 2014) 381–383.

37 See Arthur C. Hastings *A reformulation of the modes of reasoning in argumentation* (Northwestern University: unpublished PhD thesis, 1962); David Hitchcock "Good reasoning on the Toulmin model" (2005) 19 *Argumentation* 373 at 388 (modern critical questioning was pioneered by Arthur Hastings in 1963); Walton et al *Argumentation schemes*, 16–17; Ralph H. Johnson *Manifest rationality* (Mahwah: Lawrence Erlbaum Associates, 2000) 206.

in the form of intention, although many hate crime statutes do not expressly make provision for this. This conclusion is also adopted by Frederick Lawrence in his book *Punishing Hate: Bias Crimes Under American Law*.[38] Moreover, it is also not clear that the kinds of jest defences that Mari Matsuda discusses would operate to exonerate, excuse or otherwise reduce the culpability of perpetrators of hate crimes.[39] These questions are also ripe for further research. Thirdly, although this book has identified the nature and scale of processual coloniality from the Euro-American regions to the Global South in Chapter 3, it has been constrained to use periodisations (antiquity, the medieval era, and modernity) and procedural concepts ('civilian law' and 'common law') that nevertheless emerge from the Global North. This is a shortcoming or constraint for most of decolonial and post-colonial scholarship, particularly because of the difficulty of inventing something entirely new while still addressing an existing audience on some of what they already know. Fourthly, the first requirement of hate crimes generally is described as a 'base offence' that depends on the commission of an independent existing crime, such as murder, assault or arson, yet there are many examples of punishable hateful actions, especially of the non-contact kind (e.g. cross burnings, the dissemination of bigoted materials or the denials of members of protected demographic groups from accessing public facilities), contravene other non-criminal (constitutional and/or statutory) prohibitions. Therefore, the precise scope of the base requirement of hate crimes remains the subject of scholarly debate.

7.5 Bibliography

Books and Book Chapters

Aleksander Peczenik *On law and reason* 2nd ed (Dordrecht: Springer, 2009).

Anthony G. Guest "Logic in the law," in *Oxford essays in jurisprudence*, ed. Anthony G. Guest (London: Oxford University Press, 1961) 176.

Arthur C. Hastings *A reformulation of the modes of reasoning in argumentation* (Northwestern University: unpublished PhD thesis, 1962).

Charanjit Singh *Unlocking the law of evidence* 4th ed (London: Routledge, 2023).

Charles F. Chamberlayne *A treatise on the modern law of evidence* vol 3 (London: Sweet & Maxwell, 1911).

Christian Dahlman and Eivind Kolflaath "The problem of the prior in criminal trials," in *Philosophical foundations of evidence law*, eds. Christian Dahlman, Alex Stein and Giovanni Tuzet (Oxford: Oxford University Press, 2021) 287.

Dale Nance *The burdens of proof: Discriminatory power, weight of evidence and tenacity of belief* (Cambridge: Cambridge University Press, 2016).

38 Frederick M. Lawrence *Punishing hate: Bias crimes under American law* (Cambridge: Harvard University Press, 1999) 65–66.

39 See Mari J. Matsuda "Public response to racist speech: Considering the victim's story," in *Words that wound: Critical race theory, assaultive speech and the first amendment*, eds. Mari J. Matsuda et al (New York: Westview Press, 1999) 17 at 20–21.

David T. Johnson "Japan's lay judge system," in *Comparative criminal procedure*, eds. Jacqueline E. Ross and Stephen C. Thaman (Cheltenham: Elgar, 2016) 396.

Douglas N. Walton *Burden of proof, presumption and argumentation* (New York: Cambridge University Press, 2014).

Douglas N. Walton *Legal argumentation and evidence* (University Park: Pennsylvania University Press, 2002).

Douglas N. Walton "Legal reasoning and argumentation," in *Handbook of legal reasoning and argumentation*, eds. Giorgio Bongiovanni, Gerald Postema, Antonino Rotolo, Giovanni Sartor, Chiara Valentini and Douglas N. Walton (Dordrecht: Springer, 2018) 47.

Douglas N. Walton, Christopher Reed and Fabrizio Macagno *Argumentation schemes* (New York: Cambridge University Press, 2008).

Edward T. Damer *Attacking faulty reasoning: A practical guide to fallacy-free arguments* (Boston: Cengage Learning, 2013).

Floris J. Bex *Arguments, stories and criminal evidence: A formal hybrid theory* (Dordrecht: Springer, 2011).

Franco Taroni, Alex Biedermann and Silvia Bozza "The logic of inference and decision for scientific evidence," in *Philosophical foundations of evidence law*, eds. Christian Dahlman, Alex Stein and Giovanni Tuzet (Oxford: Oxford University Press, 2021) 251.

Frans H. van Eemeren, Bart Garssen, Erik C.W. Krabbe, A. Francisca S. Henkemans, Bart Verheij and Jean H.M. Wagemans *Handbook of argumentation theory* (Dordrecht: Springer, 2014).

Frans H. van Eemeren, Rob Grootendorst, Ralph H. Johnson, Christian Plantin and Charles A. Willard *Fundamentals of argumentation theory* (New York: Routledge, 1996).

Frederick M. Lawrence *Punishing hate: Bias crimes under American law* (Cambridge: Harvard University Press, 1999).

Gail Mason "Legislating against hate," in *The Routledge international handbook on hate crime*, eds. Nathan Hall et al (New York: Routledge, 2015).

Henry Prakken and Giovanni Sartor "A logical analysis of burdens of proof," in *Legal evidence and proof*, eds. Henry Prakken et al (Farnham: Ashgate, 2009) Ch 9.

Ian Dennis *The law of evidence* 6th ed (London: Sweet & Maxwell, 2017).

James B. Jacobs and Kimberly Potter *Hate crimes: Criminal law & identity politics* (New York: Oxford University Press, 1998).

James F. Stephen *A digest on the law of evidence* (London: Macmillan & Co., 1876).

James F. Stephen *The Indian Evidence Act (I of 1872): With an introduction on the principles of judicial evidence* (London: Macmillan, 1872).

Jean-Francois Blanchette *Burdens of proof: Cryptographic culture and evidence law in the age of electronic documents* (Cambridge, MA: MIT Press, 2012).

Jennifer Schweppe and Mark A. Walters, eds. *The globalisation of hate: Internationalising hate crime?* (New York: Oxford University Press, 2016).

Jeremy Bentham "An introductory view of the rationale of evidence," in *The works of Jeremy Bentham*, ed. John Bowring vol 6 (London: Simpkin, Marshall & Co., 1843) 5.

Jeremy Bentham *Rationale of judicial evidence* vol 1 (edited by J.S. Mill) (London: Hunt & Clark, 1827).

Jerome Michael and Mortimer J. Adler *The nature of judicial proof: An inquiry into the logical, legal and empirical aspects of the law of evidence* (New York: Ad Press, 1931).

John H. Wigmore *A treatise on the system of evidence in trials at common law* vol 1 (Boston: Little Brown, 1905).

John Monahan, Henry J. Steadman, Eric Silver, Paul S. Applebaum, Pamela C. Robbins, Edward P. Mulvey, Loren H. Roth, Thomas Grisso and Steven Banks *Rethinking risk*

assessment: The MacArthur study of mental disorder and violence (New York: Oxford University Press, 2001).
Jonathan O. Chimakonam and L. Uchenna Ogbonnaya *African metaphysics, epistemology, and a new logic: A decolonial approach to philosophy* (Cham: Palgrave Macmillan, 2021).
Joseph B. Kadane and David A. Schum *A probabilistic analysis of the Sacco and Vanzetti evidence* (New York: Wiley, 1996).
Kevin Clermont *Standards of decision in law: Psychological and logical bases for the standard of proof, here and abroad* (Durham: California Academic Press, 2013).
L. Jonathan Cohen *The probable and the provable* (Oxford: Oxford University Press, 1977).
Larry Laudan *Truth, error and criminal law: An essay in legal epistemology* (New York: Cambridge University Press, 2006).
Mari J. Matsuda "Public response to racist speech: Considering the victim's story," in *Words that wound: Critical race theory, assaultive speech and the first amendment*, eds. Mari J. Matsuda et al (New York: Westview Press, 1999) 17.
Mauricio Duce J. and Claudio Fuentes M., "Trials and trial by jury in Latin America," in *Göttingen handbook on Latin American public law and criminal justice*, eds. Kai Ambos and Jose Martinez (Baden-Baden: Nomos, 2023) 517.
Neil MacCormick *Legal reasoning and legal theory* (Oxford: Clarendon Press, 1978).
Neil MacCormick *Rhetoric and the rule of law: A theory of legal reasoning* (Oxford: Oxford University Press, 2005).
Nicola Monaghan *Law of evidence* (Cambridge: Cambridge University Press, 2015).
Norman Fenton and David Lagnado "Bayesianism: Objections and rebuttals," in *Philosophical foundations of evidence law*, eds. Christian Dahlman, Alex Stein and Giovanni Tuzet (Oxford: Oxford University Press, 2021) 267.
Paul Iganski and Jack Levin *Hate crime: A global perspective* (New York: Routledge, 2015).
Ralph H. Johnson *Manifest rationality* (Mahwah: Lawrence Erlbaum Associates, 2000).
Ralph H. Johnson and J. Anthony Blair *Logical self-defense* (New York: International Debate Education Association, 2006).
Ratanlal Ranchhoddas and Dhirajlal K. Thakore *Law of evidence* (PB) 27th ed (New Delhi: LexisNexis, 2020).
Richard D. Friedman *An advanced introduction to evidence* (Cheltenham: Elgar, 2024).
Richard Vogler "Introduction," in *Criminal procedure in Europe*, eds. Richard Vogler and Barbara Huber (Berlin: Duncker & Humblot, 2008) 1.
Robert J. MacCoun "Standards of proof: Theories and evidence," in *Research handbook on law and psychology*, ed. Rebecca Hollander-Blumoff (Cheltenham: Elgar, 2024) Ch 10.
Steven J. Burton *An introduction to law and legal reasoning* (Boston: Little Brown, 1985).
Terence Anderson, William Twining and David Schum *Analysis of evidence* 2nd ed (Cambridge: Cambridge University Press, 2005).
Thomas Starkie *Practical treatise of the law of evidence and digest of proofs in civil and criminal proceedings* vol 1 3rd ed (Philadelphia: T. & J.W. Johnson, 1842).
Trudy Govier *A practical study of argument* 7th ed (Boston: Cengage Learning, 2014).
William Twining "Evidence and legal theory," in *Law in context: Enlarging a discipline*, ed. Williams Twining (Oxford: Oxford University Press, 1997) 110.

Periodicals

Callie R. Snyman "The accusatorial and inquisitorial approaches to criminal procedure: Some points of comparison between the South African and the continental systems" (1975) 8(1) *Comparative and International Law Journal of Southern Africa* 100.

Chukwunweike A. Ogbuabor "Inquisitorial and adversarial process in Nigeria's criminal justice system: The dilemma of a colonised state" (2015) 38(2) *University of Western Australia Law Review* 175.
David Hitchcock "Good reasoning on the Toulmin model" (2005) 19 *Argumentation* 373.
Douglas N. Walton and Thomas F. Gordon "Formalising informal logic" (2015) 35(4) *Informal Logic* 508.
Edward J. Imwinkelried "Undertaking the task of reforming the American character evidence prohibition: The importance of getting the experiment off on the right foot" (1995) 22 *Fordham Urban Law Journal* 285.
Eric D. Green "Foreword" (1986) 66(3) *Boston University Law Review* 377.
Evode Kayitana "The accusatorial and inquisitorial models of criminal procedure: A historical and comparative approach" (2019) 3(2) *African Journal of Law and Human Rights* 187.
George A. Critchlow "Preface" (2002) 1(1) *Journal of Hate Studies* 1.
Giovanni Tuzet "Evidence assessment and standards of proof: A messy issue" (2021) 2 *Quaestio facti: International Journal on Evidential Legal Reasoning* 87.
J. Anthony Blair "Relevance, acceptability and sufficiency today" (2007) 8(1–2) *Anthropology & Philosophy* 33.
Jerome Michael and Mortimer J. Adler "The trial of an issue of fact (part 1)" (1934) 34(7) *Columbia Law Review* 1224.
Joachim Herrmann "Various models of criminal proceedings" 2(1) *South African Journal of Criminal Law and Criminology* (1978) 3.
John H. Wigmore "The problem of proof" (1913) 8 *Illinois Law Review* 77.
Kai Ambos "Intime conviction in Germany: Conceptual foundations, historical development and current meaning" (2023) 4 *Quaestio facti: International Journal on Evidential Legal Reasoning* 167.
Katherine K. Baker "Once a rapist? Motivational evidence and relevancy in rape law" (1997) 110 *Harvard Law Review* 563.
Louis T.C. Harms "Demystification of the inquisitorial system" (2011) 14(5) *Potchefstroom Electronic Law Journal* 1.
Máximo Langer "Revolution in Latin American criminal procedure: Diffusion of legal ideas from the periphery" (2007) 55 *The American Journal of Comparative Law* 617.
Michael S. Pardo "The field of evidence and the field of knowledge" (2005) 24(5) *Law and Philosophy* 321.
Michele Taruffo "Rethinking the standards of proof" (2003) 51(3) *American Journal of Comparative Law* 659.
Mike Redmayne "The relevance of bad character" (2002) 61(3) *The Cambridge Law Journal* 684.
Peter Tillers "Mapping inferential domains" (1986) 66(4) *Boston University Law Review* 883.
Roger C. Park "Character at the crossroads" (1998) 49 *Hastings Law Journal* 717.
Ronald J. Allen and Michael S. Pardo "Relative plausibility and its critics" (2019) 23 *International Journal of Evidence & Proof* 5.
Ronald Meester and Lonneke Stevens "Bayesian reasoning and the prior in court: Not legally normative but unavoidable" (2024) 23(1) *Law, Probability and Risk* 1.
Sandra F. Joireman "Inherited legal systems and effective rule of law: Africa and the colonial legacy" (2001) 39(4) *The Journal of Modern African Studies* 571.
Susan Haack "Epistemology legalized: Or, truth, justice and the American way" (2004) 49 *American Journal of Jurisprudence* 43.
Thomas O. Main "The procedural foundation of substantive law" (2003) 78 *Washington University Law Review* 801.

Tshepo B. Mosaka "Here is a table: A prolegomenon to a future new evidence scholarship in Africa" (2022) 26(2) *International Journal of Evidence & Proof* 178.
William Twining "The Boston symposium: A comment" (1986) 66(3) *Boston University Law Review* 391.
William Twining "Evidence as a multi-disciplinary subject" (2003) 2 *Law, Probability and Risk* 91.
William Twining "Some jobs for jurisprudence" (1974) 1(2) *British Journal of Law and Society* 149.

Online Resources

Judicial College *The Crown Court compendium – Jury and trial management and summing up* (July 2019), available at: judiciary.uk (accessed: 20 September 2019).

Index

Note: Page numbers in *italic* indicate a figure and page numbers in **bold** indicate a table on the corresponding page.

For Product Safety Concerns and Information please contact our EU
representative GPSR@taylorandfrancis.com
Taylor & Francis Verlag GmbH, Kaufingerstraße 24, 80331 München, Germany

www.ingramcontent.com/pod-product-compliance
Ingram Content Group UK Ltd.
Pitfield, Milton Keynes, MK11 3LW, UK
UKHW022043061126
477531UK00009B/500
9781032796208